LEAVING CERTIFICATE ECONOMICS

Revised & Updated

DENIS L. O'GRADY

FOLENS

Editor
Antoinette Walker

Layout & Design
Artwerk

Cover
Melanie Gradtke

Graphics
Philip Ryan
Alan Ryan
Turlough O'Donnell

© Denis L. O'Grady, 2002

Produced in Ireland by Folens Publishers

ISBN 1 84131 535 4

Contents

SECTION 3

Preface

This book was written specifically for students preparing for the Leaving Certificate examination at both Higher and Ordinary levels. It may also prove useful to students pursuing introductory courses at third level, and to the general reader who wishes to understand more fully the economic issues of the day.

Most Irish classes of Economics are 'mixed ability' classes, containing both Higher and Ordinary level. Accordingly, every effort has been made to keep the language as simple as possible.

As with the first edition, a feature of the book is the linking of economic theory to the real world by the use of appropriate examples, case studies and articles from current newspapers, journals, etc. A revised Appendix containing useful sources of information and helpful websites is also included.

All examples, tables and data used are denominated in euro, while the statistics used are the most up-to-date available. More headings, definition boxes and illustrations are used to make the material more easily assimilated. New material is included covering the euro changeover, European Union, EU structural funds, CAP reform, public private partnerships, the changed role of the Central Bank, globalisation, the World Trade Organisation, deregulation, the Celtic Tiger, etc.

A thorough understanding of economic terms and definitions is required for success at the subject. An accompanying workbook contains questions based on the material in the text, divided into short definition type questions (Section A) and full-length questions (Section B).

I am very grateful to Antoinette Walker for her invaluable advice and help at all stages in the preparation of this book. Also thanks is due to John O'Connor and the staff at Folens for their assistance and support.

I would also like to acknowledge the co-operation of the Central Statistics Office and the Central Bank in relation to statistical material used in the book, and all those who gave permission for articles, photographs, illustrations or extracts to be used. I am very grateful to the following for their assistance at various stages in the preparation of material – Margaret McGlynn, Mary Walton and Jim Doran.

Finally, I would like to thank Maria and Patrick for their patience and understanding during the preparation of the book.

Denis L. O'Grady
April 2002

What is Economics?

Most students approaching the study of economics for the first time are already familiar with much of its subject matter, even though they may be unaware of this fact. Every day our newspapers, magazines, radio and television programmes keep us informed about all kinds of economic issues. Unemployment, inflation, wages, strikes and industrial unrest, prices, taxation, interest rates, balance of payments – these are just some of the topics that you will read about and hear discussed. These are issues that affect all of us, either directly or indirectly.

The aim of this chapter is to define what we mean by economics, to look at the scope of the subject and the reasons for studying it, and to examine very briefly the methods used by economists to deal with these issues.

Economics is a 'social science'. A science is an organised body of knowledge. A social science is one that studies some aspect of human behaviour.

Economic activity is one aspect of human behaviour. It comprises all those economic transactions that individuals engage in, which usually involve the exchange of money. These include the production of goods and services, the sale and distribution of such goods and services, the provision of labour to be used in the production of goods and services, and the saving of money with financial institutions by some individuals that enables loans to be provided to others. The study of the nature of such activities is at the heart of economics.

Economics can be defined as the study of the production, distribution and consumption of goods and services by society.

The underlying principle in the study of economics is the concept of 'scarcity'. By scarcity we mean that the needs and wants of an individual exceed the resources available to that individual. Therefore, choices must be made. People have limited incomes and they desire to purchase more goods and services than their incomes allow. Consequently, they must decide what to buy and what to do without. The decisions of consumers concerning the allocation of their incomes are studied closely in economics.

The concept of scarcity also applies to a business. A firm has limited resources, and must make decisions concerning the type of goods to produce, what quantity should be supplied and what price should be charged. In addition, the firm must decide on the method of production to be used – should it use more workers and less machines or vice versa. As in the case with the consumer, these decisions of the producer are based on scarcity. Every firm has a limited budget, and wants to produce its output as cheaply as possible, or in such a way as to earn the most profit.

Also, governments are confronted by the problem of scarcity. A government is expected to provide many services to its citizens, for example, health, education, social welfare, defence, etc. However, the resources available to a government are limited or scarce. A government can only raise so much money through taxation. Similarly, there are definite limits to the amount of borrowing it can undertake. Once again we can see the problem of scarcity, and the need for choices to be made.

The question of choice leads us to the concept of opportunity cost.

We define the opportunity cost of an item as the alternatives that must be done without in order to have that item.

A consumer with €5,000 to spend might consider changing his car or going on a foreign holiday. If he opts for the car, the opportunity cost to him of making this choice is the holiday he must do without. In the same way, the opportunity cost to the business firm of a €1 million extension to its factory might be a €1m advertising campaign that it had planned and which it must now abandon. Finally, the expenditure of €20m more by the government on social welfare might mean €20m less available for education. In all three cases, the selection of one good or service means doing without the alternative.

We have already described economics as a social science, or one that studies some aspect of human behaviour. The laws of the social sciences are less predictable than those of the physical sciences. A physical scientist can sometimes check the accuracy of a law in a laboratory experiment, but this course of action is not open to an economist. Economic laws are statements that are generally true, even though we cannot be sure that they will hold true in 100

Fig. 1.1 The subject matter of economics confronts us every day

per cent of cases. Despite this drawback we can make fairly accurate predictions concerning the likely economic consequences of a given set of circumstances.

It is important to note that any law cannot be regarded as permanent. Circumstances can change, or new information come to light, which could make an existing law obsolete or out of date. Progress in any science involves the replacement of long-established laws by new ones, more suited to modern circumstances, and in keeping with the most up-to-date information at our disposal. Economic laws can be derived in two ways:

1. *The deductive method of analysis.* This involves reasoning from the general to the particular. A law is derived from a set of assumptions which is believed to be generally true. It is then tested to see if it is true for a particular case. For example, it might be argued that 'a rise in the price of oil on world markets will cause an increase in the quantity supplied'. Then, by examining individual cases (i.e. the output for particular oil fields), we can see if this statement is true for those cases.

2. *The inductive method of analysis.* This involves reasoning from the particular to the general. A mass of data is first collected for many cases, and then the 'hypothesis' (i.e. what we believe to be true) is drawn from this data. For example, by observing the behaviour of many consumers, who reduce their demand for a good when its price rises, we form the general conclusion that 'a rise in price will lead to a fall in the quantity demanded'.

Finally, it is important to note that the economist is concerned with 'positive statements', rather than 'normative statements'. By a positive statement we mean something which can be shown to be true or false by observing events in the real world. A normative statement involves the making of a value judgement or the expression of an opinion about what 'ought to be'. The job of the economist is to analyse all the available economic data and to state the likely outcome of each possible course of action. This involves the making of positive statements. It is then up to the decision makers (the directors in the case of a company, or the government in the case of the state) to decide what course of action should be taken. This involves the making of normative statements.

It should be obvious that a basic knowledge of economics is required if one is to be able to fully appreciate the complexities of the modern world. Whether as a consumer, a producer, a worker, a taxpayer, a borrower, a saver or simply as a well-informed citizen, each of us has a vested interest in understanding how a modern economy works, if for no other reason than to enable us to make properly informed decisions about matters affecting our own lives.

The study of economics as a subject is usually divided into the following two parts: microeconomics and macroeconomics.

MICROECONOMICS

The prefix 'micro' is derived from the Greek word *micro* meaning small. Microeconomics examines the decision-making process of small units in the economy. It is the study of economics at the level of the individual consumer, the individual supplier of factors of production and the individual producer.

MACROECONOMICS

The prefix 'macro' is derived from the Greek word *macro* meaning large. Macroeconomics is therefore concerned with the decision-making process of government as it relates to such topics as income, employment, inflation, international trade, growth, etc.

2

The Factors of Production

In *Chapter 1* we defined economics as the study of the production, distribution and consumption of goods and services by society. In this chapter, we examine the resources which are needed for the production of these goods and services. These resources are called the factors of production, and are usually classified under four headings: land, labour, capital and enterprise. To enable a firm to produce output, some combination of these four factors of production (or inputs) is required, as shown in *Figure 2.1*.

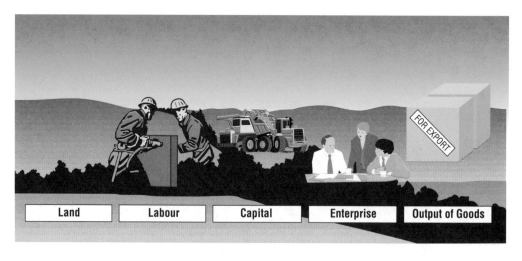

| Land | Labour | Capital | Enterprise | Output of Goods |

Fig. 2.1 The combination of land, labour, capital and enterprise is required to produce goods

If production is to take place, a factory site is required. Workers are required to apply their skills in the production of goods. Machines are required to increase the output of workers. Finally someone is required who is willing to combine the land, workers and machines with a view to making a profit. We will now examine each of the factors of production in turn and analyse its role in the production of goods and services.

LAND

The term 'land' in economics is used to describe all those things which are supplied by nature and are used in the production of goods and services.

When we define land in this way, we can see that it includes all of the following:

1. *Agricultural land* – used for the production of cereal crops, fruit and vegetables and also as pasture for animals.

2. *Rivers, lakes and seas* – used for fishing, fish farming and mariculture, and the provision of hydroelectric power for industry. Water itself is a very important raw material in the production of many goods.

3. *Mineral wealth and natural resources* – for example, oil, iron ore, coal, turf, lead, zinc, gold, etc. The earth's mineral wealth and natural resources are raw materials which are used in the production of finished goods. Some are also used as sources of power (oil, coal, natural gas, turf).

4. *The forests* supply us with timber which is an essential resource for the building industry, furniture-making and also the paper and printing industries.

5. *The atmosphere, weather and climate* are natural resources which are vital for life and the production of goods and services. Adequate rainfall and sunshine are essential for the growing of agricultural produce, while certain climatic conditions are required for the operation of a successful tourist industry (sun in the Mediterranean countries, snow in the Alps, etc.)

6. The provision of all goods and services depends on the availability of some minimum quantity of *land* itself. Sites are required for factories, shopping centres, offices, warehouses and private houses.

A modern classification of the factor of production 'land' can be made on the basis of the distinction between renewable and non-renewable resources.

Renewable resources

Renewable resources are those resources the supply of which can be replenished. An increase in the use or consumption of such resources should not be a matter of great concern since more of these resources can be made available in the future. Examples of renewable resources are water, forests, fish and soil as in *Figure 2.2*.

Fig. 2.2 Water, forests, fish and soil are renewable resources

Non-renewable resources

Non-renewable resources are those resources which, if consumed or used up now, will mean less being available for future generations. The supply of such resources is therefore limited and cannot be replaced. Examples of such resources are coal, oil, natural gas, and the mineral wealth of the earth (see *Figure 2.3*). The using up of these resources is a cause of great concern because of their importance, both as raw materials in production and also as sources of energy.

It should be clear that the over-exploitation of renewable resources (or their improper use) can cause them to become non-renewable and consequently threaten supplies for future generations. The over-fishing of our seas, over-intensive use of agricultural land, bad farming practices, lack of suitable irrigation, large-scale deforestation and pollution of our environment all represent threats to the future supply of what should be renewable resources. We shall consider 'land' as a factor of production in greater detail in *Chapter 18*.

Fig. 2.3 Natural gas from the Kinsale Gas Field is a non-renewable resource

LABOUR

The term 'labour' in economics means all human effort which goes into the production of goods and services.

The amount of labour available in a country depends not only on the population of that country but also on the number of hours worked by each worker and the extent to which people in that country seek employment.

In a modern economy the main feature of labour is its specialisation. By specialisation of labour we mean that each individual worker concentrates on one job, for which he/she receives payment, and at which he/she develops a reasonable degree of proficiency. He/she is thus able to acquire his/her needs by purchasing the goods and services provided by others. This feature of a modern economy is in marked contrast to the situation which prevails in many primitive societies where a person tries to satisfy all his needs through his own efforts (food, clothing, shelter, etc.).

It is generally accepted that specialisation of labour enables total output to be increased, that is, it makes labour more productive. The productivity of labour is further increased by education and training.

Labour is normally classified according to the type of output produced. *Table 2.1* shows the main categories of employment and the changes that have occurred in Ireland's labour force in recent years. Labour as a factor of production is considered more fully in *Chapter 19.*

Employment and Unemployment ('000s)					
Economic sector	Mar–May 1998	Mar–May 1999	Mar–May 2000	Jun–Aug 2000	Sep–Nov 2000
Agriculture, forestry & fishing	135.0	135.9	130.9	130.7	122.7
Other production industries	302.9	308.9	309.9	326.4	321.0
Construction	126.2	142.1	166.3	175.5	178.1
Wholesale & retail trade	211.4	223.3	235.8	253.4	242.6
Hotels and restaurants	98.1	102.6	109.0	118.3	110.0
Transport, storage & communication	86.9	96.0	100.8	105.9	105.2
Financial & other business services	171.8	195.8	212.1	218.8	216.3
Public administration & defence	70.7	74.4	77.8	78.8	78.5
Education & health	206.9	220.4	234.7	232.5	241.8
Other services	84.7	91.8	93.4	97.6	94.1
Total in employment	**1,494.5**	**1,591.1**	**1,670.7**	**1,737.9**	**1,710.3**
Total unemployed	126.6	96.9	74.9	77.7	68.8
Total labour force	**1,621.1**	**1,688.1**	**1,745.6**	**1,815.6**	**1,779.1**
Not in labour force	1,248.5	1,227.4	1,217.0	1,159.3	1,224.5
Population 15 years & over	**2,869.6**	**2,915.5**	**2,962.6**	**2,975.0**	**3,003.6**

International Labour Organisation (ILO) labour force classification used
Source: Central Statistics Office

Table 2.1 Employment and unemployment in Ireland, 1998–2000

CAPITAL

Capital is a word with many different meanings. However, when we speak of capital as a factor of production, it has a very precise meaning.

Capital is defined as anything made by man, which is used to produce goods and services.

It therefore includes plant and machinery, buildings, transport equipment, computers, telecommunications systems, and stocks of finished and partly finished goods. The essential feature of capital as a factor of production is that it makes labour more productive. A worker in a modern factory with proper equipment can produce much more than a worker using his bare hands. A farmer using a tractor can produce more in a given period of time than a farmer using a horse-drawn plough. An office worker can process more transactions using modern office equipment than someone without such equipment. We can identify three types of capital.

1. *Fixed capital.* This is the name given to stocks of fixed assets – for example, plant, machinery, buildings, tools, equipment, etc.

2. *Working capital.* This includes stocks of man-made raw materials, stocks of partly finished goods and stocks of finished goods.

3. *Social capital.* This term refers to the capital which is owned by the community in general – roads, harbours, communications systems, etc.

It is important to note that **money itself is not capital**. It is the means by which capital can be purchased. A country cannot increase its output of goods and services simply by printing more money. The process of adding to the stock of capital in an economy is known as investment (or capital formation). We must distinguish between gross investment and net investment.

Gross investment

Gross investment is the total amount of capital created in an economy in one year. However, some of this capital is simply replacing capital that has been used up during the year. In any year, as production takes place, machines will become worn out, damage will be done to roads, and raw materials will be used up. Capital used up in this manner is called *depreciation*.

Net investment

Net investment is defined as gross investment minus depreciation. It shows us how much the stock of capital in the economy actually increased during the year. It is an important indicator of the change in the productive capacity of the economy during that year. If net investment is low then the economy will be short the capital it requires to produce the goods which the citizens of the country desire. *Table 2.2* shows us gross investment, depreciation and net investment in Ireland in recent years. Capital as a factor of production is discussed in greater detail in *Chapter 20*.

	1998 (€m)	1999 (€m)	2000 (€m)
Gross investment	14,384	16,392	17,545
Depreciation	7,295	8,514	10,093
Net investment	7,089	7,878	7,452
Source: Central Statistics Office			

Table 2.2 Gross investment, depreciation and net investment in Ireland, 1998–2000

ENTERPRISE

Enterprise is the factor of production which takes the initiative in organising land, labour and capital, and which bears the risks involved in production.

The entrepreneur

The entrepreneur is the name given to the person who takes risks by investing his/her money in a business venture with the aim of making a profit. He/she takes the decisions regarding what is to be produced, and how it is to be produced. He/she takes the profits if the business is successful, or incurs the losses if the business is unsuccessful.

Land, labour and capital must be brought together if production is to take place. Entrepreneurs are willing to do this if they expect the demand for the goods they produce to be so high that their income from sales exceeds their costs of production. The difference represents the profit to the entrepreneur.

In a *free market economy* such as ours, the factor of production – enterprise – is provided by private individuals. The sole trader in a small shop, the partners in a partnership and the shareholders in a limited company can all be classified as entrepreneurs. In the case of a state-owned company, the taxpayers of the country can be considered entrepreneurs since any losses incurred must be paid for by the state (out of the receipts from taxation).

In the case of a '*centrally planned*' *economy*, where the state owns the means of production (e.g. China, Cuba and formerly the Soviet Union and the states of Eastern Europe), the state provides the factor of production enterprise. Any profits earned accrue to the state, while any losses incurred must be borne by the state. We shall examine the role of the entrepreneur in greater detail in *Chapter 21*.

3

The Producer

In the previous chapter, we examined the factors of production required to supply the public with goods and services. In this chapter, we will examine the role of the producer in combining these factors in such a way that the goods and services which are in greatest demand by consumers can be provided.

> A firm can be defined as an individual unit of business which produces output and sells its product in the market.

We define an industry as the group of firms which produce the entire output of a particular good. Ford, Toyota and Nissan are firms which produce part of the output of the motor industry.

We can distinguish between private sector firms and public sector firms. Private sector firms are privately owned businesses engaged in the production of goods and services. The following are the main categories of private sector firms:

1. *Sole traders*. The business is owned by a single individual, for example, a shop or farm.
2. *Partnerships*. A minimum of two and a maximum of 20 individuals join together to run the business and share profits in an agreed manner.
3. *Private limited companies*. Business units owned by shareholders who have limited liability, but whose shares are not traded on the stock exchange. There must be a minimum of one and a maximum of 50 shareholders.
4. *Public limited companies* (plcs). Usually large businesses with many shareholders who have limited liability and whose shares can be bought and sold on the stock exchange. There must be at least seven shareholders (and no maximum).
5. *Co-operatives*. Business units where each member's profit depends on the volume of business he/she carries on with the co-operative.

The public sector firms are the semi-state bodies which are owned by the state and which supply goods and services to customers, for example, Bord na Móna, Aer Lingus, CIE, etc. In this chapter, we shall devote our attention to private sector firms. We shall consider semi-state bodies separately in *Chapter 27*. The firm is the basic unit of production and has the following three main aims:

1. To produce goods and services that consumers want.

2. To produce goods and services at prices consumers are willing to pay.

3. To organise production in such a way that revenue from sales exceeds the cost of production so that profits can be made.

It is obvious from these aims that each firm must be able to operate at its most efficient size, that is, where its unit costs are at a minimum. Such a position is referred to as the optimum size of the firm.

The optimum size of the firm will vary from industry to industry. For example, the optimum size of a car-manufacturing firm will be very large. Mercedes-Benz, the German car and truck manufacturer, is now part of the giant DaimlerChrysler Motor Company, which in 2000 employed 416,000 people and had total revenues of €162 billion.

At the other end of the scale, a firm producing handcrafts for the tourist trade might be at its optimum size with less than a dozen workers.

Fig. 3.1 A view of the Mercedes-Benz plant near Stuttgart, which is the European headquarters for DaimlerChrysler

INTERNAL ECONOMIES OF SCALE

The internal economies of scale are the forces at work within a firm which lower the average cost of production as the firm expands in size. In other words, the internal economies of scale represent the advantages to the firm of large-scale production.

Such economies can be classified along the following lines:

1. *Technical economies of scale.* A large firm can justify the purchase of the most technically advanced machines because it can spread the cost of such equipment over a large quantity of output. The output of small firms would not make the purchase of such machines worthwhile.

2. *Construction economies.* Building costs do not increase in proportion to the size of the firm. A simple example will illustrate this. In *Figure 3.2*, Factory B is four times the size of Factory A but only needed twice the quantity of building blocks (800 metres and 400 metres, respectively).

3. *Economies in the use of labour.* A large firm is more likely to be able to engage in the specialisation and division of labour. Each worker can concentrate on a specific task at which he/she becomes very skilled.

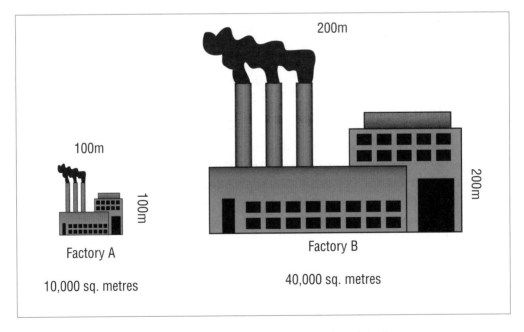

Fig. 3.2 Building costs do not increase in proportion to the size of the firm

Therefore output per worker is increased, and the cost per unit of output is reduced. Also a large firm can employ more marketing managers, sales personnel and production engineers each of whom can increase the output of the company still further.

4. *Production economies*. Large firms can keep the production process continuous. This is done by operating three eight-hour shifts so that output is produced 24 hours a day. As a result there is no interruption to production while machines heat up, etc.

5. *Integrated production*. A large firm can reduce cost per unit by involving itself at more than one stage in the production process. For example, a large supermarket may have an in-store bakery, enabling it to sell bread and confectionery more cheaply than its rivals. However, a small family-run grocery shop would not find this practice worthwhile.

6. *Economies in the use of raw materials*. The larger the firm, the more likely it is to be producing a wide range of goods. A large firm is, therefore, less likely to have waste, since any raw material not used up in the production of one good can be used in making related products.

7. *Financial economies*. A large firm has a greater choice of sources of finance than a small firm. Furthermore, the large firm is likely to be able to borrow at lower rates of interest because it is seen as more secure by the banks.

8. *Purchasing economies*. Large firms are more likely to secure favourable trading terms (i.e. discounts) because they buy in bulk.

9. *Economies in distribution*. A firm with a high volume of sales can organise a more efficient transport and distribution system than a small firm with only a few deliveries to make.

10. *Advertising economies*. Advertising costs per unit of output are lower for a large firm. For example, a €50,000 TV advertisement by Guinness would only cost 5c per pint if the daily sales of Guinness were 1 million pints. A similar advertisement by Murphy's would cost 50c per pint if its daily sales were 100,000 pints.

EXTERNAL ECONOMIES OF SCALE

External economies of scale are those forces at work which benefit all firms in an industry as it grows in size. While internal economies of scale refer to what happens within the individual firm, external economies are the advantages of large-scale production which are common to all firms in the industry.

External economies of scale can be classified as follows:

1. Economies in the supply of *component parts*. As an industry expands, other firms may be established to supply it with component parts. For example, the growth of shipbuilding as a major industry was accompanied in many centres by the setting up of firms supplying component parts or related products, such as paint, ropes, nautical equipment, etc. Similarly, the development of Detroit as the major centre of the motor industry in the United States has been accompanied by the growth of many firms supplying a wide range of 'inputs' such as tyres, batteries, glass and upholstery.

2. As an industry expands, it may become worthwhile for firms to be established to supply *specialised machinery* to be used in the production process itself.

3. As an industry expands, local educational institutions may provide *training courses* for workers to develop skills related to that industry.

4. *Marketing agencies* may be established to sell the increased output as the industry expands. Also technical information and market trends may become available through a trade association. Such an association may undertake activities (such as trade fairs) outside the scope of the individual firm.

5. The costs of product design, research and the introduction of new technology may be shared by firms as the industry expands.

6. As the economy expands, the *'back-up facilities'* available to firms improve. Better roads, railways, ports, communications, etc. are provided. Such improved facilities confer benefits on already established firms.

The economies of scale (internal and external) are shown in summary form in *Figure 3.3*.

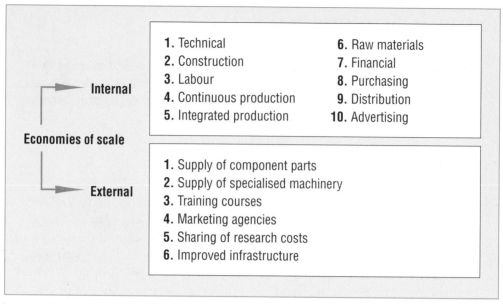

Fig. 3.3 Summary of internal and external economies of scale

INTERNAL DISECONOMIES OF SCALE

Internal diseconomies of scale are the factors within the firm which cause unit cost to rise again once the firm reaches a certain size. In other words, internal diseconomies of scale are the disadvantages within the firm of large-scale production.

1. *Managerial diseconomies.* The bigger the firm the more difficult it is to manage. Even in a very large firm the decision-making is done by a relatively small group of people. It is more difficult in a large company for such a group to gather together all the information necessary to make the correct decisions. Also problems may arise in the communication of information from management to worker.

2. As a firm expands, the interests of workers and management may *conflict*, and industrial relations problems could result. Workers may see themselves as merely 'cogs in the wheel of production'. Workers' morale may suffer as a result, leading to absenteeism and an increase in costs within the company.

3. A large firm is usually characterised by a high degree of specialisation of labour. While this usually leads to increased output, there are possible

disadvantages. Workers can become *bored with the constant repetition of the same tasks* and the quality of work may suffer. Also workers may not be open to new work practices if they have been trained to perform only a few tasks.

4. In a large company there tends to be a higher proportion of '*non-productive' workers*. More foremen and supervisors are required, as well as administrators, clerical staff, etc.

5. A large firm may be more exposed to *unreasonable demands by workers*. Workers may feel that, because of its size, the company can more easily give in to their demands.

EXTERNAL DISECONOMIES OF SCALE

External diseconomies of scale are the forces at work which cause unit cost to rise as output expands, and which are common to all firms in the industry. In other words, external diseconomies are the disadvantages of large-scale production which apply to all firms in the industry.

1. As the industry expands, the *amount of raw materials required by firms increases*. This can have two negative effects. First, the cost of raw materials will rise because of the increased demand. Second, poorer quality materials may have to be used.

2. A similar problem can arise in the case of labour. As the industry expands, *more labour is required*. Skilled labour may be in short supply so wage rates are forced up. Alternatively, the firm may be forced to employ less skilled workers. In either case, costs will rise.

3. As industry expands, *greater demands are made on a country's infrastructure*. The existing infrastructure may be inadequate to cope with the demands of expanding industries. Roads, harbours and airports may be too small to service the growing needs of industry.

The diseconomies of scale (internal and external) are shown in summary form in *Figure 3.4*.

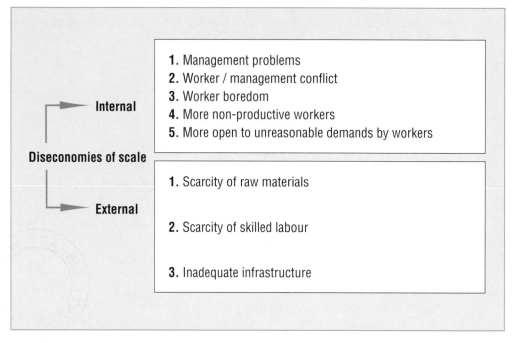

Fig. 3.4 Summary of internal and external diseconomies of scale

THE SIZE OF FIRMS

A marked feature in advanced economies in recent years has been the growth in the size of firms. This trend is most noticeable in the US and Europe, where many mergers and acquisitions have occurred.

The average size of a firm in Ireland is typically smaller than that of our European neighbours. There are many reasons for this, but the main cause is the fact that many Irish owned ('indigenous') firms supply only the home market. Therefore, they have not been able to reach the size where economies of scale are large and unit cost is low.

In 2001, there were over 1,200 multinational companies (i.e. companies with operations in many different countries) operating in Ireland, employing over 140,000 people. This represents a very sizeable proportion of our total industrial employment, and it has long been part of government policy in Ireland to seek out foreign companies to locate here.

An examination of *Table 3.1* shows that the largest companies operating in Ireland (whether Irish or foreign owned) are involved in the supply of goods and services both at home and abroad.

Rank	Company Name	Turnover (€m)	Profit (Loss) (€m)	Activity	Jobs
1	CRH	8,863	740	Building materials	36,665
2	Intel Ireland	6,031	n/d	Computers	4,500
3	Dell	5,390	91	Computers	4,525
4	Jefferson Smurfit	4,571	485	Print & packaging	6,000
5	Microsoft	4,488	n/d	Computer software	1,592
6	Kerry Group	2,603	173	Food processing	14,000
7	Glanbia	2,401	80	Food processing	7,500
8	Dunnes Stores	2,095	n/d	Retailing	18,000
9	Eircom	1,955	336	Telecommunications	12,606
10	Fyffes	1,886	84	Fruit importing	3,595
11	EMC Ireland	1,821	n/d	Computer data storage	1,100
12	Irish Dairy Board	1,809	30	Dairy exports	2,633
13	Oracle Europe	1,778	n/d	Computer software	800
14	Musgrave	1,730	33	Wholesale distribution	2,600
15	ESB	1,720	337	Electricity	9,319
16	Elan Corporation	1,651	452	Pharmaceuticals	1,600
17	Irish Distillers	1,587	n/d	Distilling	2,000
18	DCC	1,527	139	Food, oil, computers	2,933
19	Guinness Ireland	1,251	264	Brewing	2,200
20	Tesco	1,213	n/d	Retailing	10,000
21	Independent News	1,168	n/d	Printing & publishing	10,806
22	Aer Lingus	·1,157	(61)	Air transport	5,500
23	Janssen (Irl)	1,149	n/d	Pharmaceuticals	780
24	Waterford Wedgewood	1,084	86	Crystal & ceramics	9,116
25	3Com Ireland	1,009	n/d	PC adaptor card Mfr	1,800
26	IAWS	982	56	Agri-business	950
27	Irish Food Processors	914	n/d	Meat process/export	3,350
28	Greencore	906	71	Food processing	3,682
29	Glen Dimplex	889	n/d	Domestic appliances	6,000
30	Swords Laboratories	889	n/d	Pharmaceuticals	360

Source: Business & Finance, February 2001

Table 3.1 Ireland's top companies

It has been the aim of successive Irish governments to expand the exports of indigenous Irish firms so as to increase income and employment in Ireland. Only by supplying the export market can such companies hope to achieve economies of scale. At the same time it is recognised that small firms have a very important role in economic growth and the provision of employment in Ireland.

In the National Development Plan 2000–2006, the Irish Government set out to tackle the weaknesses of the indigenous manufacturing sector, which it identified as follows:

- Gross output per person in Irish-owned manufacturing plants is only 45 per cent of that of workers in foreign owned plants

- The average size of plant in terms of persons employed is five times greater in foreign-owned plants

- Indigenous firms spend little on research and development.

THE LOCATION OF INDUSTRY

The choice of one location over another by the management of a firm can have a very significant effect on its prospects for growth and long-term survival. The following are the main factors affecting the location of firms:

The nature of the industry

Industries can be classified as supply oriented, market oriented or footloose.

1. *Supply-oriented industries* are also known as weight-losing industries. For firms in such an industry, access to raw materials is more important than closeness to the market. The raw material is more bulky than the finished product, so that transport costs for the individual firm are minimised when it locates close to the source of the raw material. Examples of supply-oriented industries are steel plants (located near deposits of iron ore), sugar beet factories (located in areas where sugar beet is a major crop) and briquette factories (located close to bogs).

2. *Market-oriented industries* are also known as weight-gaining industries. For firms in such an industry, closeness to the market is more important than access to raw materials. The finished product is more bulky than the raw material because weight is added during production. In some cases the product may require special packaging if the goods are fragile and/or

perishable. Therefore, firms in such industries will tend to locate close to the market. Examples of such industries are spirits and beers, soft drinks, ice creams and bread. Most service industries are market orientated. They require large centres of population to function effectively, and consequently are to be found mostly in large towns and cities. Examples of such services are banks and other financial institutions, third-level colleges, law and accounting practices, etc.

3. *Footloose industries* are those industries which can locate anywhere. They are not obliged to locate close to the market. Therefore, there are many locational options available to firms in such industries. The location chosen by a firm will depend on some of the other factors which we will now consider.

The availability of labour

The availability of suitable skilled labour at competitive wage rates is a very important locational consideration for most firms. The recent growth in the Irish economy has been heavily dependent on foreign high technology firms. The availability of skilled labour has been crucial to our ability to attract such firms here to locate or expand their operations.

In addition, the viability of the firm can be affected by how close workers are to the firm. Workers living long distances from the factory may require travel allowances, canteen facilities, etc. and may be more likely to arrive late for work.

The closeness to similar firms and/or related research facilities

Many firms may wish to engage in joint projects with other firms, or avail of research and technological facilities in third-level colleges and specialist research institutes.

The availability of suitable transport

The availability of good transport facilities at a reasonable cost is one of the main determinants of the location of industry in Ireland. Firms will wish to minimise transport costs and consequently tend to locate in areas where good road, rail, sea and air transport facilities are available.

Roads are the dominant mode of internal transport in Ireland, accounting for 90 per cent of freight traffic and 96 per cent of passenger traffic. These figures are very high by European standards and reflect a poorly developed public transport system. An underdeveloped public transport system can hinder growth and discourage the location of industry in such areas. For an exporting firm, a location close to an airport or a seaport is obviously a very strong attraction. Ireland suffers a competitive disadvantage on European markets because of its peripheral location.

Telecommunications and energy

The availability of good telecommunications and energy services is a vital requirement for firms, particularly those engaged in the export trade. The deregulation of the telecommunications services and energy sectors means that the market should supply such services. However the lack of such services in less developed areas will discourage firms from locating there.

Government policy

The government can give higher grants to companies locating in certain designated areas, in an attempt to spread the benefits of industry as evenly as possible throughout the country. A firm in a more remote area, which is at a competitive disadvantage in relation to transport costs, may benefit from 'positive discrimination' by government in the form of extra grants or tax allowances.

The government can also attract industry to a particular area by providing advance factories, rates relief, training schemes for workers, subsidised housing and a good infrastructure. Industry can be discouraged from locating in a particular area by restrictive planning regulations, high rates and a poor infrastructure.

Ireland possesses a number of characteristics which make it a very attractive location for foreign direct investment (FDI), especially from the US which is the largest global source of such investment. These include:

- An adequate supply of skilled English-speaking labour
- Unrestricted access to a large European market
- A stable business environment
- Attractive tax rates
- A pro-business outlook from government
- An overall welcoming attitude to foreign investors.

4

The Consumer

In this chapter we will examine the role of the consumer.

> In economics, the decision-making unit that buys goods and services is known as the consumer.

The consumer can be a single individual purchasing things for him/herself, or a member of a household making purchasing decisions on behalf of the family. The members of the household will have a variety of wants, and the decision maker (or consumer) will spend the household income on goods and services which will satisfy those demands. Thus, the wants of households are turned into a demand for goods and services, which firms in the economy will try to provide. Consumers are able to purchase the output of firms because they have incomes. These incomes are earned by consumers as a result of supplying factors of production to firms. This important relationship between firms and consumers is shown in *Figure 4.1*.

Consumers supply land, labour, capital and enterprise to firms. Those supplying land receive rent in return. Most consumers supply their labour and receive wages in return. Some supply capital and receive interest. Those who bear the risk involved in production by becoming entrepreneurs earn profit in return. It is obvious that in order to purchase goods and services a consumer requires a certain quantity of money. Those consumers who do not earn income receive *transfer payments* from the state (i.e. social welfare). This allows them to purchase goods and services.

> We can define transfer payments as payments made to individuals for which no factor of production is supplied in return.

No consumer, no matter how wealthy, has an unlimited income. Every person has a finite budget within which to purchase his/her needs. In economics, we make certain assumptions about the way consumers behave, that is, on the way they spend their incomes.

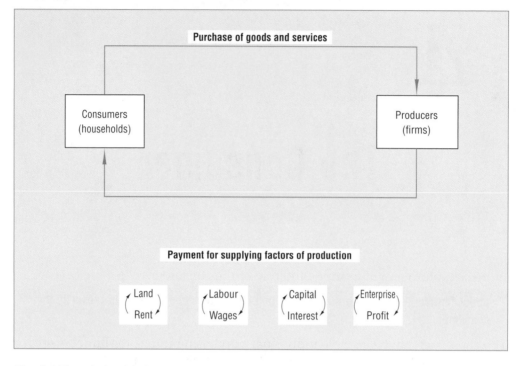

Fig. 4.1 The relationship between consumers and producers

ASSUMPTIONS CONCERNING CONSUMER BEHAVIOUR

1. Consumer income

The ability of a consumer to purchase goods and services depends on his/her income. This income is finite or limited.

2. Consumer choice

The consumer's income is limited, but his/her wants are infinite. Once the basic needs of food, clothing and shelter have been provided, the consumer is faced with a huge range of goods and services which he/she can buy. Thus, the consumer is faced with choices. A decision to purchase one item often means that it is impossible to buy another.

3. Consumer rationality

The consumer is said to act rationally. This means that the consumer will spend his/her income on the goods and services that give the greatest satisfaction. The satisfaction a consumer gets from a good is called the utility of that good.

The consumer spends his/her income so as to get the greatest possible total utility.

It should be obvious that utility is a subjective concept. It varies from person to person. A visit to your local music store will convince you of this. Thousands of CDs and tapes will be available, yet you will probably only derive satisfaction from listening to a fraction of these. However, some customers must derive pleasure from the others, since otherwise the store would not stock them.

Even for one individual, utility is not constant. It can vary over time. What you liked two years ago, you may not like now. What is to your taste now may be totally objectionable to you in another two years.

Two very important points need to be made here regarding utility and the behaviour of consumers. First, utility is not measurable. It is not possible for me to say that one item gives me 10 units of utility and another item only five. Second, it is not suggested that every consumer carefully plans his/her spending so as to get the maximum possible utility from every penny spent. We all can remember times when we foolishly bought things on the spur of the moment, without considering did we really need them and without estimating their usefulness to us. What is being said is that each consumer can rank his/her preferences. A consumer can say that Good X is preferable to Good Y because it yields more satisfaction.

> A rational consumer can be defined as one who spends his/her income on the goods and services that give him/her the most utility.

4. Economic goods

The consumer will spend his/her income on 'economic goods' only. An economic good is defined as any physical object, or any service rendered, which possesses the following three characteristics:

(a) *It must give utility or satisfaction.* Otherwise there would be no demand for it.

(b) *It must be scarce in relation to the demand for it,* i.e. there must be less of it available than would satisfy all possible wants for it. If this were not so, no one would be willing to pay a price for it.

(c) *It must be transferable.* It must be possible for one person to sell it to another. Good health, beauty and intelligence satisfy points (a) and (b) but not (c), so they cannot be classified as economic goods.

5. The Law of Diminishing Marginal Utility

The consumer is subject to the Law of Diminishing Marginal Utility, which states that:

> As extra units of a good are consumed, the satisfaction gained from each extra unit of that good falls.

We have already defined the utility of a good as the satisfaction a consumer gets from using that good. We now define the marginal utility of a good as the extra satisfaction a consumer derives from consuming an extra unit of that good.

Put in its simplest form, this law states that the more of any item an individual has, the less satisfaction he gets from having more of it. An extra pair of shoes would yield more satisfaction to a man with only one pair than to a man who already has 10 pairs. An extra bar of chocolate will mean less to a child who has already had six bars than to a child who has already consumed only one bar.

Two features of economic behaviour confirm that the Law of Diminishing Marginal Utility does indeed hold true in the vast majority of cases.

1. Producers often offer quantity discounts to consumers. For example, a shop might offer chocolate at 40c a bar or three for €1. This is a recognition by the producer or seller that the consumer is less likely to buy more units, unless a lower price is charged for additional units. This must mean that additional units of the good are less attractive to the consumer. If the second and third bars of chocolate gave the same utility as the first, there would be no need for the seller to offer quantity discounts.

2. There is a limit to the amount of a good which people will consume, even if no additional charge is made for extra units of the good.

There are very few exceptions to the Law of Diminishing Marginal Utility. One possible exception is in the case of addictive drugs or medicine. A second or third dose of medicine may be as important as the first in the treatment of a particular complaint and so may yield the same (or even higher) utility than the first.

HOW WILL A UTILITY-MAXIMISING CONSUMER SPEND HIS/HER INCOME?

We now turn our attention to the way in which a utility-maximising consumer spends his/her income. Based on our observations above concerning consumer behaviour, we are able to make the following precise statement:

> In order to enjoy maximum utility, a rational consumer will spend his/her income in such a way that the ratio of marginal utility to price is the same for all the goods he/she buys. This law is known as the Law of Equi-Marginal Returns (or the Equi-Marginal Principle).

It is often expressed in the following notation:

$$\frac{MU_1}{P_1} = \frac{MU_2}{P_2} = \ldots\ldots \frac{MU_n}{P_n}$$

where MU = marginal utility

P = price

1, 2, ...n = the goods that are bought

If this relationship did not hold true, it would be possible for the consumer to increase his/her total satisfaction (or utility) by changing his/her spending pattern so that he/she spends more on the goods yielding higher marginal utility and less on the goods yielding lower marginal utility.

It has already been pointed out that utility cannot be measured. The following example assumes that we can measure utility. Unless we make this assumption, we cannot show how the Law of Equi-Marginal Returns works.

Suppose a girl gets weekly pocket money of €10 which she spends on two goods, cans of minerals and bars of chocolate. Minerals cost €1 per can and chocolate 50c per bar. The marginal utility and the total utility she derives from consuming various quantities of the two goods are as shown in *Table 4.1*.

Quantity consumed per week	Cans of minerals		Bars of chocolates	
	Total utility	Marginal utility	Total utility	Marginal utility
1	100	–	80	–
2	190	90	155	75
3	269	79	219	64
4	335	66	270	51
5	392	57	315	45
6	432	40	358	43
7	467	35	396	38
8	487	20	416	20
9	504	17	434	18
10	519	15	448	14
11	529	10	458	10
12	533	4	464	6

Table 4.1 The Law of Equi-Marginal Returns: how a girl allocates her pocket money between two goods

The total utility the girl gets from consuming one bar of chocolate is 80 units. The total utility she gets from consuming two bars is 155 units, so the marginal utility of the second bar is 75 (155 – 80) units, and so on. Notice that the marginal utility of both products is declining as extra units are consumed – this is the Law of Diminishing Marginal Utility in operation. Total utility, therefore, increases but at a declining rate.

How should this girl spend her weekly pocket money of €10 to gain the greatest satisfaction? According to the Law of Equi-Marginal Returns, she should spend her income so that the ratio of marginal utility to price is the same for both goods. Therefore, she should buy six cans of minerals and eight bars of chocolate weekly, since for this combination of the two goods:

$$\frac{MU(minerals)}{P(minerals)} = \frac{MU(chocolate)}{P(chocolate)}$$

$$\frac{40}{€1} = \frac{20}{50c}$$

Spending her income in this way gives her a total of 848 (432 + 416) units of utility. By examining any other combination of the two goods, we can see that her total utility will be less. For example, buying eight minerals and four bars of chocolate would give her 757 (487 + 270) units of utility. Alternatively, if she were to spend her weekly income on four cans of minerals and 12 bars of chocolate, her total utility would be 799 (335 + 464) units. There is no other possible combination of the two products that would yield a higher total utility than would apply when six cans of minerals and eight bars of chocolate are consumed.

REASONS WHY CONSUMERS BUY CERTAIN GOODS AND SERVICES

Producers are always interested in the reasons why consumers buy goods and services. By examining these reasons, they hope to increase their own sales (and profits). The following are the main sources of demand which are usually identified:

1. *Functional demand.* This is the most basic source of demand. People buy products to perform specific tasks, e.g. a camera to take photographs, a cooker to prepare meals, etc.

2. *The bandwagon effect.* People sometimes buy goods because others (their neighbours perhaps) have bought similar items. For example, if one householder in a particular area installs new PVC windows, his/her neighbour may be tempted to do likewise.

3. *Exclusive demand.* Sometimes expensive goods are bought because of the status attached to them, e.g. designer clothes, expensive jewellery, etc.

4. *Speculative demand.* Sometimes people purchase items because they believe these items will go up in value over a period of time. This usually applies to land, housing, antiques and stocks and shares.

5. *Impulse buying.* Sometimes people purchase goods on the spur of the moment, possibly as a result of a very persuasive advertising campaign.

INCOME, WEALTH, UTILITY AND WELFARE

It is opportune at this point to clarify a few words that have very precise meanings in economics and which are used in explaining consumer behaviour. First we must distinguish between income and wealth.

> **Wealth is the total stock of assets which a person owns.**

Wealth includes money and physical assets like land, property and household goods.

> **Income is the flow of wealth which is earned by an individual over a period of time, usually one year.**

This is received by the individual in exchange for supplying one or more of the factors of production. So while wealth is a stock measured at a particular point in time, income is a flow over a period of time. Income is usually received in money, but sometimes people can receive part of their incomes 'in kind', that is, in the form of goods and services.

Similarly, we must distinguish between utility and welfare.

> **Utility is the satisfaction a consumer enjoys by using goods.**

> **Welfare refers to the overall well-being of an individual.**

It should be obvious that these two terms do not mean the same thing. In economics, we concentrate on the satisfaction a person gets from consuming economic goods. However, it is important to remember that this represents only part of a person's welfare. Good health, intelligence, a positive attitude to life and an ability to get on well with others are all desirable qualities which determine a person's welfare; but because they are not economic goods, they do not form part of the subject matter of economics.

5

Markets

In economics we define a market as the mechanism by which potential buyers of a good or service are brought into contact with potential sellers of that good or service.

A market includes all the individuals and institutions involved in buying or selling a good or service.

Markets provide the answers to four fundamental economic questions:

1. What goods should be produced (and in what quantities)?
2. For whom are the goods produced?
3. How are the goods to be produced (i.e. what combination of factors of production should be used)?
4. What rewards should be given to those who supply the factors of production.

When defined in this way, it is obvious that a market is a group of people rather than a particular place. While a market may be confined to one particular location, such as the stock exchange (where company shares and government securities are traded), it may be dispersed, as is the market for foreign currencies that extends worldwide (and is known as the foreign exchange market).

In this chapter, we shall examine the way in which a market works, and show how the desires of consumers (as expressed in their demand for goods and services) are brought into harmony with the output decisions of producers (as expressed in their supply of goods and services). We shall then examine different types of markets, and analyse the special features of each so that we can more clearly understand its role in our lives.

How a Market Works

Every market works through the interaction of supply and demand. By the demand for a good we mean the quantity consumers would be willing to buy at different prices. By the supply of a good we mean the quantity that producers would be willing to make available at different prices. A market works on the principle that there is some price that satisfies both consumers and producers.

Let us first turn our attention to consumers. We can make two statements which are true in the vast majority of cases:

> If price rises, quantity demanded falls.
> If price falls, quantity demanded rises.

So if we look at the market for coffee in Ireland, we might find the following relationship between price and quantity demanded.

Price per 100 g jar (€)	Number of jars demanded
1.00	50,000
1.50	40,000
2.00	35,000
2.50	25,000
3.00	20,000
3.50	15,000

Table 5.1 Weekly demand schedule for coffee in Ireland

A list showing the quantities that would be demanded at a number of different prices is called a demand schedule. When the same information is presented

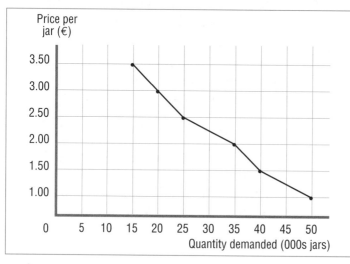

Fig. 5.1 Demand curve showing weekly demand for coffee in Ireland

graphically, it is known as a demand curve. *Figure 5.1* shows the demand curve which is drawn from the demand schedule in *Table 5.1*. We measure quantity demanded along the horizontal (or X) axis and price per jar along the vertical (or Y) axis.

Now let us examine the situation from the point of view of the producers. The following two statements are true for the vast majority of producers:

If price rises, quantity supplied rises.
If price falls, quantity supplied falls.

Staying with our example of the market for coffee in Ireland, we might find the relationship between price and quantity supplied to be that shown in *Table 5.2*.

Price per 100 g jar (€)	Number of jars demanded
1.00	5,000
1.50	10,000
2.00	15,000
2.50	25,000
3.00	35,000
3.50	45,000

Table 5.2 Weekly supply schedule for coffee in Ireland

A list showing the quantities that producers are willing to supply at each price is known as a supply schedule. When the same information is presented graphically, it is known as a supply curve.

Figure 5.2 shows the supply curve which is drawn from the supply schedule in *Table 5.2*. Again we measure quantity along the horizontal axis, but 'quantity'

Fig. 5.2 Supply curve showing weekly supply of coffee in Ireland

in this case represents the output that producers are prepared to supply. Price is again measured along the vertical axis.

Suppose the price of coffee now is €3.00 per jar. Producers would be willing to supply 35,000 jars weekly at that price, but consumers are prepared to buy only 20,000 jars. Producers would be left with 15,000 jars per week that could not be sold. There is excess supply. Excess supply exists when quantity supplied is greater than quantity demanded. Producers have no option but to lower price. So a price of €3.00 per jar could only last for a short period of time.

The same could be said for a price of €1.50 per jar. At this price, consumers are willing to buy 40,000 jars per week, but producers are prepared to supply only 10,000 jars per week. There is excess demand. Excess demand exists when quantity demanded is greater than quantity supplied. In this case, consumers would compete against each other for the available supply and price would be forced upwards. Therefore, a price of €1.50 could only exist for a short period of time.

At a price of €2.50 per jar, the weekly demand for coffee is exactly equal to the quantity producers are willing to supply. That is, at a price of €2.50 per jar, supply equals demand. This price is called the equilibrium price, and 25,000 jars per week represent the equilibrium quantity. By equilibrium we mean a situation from which there is no tendency to change.

If the price on the market is above the equilibrium price, there will be downward pressure on price. Quantity supplied will exceed quantity demanded, and producers will lower price to get rid of surplus stock.

If the price on the market is below the equilibrium price, there will be upward pressure on price. Quantity demanded will exceed quantity supplied, and consumers will be competing for a limited supply of the good. Scarcity would exist and price would increase. We can now summarise the above analysis by making the following observation:

> If no interference in the market occurs (by government or other agency), price will eventually settle at the level where quantity demanded equals quantity supplied. This position is called the market equilibrium.

TYPES OF MARKETS

1. *Factor markets.* A factor market is a market where a factor of production is bought and sold. The buyer is the entrepreneur who wishes to use that factor in the production of goods and services. The seller is the owner of the factor of production in question. The price is determined in the way

just described, and represents income to the owner of the factor of production. Rent is income to the owner of land, wages the reward to the supplier of labour, and interest the return to the owner of capital.

2. *Intermediate markets*. An intermediate market is one where the output is sold to be used as an 'input' (i.e. component or raw material) in the production of another good. For example, the output of the steel industry is bought by car manufacturing firms and shipyards to be used in the making of cars and ships. Intermediate goods are also known as producer goods.

3. *Final markets*. Final markets are markets which deal with goods and services that give consumers utility, and for which they are therefore prepared to pay a price. These are known as consumer goods. Whereas producer goods are traded on intermediate markets, consumer goods are traded on final markets. Examples of final markets are the markets for food, drink, clothing, cars, furniture and household appliances.

Examples of markets in operation

1. A RETAIL SHOP

This is the market that most people are familiar with. A vast range of consumer goods is offered for sale to the public. Shops range in size from small family-run businesses serving the local community to the huge retail units located in large shopping centres serving an extended catchment area (see *Figure 5.3*).

Fig. 5.3 Blanchardstown Centre: Ireland's biggest shopping centre opened in 1997 with 61,000 square metres of shops in 113 retail units

Most shops find it convenient to fix the price of each good, so that every consumer is then free to decide the quantity he/she wishes to buy (if any) at that price. If the price is set too high, supply will exceed demand. In that case, the producer/seller must lower the price to attract more customers or else go out of business altogether. If the price is set too low, demand will exceed supply. The producer/seller will find that profits can be increased by increasing price. Thus, the price of a good is always tending towards equilibrium, where supply is equal to demand.

2. An Auction

In an auction, the supply is restricted to one unit (or 'lot') which is sold to the highest bidder. There is one seller but many would-be buyers. The auctioneer progressively raises the asking price until demand is made equal to supply, that is, until there is only one would-be buyer prepared to offer this price. In some cases the seller specifies a minimum (or reserve) price, below which he/she is not prepared to sell the good.

3. Haggling

This is the name given to the practice whereby the buyer and seller argue over the price of an item. The price is not fixed beforehand, and bargaining takes place on a one-to-one basis between buyer and seller.

The seller tries to sell the item at the highest possible price and has a minimum price below which he/she is not prepared to sell. The buyer tries to purchase the item at the lowest possible price and has a maximum price above which he/she is not prepared to buy.

If the seller's minimum price exceeds the buyer's maximum price, the good will not be exchanged. If the seller's minimum price is less than or equal to the buyer's maximum price, then there is said to be 'a bargaining range' and the good can be exchanged. The actual price in this case will depend on the relative bargaining skills of the buyer and seller.

Two related concepts need to be explained at this point.

(a) *Consumer's surplus.* This is the difference between the highest price a consumer is prepared to pay for an item, and the price he/she actually pays. For example, if I am prepared to pay €20,000 for a particular second-hand car, but able to buy it for €15,000, then I am said to enjoy a consumer's surplus of €5,000.

(b) *Producer's surplus.* This is the difference between the lowest price a producer/seller is prepared to accept for a good, and the price he/she actually receives. For example, if a farmer is prepared to supply potatoes at €600 per tonne but receives €700 per tonne, he is said to enjoy a producer's surplus of €100 per tonne.

In haggling the existence of consumer's surplus/producer's surplus is an indication of the relative bargaining strengths of the buyer/seller. An example of a market where haggling takes place in Ireland is the second-hand car market (see *Fig. 5.4*). Advertisements are placed in the pages of newspapers by would-be sellers, who are then contacted by would-be buyers. Bargaining then takes place in an effort to fix a price acceptable to both parties.

Fig. 5.4 The second-hand car market in Ireland operates through the pages of newspapers. (Source: *Evening Herald*, 17 November 2001)

4. THE STOCK EXCHANGE

This is a market where shares in public companies and units of government stock are bought and sold. The purchase of shares by an individual gives him/her part ownership of the company and the right to an annual dividend based on company profits. Buyers of government stock can be considered as lenders to the government, who receive a fixed rate of return on their money each year, together with the guaranteed repayment of the purchase price of the stock at an agreed future date.

As was the case in other markets, a change in price is the mechanism by which demand is made equal to supply on the stock exchange. If a company is doing well and expected to make good profits, there will be many would-be buyers of its shares but few shareholders will be willing to sell their shares. Therefore, demand exceeds supply and the price of the share will rise. The opposite will apply if the company is doing badly.

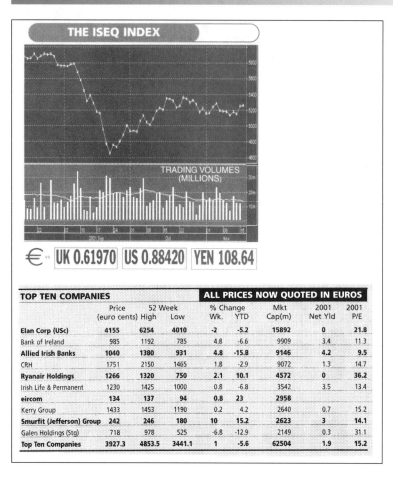

Fig. 5.5 The Irish Stock Exchange – details for top ten companies and the ISEQ Index. (Source: *The Sunday Tribune*, 18 November 2001)

TOP TEN COMPANIES	Price (euro cents)	52 Week High	Low	% Change Wk.	YTD	Mkt Cap(m)	2001 Net Yld	2001 P/E
Elan Corp (USc)	4155	6254	4010	-2	-5.2	15892	0	21.8
Bank of Ireland	985	1192	785	4.8	-6.6	9909	3.4	11.3
Allied Irish Banks	1040	1380	931	4.8	-15.8	9146	4.2	9.5
CRH	1751	2150	1465	1.8	-2.9	9072	1.3	14.7
Ryanair Holdings	1266	1320	750	2.1	10.1	4572	0	36.2
Irish Life & Permanent	1230	1425	1000	0.8	-6.8	3542	3.5	13.4
eircom	134	137	94	0.8	23	2958		
Kerry Group	1433	1453	1190	0.2	4.2	2640	0.7	15.2
Smurfit (Jefferson) Group	242	246	180	10	15.2	2623	3	14.1
Galen Holdings (Stg)	718	978	525	-6.8	-12.9	2149	0.3	31.1
Top Ten Companies	3927.3	4853.5	3441.1	1	-5.6	62504	1.9	15.2

All prices now quoted in euros

€ vs UK 0.61970 US 0.88420 YEN 108.64

The price of shares on the stock exchange is an indicator of the overall well-being of the economy. On the Irish Stock Exchange movements in the general level of share prices are reflected in the ISEQ Index (see *Fig. 5.5*). If share prices in general are rising, this reflects confidence in the economy and an expectation that firms will be profitable. A fall in share prices reflects a gloomy outlook for business and a desire by existing shareholders to convert their shares into cash.

5. THE FOREIGN EXCHANGE MARKET

This is an international market where the currencies of the world are bought and sold. It is not located in any one place since transactions are conducted electronically right across the world. The buyers and sellers are those individuals and institutions who trade in currencies to make profits (speculators) or to facilitate international trade (importers and exporters).

The price in this case is known as the exchange rate of a currency. As in other markets, it is determined by the interaction of demand and supply. Foreign exchange markets will be examined more fully in *Chapter 29*.

Euro Exchange Rates

Currency	Yesterday	Previous
Sterling	0.6149	0.6154
US Dollar	0.8972	0.8968
Japanese Yen	108.69	109.11
Danish krone	7.4475	7.4475
Swedish krone	9.4737	9.4966
Swiss franc	1.4719	1.4727
Norwegian krone	7.945	7.928
Canadian dollar	1.4296	1.4301
Australian dollar	1.7496	1.7675
Polish zloty	3.67	3.6843
Hungarian forint	251.48	253.1
Hong Kong dollar	6.9973	6.9945
Singapore dollar	1.6331	1.6345

Fig. 5.6 The foreign exchange market – the value of the euro in terms of other currencies. (Source: *The Irish Times*, 7 November 2001 – *www.ireland.com*)

6. COMMODITY MARKETS

Like the foreign exchange market, the markets for major commodities (crude oil, sugar, metals, cocoa, coffee, grain crops, etc.) are worldwide with price changes reflecting the relative scarcity or abundance of the good (see *Fig. 5.7*). Any interruption of supply, such as bad weather, transport difficulties, strikes, etc. will cause the price of a commodity to rise worldwide, while overproduction will cause a 'glut' or surplus which will result in a fall in price.

Commodities, like currencies and shares, can be traded on the 'spot' market or the 'futures' market. The spot market is the market for immediate delivery, and the spot price is the price that prevails at the moment. Futures markets (also called forward markets), on the other hand, allow manufacturers and traders to hedge against changes in the price of their raw materials. This is done by making contracts at an agreed price now for the supply of these commodities at a specified future date.

Fig. 5.7 Commodity markets – details of commodity prices on world markets. (Source: *Financial Times*, 3 November 2001)

WEEKLY PRICE CHANGES

	Latest prices	Change on week	Year ago	2001 High	2001 Low
Gold per troy oz.	$280.30	+3.5	265.15	291.125	256.70
Silver per troy oz	288.05p	-5.7	328.49	329.47	287.78
Aluminium 99.7% (cash)	$1253.25	-25.25	1475.5	1690	1265.5
Copper Grade A (cash)	$1399.5	+33.75	1824.5	1831	1360.25
Lead (cash)	$478.75	-1.75	491.5	519	437.5
Nickel (cash)	$4437.5	-130	7360	6335	4567.5
Zinc SHG (cash)	$747.5	-15.75	1093	1044.5	746.25
Tin (cash)	$3815	-2.5	5170.0	5250	3622.5
Cocoa Futures Dec	#733	-4	582	925	615
Coffee Futures Nov	$377	-17	710	1231	358
Sugar (LDP Raw)	$176.1	-3.5	255.5	259.00	170.00
Barley Futures Nov	#63.00	+0.75	64.5	72.50	60.50
Wheat Futures Nov	#76.00	-0.7	60.0	80.00	67.00
Cotton Outlook A Index	34.95c	-0.55	61.75	76.50	35.50
Wool (64s Super)	352p	+3	312	388	324
Oil (Brent Blend)	$19.55x	-1.65	31.53	30.95	19.50
Sovereigns	$68.5	+1	66	71	64
Kruggerands	$280.4	+0.4	280.5	290.50	255.75

Per tonne unless otherwise stated. p Pence/kg. c Cents/lb. x Nov

7. TELEMARKETING

According to IDA Ireland, Ireland has established itself as the undisputed leader in the field of European call centres in the last five years, with over 60 major world companies selecting this country as the base for their European operations. These centres, which employed over 6,000 people in 2002, carry out a range of functions such as direct selling, handling customer queries, providing technical support and advice, and handling reservations for airlines, car hire, hotels and other accommodation.

8. BUYING AND SELLING ON THE INTERNET

The growth of the internet has provided a new and powerful method of bringing buyers and sellers of goods and services together. Most major retailers now provide online shopping facilities, while banking, insurance and financial service companies have also been quick to embrace the new technology in their efforts to increase sales.

Commodity markets at work

The following market report from the *Financial Times*, 3 November 2001, outlines some important features of markets:

- The price of any product depends on supply and demand

- Supply can be restricted by producers in an effort to increase price

- An increase in unemployment will usually lead to a fall in demand.

Weak US data bring down oil

By Sarah Ross

Oil prices fell to their lowest level since August 1999, weighed down by weak US economic data, a lack of agreement to cut supply by OPEC producers and signs of higher crude oil stocks in the US.

Signs of deepening malaise in the world's largest economy – declining gross domestic product growth, higher unemployment and falling consumer confidence – increased fears that demand for oil would weaken.

Meanwhile, OPEC's attempts to shore up the price by seeking agreement for a production cut of 1m barrels a day had little effect. Although it seems probable that cuts will be announced at OPEC's next ministerial meeting on November 14, the cartel is finding it difficult to persuade non-members to support its efforts.

Oil price bulls are hoping that an OPEC output cut as well as better compliance with production limits by members will boost prices. There are also expectations that the White House will announce an increase in its Strategic Petroleum Reserve – possibly of 100,000 b/d over the next three years.

Late in London December Brent was down 52 cents at $19.10. In early afternoon in New York, WTI was down 57 cents at $19.82.

Gold rose briefly above $280 an ounce on Tuesday after sharp equity market falls the day before. A weaker US dollar also helped support prices.

Spot gold fixed at $279.90 a troy ounce in London afternoon trade, compared with last Friday's $277.25.

Copper prices fell to their lowest level since February 1987 following disapppointment over producer's unwillingness to curb output and concerns over global oversupply. LME three-month copper closed the afternoon session at $1355.50, down $41 over the week.

The decision by Outokumpu, the Finnish mining company, to close its Tara mine in Ireland helped zinc prices recover from their lowest ever in real terms. But the rally fizzled out on concerns that mine shutdowns would not be enough to address the supply/demand imbalance.

LME three-month zinc fell $15 over the week to $767.50.

Demand

In *Chapter 5* we examined how markets work. We noted that price was determined by the interaction of demand and supply. From demand and supply schedules, we drew demand and supply curves. We saw that the price eventually settles at the level which equates demand and supply. In the next two chapters we shall deal in turn with the factors affecting demand and supply. In *Chapter 8* we shall examine how changes in demand and supply affect equilibrium price and quantity.

At the outset, we must distinguish between 'desire' and 'demand'. When we speak of 'the demand for a good', we do not mean the desire of individuals to own that good. We are referring to their ability and willingness to purchase a good. This is known as effective demand.

INDIVIDUAL DEMAND AND MARKET DEMAND

An *individual demand schedule* lists the different quantities of a good that an individual consumer is prepared to buy at each price.

An *individual demand curve* is a graph showing how much of a good a consumer is prepared to buy at each price. It is derived from the individual's demand schedule for that good.

A *market (or aggregate) demand schedule* lists the different quantities of a good that all consumers in the market are prepared to buy at each price. It is derived by adding together all the individual demand schedules for the good.

A *market (or aggregate) demand curve* is a graph showing the total demand in the market for that good at each price. It is derived by adding together (horizontally) all the individual demand curves for that product.

Price per item (cent)	Individual demand schedules			Market demand schedule
	A	B	C	
20	10	10	9	29
40	8	8	7	23
60	7	6	5	18
80	6	4	4	14
100	5	2	3	10

Table 6.1 Individual demand schedules and market demand schedule for Good X

Example: To make the explanation easier, we will assume that in the case of Good X, there are only three consumers in the market, namely A, B and C. Their individual weekly demand schedules for Good X are given in *Table 6.1*, together with the market (or aggregate) schedule. *Figure 6.1* shows the individual demand curves of the three consumers A, B and C for Good X.

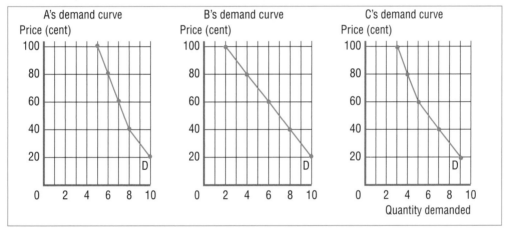

Fig. 6.1 Individual demand curves of consumers A, B and C for Good X

The market demand curve for Good X is derived by horizontally adding the individual demand curves of the three consumers. This is shown in *Figure 6.2*.

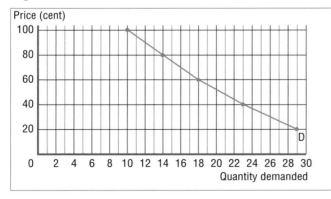

Fig. 6.2 Market (aggregate) demand curve of Good X

FACTORS AFFECTING THE DEMAND FOR A GOOD

1. Demand for a good depends on its own price

GOODS WHICH OBEY THE LAW OF DEMAND

In *Chapter 5* we made two statements, which we said were true for most goods.

> If price rises, quantity demanded falls.
> If price falls, quantity demanded rises.
> That is, if P rises, Q falls.
> If P falls, Q rises.
> P and Q refer to price and quantity demanded, respectively.

This is known as the Law of Demand. Goods which obey this law have, therefore, an inverse (i.e. negative) relationship between price and quantity demanded. The demand curve for such goods will be downward sloping from left to right, as shown in *Figure 6.3*. At price P_1, quantity demanded is Q_1. If price is increased to P_2, quantity demanded falls to Q_2.

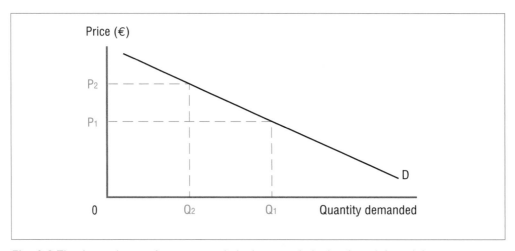

Fig. 6.3 The demand curve for most goods is downward sloping from left to right

GOODS WHICH DO NOT OBEY THE LAW OF DEMAND

All the demand curves drawn so far reflect the usual pattern of demand, i.e. they are downward sloping, indicating that the higher the price, the lower the quantity demanded. However, there are a number of important exceptions to this pattern, i.e. there are some goods that do not obey the Law of Demand.

1. *Giffen goods.* These goods are named after Sir Robert Giffen (1837-1910), a Scottish economist. He observed that in the case of certain necessities, such

as bread, a rise in price caused an increase in demand, while a fall in price caused a fall in demand. Giffen explained this as follows. Poor people spend their incomes mostly on bread and on a few luxury goods, such as meat. As the price of bread rises, they have less income to spend on other types of food, so they tend to increase their demand for bread. Similarly, because bread constitutes such a large part of the spending of the poor, a fall in its price will enable them to spend more on other food items, while spending less on bread. Rice is the staple diet of the poor in many countries today and is often cited as an example of a Giffen good.

2. *Snob goods.* These are goods which are attractive to some consumers because they are expensive. The price is considered to be an indication of their exclusive nature or of their quality. For example, in a top class restaurant, the most expensive wine is often the one most in demand. The same point can be made in the case of expensive cars, fur coats, jewellery, etc. A rise in price may make them more exclusive, and therefore, more attractive to those with the incomes to purchase them. A fall in price may lead to a fall in quantity demanded. This is because they no longer appear as exclusive to the rich, but are still outside the price range of the poor. Snob goods are sometimes referred to as 'status symbols'. The purchase of such goods is often called 'conspicuous consumption'.

3. *Goods affected by consumers' expectations.* Expectations of a further price rise may cause people to increase their demand for a good following an initial price rise. Similarly, a fall in price may lead to a fall in quantity demanded if people think that the price of the good will fall further. This can be seen in the case of shares on the stock exchange, and also speculation in land and foreign currencies. When the price of a company's shares falls, people may buy fewer shares if they think that the price will fall even further.

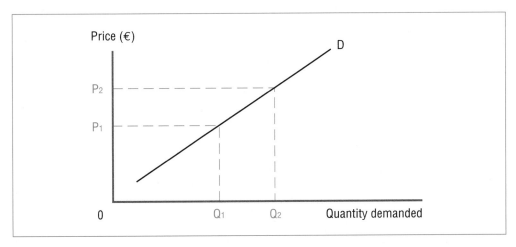

Fig. 6.4 Goods which do not obey the Law of Demand have upward sloping demand curves

A rise in the price of a company's shares will cause people to increase their demand for shares if they expect further price increases. In each of these three cases, the demand curve for the good will be upward sloping from left to right, as shown in *Figure 6.4*. A rise in price from P_1 to P_2 will cause an increase in quantity demanded from Q_1 to Q_2, while a fall in price will lead to a reduction in quantity demanded. Such goods are said to have 'perverse' or 'regressive' demand curves.

Summary

The statement, 'The quantity demanded of Good X depends on the price of Good X', can be written more concisely as:

$Q_X = f(P_X)$, where f means 'is a function of ' or 'depends on'.

For goods which obey the Law of Demand:
If P_X rises, Q_X falls.
If P_X falls, Q_X rises.

For goods which do not obey the Law of Demand:
If P_X rises, Q_X rises.
If P_X falls, Q_X falls.

---

2. Demand for a good depends on price of other goods

The demand for a good may change if the price of complementary or substitute goods change.

> Complementary goods are goods which are used jointly. The use of one involves the use of the other.

Examples of complementary goods are cars and petrol, cameras and film, gin and tonic, bread and butter, tennis racquets and tennis balls. Complementary goods are said to be in 'joint demand'. If an increase in the price of one good leads to a decrease in the demand for another good, then the two goods are said to be complementary goods (or complements).

> Substitute goods are goods which satisfy the same need, and thus can be considered as alternatives to each other.

Examples of substitute goods are coffee and tea, butter and low-fat spreads, compact discs and cassettes. If an increase in the price of one good leads to an increase in the demand for another good, then the two goods are said to be substitute goods. When the demand for a good increases we must draw a new demand curve, to the right of the existing one (i.e. further away from the origin). When the demand for a good falls we must draw a new demand curve, to the left of the existing one (i.e. closer to the origin).

Change in Price of Complementary Good

An increase in the price of a complementary good causes the demand for our good (Good X) to fall. This is shown in *Figure 6.5*. The demand curve shifts to the left. D_1 represents the original demand curve and D_2 the new demand curve.

A fall in the price of a complementary good causes the demand for our good (Good X) to rise. This is shown in *Figure 6.6*. The demand curve shifts to the right. D_1 represents the original demand curve and D_2 the new demand curve.

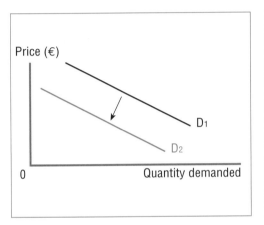

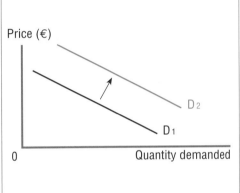

Fig. 6.5 An increase in the price of a complementary good causes the demand for Good X to fall

Fig. 6.6 A fall in the price of a complementary good causes the demand for Good X to rise

Change in Price of Substitute Good

An increase in the price of a substitute good causes the demand for our good (Good X) to rise. This is shown in *Figure 6.7*. The demand curve shifts to the right. D_1 represents the original demand curve and D_2 the new demand curve.

A fall in the price of a substitute good causes the demand for our good (Good X) to fall. This is shown in *Figure 6.8*. The demand curve shifts to the left. D_1 represents the original demand curve and D_2 the new demand curve.

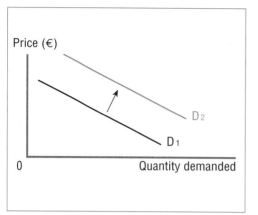

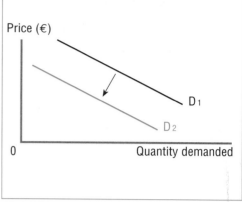

Fig. 6.7 An increase in the price of a substitute good causes the demand for Good X to rise

Fig. 6.8 A fall in the price of a substitute good causes the demand for Good X to fall

Summary

The demand for Good X, therefore, depends on the price of complementary and substitute goods. We can express this concisely as follows:

$D_X = f (P_C, P_S)$, where

P_C = the price of complementary goods

P_S = the price of substitute goods

For complementary goods:
If P_C rises, D_X falls.
If P_C falls, D_X rises.

For substitute goods:
If P_S rises, D_X rises.
If P_S falls, D_X falls.

3. Demand for a good depends on level of income

We must initially make a distinction between *money income* and *real income*. A person's money income is simply his/her earnings expressed as euro per week/month/year. A person's real income is the purchasing power of his/her money income. It is possible for a person to get a rise in his/her money income, and still suffer a decline in real income. This happens if the rise in the cost of living exceeds the rise in his/her money income, so that his/her purchasing power (i.e. the amount of goods and services that he/she can buy) has fallen. In the explanation that follows, 'income' refers to 'real income'.

NORMAL GOODS

For most goods, a rise in incomes will lead to an increase in demand. As our incomes increase, we buy more goods and services. If our incomes fall, we buy less goods and services. Therefore, most goods will have a positive relationship between income and quantity demanded. Such goods are called normal goods.

> A normal good is a good with a positive income effect. A rise in income causes more of it to be demanded, while a fall in income causes less of it to be demanded.

An increase in income will, therefore, cause the demand curve for a normal good to shift to the right, outwards from the origin, i.e. there will be an increase in demand. This is shown in *Figure 6.9*.

Conversely, a reduction in income will cause the demand curve for a normal good to shift to the left, closer to the origin, i.e. there will be a decrease in demand. This is shown in *Figure 6.10*.

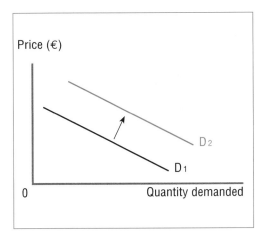

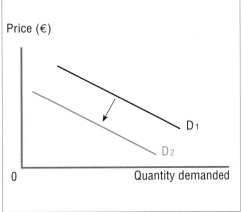

Fig. 6.9 A rise in income causes the demand for a normal good to increase from D_1 to D_2

Fig. 6.10 A fall in income causes the demand for a normal good to fall from D_1 to D_2

INFERIOR GOODS

> An inferior good is a good with a negative income effect. A rise in income causes less of it to be demanded, while a fall in income causes more of it to be demanded.

Inferior in this sense does not refer to the quality of the good, but only to the reaction of consumers to the good as their incomes rise. Potatoes and white bread are considered inferior goods in Ireland. These goods are less attractive at high incomes and tend to be replaced by more expensive substitutes. An increase in income will, therefore, cause the demand curve for an inferior good to shift to the left, closer to the origin, i.e. there will be a decrease in demand. This is shown in *Figure 6.11*.

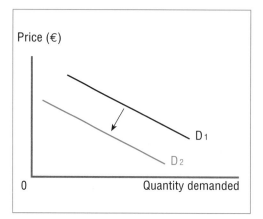

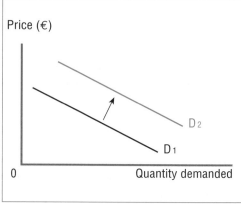

Fig. 6.11 A rise in income causes the demand for an inferior good to fall from D_1 to D_2

Fig. 6.12 A fall in income causes demand for an inferior good to rise from D_1 to D_2

Conversely, a fall in income will cause the demand curve for an inferior good to shift to the right, away from the origin, i.e. there will be an increase in demand. This is shown in *Figure 6.12*.

Summary

$$D_X = f(Y)$$
Where Y = income

For normal goods:
If Y rises, D_X rises.
If Y falls, D_X falls.

For inferior goods:
If Y rises, D_X falls.
If Y falls, D_X rises.

4. Demand for a good depends on taste

Goods may become more or less appealing to consumers with the passing of time. Some goods which were very much in demand in the past have gone out of fashion completely (e.g. certain types of clothes). To convince yourself of this, look at videos of 1970's rock groups (or ask your teacher for some old photographs!).

If the movement in taste is in favour of the good, it causes an increase in demand, which shifts the demand curve to the right (from D_1 to D_2 as shown in *Figure 6. 13*). The aim of advertising is therefore to shift the firm's demand curve to the right. If the movement in taste is against the good, it causes a fall in demand, which shifts the demand curve to the left (from D_1 to D_2 in *Figure 6. 14*).

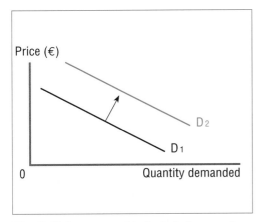

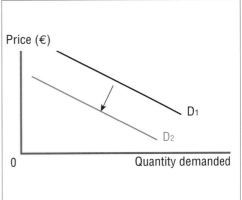

Fig. 6.13 A movement in taste in favour of a good causes demand to increase (from D_1 to D_2)

Fig. 6.14 A movement in taste against a good causes demand to fall (from D_1 to D_2)

Summary
$$D_X = f(t)$$
where t = tastes of consumers.

For all goods:
If t rises (i.e. taste moves to Good X), D_X rises.
If t falls (i.e. taste moves from Good X), D_X falls.

5. Demand for a good depends on expectations of consumers concerning future prices, availability or incomes

The demand curve for Good X will shift to the right (from D_1 to D_2 in *Figure 6.15*) if consumers expect: (a) the price of Good X to be higher in future, or (b) a scarcity of Good X in future, or (c) their incomes to be higher in future.

The demand curve for Good X will shift to the left (from D_1 to D_2 in *Figure 6.16*) if consumers expect: (a) the price of Good X to be lower in future, or (b) a more plentiful supply of Good X in future, or (c) their incomes to be lower in future.

Summary
Dx = f (E), where E = the expectations of consumers concerning future prices, availability or incomes.

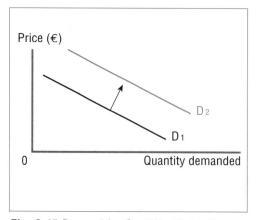

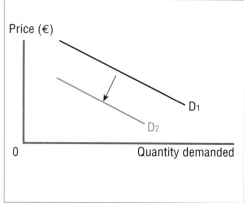

Fig. 6.15 Demand for Good X will rise if consumers expect higher future price, scarcity or higher future incomes

Fig. 6.16 Demand for Good X will fall if consumers expect lower future price, abundance or lower future incomes

Overall summary of factors affecting demand

The demand function is the name given to the list of factors which affect the demand for a good. The full demand function for Good X can be expressed as follows:

$$D_X = f\ (P_X,\ P_C,\ P_S,\ Y,\ t,\ E)$$

If P_X changes, there is said to be 'a change in the quantity demanded of Good X'. This is a movement along the existing demand curve. We use Q_x to denote 'quantity demanded of Good X'. If any of the other variables change, there is said to be 'a change in demand'. This involves a shift to a new demand curve. We use D_x to denote 'the demand for Good X'. *Table 6.2* shows a summary of the demand function for Good X.

Factor	Symbol	Explanation

Price of Good X	P_X	Goods that obey the law of demand:
		     If P_X rises, Q_X falls
		     If P_X falls, Q_X rises
		 Goods that do not obey the law of demand:
		     If P_X rises, Q_X rises
		     If P_X falls, Q_X falls

Price of complementary goods	P_C	If P_C rises, D_X falls If P_C falls, D_X rises
Cost of substitute goods	P_S	If P_S rises, D_X rises If P_S falls, D_X falls

Income	Y	Normal good:
		     If Y rises, D_X rises
		     If Y falls, D_X falls
		 Inferior good:
		     If Y rises, D_X falls
		     If Y falls, D_X rises

Tastes	t	If taste moves towards Good X, D_X rises If taste moves against Good X, D_X falls

Expectations	E	D_X rises if people expect:
		     1. Future price rise
		     2. Future scarcity
		     3. Future income rise
		 D_X falls if people expect:
		     1. Future price fall
		     2. Future abundance
		     3. Future income fall

Table 6.2 Summary of factors affecting demand for Good X

SUBSTITUTION EFFECTS AND INCOME EFFECTS

If the price of a good falls, two things happen.

1. The good becomes cheaper relative to other goods. This is called the *substitution effect*.

2. The real income of the consumer is increased. This is called the *income effect*.

The substitution effect will always push the consumer in one direction – he will tend to buy more of the relatively cheaper good (see column 2 in *Table 6.3*).

1 Good	2 Substition effect	3 Income effect	4 Price effect	5 Type of good
A	More	More	More	Normal good
B	More	Less	More	An inferior good which is not a Giffen good
C	More	Less	Less	An inferior good which is also a Giffen good

Table 6.3 The substitution and income effects of a fall in the price of a good

The income effect can work in two directions. If the good is a normal good, the fact that real income has increased will cause the consumer to buy more (see column 3 for Good A). If the good is an inferior good, the increase in real income will cause the consumer to buy less (see column 3 for Goods B and C). The price effect is the sum of the substitution effect and the income effect.

NORMAL GOODS

For a normal good, the price effect must indicate that more will be bought. (Read across *Table 6.3* for Good A.)

INFERIOR GOODS

In the case of an inferior good, if the substitution effect is stronger than the income effect, more will be bought. This is the case with Good B. Therefore, Good B is an inferior good but not a Giffen good. If the substitution effect is weaker than the income effect, less will be bought. This is the case with Good C. Therefore, Good C is an inferior good and also a Giffen good. By examining Goods B and C in *Table 6.3*, we can see that all Giffen goods are inferior goods, but not all inferior goods are Giffen goods.

7

Supply

By supply we mean the quantity of a good that firms are willing to make available over a particular period of time. Just as the individual consumer was the basic unit responsible for making decisions in relation to demand, the single firm is the basic unit which makes the decisions in relation to supply. For the purposes of this chapter, when we use words like 'seller', 'supplier' or 'producer', we are referring to the individual firm which decides on the level of output it is willing to supply at the prevailing market price.

INDIVIDUAL SUPPLY AND MARKET SUPPLY

An *individual supply schedule* is a list which shows the different quantities of a good an individual firm is willing to make available at each price.

An *individual supply curve* is a graph showing how much of a good an individual firm is willing to make available at each price. It is derived from that firm's supply schedule for that good.

A *market (or aggregate) supply schedule* is a list showing the total quantities of a good that all firms are willing to make available at each price. It is derived by adding together all the individual supply schedules for that good.

A *market (or aggregate) supply curve* is a graph showing the total quantities of a good that all firms are willing to make available at each price. It is derived by adding together (horizontally) all the individual supply curves for that good.

Example: In the case of Good Y, we will assume that there are only three firms involved in its production, namely Firms A, B and C. Their individual weekly supply schedules for Good Y are shown in *Table 7.1*, together with the market (or aggregate) supply schedule.

Price per item (€)	Individual supply schedules			Market supply schedule
	Firm A	Firm B	Firm C	
20	3,000	4,000	1,000	8,000
40	4,000	5,000	3,000	12,000
60	5,000	6,000	5,000	16,000
80	7,000	7,000	7,000	21,000
100	8,000	8,000	9,000	25,000

Table 7.1 Individual supply schedules and market supply schedule for Good Y (items per week)

It is obvious from these supply schedules that the higher the price of the good, the greater the quantity that each firm is willing to supply. This is simply because the higher the selling price, the greater the profit per item that can be earned. This gives us the *Law of Supply*, which we can now state as follows:

If the price of a good increases, more of it will be supplied, while if the price of a good falls, less of it will be supplied. That is:

If P rises, Q rises.
If P falls, Q falls.

P and Q refer to price and quantity supplied, respectively.

There is, therefore, a positive relationship between price and quantity supplied. The typical supply curve will be upward sloping from left to right.

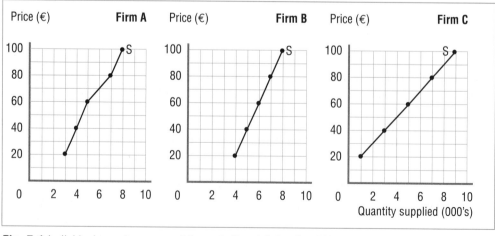

Fig. 7.1 Individual supply curves of firms A, B and C for Good Y

Figure 7.1 shows the individual supply curves for Good Y of Firms A, B and C. The market supply curve for Good Y is shown in *Figure 7.2.*

Fig. 7.2 Market supply curve for Good Y

OTHER SUPPLY CURVES

While the supply curves shown in *Figures 7.1* and *7.2* represent the usual pattern, there are some exceptions.

Case 1: Perfectly inelastic supply

Figure 7.3 depicts a situation where the quantity supplied of a product is fixed, so that an increase in price will not bring forth further supplies, while a fall in price will not result in less being supplied.

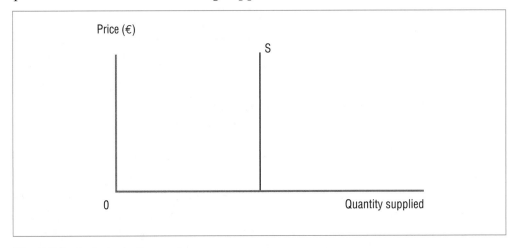

Fig. 7.3 Perfectly inelastic supply

An example of this would be the daily supply of fresh fruit, vegetables or flowers at open-air markets in certain cities. If a street trader has bought a certain quantity from a wholesaler, e.g. 300 bunches of flowers, then this is the quantity he must dispose of on that day. If demand is brisk, he will be able to charge a high price. If demand is slow, he will sell them at a reduced price (since a low price is better than no price at all). The goods are perishable, so he will not be able to keep them until the following day.

Case 2: A minimum price is established below which supply will be zero

Figure 7.4 depicts a situation where the suppliers are able to impose a minimum price (P_1). At prices below P_1, nothing will be supplied. At price P_1, Q_1 units will be supplied. At prices above P_1, the supply curve again assumes its normal (upward sloping) appearance, indicating that the higher the price, the greater the quantity supplied. An example of where such a supply curve might apply is in the case of a trade union which represents all the workers in a particular trade. It might enforce a minimum wage, below which no labour will be supplied.

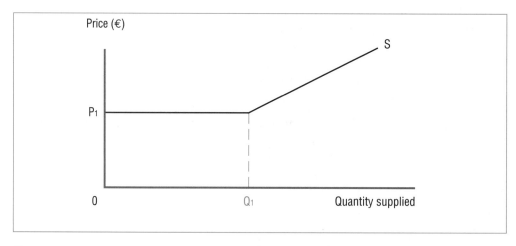

Fig. 7.4 A minimum price (P_1) is established by suppliers

Case 3: The firm reaches its maximum (or capacity) output

Figure 7.5 depicts a situation where the firm increases output as price increases, up to its maximum level of output, Q_1. Any increase in price above P_1 will have no effect on quantity supplied because the firm is operating at full capacity. Q_1 represents its maximum level of output, given its existing factory size. A *capacity constraint* (or limit to output) is said to exist.

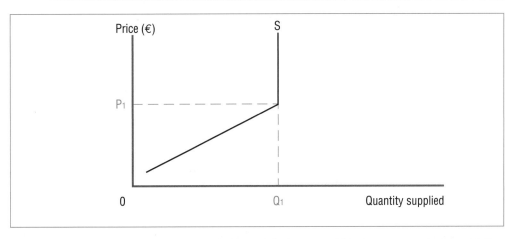

Fig. 7.5 Firm is unable to increase supply beyond Q_1 because this represents capacity output

FACTORS AFFECTING THE SUPPLY OF A GOOD

1. Supply of a good depends on its own price

As we have already seen, most goods obey the Law of Supply. If price rises, more will be supplied, and if price falls, less will be supplied. This gives us the usual upward sloping supply curve, as seen in *Figure 7.2*. We can express this concisely as follows:

$$Q_Y = f(P_Y), \text{ where}$$
$$Q_Y = \text{the quantity supplied of Good Y, and}$$
$$P_Y = \text{the price of Good Y}$$

A change in the price of Good Y will cause a movement along the existing supply curve, while a change in any of the other factors below causes a shift to a new supply curve. We use the term 'change in quantity supplied' to indicate a movement along the existing supply curve, while a 'change in supply' means a shift to a new supply curve.

2. Supply of a good depends on prices of related goods

By related goods we mean goods that the firm could produce instead of its own good.

If the price of a related good rises, while the price of the good the firm is making now remains the same (or falls), it becomes more attractive for the firm to supply the good that has increased in price. Consequently, it will switch its resources to the production of the relatively more highly priced good. For

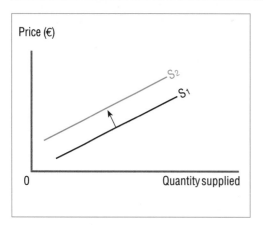

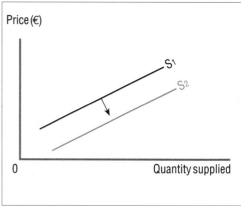

Fig. 7.6 An increase in the price of a related good will cause a fall in the supply of Good Y

Fig. 7.7 A fall in the price of a related good will cause an increase in the supply of Good Y

example, if a farmer is currently producing both sugar beet and wheat, an increase in the price of wheat (while the price of sugar beet remains unchanged) will cause him to supply more wheat and less sugar beet.

If the price of a related good rises, there will be a reduction in the supply of Good Y, as shown in *Figure 7.6*. If S_1 represents the original supply curve for Good Y, S_2 represents the new supply curve. If the price of a related good falls, there will be an increase in the supply of Good Y, as shown in *Figure 7.7*. If S_1 represents the original supply curve, S_2 represents the new supply curve in this case. Note that a shift of the supply curve to the left means a reduction in supply, while a shift of the supply curve to the right represents an increase in supply.

We can express this more concisely as follows:

S_Y = $f(P_R)$, where
S_Y = the supply of Good Y, and
P_R = the price of related goods
More precisely:
If P_R rises, S_Y falls.
If P_R falls, S_Y rises.

3. Supply of a good depends on cost of production

If there is an increase in the cost of production of Good Y, there will be a reduction in supply. The supply curve will shift from S_1 to S_2 as shown in *Figure 7.8*. Possible causes of an increase in the cost of production are:

1. A rise in labour costs
2. A rise in the cost of raw materials
3. An increase in tax
4. A reduction in subsidies

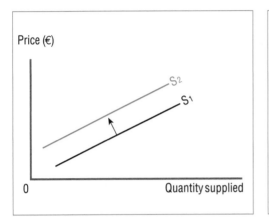

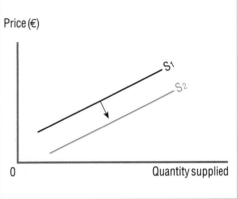

Fig. 7.8 An increase in the cost of production will cause a fall in the supply of Good Y

Fig. 7.9 A fall in the cost of production will cause an increase in the supply of Good Y

Similarly, if there is a reduction in the cost of production of Good Y, there will be an increase in supply. The supply curve will shift from S_1 to S_2 in *Figure 7.9*. Possible causes of a reduction in the cost of production are:

1. A fall in labour costs
2. A fall in the cost of raw materials
3. A reduction in tax
4. An increase in subsidies

We can express the relationship between supply and cost of production concisely as follows:

$$S_Y = f(C), \text{ where}$$
$$C = \text{cost of production}$$
More precisely:
If C rises, S_Y falls.
If C falls, S_Y rises.

4. Supply of a good depends on the state of technology

By the state of technology we mean the methods of production available to a firm. As technology advances, it improves the productivity of the firm and therefore increases supply. The supply curve shifts to the right (from S_1 to S_2 in *Figure 7.10*).

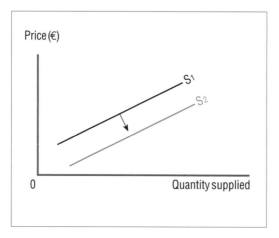

Fig. 7.10 An improvement in the state of technology will cause an increase in the supply of Good Y

We can express this more concisely as follows:

$$
\begin{aligned}
S_Y &= f(T) \text{ where} \\
T &= \text{the state of technology}
\end{aligned}
$$

(**Note:** We do not discuss a 'fall' in the state of technology. This is because we assume that any method of production available to a firm now will always remain an option to the firm.)

5. Supply of a good depends on factors outside control of firm

Sometimes the supply of a good can be influenced by factors which are not planned in advance by the producer. For example, a strike or a shortage of raw materials will cause the supply to be less than originally expected. Similarly, in the case of agricultural produce, output can be affected by the weather. Very favourable weather conditions (adequate rainfall and sunshine) can lead to a bumper crop, while unfavourable conditions (e.g. drought) can lead to output being less than expected. These factors outside the control of the producer can be termed unplanned factors. Unplanned factors can be favourable or unfavourable.

In *Figure 7.11* a favourable unplanned factor causes a shift in the supply curve to the right from S_1 to S_2 (i.e. an increase in supply). In *Figure 7.12* an unfavourable unplanned factor causes a shift in the supply curve to the left from S_1 to S_2 (i.e. a fall in supply). We can express this more concisely as follows:

S_Y = f (U), where
U = unplanned factors
More precisely:
If U is favourable, S_Y rises.
If U is unfavourable, S_Y falls.

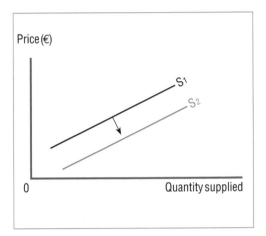

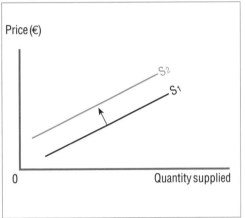

Fig. 7.11 A favourable unplanned factor causes an increase in the supply of Good Y

Fig. 7.12 An unfavourable unplanned factor causes a fall in the supply of Good Y

OVERALL SUMMARY OF FACTORS AFFECTING SUPPLY

The supply function is the name given to the list of factors which affect the supply of a good. It can be expressed as follows, where the symbols have the same meaning as before:

$$S_Y = f(P_Y, P_R, C, T, U)$$

Table 7.2 (overleaf) contains the supply function in summarised form.

We must distinguish between 'a change in the quantity supplied of Good Y' and 'a change in the supply of Good Y'. If P_Y changes, there is said to be 'a change in the quantity supplied of Good Y'. This is simply a movement along the existing supply curve. We use 'Q_Y' to mean 'quantity supplied of Good Y'. If any of the other factors change, there is said to be 'a change in the supply of

Good Y'. This involves a shift to a completely new supply curve. We use 'S_Y' to mean 'change in supply'.

Table 7.2 Summary of factors affecting supply of Good Y

Factor	Symbol	Explanation
Price of Good Y	P_Y	If P_Y rises, Q_Y rises (unless subject to capacity constraint) If P_Y falls, Q_Y falls
Price of related goods	P_R	If P_R rises, S_Y falls If P_R falls, S_Y rises
Cost of production	C	If C rises, S_Y falls If C falls, S_Y rises
State of technology	T	If T improves, S_Y rises
Factors outside the control of the supplier (i.e. unplanned factors)	U	If U is favourable, S_Y rises If U is unfavourable, S_Y falls

Demand and Supply Combined – Market Equilibrium

In this chapter we shall examine how shifts in the demand and supply curves of a good can affect the market equilibrium price and quantity.

We already introduced the concept of market equilibrium in *Chapter 5*. Refer again to *Tables 5.1 and 5.2*. We saw that at a price of €2.50, 25,000 jars of coffee were demanded and this was exactly the quantity that producers were willing to supply at that price. *Figure 8.1* combines on one graph, the market demand curve from *Figure 5.1* and the market supply curve from *Figure 5.2*. At any price above €2.50, excess supply exists, i.e. quantity supplied exceeds quantity demanded. At any price below €2.50, excess demand exists, i.e. quantity demanded exceeds quantity supplied.

From an initial equilibrium position, we shall now examine the effects of changes in demand and supply on the equilibrium price and quantity.

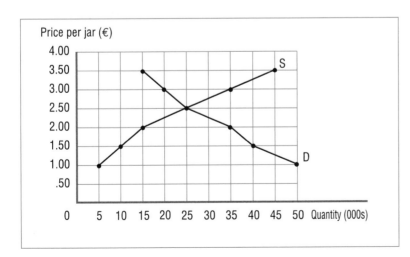

Fig. 8.1 Market demand and supply curves (based on data in *Tables 5.1* and *5.2*)

Case 1: An increase in demand

Let D_1 and S_1 in *Figure 8.2* be the original demand and supply curves, respectively. P_1 was the original equilibrium price, and Q_1 the original equilibrium quantity. Now suppose there is an increase in demand, i.e. a shift of the demand curve to the right from D_1 to D_2. This may be caused by:

1. An increase in the price of a substitute
2. A fall in the price of a complement
3. An increase in income (if the good is a normal good)
4. A change in taste in favour of the good, or
5. Expectations of higher prices in future or scarcity.

The increase in demand leads to a new equilibrium price (P_2) and a new equilibrium quantity (Q_2).

$$Q_2 > Q_1 \text{ and } P_2 > P_1$$

An increase in demand causes an increase in the equilibrium price and the equilibrium quantity.

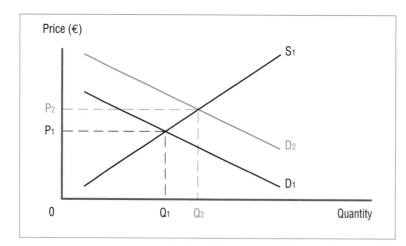

Fig. 8.2 An increase in demand causes an increase in equilibrium price and equilibrium quantity

Case 2: A fall in demand

Figure 8.3 deals with a fall in demand. Let D_1 and S_1 be the original demand and supply curves, respectively. P_1 is the original equilibrium price and Q_1 the original equilibrium quantity. Now suppose there is a fall in demand, i.e. a shift of the demand curve to the left from D_1 to D_2. This may be caused by:

1. A fall in the price of a substitute
2. A rise in the price of a complement
3. A fall in income (if the good is a normal good)
4. A change in taste away from the good, or
5. Expectations of lower prices in future or greater supplies.

The fall in demand leads to a new equilibrium price (P_2) and a new equilibrium quantity (Q_2).

$$Q_2 < Q_1 \text{ and } P_2 < P_1$$

A fall in demand causes a reduction in the equilibrium price and the equilibrium quantity.

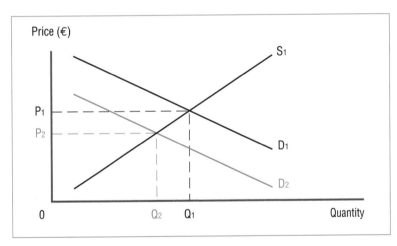

Fig. 8.3 A fall in demand causes a fall in equilibrium price and equilibrium quantity

Case 3: An increase in supply

Figure 8.4 deals with an increase in supply. Let D_1 and S_1 be the original demand and supply curves, respectively. P_1 is the original equilibrium price and Q_1 the original equilibrium quantity. Now suppose there is an increase in supply, i.e. a shift of the supply curve to the right from S_1 to S_2. This may be caused by:

1. A fall in the price of a related good
2. A fall in the cost of production
3. An improvement in technology, or
4. Favourable unplanned factors.

The increase in supply leads to a new equilibrium price (P_2) and a new equilibrium quantity (Q_2).

$$Q_2 > Q_1 \text{ and } P_2 < P_1$$

An increase in supply leads to a fall in the equilibrium price and an increase in the equilibrium quantity.

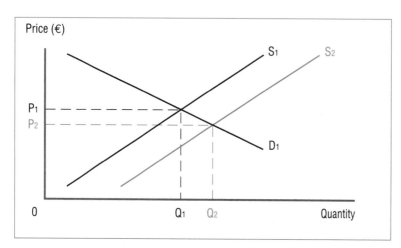

Price (€)

S_1 S_2

P_1

P_2

D_1

0   Q_1 Q_2 Quantity

Fig. 8.4 An increase in supply lowers equilibrium price and increases equilibrium quantity

Case 4: A fall in supply

Figure 8.5 deals with a fall in supply. Let D_1 and S_1 be the original demand and supply curves, respectively. P_1 is the original equilibrium price and Q_1 the original equilibrium quantity. Now suppose there is a fall in supply, i.e. a shift of the supply curve to the left from S_1 to S_2. This may be caused by:

1. A rise in the price of a related good
2. A rise in the cost of production, or
3. Unfavourable unplanned factors.

The fall in supply leads to a new equilibrium price (P_2) and a new equilibrium quantity (Q_2).

$$Q_2 < Q_1 \text{ and } P_2 > P_1$$

A fall in supply leads to a rise in the equilibrium price and a fall in the equilibrium quantity.

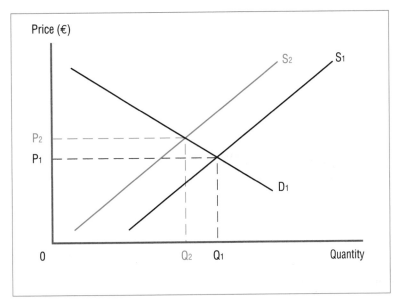

Fig. 8.5 A fall in supply raises equilibrium price and lowers equilibrium quantity

Table 8.1 gives the above conclusions in summarised form.

Change	Equilibrium price	Equilibrium quantity
An increase in demand	Rises	Rises
A fall in demand	Falls	Falls
An increase in supply	Falls	Rises
A fall in supply	Rises	Falls

Table 8.1 Effects of changes in demand and supply on equilibrium price and quantity

Elasticity

PRICE ELASTICITY OF DEMAND

We have already seen that for most goods a rise in price will cause a fall in quantity demanded, while a fall in price usually leads to an increase in the quantity demanded. However, this information is not sufficient to enable a producer to decide what price changes (if any) he should make in order to maximise his revenue and/or profits. Similarly, knowing that a price rise will lead to a fall in quantity demanded will, in itself, be of little use to the government in calculating its revenue from taxation. The concept of price elasticity of demand will enable the producer (and the government) to make accurate predictions as to the likely outcome of price changes.

> Price elasticity of demand is defined as 'the degree of responsiveness of quantity demanded of a good to a change in the price of that good'.

Put more simply it measures what happens to the quantity demanded of a good when the price of the good is changed. Numerically, price elasticity of demand (PED) is measured as:

$$PED = \frac{\text{Proportionate change in quantity demanded}}{\text{Proportionate change in price}}$$

Consider the following situation:

Price per unit (€)	Quality demanded
10	100
12	60

Table 9.1 Market demand schedule of Good A

Example 1: Suppose the producer of Good A is charging €10 per unit now and is considering raising his price to €12 each. He calculates price elasticity according to the following formula:

$$PED = \frac{\text{Proportionate change in quantity demanded}}{\text{Proportionate change in price}}$$

$$= -\frac{40}{100} \div \frac{2}{10}$$

$$= -\frac{40}{100} \times \frac{10}{2}$$

$$= -\frac{400}{200}$$

$$= -2$$

Example 2: Suppose the producer of Good A is presently charging €12 per unit and is considering a price reduction to €10. In this situation he calculates price elasticity of demand as follows:

$$PED = +\frac{40}{60} \div \frac{-2}{12}$$

$$= +\frac{40}{60} \times \frac{12}{-2}$$

$$= \frac{480}{-120}$$

$$= -4$$

It is clear from the above that we get two different answers for price elasticity of demand, one associated with a price increase and the other with a price reduction. To avoid the confusion of different answers we will now use a formula that gives us the same measure for price elasticity, irrespective of whether a price increase or decrease is involved.

We will take the price change as a proportion of the average of the higher and the lower prices; and take the quantity change as a proportion of the average of the higher and the lower quantities. Now our formula can be expressed as follows:

$$PED = \frac{\Delta Q}{\frac{1}{2}(Q_1 + Q_2)} \div \frac{\Delta P}{\frac{1}{2}(P_1 + P_2)}$$

Where PED	=	price elasticity of demand
ΔQ	=	change in quantity demanded
Q_1	=	original quantity demanded
Q_2	=	new quantity demanded (i.e. after price change)
ΔP	=	change in price
P_1	=	original price
P_2	=	new price (i.e. after price change)

Using this formula for *Example 1* above, we get:

$$ PED \; = \; \frac{-40}{\frac{1}{2}(100+60)} \; \div \; \frac{2}{\frac{1}{2}(10+12)} $$

$$ = \; \frac{-40}{80} \; \div \; \frac{2}{11} $$

$$ = \; \frac{-40}{80} \; \times \; \frac{2}{11} $$

$$ = \; -2.75 $$

Using the same formula for *Example 2* above, we get:

$$ PED \; = \; \frac{-40}{\frac{1}{2}(60+100)} \; \div \; \frac{-2}{\frac{1}{2}(12+10)} $$

$$ = \; -2.75 $$

Significance of plus (+) or minus (−) sign

All goods which obey the Law of Demand have a negative price elasticity of demand.

We have already seen that all goods which obey the Law of Demand have an inverse relationship between price and quantity demanded, i.e. an increase in price will lead to a fall in quantity demanded, while a reduction in price will cause an increase in quantity demanded. Because of this ΔQ and ΔP will always move in opposite directions. This can be expressed in the following way.

> If ΔP is positive, then ΔQ will be negative.
> If ΔP is negative, then ΔQ will be positive.

Therefore, for such goods, when we use the formula for price elasticity of demand, we have a positive number divided by a negative number, or a negative number divided by a positive number. In either case, the answer will always be negative.

> **All goods which do not obey the Law of Demand have a positive price elasticity of demand.**

We have already seen that all goods which do not obey the Law of Demand have a positive relationship between price and quantity demanded, i.e. an increase in price will lead to an increase in quantity demanded, while a reduction in price will lead to a fall in quantity demanded. Because of this ΔQ and ΔP always move in the same direction. This can be expressed more specifically in the following way.

> If ΔP is positive, then ΔQ will be negative.
> If ΔP is negative, then ΔQ will be negative.

Therefore, for such goods, when we use the formula for price elasticity of demand, we have a positive number divided by a positive number, or a negative number divided by a negative number. In either case, the answer will always be positive. Since Giffen goods are included in this category, we can say that all Giffen goods have a positive price elasticity of demand.

Significance of size of number

When the application of the formula for price elasticity of demand gives us an answer greater than 1 in absolute terms (i.e. ignoring the sign), the good is said to be price elastic. The proportionate change in quantity demanded is greater than the proportionate change in price in this case.

When the application of the formula for price elasticity of demand gives us an answer less than 1 in absolute terms, the good is said to be price inelastic. The proportionate change in quantity demanded is less than the proportionate change in price in this case.

When the application of the formula for price elasticity of demand gives us an answer equal to 1, the good is said to be of unit elasticity. The proportionate change in quantity demanded is equal to the proportionate change in price in this case.

Price elasticity of demand for goods obeying Law of Demand

Let us look in greater detail at five cases which cover the full range of possibilities in relation to price elasticity of demand for goods which obey the Law of Demand.

CASE 1: A GOOD WITH A PERFECTLY INELASTIC DEMAND

A good is said to have a perfectly inelastic demand if a change in its price will cause no change in the quantity demanded. The demand curve for such a good is illustrated in *Figure 9.1*.

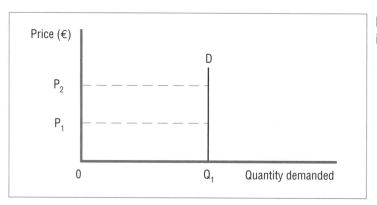

Fig. 9.1 Perfectly inelastic demand

It can be seen that the quantity demanded of such a good will not change even if price changes. Q_1 is demanded at a price of P_1, and even if price is increased to P_2, exactly the same quantity will be demanded. Examples of such goods are life-saving drugs and essential medical equipment where the consumer (in this case, the patient) is not in a position to reduce his/her demand for the product, since a certain quantity has been prescribed. The numerical measure for price elasticity of demand in this case is 0 (zero) since $\Delta Q = 0$.

To achieve maximum revenue

It is obvious in this case that in order to maximise his total revenue the producer will increase his price as much as possible.

$$
\begin{aligned}
\text{Let } TR_1 &= \text{total revenue before price increase} \\
TR_2 &= \text{total revenue after price increase} \\[6pt]
TR_1 &= P_1 \times Q_1 \\
TR_2 &= P_2 \times Q_1 \\
TR_2 &> TR_1 \ (\text{since } P_2 > P_1)
\end{aligned}
$$

To achieve maximum profit

Profit is equal to total revenue minus total cost. That is, Profit = TR – TC. To maximise profit the producer should increase price as much as possible. By doing so, his total revenue is raised while his total cost remains unchanged (since $\Delta Q = 0$). The government may sometimes consider it necessary to intervene in the market for such goods in order to prevent exploitation of consumers by the producer. Such intervention usually takes the form of a maximum price order, which fixes an upper limit to the prices that can be charged for such goods.

CASE 2: A GOOD WITH A RELATIVELY INELASTIC DEMAND

A good is said to have a relatively inelastic demand when the proportionate change in quantity demanded is less than the proportionate change in price. The demand curve for such a good is shown in *Figure 9.2*.

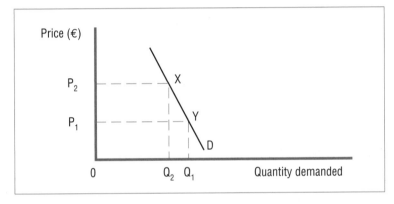

Fig. 9.2 Relatively inelastic demand

It can be seen from the graph that an increase in price from P_1 to P_2 will lead to a much smaller drop in quantity demanded from Q_1 to Q_2. In this case it should be obvious that quantity demanded is not very responsive to changes in price. Examples of goods which have an inelastic demand are petrol, alcohol and tobacco. A rise in the price of these goods will lead to a less than proportionate fall in the quantity demanded. It is for this reason that governments tend to select inelastic goods as suitable for taxation. The numerical measurement for price elasticity of demand in this case is greater than zero but less than 1 ($0 <$ PED < 1).

To achieve maximum revenue

In order to maximise his total revenue in this case the producer should raise his price as much as possible. This is obvious if we examine *Figure 9.2*.

Rectangle $0Q_2XP_2$ represents total revenue at price P_2

Rectangle $0Q_1YP_1$ represents total revenue at price P_1

It is clear that:

Rectangle $0Q_2XP_2$ > Rectangle $0Q_1YP_1$

To achieve maximum profit

We can also be certain that total profit would rise in this case if the producer raises his price.

$$\text{Profit} = \text{total revenue (TR)} - \text{total cost (TC)}$$

At price P_1, $\text{profit}_1 = TR_1 - TC_1$

where $TR_1 = P_1 \times Q_1$

$TC_1 = $ total cost of producing Q_1 units of output

At price P_2, $\text{profit}_2 = TR_2 - TC_2$

where $TR_2 = P_2 \times Q_2$

and $TC_2 = $ total cost of producing Q_2 units of output

We have already seen that $TR_2 > TR_1$

Also, $TC_2 < TC_1$ since Q_2 represents a smaller quantity of output than Q_1

Therefore, $\text{profit}_2 > \text{profit}_1$

CASE 3: A GOOD WITH UNIT ELASTICITY OF DEMAND

A good is said to have unit elasticity of demand if the proportionate change in quantity demanded is equal to the proportionate change in price. For example, a 10 per cent increase in price would lead to a 10 per cent fall in quantity demanded. The numerical measure for price elasticity of demand in this case is –1. The demand curve for such a good is shown in *Figure 9.3*.

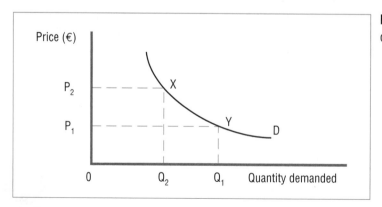

Fig. 9.3 Unit elasticity of demand

To achieve maximum revenue

If price is increased from P_1 to P_2, quantity demanded fall[...]
revenue remains constant. Rectangle $0Q_1YP_1$ = Rectangle [...]
the firm cannot increase its total revenue by making any pri[...]

To achieve maximum profit

However, the firm can maximise its profit by increasing price a[...]
possible. For example, if the firm sells 500 units at a price of €4 each, a[...]
increases its price to €5 each, at which it sells 400 units, its total re[...]
remains constant at €2000. However, its profit would be higher if it charge[...]
per unit since it costs less to produce 400 than 500 units. Suppose each ite[...]
costs €2 to produce. At a price of €4 each, total revenue is €2,000, while tota[...]
cost is €1,000 (i.e. 500 x €2). Therefore profit is €1,000. At a price of €5
each, total revenue is €2,000 while total cost is €800 (i.e. 400 x €2).

CASE 4: A GOOD WITH A RELATIVELY ELASTIC DEMAND

A good is said to have a relatively elastic demand if the proportionate change
in quantity demanded is greater than the proportionate change in price. This
case is shown in *Figure 9.4*. If price is increased from P_1 to P_2, quantity
demanded falls from Q_1 to Q_2 and total revenue is reduced accordingly.
Rectangle $0Q_2XP_2$ is clearly smaller than rectangle $0Q_1YP_1$. It is clear that the
demand for such goods will be very responsive to price changes. The numerical
measure for elasticity of demand in this case is greater than 1 (PED > 1).

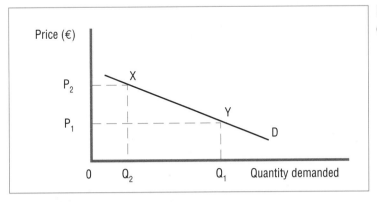

Fig. 9.4 Relatively elastic demand

To achieve maximum revenue

As a general rule, when price elasticity of demand is greater than 1 (in absolute
terms), a price increase will lead to a fall in total revenue while a price
reduction will lead to a rise in total revenue. Therefore, the firm which has a
relatively elastic demand for its product will maximise its total revenue by
lowering its price as much as possible.

costs of production will be increased
crease in the quantity of output). Since
e increased, it is not possible to state
(unlike Cases 2 and 3 above). To state
take we would need to know exactly
els of output.

ND

price elasticity of demand for a
apply if consumers are prepared
a price of P_1, while any increase in price
and to fall to zero. We will return to this case of a
curve in *Chapter 12* when we examine the market structure
competition. A summary of the relationship between price elasticity
demand and total revenue is given in *Table 9.2*.

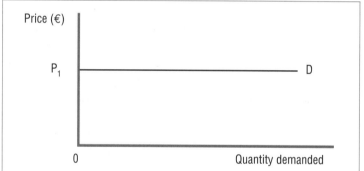

Fig. 9.5 Perfectly elastic demand

Description	Elasticity value	Total revenue (TR)	Profit (TR − TC)
Elastic	Greater than 1 (PED > 1)	Rises if price is reduced Falls if price is increased	Not conclusive
Inelastic	Less than 1 (PED < 1)	Falls if price is reduced Rises if price is increased	Falls if price is reduced Rises if price is increased
Unity	Equal to 1 (PED = 1)	Is constant, i.e. does not change as price is increased or reduced	Falls if price is reduced Rises if price is increased

Table 9.2 Summary of the relationship between price elasticity of demand, total revenue and profit

What determines price elasticity of demand?

1. **Are close substitutes available?**

   In general, the greater the number of close substitutes available for a product, the more likely demand for that product will be responsive to changes in its own price. This is because a price increase for such a good will lead many customers to switch to the cheaper substitute goods. For example, an increase in the price of butter will cause a large reduction in the demand for butter as customers switch to butter substitutes such as dairy spreads, low-fat spreads, etc. On the other hand, an increase in the price of petrol will not result in a significant reduction in quantity demanded, because of the absence of any substitute for petrol, as far as most motorists are concerned. Therefore, as a general rule, we can say that goods with many close substitutes will be price elastic while goods with few close substitutes (or none at all) will be price inelastic.

2. **Is the good expensive?**

   The more expensive the good, the more likely it is to be elastic with respect to changes in its own price. The less expensive the good, the more likely it is to be inelastic with respect to changes in its own price. If a product is already expensive, a further price rise may put it outside the reach of many customers, so that a large reduction in demand results. On the other hand, a price increase on goods which are fairly cheap now (e.g. newspapers, boxes of matches, etc.), or which account for only a small fraction of a customer's weekly expenditure, is likely to result in little or no change in quantity demanded.

3. **Is the product durable?**

   If the product is durable or long lasting (e.g. cars, TVs, hi-fi equipment, etc.), an increase in its price may cause the consumer to postpone the replacement of his/her existing model. If most customers behave in this way the price increase may lead to a more than proportionate fall in quantity demanded. Therefore, the more durable the good, the more likely it is to be price elastic.

4. **Are habits and brand loyalty important elements of consumer behaviour?**

   A customer may become strongly attached to a particular product either through habit or loyalty to that particular brand, so that a price increase on that good will not cause him/her to consume less of the product or to switch to other cheaper substitutes. The demand for such goods will therefore be price inelastic.

5. **Is the product the cheaper of two goods which are in joint demand?**

   If two goods are in joint demand (i.e. if they are complimentary goods), the demand for the cheaper of the two goods is likely to be inelastic. For example, golf balls and sets of golf clubs are complimentary goods. A 50 per cent increase in the price of golf balls is not likely to lead to a 50 per cent fall in the demand for sets of golf clubs. This is because, in relation to the overall cost of playing the game of golf, the cost of golf balls is not a major element.

INCOME ELASTICITY OF DEMAND

The responsiveness of demand for a good to changes in income is measured by income elasticity of demand. This is calculated by the formula:

$$YED = \frac{\Delta Q}{\frac{1}{2}(Q_1 + Q_2)} \div \frac{\Delta Y}{\frac{1}{2}(Y_1 + Y_2)}$$

where YED	=	income elasticity of demand
ΔQ	=	change in quantity demanded
Q_1	=	original quantity demanded
Q_2	=	new quantity demanded (after the change in income)
ΔY	=	change in income
Y_1	=	original level of income
Y_2	=	new level of income

Income elasticity of demand for normal goods

For the vast majority of goods, an increase in income will lead to an increase in the demand for the good, while a fall in income will lead to a fall in the demand for the good. Therefore, when we use the above formula, we get a positive answer for income elasticity of demand. This is because ΔQ and ΔY will either be both positive or both negative.

We define a normal good as one which has a positive income effect, i.e. more of it will be bought as income rises.

A normal good, therefore, has a positive income elasticity of demand.

If the application of the above formula yields an answer greater than 1 (in absolute terms), then the good is said to be a luxury good. Therefore, a luxury good is one on which a greater proportion of income is spent as income rises. For example, suppose my income is €500 per week, and I spend €25 per week on Good X. If my income increases to €600 per week and I now spend €60 per week on this good, it is a luxury good, as far as I am concerned. I am now spending 10 per cent of my weekly income on this good, compared to only 5 per cent before the increase in income.

Income elasticity of demand for inferior goods

An inferior good is defined as one which has a negative income effect. As income rises, less of an inferior good will be bought.

It follows that an inferior good has a negative income elasticity of demand. The application of the above formula will give a negative answer. This is because

ΔQ and ΔY are moving in opposite directions. Own-brand food products in our larger supermarkets are sometimes cited as examples of inferior goods. A low-income family may purchase own-brand cornflakes. A rise in income may cause them to switch to the more well-known brand of cornflakes. Remould tyres and 'off the peg' suits are often cited as examples of inferior goods.

Goods with low-income elasticity of demand

In wealthier countries today, the demand for food products and basic items of clothing does not rise pro rata with increases in income. Consequently, these goods are considered to have a low-income elasticity of demand.

Goods with high-income elasticity of demand

Most consumer-durable products, for example, video recorders, hi-fi systems, dishwashers and kitchen appliances exhibit a high-income elasticity of demand.

CROSS ELASTICITY OF DEMAND

A businessman will want to know what will happen to the quantity demanded of his good when the prices of other goods change. The concept of cross elasticity of demand is useful for this purpose. Cross elasticity of demand (CED) measures the effect of a change in the price of one good (for example, Good B) on the quantity demanded of another good (Good A). The formula for cross elasticity of demand is:

$$CED = \frac{\text{Proportionate change in quantity demanded of Good A}}{\text{Proportionate change in price of Good B}}$$

$$= \frac{\Delta Q_A}{\frac{1}{2}(Q_{1A} + Q_{2A})} \div \frac{\Delta P_B}{\frac{1}{2}(P_{1B} + P_{2B})}$$

Where
ΔQ_A = change in the quantity demanded of Good A
$Q1_A$ = original quantity demanded of Good A
$Q2_A$ = quantity demanded of Good A after the price of Good B has changed
ΔP_B = change in the price of B
$P1_B$ = original price of Good B
$P2_B$ = new price of Good B

Negative cross elasticity of demand for complementary goods

If a rise in the price of Good B leads to a fall in the demand for Good A, then goods A and B are complementary goods. The use of the above formula will always produce a negative cross elasticity of demand in such cases. For example, if the price of gin rises, we could expect a fall in the quantity demanded of tonic water. Gin and tonic water would then be complementary goods. The higher the negative value of the cross elasticity of demand, the more complementary are the two goods.

Positive cross elasticity of demand for substitute goods

If a rise in the price of Good B leads to a rise in the demand for Good A, then the two goods are substitute goods. The use of the above formula in this case will lead to a positive cross elasticity of demand. For example, if the price of butter rises, we would probably witness a rise in the quantity demanded of non-dairy spreads. These goods could then be classified as substitutes. Again we can say that the greater the positive value of the cross elasticity of demand, the closer are the substitutes. If the cross elasticity of demand is zero, we can say that there is no relationship between the two goods, since a change in the price of one will have absolutely no effect on the quantity demanded of the other.

PRICE ELASTICITY OF SUPPLY

The concept of elasticity can be applied to supply as well as to demand.

Price elasticity of supply (PES) measures the degree of responsiveness of the supply of a good to changes in its own price.

It is calculated as follows:

$$PES = \frac{\text{Proportionate change in quantity supplied}}{\text{Proportionate change in price}}$$

$$= \frac{\Delta Q}{\frac{1}{2}(Q_1 + Q_2)} \div \frac{\Delta P}{\frac{1}{2}(P_1 + P_2)}$$

$$Q = \text{quantity supplied}$$

Positive price elasticity of supply

We have already seen that a rise in price will usually lead to an increase in quantity supplied. A producer will always be willing to put more units of his product on the market if the price has risen since he will increase his profit by so doing. Therefore, quantity supplied and price move in the same direction, so the application of the above formula gives a positive answer.

The bigger the numerical value of PES, the more responsive the producer is to a change in the price of the good. If the producer is operating at full capacity, his price elasticity of supply is zero (PES = 0). No matter how much a producer may wish to increase output in response to a price rise, he will not be able to do so if he is currently producing the maximum possible level of output (given his existing scale of operation). ΔQ is zero, therefore PES = 0.

Factors affecting price elasticity of supply

1. **Is the firm operating close to full capacity?**
   The closer the firm is to its maximum level of output, the less likely it will be able to respond to a price increase, and therefore, the more inelastic supply will be.

2. **Mobility of factors of production.**
   The easier it is for the producer to switch resources from the production of one good to another, the more elastic the supply of these goods will be. The firm will devote more resources to the production of the good with the higher selling price and less resources to the production of the good with the lower selling price.

3. **The time period under consideration.**
   The longer the time period under consideration the more elastic supply will be. This is because with certain goods (e.g. agricultural produce) a rise in price cannot bring forth an immediate increase in quantity supplied.

4. **The nature of the product.**
   If the product is a perishable one, or one that deteriorates over time, the supply is likely to be inelastic. For example, a fall in the price of wheat will not cause less of the crop to be released on the market, since a low price is better than no price at all. Conversely, in the case of oil or minerals, supply is likely to be highly elastic as producers withdraw supplies (or slow down production) if price falls, and increase supply in response to a price rise.

10

Costs, Revenue and Profit

This chapter looks at the costs of production of the firm, its revenue from sales and the profit it earns. We shall consider the short-run and long-run production periods, and distinguish between fixed and variable costs. We shall then consider the revenue conditions of the firm and establish the rules which determine the most profitable level of output of the firm.

COSTS OF PRODUCTION – FIXED COSTS AND VARIABLE COSTS

The higher the level of output of the firm, the greater will be its total costs of production. Total costs can be broken down into fixed costs and variable costs.

Fixed costs are those costs which do not change as output changes.

These costs are fixed regardless of the level of output produced. If output is zero, fixed costs must still be paid. Examples of fixed costs are:

1. Rent of factory
2. Rates (payable to a local authority)
3. Costs of maintenance of a factory, e.g. cleaning, security, etc.
4. Salaries of certain members of staff, e.g. accountant, management, etc.
5. Interest on money borrowed.

Variable costs are those costs which do change as output changes.

As output increases, variable costs increase. Examples of variable costs are:

1. Cost of raw materials
2. Cost of electricity (to run machines)
3. Wages of most workers directly involved in production.

Figure 10.1 shows fixed costs, variable costs and total costs for one firm. Notice that when output is zero, variable costs are zero, but fixed costs must still be paid.

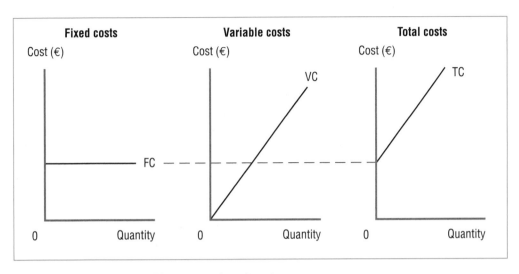

Fig. 10.1 Fixed costs, variable costs and total costs

THE SHORT RUN AND LONG RUN

We define the short run as a period of time within which at least one factor of production is fixed in quantity.

If the firm wishes to increase output in the short run, it has no option but to increase the amount of the variable factors employed. In most cases, land or capital are the fixed factors, while labour is the variable factor. It is easier for a firm to expand output by employing more workers than by building (and equipping) a larger factory.

We define the long run as the period of time long enough for all the factors of production to be varied.

If the firm wishes to increase output in the long run it can vary the inputs of all the factors of production. Additional workers can be hired, a bigger factory unit can be built, more machines can be installed and additional management personnel may be taken on.

It is important to understand that the short run and the long run do not refer to fixed specific lengths of time, but will vary from industry to industry. A self-employed craftsman making items individually for tourists visiting his area may be able to vary all his inputs in a matter of days. On the other hand, a car manufacturing plant may have a short-run period of several years, since an increase in factory size and the installation of the sophisticated machinery required for car assembly cannot be achieved in a shorter period of time.

THE COST STRUCTURE OF A FIRM

We will begin our analysis of costs by examining the details for the Southern Furniture Company given in *Table 10.1*. This is a small business which specialises in the manufacture of coffee tables, and is run by Tom Fahy, a skilled woodworker.

1 Quantity (units of output)	2 Fixed cost	3 Variable cost	4 Total cost	5 Average fixed cost	6 Average variable cost	7 Average cost	8 Marginal cost
			(2 + 3)	(2 ÷ 1)	(3 ÷ 1)	(4 ÷ 1)	ΔTC
1	30	40	70	30.00	40.00	70.00	—
2	30	60	90	15.00	30.00	45.00	20
3	30	90	120	10.00	30.00	40.00	30
4	30	130	160	7.50	32.50	40.00	40
5	30	180	210	6.00	36.00	42.00	50
6	30	250	280	5.00	41.67	46.67	70
7	30	350	380	4.29	50.00	54.29	100

Table 10.1 Cost conditions of Southern Furniture Company (all figures in euro)

Table explanation

Column 1 is simply the number of tables produced (per day).
Column 2 is the total fixed costs (TFC) of the business. We will assume that Tom rents a small workshop for €30 per day and has no other fixed costs.
Column 3 is the total variable costs (TVC) of the business.
Column 4 is total cost (TC), i.e. TFC + TVC.
Column 5 is average fixed cost (AFC). This is fixed cost per unit of output produced, i.e. AFC = TFC/Q.
Column 6 is average variable cost (AVC). This is variable cost per unit of output produced, i.e. AVC = TVC/Q.
Column 7 is average cost (AC), i.e. TC/Q or AFC + AVC.
Column 8 is marginal cost (MC), i.e. the change in total cost as a result of

producing an extra unit of output. For example, the total cost of producing two units is €90, and the total cost of producing three units is €120, so the marginal cost of the third unit is €30 (€120 – €90).

We have already examined the total costs above in *Figure 10.1*, so we will now concentrate on average and marginal cost.

AVERAGE FIXED COST

Figure 10.2 is a graph of average fixed cost, based on the data in *Table 10.1*. We can see that AFC always slopes downward. This is simply because we are dividing a fixed number (TFC) by an increasing number (Q), so we must get a smaller figure each time. When fixed costs are shared out over a larger quantity in this way, this is known as the 'spreading of overheads'. Also we can see that the fall in AFC is more marked at lower levels of output, and then the graph flattens out at higher levels of output. However, it can never rise.

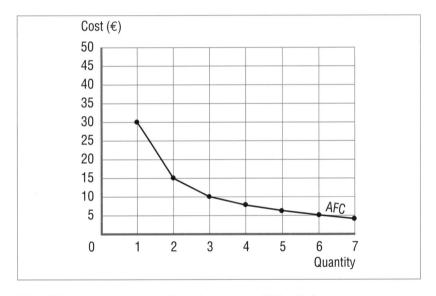

Fig. 10.2 Average fixed cost (based on data in *Table 10.1*)

AVERAGE VARIABLE COST

Figure 10.3 is a graph showing average variable cost. We can see that average variable cost falls at first and then rises when four units of output are produced. 'Diminishing returns' set in after three units of output have been produced. We will return to this later.

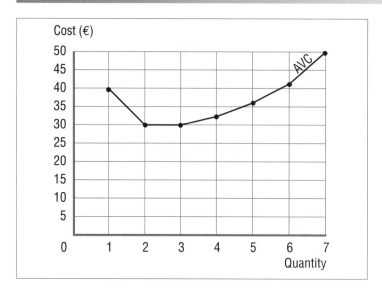

Fig. 10.3 Average variable cost (based on data in *Table 10.1*)

AVERAGE COST AND MARGINAL COST

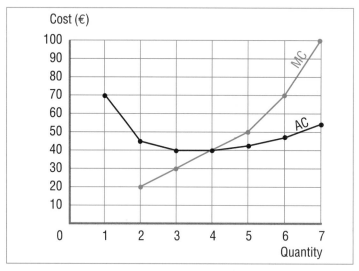

Fig. 10.4 Average cost and marginal cost (based on data in *Table 10.1*)

Figure 10.4 shows both average cost (AC) and marginal cost (MC) based on the data in *Table 10.1*. There is a very important relationship between average cost and marginal cost, which we will now explain.

1. When marginal cost is lower than average cost, average cost is falling

Suppose Tom Fahy's furniture company is producing two tables a day. Average cost is €45. Tom is considering the production of a third table. The extra (marginal) cost of doing so is €30. Because this is less than the average cost of producing two units (€45), the average cost will fall (to €40) if three units are produced.

2. When marginal cost is equal to average cost, average cost will remain the same

Suppose Tom is producing three tables. Average cost is €40. He is considering the production of a fourth table. The extra (marginal) cost of doing so is €40. Because this is the same as the average cost of producing three tables, the average cost will remain the same (at €40) if four units are produced.

3. When marginal cost is greater than average cost, average cost is rising

Suppose Tom is producing four tables. Average cost is €40. He is considering the production of a fifth table. The extra (marginal) cost of doing so is €50. Because this is more than the average cost of producing four tables, the average cost will rise (from €40 to €42) if five units are produced.

If (1), (2) and (3) above are true, then the marginal cost curve must cut the average cost curve at the lowest point of the average cost curve. This can be seen in *Figure 10.4* at a level of output of four units.

If the marginal cost is less than the average cost so far, it will drag the average down. If the marginal cost is equal to the average cost so far, the average stays the same. If the marginal cost is more than the average cost so far, it will drag the average up.

We can see this relationship between 'marginal' and 'average' in many different situations. If you have received 40 per cent in each of three exams, your average mark is 40 per cent. If you get 60 per cent in a fourth exam, your average mark is now 45 per cent. Because the marginal mark (60%) was higher than the average so far (40%), it dragged your average up to 45 per cent.

If your friend got 50 per cent in each of the first three exams, his average mark is 50 per cent. If he receives only 30 per cent in the fourth exam, his average is now 45 per cent. Because his marginal mark (30%) was less than his average so far (50%), it dragged his average down to 45 per cent.

Summary of the relationship between marginal cost and average cost:

When MC < AC, AC is falling
When MC = AC, AC stays the same
When MC > AC, AC is rising

THE SHAPE OF THE SHORT-RUN AVERAGE COST CURVE (SRAC)

Returning to *Figure 10.4*, we can see that average cost (AC) falls initially and then after a certain level of output has been reached, it rises again. Both average variable cost (AVC) and average cost (AC) have this 'U' shape. In the case of our furniture factory, AVC and AC rise once the fourth unit of output is produced.

Most firms have a short-run average cost curve which is U-shaped. There are two reasons why the average cost curve slopes downward at low levels of output, and one reason why it eventually slopes upwards.

1. Better spread of fixed costs

AC includes both AFC and AVC. As output rises, the fixed costs are spread out over a greater output. When output rises, AFC falls, very much at first and then by smaller amounts. Therefore, AFC as a fraction of AC gets smaller as output expands.

2. Specialisation of labour

When output is small, the production of extra units of output will allow the firm to allocate its labour (and other resources) in a more efficient manner. The division of labour (i.e. specialisation) can be practised, and as we saw already, this can greatly increase output per worker. Each extra worker adds the same amount to cost but a different amount to output. When output per worker is rising, the cost per unit of output (i.e. AC) is falling.

3. The Law of Diminishing Returns

AC will eventually slope upwards because output per worker will not keep rising as output expands. At some stage, output per worker will fall. This is due to the operation of the Law of Diminishing Returns which we will now consider.

> The Law of Diminishing Returns states that if increasing quantities of a variable factor are combined with a given amount of a fixed factor, eventually a stage will be reached where the addition to total output ('marginal output') will decline.

This law is most clearly understood if we take the example of a farmer with a given amount of land, say 100 acres, who specialises in the production of potatoes. He is considering the employment of extra workers in order to increase output. Suppose the position facing the farmer is as shown in *Table 10.2*.

Units of land	Units of labour	Total output	Marginal output	Average output
1	1	200	–	200
1	2	450	250	225
1	3	750	300	250
1	4	1100	350	275
1	5	1300	200	260
1	6	1400	100	233

Table 10.2 The operation of the Law of Diminishing Returns

If he operates on his own, his total output is 200 tonnes. If he takes on one extra man, the combined total output is 450 tonnes. The marginal output of the second man is 250 units. If a third man is taken on, the total output rises by 300 units. A fourth man causes output to rise by 350 tonnes, while a fifth adds 200 tonnes to total output. Therefore, diminishing returns set in after the fourth man is employed.

Diminishing returns is the same as increasing costs. When output per worker (average output) is falling, average costs of production are rising. In our example, when the fifth man is employed, average output falls from 275 tonnes to 260 tonnes. (In *Table 10.1*, AC began to rise once four units of output were produced.) It is important to note that the Law of Diminishing Returns only applies in the short run. In the long run, all the factors of production are variable.

Figure 10.5 shows a typical short-run average cost curve, which is U-shaped. It slopes downwards initially, because fixed costs are spread out over a larger output and because the firm can use its labour more efficiently as output increases. It eventually slopes upwards because of the operation of the Law of Diminishing Returns.

THE LONG-RUN AVERAGE COST CURVE (LRAC)

We have already seen that in the short run, at least one factor of production is fixed. In the case of our farmer above, if he wanted to increase his output of potatoes, he had to take on extra workers. In the long run, all his factors of production are variable, so he could use any combination of land, labour, capital and enterprise to achieve his desired level of output. It should be obvious, therefore, that each short-run average cost curve relates to one particular scale of operation.

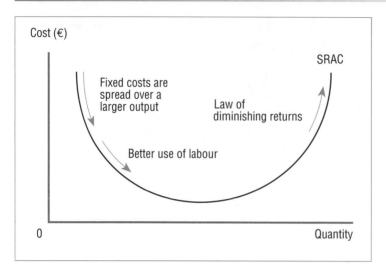

Fig. 10.5 The short-run average cost curve is U-shaped

Figure 10.6 shows four different short-run average cost curves for a particular firm. Each one relates to one particular scale of operation (i.e. factory size). When a firm starts production, it will be unwilling to take the risks associated with a large scale of operation, since it will be unsure about the demand for its product in the long term. A large scale of operation will involve more fixed costs. It costs more to rent a large factory than a small one.

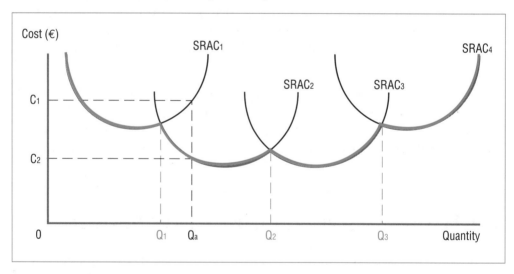

Fig. 10.6 The long-run average cost curve of a firm

Consequently, in the initial stages of production, the firm will produce a small output, which requires a small factory. $SRAC_1$ is the average cost curve which applies to this factory size. $SRAC_2$, $SRAC_3$ and $SRAC_4$ represent the short-run average cost curves associated with larger factory sizes. For any chosen level of output, the firm will wish to produce that output at the lowest possible average cost. Our firm will start production at a level of output below Q_1. As the level of demand expands, the firm will increase its output. If output expands beyond Q_1, say to Q_a, average cost will be higher than necessary if the firm remains at its existing size. This is because at its existing factory size, it costs on average C_1 to produce each unit of output, while by expanding to the factory size represented by $SRAC_2$, average cost would fall to C_2.

Consequently, the firm would be better off producing any level of output between Q_1 and Q_2 by using the scale of operation represented by $SRAC_2$. Similarly, if the chosen level of output is between Q_2 and Q_3, the firm would achieve a lower average cost by expanding its scale of operation to that represented by $SRAC_3$, and so on.

For any firm, there are very many possible factory sizes. Each scale of operation will be governed by a short-run average cost curve. At that scale of operation, output can be increased by using more of the variable factors (e.g. labour), while the amount of the fixed factor (i.e. the factory itself) remains unchanged. In the long run the firm will be free to change the inputs of all factors, and will select that scale of operations where average cost is at a minimum for the level of output it has chosen.

The long-run average cost curve comprises all the lowest points on the short-run cost curves.

This is shown in *Figure 10.6* by the thick red line. We can say that a firm will never select a scale of operation in the long run where average cost is higher than it had been in the short run.

Like the short-run curve, the long-run average cost curve will be U-shaped. However the reasons for this are different. The relative importance of economies and diseconomies of scale will decide whether long-run average cost will rise or fall. You will remember that economies of scale were the advantages of large-scale production while diseconomies of scale were the disadvantages of large-scale production (see *Chapter 3*).

If economies of scale outweigh diseconomies of scale over a particular range of output, then long-run average cost will fall over that range of output. If diseconomies of scale outweigh economies of scale over a particular range of output, then long-run average cost will rise over that range of output. *Figure 10.7* illustrates this fact.

At any level of output between 0 and Q_1, economies outweigh diseconomies and LRAC falls. At any level of output above Q_1, diseconomies outweigh economies and LRAC rises. Q_1 is the output where LRAC is at a minimum, and is known as the optimum size for that firm.

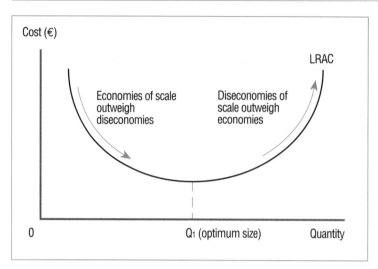

Fig. 10.7 The long-run average cost curve is U-shaped

TOTAL REVENUE, AVERAGE REVENUE AND MARGINAL REVENUE

Total revenue (TR) is the total amount of money received by the firm from the sale of its goods.

It is derived by multiplying the price of the good by the number of goods sold. Total revenue rises as output increases, as shown in *Figure 10.8*.

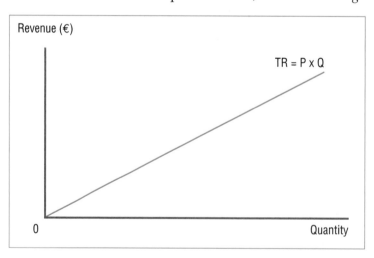

Fig. 10.8 Total revenue rises as output increases

$$TR = P \times Q$$

Average revenue (AR) is the total revenue divided by the number of units of the good sold. It is the same as the price of the good.

$$AR = \frac{TR}{Q} = \frac{P \times Q}{Q} = P$$

Average revenue can be constant or falling as shown in *Figure 10.9*. If average revenue is constant, it means the firm will not have to lower price to sell extra output. If average revenue is falling it means the firm must lower price to sell extra output.

Marginal revenue (MR) is the change in total revenue as a result of the sale of one extra unit of output.

For example, if I can sell 10 units at €20 each and 11 units at €19.50 each, the marginal revenue of the 11th unit is €14.50 (i.e. €214.50 – €200).

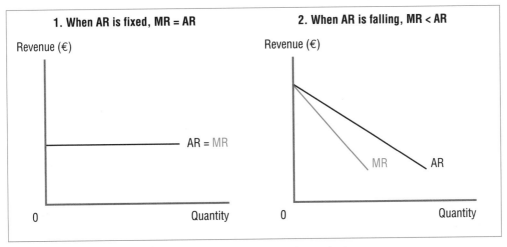

Fig. 10.9 The relationship between average revenue and marginal revenue

The relationship between average revenue and marginal revenue is the same as that between average cost and marginal cost.

When average revenue is fixed, marginal revenue is equal to average revenue.

If I sell two books at €5 each, my average revenue is €5 (€10/2). If I now sell a third book for €5, my marginal revenue is €5 (€15 – €10), and my average revenue remains €5 (€15/3).

When marginal revenue is less than average revenue, average revenue is falling.

If I sell two books at €5 each, my average revenue is €5 (€10/2). If I now sell a third book for €3, my marginal revenue is €3 (€13 – €10), and my average revenue is €4.33 (€13/3). Another way of saying this is that when a firm has to reduce price in order to sell extra output, marginal revenue will be less than average revenue.

PROFITS

The aim of all production is to make a profit.

Profit is defined as the difference between total revenue and total cost.

$$\text{Profit} = \text{TR} - \text{TC}$$

Included in total costs is the minimum amount of profit the entrepreneur is prepared to accept for his/her efforts. This is known as *normal profit*. Unless this is received, the firm will go out of business. Any profit received in excess of normal profit is called *supernormal profit (SNP)*. It is a bonus to the firm, since production would still take place if it were not earned.

RULES FOR PROFIT MAXIMISATION

1. Marginal cost must equal marginal revenue

For maximum profit to be earned, marginal cost must be equal to marginal revenue. Let us return to the Southern Furniture Company, and add the following revenue information to the cost information contained in *Table 10.1*. We will assume that additional units can be sold at the same price of €70, that is, average revenue is constant.

When average revenue is constant, marginal revenue is equal to average revenue. Therefore, marginal revenue is €70.

1 Quantity	2 Total cost	3 Marginal cost (price)	4 Average revenue (P x Q)	5 Total revenue (ΔTR)	6 Marginal revenue (TR – TC)	7 Profit
1	70	–	70	70	–	0
2	90	20	70	140	70	50
3	120	30	70	210	70	90
4	160	40	70	280	70	120
5	210	50	70	350	70	140
6	280	70	70	420	70	140
7	380	100	70	490	70	110

Table 10.3 Cost and revenue conditions for Southern Furniture Company

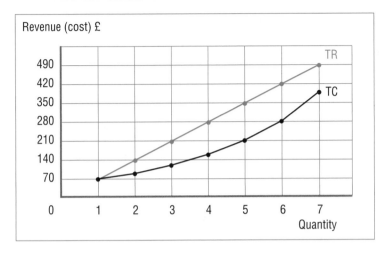

Fig. 10.10 Total revenue and total cost (based on data in *Table 10.3*)

Table 10.3 contains cost and revenue information for the company. By looking at Column 7, we can see that profit (TR – TC) is maximised at €140 when six units are produced per day. *Figure 10.10* shows total revenue and total cost. The vertical distance between the two graphs at each level of output represents the profit that is earned at that level of output. The greatest vertical distance between TR and TC occurs at six units of output.

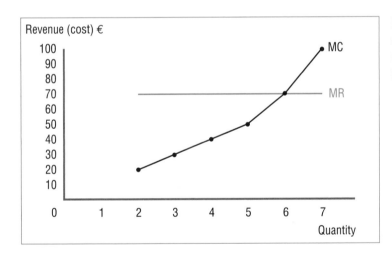

Fig. 10.11 Marginal cost and marginal revenue (based on data in *Table 10.3*)

We can arrive at the same conclusion by comparing marginal cost with marginal revenue, as shown in *Figure 10.11*. At any level of output below that at which MR = MC, total profit could be increased by expanding output.

For example, if the firm is producing three tables a day, it is making a profit of €90. However, by producing an extra table, the marginal (or extra) revenue earned is €70 but the extra cost is only €40. Total profit can be increased by €30 by the production of the fourth table. Therefore, the production of three tables could not represent the most profitable level of output. Similarly an extra €20 could be earned by the making of the fifth table (since MR = €70 but MC = €50). At a level of output of six units per day, the marginal revenue is equal to the marginal cost and this is the most profitable level of output. In fact it does not matter whether this unit is made or not since it adds €70 to total revenue and €70 to total cost. So we could say that the most profitable output is 'one unit less than that at which MC = MR' but this is too awkward. If the firm produces seven units of output, MC > MR, so a loss is made on the seventh unit.

> The first rule of profit maximisation is 'produce that level of output where MC = MR'. This is an extremely important rule and applies in all market structures.

2. MC must cut MR from below

For maximum profit to be earned, MC must cut MR from below. In *Figure 10.12*, MC cuts MR at two levels of output. Which is the most profitable? The answer is Q_2. If the firm produced only Q_1 units, it would have failed to earn the extra profit indicated by the shaded area. Therefore, it could not have been maximising its profits.

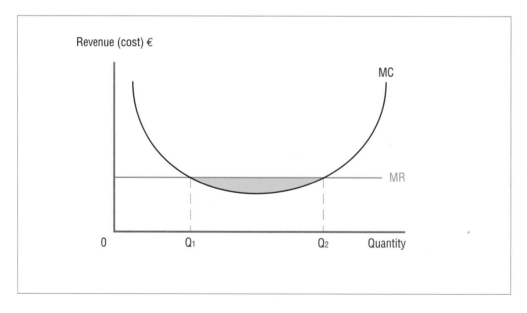

Fig. 10.12 For profit maximisation, MC must cut MR from below

3. Revenue must exceed variable costs

In the long run, the firm must cover all its costs but it can survive in the short run if revenue exceeds variable costs. In the case of our furniture factory if the price of coffee tables fell to €35 each, it would still pay the firm to produce either two, three or four units of output in the short run. This is because AR > AVC at each of these outputs. If the firm goes out of production, the fixed cost must still be paid. Therefore the loss per day is €30.

If the firm produces three units of output, total cost is €120, and total revenue would be €105 (3 x €35). Therefore the loss per day is €15. The firm would be better off (by €15) if it continued in production in the short run. However, in the long run, the firm must cover all its costs.

Summary of profit-maximising conditions

In the short run:
1. MC = MR
2. MC must cut MR from below
3. AR > AVC

In the long run:
1. MC = MR
2. MC must cut MR from below
3. AR must be greater than or equal to AC

11

Market Structures – An Introduction

In *Chapter 5* we considered the concept of a market. We defined a market as a means by which buyers and sellers are brought together so that goods and services (and factors of production) can be bought and sold.

In *Chapter 3* we defined an industry as a group of firms selling goods on a particular market. This means that all of the firms in an industry are engaged in the production of similar goods.

Because the range of goods and services being produced in a modern economy is so vast, it is only to be expected that the type of market in which goods are sold will differ greatly from industry to industry.

One type of product or service (for example, electricity) may be provided in a market where only one very large firm exists which completely controls output, while another type of product (for example, potatoes) may be supplied by thousands of different producers, each one of which has little or no influence on the price or total output of that good.

The economic circumstances under which a good or service is traded constitute the market structure of that good or service. In the next five chapters we will consider five different forms of market structure, which cover the complete range of goods and services that are traded in a modern economy. We will list the characteristics of these market structures and then explain how a firm operating in that type of market will achieve its goal of profit maximisation, what quantity it will produce, what price it will charge and how it will deal with rival firms in the same industry. We will analyse what factors may cause a change in the price/output combination of the firm and we will differentiate between the short run and long run. *Table 11.1* gives an indication of the range of market structures that we will examine.

Monopoly	Imperfect competition	Perfect competition
One firm supplies all of the goods	Many different firms producing similar but not identical goods: **Duopoly** – two firms produce total output **Oligopoly** – a few firms produce total output	Lots of firms producing identical goods

Table 11.1 Types of market structure

In perfect competition, there are very many firms selling the same good. In *monopoly*, there is only one producer supplying the good. In between these two extremes, there is a wide range of imperfectly competitive markets. *Duopoly* is a name given to a market consisting of only two firms. *Oligopoly* is the term used to describe a market where only a few firms supply similar products.

The term imperfect competition is used to describe the market structure where a large number of firms are producing similar but not identical goods. It is important to stress here that using terms like 'imperfect' and 'perfect' does not imply any notion of desirability or undesirability. Perfect competition refers to the complete or highest form of competition, not the most desirable form of competition.

12

Perfect Competition

Perfect competition is the most extreme form of market structure. It is characterised by the following set of assumptions.

1. The product is homogeneous

Each firm in the industry is producing an identical product. Consumers are unable to distinguish the output of one firm from that of any other firm. For example, a consumer buying potatoes in a shop does not care whether they were grown by Farmer A or Farmer B.

2. No one seller can influence market price

There are so many sellers of the good in the market that no one seller is able to influence the market price of the good. If we take potato production as our example again, this means that if a farmer ceases to produce potatoes, the market price will not rise as a result. Similarly, if he doubles his output of potatoes, the price of potatoes will not fall. This is because there are so many thousands of farmers producing potatoes that any one farmer's output represents only a tiny fraction of the total output. For this reason every firm in perfect competition is a price taker (i.e. each producer regards the market price as fixed).

3. No one buyer can influence market price

There are so many buyers of the good in the market that no one buyer is able to influence the market price of the good. Each buyer purchases such a tiny fraction of total output that his/her actions have no effect on market price.

4. Individual buyers and sellers act independently

This is related to (2) and (3) above. The market is such that there is no scope for groups of buyers and/or sellers to come together with a view to changing the market price.

5. No barriers to entry

By barriers to entry we mean restrictions on new firms entering the industry. In perfect competition existing firms cannot stop new firms entering into competition with them. In addition, it is possible for any existing firm to cease production and leave the industry if it so wishes.

6. Perfect knowledge exists in the market

This means every buyer and seller is fully informed concerning price, quality and profit levels in the industry.

7. Each firm aims to achieve the maximum level of profit

We assume that the sole objective of each producer is to earn maximum profit, and that each firm will want to produce that quantity which achieves this aim.

IMPLICATIONS OF THESE ASSUMPTIONS

A brief look at the above assumptions shows that markets like this are not very common. Most manufactured products contain brand names by which they can be distinguished from other similar products, so that perfect competition describes a situation which applies to only a small proportion of the goods and services supplied on markets today.

However, the above conditions do represent the market situation for many agricultural products. The sale of fresh fruit and vegetables in shops or in markets reflects the market characteristics of perfect competition. Also the organised commodity markets for primary products (wheat, coffee, tea, rubber, etc.) are such that a price may be fixed for grade or quality of the product, and an individual producer, no matter how large his output, represents only a small fraction of total output.

Similarly, the markets for stocks and shares (i.e. the stock exchange) and the markets for foreign currencies (i.e. foreign exchange markets) may be seen as 'perfect' in that the products traded are identical. However, caution must be exercised here because sometimes large institutional investors can influence market price by buying and selling large amounts of the good.

Even though the above assumptions apply to only a limited number of cases, and despite the fact that some of the assumptions may be considered unrealistic, the perfectly competitive market structure is usually the starting point chosen in any analysis of how markets work, and is the yardstick by which the other market structures are evaluated.

EQUILIBRIUM OF FIRM UNDER PERFECT COMPETITION IN THE SHORT RUN

In assumption (2) above, the firm was shown to be a price taker. This means that the firm has no option but to sell its output at the prevailing market price. Therefore, the demand curve facing the individual firm in perfect competition is a horizontal straight line as shown in *Figure 12.1*.

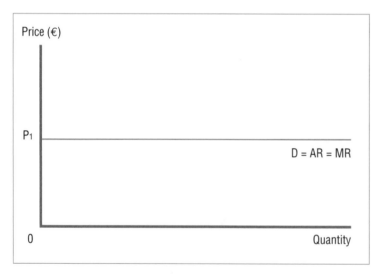

Fig. 12.1 Demand curve facing the individual firm in perfect competition

If the firm tries to raise price above P_1, demand will fall to zero because consumers will buy the identical goods of other producers.

We have shown in *Chapter 10* that average revenue is another name for price. Therefore this demand curve also represents the average revenue curve of the firm since price is fixed, irrespective of the quantity produced.

Remember that we have already defined marginal revenue as 'the change in total revenue resulting from the sale of one extra unit of output'. Since the firm can sell any quantity it likes at the given market price, marginal revenue must be equal to average revenue. Let us look at the following table which shows revenue information for a firm in perfect competition.

Average revenue (P) (€)	Quantity demanded	Total revenue (€)	Marginal revenue (€)
5	1	5	5
5	2	10	5
5	3	15	5
5	4	20	5
5	5	25	5

Table 12.1 Revenue figures for a firm in perfect competition

It can be seen that when price (average revenue) is fixed, marginal revenue equals average revenue. Every extra unit sold will add the same amount to the total revenue of the firm. Under perfect competition:

$$MR = AR = P$$

All three coincide in the same horizontal line as shown in *Figure 12.1*. As far as the producer is concerned, all are constant regardless of the output produced. Of course, it is important to note that total revenue of the firm is not constant. It increases as output increases.

$$\text{Remember } TR = P \times Q$$

Since P is fixed, TR varies directly with Q. This is shown in *Figure 12.2*.

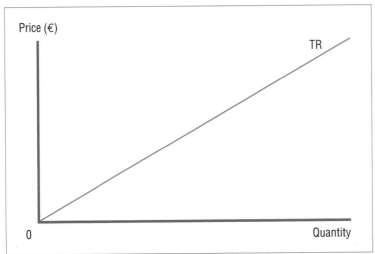

Fig. 12.2 Total revenue of a firm in perfect competition

Let us now turn our attention to the costs of production of the perfectly competitive firm. We have seen in *Chapter 10* that a typical short-run average cost curve of a firm in any type of market is U-shaped. We have also learned that the marginal cost curve must always cut the average cost curve at the lowest point of the average cost curve. *Figure 12.3* shows us the cost and revenue graphs for the perfectly competitive firm in the short run.

Note:
(a) As already explained in *Chapter 10* average cost includes normal profit.
(b) Profit maximisation always occurs at the level of output where MR = MC.

> The most profitable level of output for the firm is Q_1 where MR = MC.

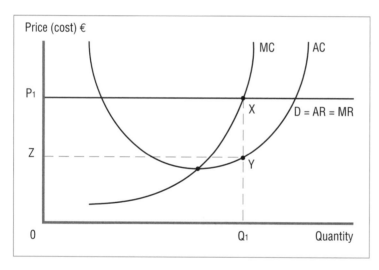

Fig. 12.3 Short-run equilibrium position of a firm in perfect competition

Therefore the equilibrium position of the firm is at quantity Q_1 and price P_1. At quantity Q_1, average revenue is $0P_1$, but average cost is only $0Z$. Therefore:

> Supernormal profit per unit = AR − AC = XY
> Total supernormal profit = rectangle $XYZP_1$

If the prevailing situation in the market is as depicted in *Figure 12.3*, the existence of supernormal profit will have the effect of attracting other producers into the industry. Remember there is perfect knowledge and free entry to (and exit from) the industry.

Producers of other less profitable products will divert resources to the production of goods on this market. To return to the case of agricultural output, the existence of high levels of supernormal profit in wheat production may cause farmers to increase the output of wheat by decreasing the output of other crops.

This will have the effect of increasing the supply of the product on the market, with a consequent reduction in the equilibrium price (as shown in *Fig. 12.4*) from P_1 to P_2.

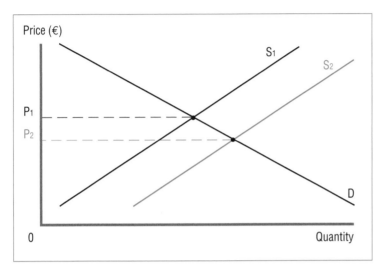

Fig. 12.4 The existence of supernormal profits attracts new firms to the market, causing the industry supply curve to move to the right, and market price to fall

Note from this graph that although the individual producer faces a horizontal straight line demand curve (since he takes price as given), the market demand curve under perfect competition is the normal downward sloping curve from left to right. This indicates that the lower the market price, the greater the total (or aggregate) demand for the product.

EQUILIBRIUM OF FIRM UNDER PERFECT COMPETITION IN THE LONG RUN

The existence of supernormal profits in the short run will attract new entrants to the industry, forcing market price to fall (from P_1 to P_2) as shown in *Figure 12.4*. When market price falls, the horizontal demand curve facing each existing firm, as well as each new entrant, also falls. Each firm adjusts its output to its new profit-maximising position, where marginal cost equals marginal revenue.

If a firm's cost and revenue situation as a result of this fall in market price is as depicted in *Figure 12.5*, then this firm will have no option but to leave the industry. This is because average cost is higher than average revenue at every possible level of output. Therefore, there is no level of output at which the firm can make even normal profits (i.e. where AC = AR), so the firm has no option but to cease production and leave the market.

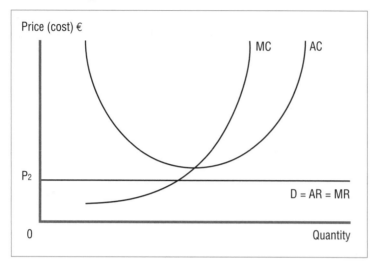

Fig. 12.5 A firm making losses (i.e. AC > AR at all levels of output) has no option but to leave the industry

The entry and exit of firms is the mechanism by which the industry equilibrium is eventually reached. The existence of supernormal profits attracts new firms into the industry which increases market supply and lowers market price. If firms are experiencing losses at the new lower market price, these firms will leave the industry, causing market price to rise. This process will continue until all supernormal profits have been eliminated, and all loss-making firms have left the industry.

Therefore, the long-run equilibrium of the firm under perfect competition is as depicted in *Figure 12.6*. At the new market price of P_3 the firm will produce Q_3, because this level of output satisfies the profit-maximising condition of marginal cost being equal to marginal revenue.

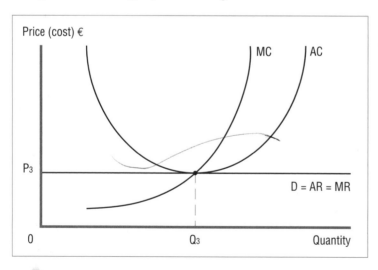

Fig. 12.6 Long-run equilibrium position of a firm in perfect competition

At the level of output Q_3:

$$MR = MC = AR = AC$$

MR = MC ensures that profit maximisation occurs
and
AR = AC ensures that the firm is making normal profits

The absence of supernormal profits means there is no incentive for new firms to enter the industry, while the existence of normal profits ensures that existing firms will not be forced to leave the industry. The industry is therefore at long-run equilibrium. There is no incentive for the number of firms in the industry to change.

SUMMARY AND EVALUATION OF PERFECT COMPETITION

1. In the long run the firm produces at the minimum point on its average cost curve. This equilibrium position of AR = AC ensures that price is at the lowest possible level.

2. Because price is at a minimum, and no supernormal profits are being made, there is no waste of resources from the point of view of society as a whole. Consumers are not exploited by the charging of unneccessarily high prices.

3. Only the most efficient firms survive, since any firms whose costs are such that AC exceeds AR will be forced out of the industry in the long run.

4. No barriers to entry exist which could have the effect of reducing competition or distorting the market.

5. There is no competitive advertising undertaken in perfect competition, since such advertising would only raise costs while not increasing a firm's sales. This is because consumers are unable to distinguish the output of one firm from that of any other firm. However, generic advertising may occur. This means that all firms advertise with a view to increasing market demand, while no specific brand names are mentioned.

6. At long-run equilibrium under perfect competition:

    $$MR = MC = AR = AC$$

SUPPLY CURVE OF A FIRM IN PERFECT COMPETITION

The supply curve of a firm shows the quantity of the good the firm is willing to supply at each price. Under perfect competition a firm always produces where marginal cost is equated with price (i.e. AR = MC). This is because profit maximisation occurs where MC = MR:

> But MR = AR (price)
> Therefore MC = AR

Using this information we can derive the supply curve of a firm under perfect competition. You will remember that in *Chapter 10* it was shown that for a firm to survive in the long run it must cover its total costs, but should continue in production in the short run if it can cover its variable costs and make some contribution to its fixed costs (which must be paid even if no output is produced).

> The short-run supply curve of a firm under perfect competition is that part of its marginal cost curve which lies above the average variable cost curve.

This is shown in *Figure 12.7* by the thick red line.

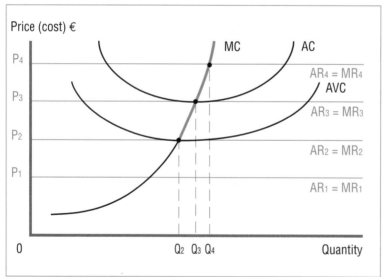

Fig. 12.7 The short-run supply curve of a perfectly competitive firm

If the price is P_2, the firm will supply Q_2
If the price is P_3, the firm will supply Q_3
If the price is P_4, the firm will supply Q_4

However at a price below P_2 (say P_1) the firm will not supply any output since at such a price AVC exceeds AR. The firm will go out of production in such circumstances. In the long run the firm will need to cover all its costs (both fixed and variable). No output will be supplied at any price (AR) which is below average total cost (AC).

Therefore the long-run supply curve of a firm under perfect competition is that part of its marginal cost curve which lies above average (total) cost. This is shown in *Figure 12.8* by the thick red line.

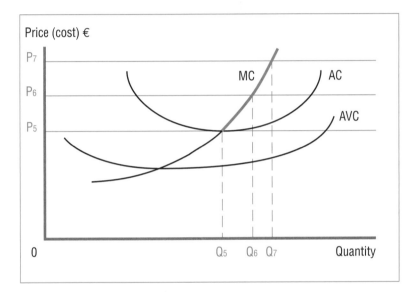

Fig. 12.8 The long-run supply curve of a perfectly competitive firm

At a market price below P_5, the firm will not continue production in the long run, since AC would be greater than AR at any such price and, therefore, the firm would incur losses.

At a price P_5, Q_5 will be supplied
At a price P_6, Q_6 will be supplied
At a price P_7, Q_7 will be supplied
... and so on.

113

13

Monopoly

In *Chapter 12* we commenced our examination of market structures by considering the case of perfect competition. Monopoly is at the other end of the spectrum of market structures. While perfect competition has thousands of firms operating in the same industry the essence of monopoly is that a single producer has entire control over the output of the industry.

> Monopoly is where there is only one producer, so that 'the firm' and 'the industry' have the same meaning.

It is very difficult to envisage an absolute monopoly, because all products are competing against each other to a greater or lesser extent. No firm, even if it is the sole supplier of a product or service, is without competition from suppliers of other products or services. This is so because consumers' incomes are limited.

However for the purposes of this chapter, when we use the term 'monopoly' we are speaking of a firm which controls the entire output of a particular industry. There are no close substitutes available for the product.

ASSUMPTIONS OF MONOPOLY

1. There is only one firm in the industry, i.e. the firm equals the industry.
2. Like perfect competition, the aim of the firm is to maximise its profits.
3. There are barriers to entry which prevent other firms entering the market and competing with the monopolist.
4. Because of the existence of barriers to the entry of new firms, supernormal profits can be earned in both the short run and the long run.
5. No matter how powerful a monopolist is, he cannot control both price and quantity.

The monopolist has two options. He can fix the price and let the market decide what quantity will be demanded. Alternatively, he can decide on a certain quantity to be produced and let the market decide on the price. He cannot control both price and quantity demanded.

Implications of these assumptions

The most obvious implication of the above characteristics is that a separate analysis of the short-run and long-run equilibrium positions of the monopolist is not necessary. Because of barriers to entry, the short-run profit maximising position of the monopolist may be maintained in the long run.

Second, the monopolist is not faced with a horizontal demand curve for his product. If he wants to sell more he must lower his price, therefore, a downward sloping demand curve applies to the monopolist.

Third, because of the nature of monopoly, government monitoring is much more likely than is the case under any other form of market structure. This is to ensure that the monopoly firm does not abuse its dominant and powerful position by charging very high prices or engaging in practices which the government might consider to be against the public interest.

HOW 'BARRIERS TO ENTRY' ARISE

The survival of a firm as a monopoly depends very much on the existence of barriers to entry which prevent the emergence of competition in the market supplied by the monopolist. These barriers to entry may arise in the following ways:

1. Legal monopoly

The state may confer on some companies the exclusive right to supply a particular good or service. This is usually done by the passing of an Act of the Oireachtas, giving a semi-state body the sole right to supply a particular market. When the state grants a monopoly to a company in this manner, it is referred to as a *legal monopoly*. For example, only Dublin Bus is authorised to provide bus services in Dublin, and Iarnród Éireann has a monopoly in rail transport.

2. Monopoly arising from granting of patents or copyrights

If a company invents a new product or develops a new method of production, it may be granted a *patent* which prevents rival firms from copying such products or processes for a certain period of time. This is to provide a pay-back period for progressive firms, i.e. to compensate them for the costs of the research and development involved in designing, manufacturing and bringing these products to the market.

3. Sole ownership of essential raw material

It might be the case that one firm has acquired sole ownership of an essential raw material and thus has a *natural monopoly* in the production of a good. This might apply in the case of mineral wealth, where one company owns the only source of a particular mineral.

4. Significant economies of scale

If economies of scale are significant, monopoly may arise. In some industries, the minimum size of a firm required to operate efficiently is so large that there is no room for competitors once one firm has managed to successfully establish itself. Potential rivals are discouraged from entering the industry by the high initial start-up costs.

5. Monopolies created by product differentiation

A firm may gain monopoly power if its advertising and marketing is so successful that it can convince customers that there is no alternative to its product.

6. Mergers and takeovers

A company may achieve monopoly power by merging with other companies in the same line of production or by taking over rival companies so that competition is eliminated.

7. Trade agreements, cartels or collusion lead to monopolies

Some companies might agree to share out the market in some way which restricts or eliminates competition, so that each can gain a monopoly in some segment of the market. Such arrangements (or cartels) are forbidden in many countries because they are considered to be against the public interest.

How the Monopoly Firm Reaches Equilibrium

Since the firm equals the industry in monopoly, the monopolist faces a downward sloping demand curve for his product. To sell more he must lower his price. Note that this demand curve is also the average revenue curve (as was the case under perfect competition – see *Chapter 12*). When price (AR) is reduced to sell more output, marginal revenue will be less than price. That is, when AR is falling, MR < AR. A simple example will illustrate this point. Suppose the position for the monopolist is as depicted in *Table 13.1* below.

Units of output	Average revenue (€)	Total revenue (€)	Marginal revenue (€)
1	10.0	10.00	10.0
2	8.50	17.00	7.00
3	7.00	21.00	4.00
4	5.50	22.00	1.00

Table 13.1 Average revenue, total revenue and marginal revenue for a monopoly firm

When price is reduced from €10.00 to €8.50 to sell more, AR is now €8.50. MR is €7. When price is reduced from €8.50 to €7.00 to sell more, AR is now €7.00 but MR is only €4.00 and so on. It should be clear (from *Table 13.1*) that in each case of a price reduction, MR will be less than AR. This is shown graphically in *Figure 13.1*.

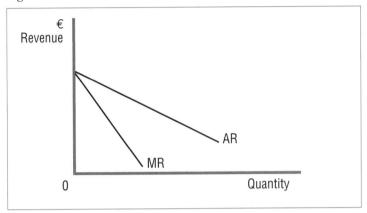

Fig. 13.1 Average and marginal revenue for the monopolist

Let us now turn our attention to the cost structure of the firm under monopoly. Like perfect competition, the average cost (AC) curve will be U-shaped for the monopolist, for the reasons already given in *Chapter 10*. Again, by definition, marginal cost (MC) must cut average cost at the lowest point on the average cost curve. Therefore average cost and marginal cost for the monopolist are as shown in *Figure 13.2*. We will assume that the curves drawn represent the cost situation in the long run.

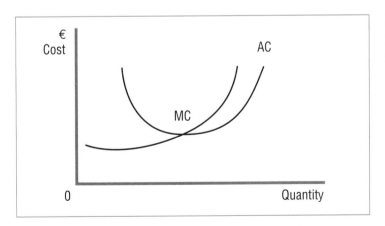

Fig. 13.2 Average and marginal cost for the monopolist (in the long run)

Let us now put our cost and revenue information together in one diagram as shown in *Figure 13.3*. We have already seen that the basic requirement for profit maximisation in any type of market structure is to produce that quantity at which marginal cost is equal to marginal revenue. Therefore, the monopolist should produce Q_1 units of output at a market price of P_1.

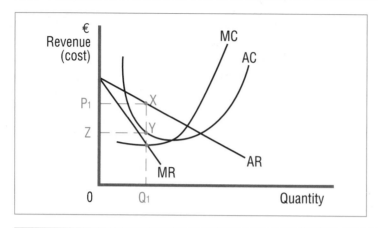

Fig. 13.3 Long-run equilibrium position of a monopolist

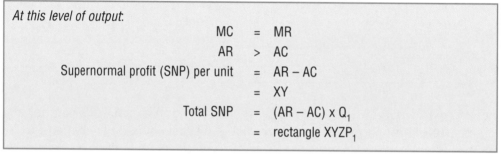

At this level of output:

$$MC = MR$$
$$AR > AC$$
$$\text{Supernormal profit (SNP) per unit} = AR - AC$$
$$= XY$$
$$\text{Total SNP} = (AR - AC) \times Q_1$$
$$= \text{rectangle } XYZP_1$$

Due to the presence of barriers to entry this supernormal profit will not be competed away in the long run by other firms.

COMPARISON OF PRICING AND OUTPUT POLICY IN PERFECT COMPETITION AND MONOPOLY

We are now in a position to compare the quantities produced and the prices charged in perfect competition and monopoly (if cost and revenue conditions are the same). Look carefully at *Figure 13.4*.

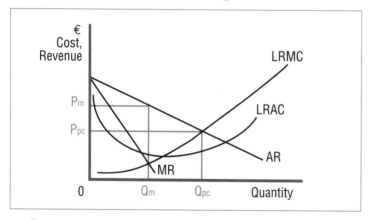

Fig. 13.4 Price and output in perfect competition and monopoly – long-run equilibrium positions compared

In perfect competition, a firm in long-run equilibrium produces that level of output where MC = AR (since AR = MR). Therefore in *Figure 13.4*, the perfectly competitive firm produces Q_{pc} units of output at a price of P_{pc}. In monopoly, a firm in long-run equilibrium produces that level of output where MC = MR. Therefore in *Figure 13.4*, the monopolist produces Q_m units of output at a price of P_m.

We can now conclude that if cost conditions are the same, a monopolist will produce a smaller quantity at a higher price than would a perfectly competitive firm.

SUMMARY AND EVALUATION OF MONOPOLY

1. Unlike a perfectly competitive firm, the monopolist does not produce that level of output where average cost is at a minimum. Therefore, it can be argued that the monopolist is inefficient, with average cost higher than it would have been in a competitive market.

2. A monopolist can earn supernormal profit in both the short run and the long run. This is because of the existence of barriers to entry which prevent new firms entering the market and competing SNP away in the long run.

3. A monopolist can control price or output but not both.

4. In defence of monopoly, it is sometimes argued that because of the benefits of economies of scale, the monopolist can sell his product at a lower price than might be the case under other forms of competition. In other words, the existence of supernormal profits in monopoly does not always imply that the consumer is being exploited by high prices. Such supernormal profits could have arisen through the achievement of lower costs of production brought about by the advantages of producing on a large scale.

5. Not all monopolies are certain to enjoy large supernormal profits. The government, if it considers it to be in the public interest to do so, may force a monopoly firm to charge a price close to average cost (or marginal cost). Alternatively, the government may impose a lump sum tax on a monopoly firm which may reduce or eliminate any supernormal profits.

6. There is a restriction of consumer choice. The consumer cannot transfer his/her demand to a good (or service) supplied by another firm if he/she considers the price charged by the monopolist to be too high, or the good (or service) to be unsatisfactory.

7. No incentive to innovate exists under monopoly. Because of the absence of competition, there is no pressure on the monopolist to introduce new improved methods of production or to undertake research and development.

8. The monopolist may be in a position to separate parts of the market and charge a higher price to one sector than another. This is referred to as price discrimination and is dealt with in greater detail in *Chapter 14*.

9. It is sometimes argued in favour of monopoly that it avoids wasteful duplications of facilities. The benefits of this are perhaps most obvious in the case of public utilities such as water supply, gas and electricity.

10. The monopoly firm may be more resistant to fluctuations in demand than a firm operating on a small profit margin in a competitive environment. With a greater chance of survival, it is sometimes argued that the monopolist gives greater job scrutiny to the workforce and better returns to the shareholders.

11. Highly competitive markets are often characterised by significant advertising costs, which are usually passed on to the consumer. However, no such advertising is necessary for the monopolist.

CONTROL OF MONOPOLIES AND PROMOTION OF COMPETITION

Most monopolies which existed in Ireland in the past arose as a result of the establishment of semi-state bodies in those industries in which the Irish Government felt that such a monopoly was appropriate and in the public interest. In many cases this involved the exploitation of natural resources or the provision of services which the private sector was reluctant to provide. However in recent years the Irish Government, in accordance with EU policy, has undertaken major market deregulation and liberalisation, and now many semi-state companies which previously operated as monopolies have been exposed to competition. This has come about either through privatisation (e.g. Eircom) or through the granting of licences to competitors (e.g. TV3).

Fig. 13.5 Irish television stations now compete for viewers – TV3 newscasters Gráinne Seoige and Alan Cantwell in action.

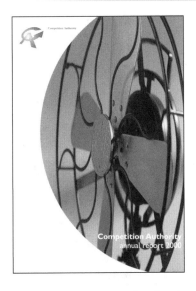

Fig. 13.6 Annual Report 2000 of the Competition Authority.

The Competition Authority, established in the Competition Act 1991, has responsibility for promoting greater competition in every sector of the Irish economy by tackling anti-competitive practices. In its *Annual Report 2000 (Figure 13.6)* it argued that many constraints on competition in Ireland are the result of legislation or regulation and are therefore caused by government rather than private firms. Pubs and taxis are given as examples of services where anti-competitive regulation has worked against the interests of consumers.

In 2002 the Government announced its intention to appoint a Transport Regulator to supervise competition. CIE would be broken up and more competition allowed. This is likely to lead to an immediate scramble among bus companies for licences to operate in Dublin. Another state company facing the cold winds of competition is the ESB. The EU Directive on liberalisation of the electricity market requires an independent electricity transmission system operator (TSO) to be set up in each member country. In 2002, EirGrid plc took over the operation of Ireland's electricity transmission system from the ESB, and in that year over 40 per cent of the electricity market was opened up to competition, with full liberalisation expected in 2005.

In the case of the postal service, the state monopoly, An Post, which lost €7.2m in 2001, sought permission from the Office of the Director of Telecommunications Regulation (ODTR) for substantial rises in postal charges. Postal services are under threat from e-mail and from phone-based communications. The Irish postal market is being opened up to more competition and it seems likely that An Post's delivery service monopoly will be ended, with other EU postal companies gaining access to the Irish market. It seems certain that the era of state monopolies is coming to an end.

A report in the *Irish Examiner* (21 November 2001) highlights the impact of competition on jobs.

COMPETITION CREATES JOBS, SAYS SOLICITOR

By Ian Guider

Increased competition in all sectors of the Irish economy would stimulate economic growth, according to a leading competition solicitor, Vincent Power. Mr Power, a competition law solicitor at leading firm A & L Goodbody says it is more important than ever anti-competitive practices be outlawed to boost job creation as the economy faces a downturn.

He said: "We all believed in opening Ireland to competition during the Celtic Tiger and what is important is that we continue to open up the different industries to competition to avoid a recession."

"If we are facing a recession, we need more competition to lower prices, fight inflation and bring back our competitiveness to attract jobs and industry."

"Among the areas in urgent need of being opened up are airports and the lifting of the Groceries Order."

Mr Power said that while the number of low cost and traditional airlines flying in and out of Ireland has risen, larger airports were still in the hands of the State. He said he favours removing the Groceries Order as it prevents price competition in the sector.

"Our experience has shown competition creates jobs and benefits consumers. The best example of this is teleco-mmunications. Five years ago we had one operator, now we have a handful and prices have come down. There have been no job losses, but job creation."

He said State aid to prop up loss-making businesses must end. "There is some room for State aid but it has to be associated with radical once-off surgery and no on-going link between the State and the recipient of the State aid."

There was also a need to increase the powers of industry regulators, such as the telecoms and electricity regulators, to give them greater muscle to deal with breaches of competition law. He said they should be given the power to levy fines on individual companies.

14

Price Discrimination

In our summary and evaluation of monopoly in the previous chapter, we referred to the fact that it is sometimes possible for a monopolist to divide his market into separate components in such a way that he can increase his profits. By doing so, he is discriminating against consumers in one section of the market by charging them higher prices, even though no extra costs have been incurred in supplying such consumers. A producer is said to be engaging in price discrimination when he behaves in such a manner.

> Price Discrimination is defined as the selling of the same good (or service) to different customers at different prices, where such price differences are not caused by differences in costs.

It is clear from this definition that all price differences are not a result of price discrimination. For example, a producer will usually charge more for a good sold in a distant market than in a nearby market.

This is not price discrimination. It is simply because it costs more to transport the good and sell it in the distant market than it does to sell the same good in the nearby market. However, when surplus EU agricultural products are sold outside the EU at prices lower than within the EU, this is price discrimination, because the price differences are not caused by cost differences.

TYPES OF PRICE DISCRIMINATION

It is possible to distinguish two types of price discrimination.

1. Sale of identical goods (or services) to different customers at different prices

> **EXAMPLES**
>
> (a) A doctor may charge a rich patient €30 for a consultation, while a poor person may be charged €15 for the same service.
>
> (b) A young boy may be admitted to a football match for €5, while an adult might have to pay €15.
>
> (c) Iarnród Éireann might charge an adult €30 for a return fare from Dublin to Cork, while a teenager might only be charged €18.
>
> (d) An 'industrial user' (i.e. a manufacturing firm) is charged a lower rate per unit for electricity than a 'domestic user' (i.e. a householder).
>
> (e) Old age pensioners are sometimes offered services at reduced rates, for example, dry cleaning and hairdressing.

In each of the above examples, the underlying feature is that the seller (or producer) charges higher prices for the same good to those customers perceived to be in the best position (i.e. willing and/or able) to pay such prices, and lower prices to those customers whose demand is not seen to be as strong.

2. Sale of different quantities of a good (or service) to same consumer at different prices

> **EXAMPLES**
>
> (a) A publisher charges €3 per issue for a weekly magazine, but is willing to offer an annual subscription for €100.
>
> (b) A grocer sells a packet of biscuits at €2, or two for €3.
>
> (c) A hotel charges €60 per night for bed and breakfast, but has a special weekend rate of €90 (to cover two nights).

The above price concessions or discounts are a recognition by the seller that the buyer is subject to the Law of Diminishing Marginal Utility. In order to persuade the buyer to purchase more of the good (or service), the seller must make additional units available at a lower unit price.

CONDITIONS NECESSARY FOR PRICE DISCRIMINATION

The following conditions must be present if price discrimination is to exist.

1. Element of monopoly power

The firm wishing to engage in price discrimination must have some element of monopoly power. There must be some barriers to entry to the market. If this were not so, new firms would attempt to supply a similar good (or service) on the higher priced market, at a price lower than that being charged by the price-discriminating monopolist. This would force the monopolist to abandon his discriminatory pricing policy, or at the very least, lower the price charged to that section of the market.

2. Distinct and separate markets

The markets must be distinct and separate. Consumers in the market where price is relatively low must not be able to resell to consumers in the high priced market. If this were not the case, the transfer of goods purchased in the lower priced market to the higher priced market would make the charging of different prices in the two markets impossible.

The above condition is perhaps more easily seen to apply to services rather than goods. For example, services by doctors, lawyers, accountants, etc. are usually supplied on a one-to-one basis, so that they are not readily transferable from one buyer to another. If Mr Murphy visits his doctor because he is worried about his health, the information he receives is of no use to Mr O'Brien, who might have concerns about his own health. Because a service bought by one person is of no use to anyone else, it cannot be resold. This allows the seller to charge different prices to different customers, based on his perception of their willingness (or ability) to pay.

In the case of goods, certain features of the market may make separation into high priced and low priced segments possible. Transport costs, tariff barriers and import quotas are examples of such features which can make price discrimination possible, by ensuring that the monopolist does not face much of a threat from foreign competition. The firm can thus charge a high price on the home market, which is protected, and sell at a low price abroad, where it faces competition from other suppliers.

3. Different elasticities of demand

The firm must be able to identify different elasticities of demand for the good or service. The price-discriminating monopolist will be aware that not all his potential customers have the same strength of demand for his good or service. It is important for the firm to be able to distinguish those customers with a strong demand from those with a weak demand.

For example, a business person travelling by air from Dublin to London might be willing to pay €200 for this service, while a student, wishing to avail of the same service, might not be willing to pay more than €100.

Old age pensioners and children often get reductions on admission charges to certain sporting events because they are seen to have less strong a demand. Not many pensioners or children are willing (and/or able) to pay full admission prices for such events. Their demand for such events is therefore elastic with respect to price. For the same reason, many shops are prepared to give discounts, ranging from 5 to 25 per cent, to full-time students (on production of a student identity card).

The underlying feature in each of the above examples is that the seller can clearly identify different categories of buyers. Those with a greater willingness and ability to pay (i.e. those with a relatively inelastic demand) will be asked to pay more. Those who are less willing and less able to pay (i.e. those with a relatively elastic demand) will be charged a lower price.

Characteristics of consumers

Certain characteristics of consumers make the practice of price discrimination more likely:

1. **Consumer ignorance.** Consumers may not be aware that the good or service is available from another supplier at a lower price.

2. **Consumer inertia.** Even if they are aware of its availability at a lower price, consumers may regard the difference in price as insignificant. Therefore, they may be reluctant to change from one supplier to another.

3. **Consumer attitude to the goods or services in question.** Consumers may be willing to pay a higher price for the good or service supplied by one firm because of a certain status or prestige attaching to that firm.

HOW A PRICE-DISCRIMINATING MONOPOLIST REACHES EQUILIBRIUM

We will now find out how a price-discriminating monopoly, selling on two markets, decides what price to charge in each market and how it allocates its output between the two markets. Let us assume that our firm is a manufacturing firm, selling its product on the home and the foreign markets. We will also assume that our firm faces a downward sloping demand curve for the product on both markets. In order to sell more, price will have to be reduced. Suppose our revenue conditions are as shown in *Tables 14.1* and *14.2*.

Units of output (Q)	Average revenue (€) (AR = P)	Total revenue (€) (TR = P x Q)	Marginal revenue (€) (MR = ΔTR)
1	50	50	50
2	45	90	40
3	39	117	27
4	35	140	23
5	31	155	15

Table 14.1 Revenue conditions in the home market for a price-discriminating monopolist

Units of output (Q)	Average revenue (€) (AR = P)	Total revenue (€) (TR = P x Q)	Marginal revenue (€) (MR = ΔTR)
1	42	42	42
2	38	76	34
3	32	96	20
4	28	112	16
5	25	125	13

Table 14.2 Revenue conditions in the foreign market for a price-discriminating monopolist

Firm produces one unit of output

If the firm decides to produce only one unit of output, it is obvious that this unit will be supplied to the home market, where the selling price is €50, and not to the foreign market, where the selling price is only €42.

Firm produces two units of output

If the firm's total output is two units, one unit will be supplied to the home market (at €50) and one unit to the foreign market (at €42). In this way total revenue is maximised at €92. If both units had been supplied to the home market, total revenue would have been €90 (i.e. two units at €45 each). If both units had been supplied to the foreign market, total revenue would have been €76 (i.e. two units at €38 each).

Another way of arriving at this conclusion is by examining marginal revenue in each market. The marginal revenue of the second unit of output produced would be €40 if sold at home, while it would be €42 if sold abroad. Note that the second unit of output produced would be the first unit of output sold abroad, hence marginal revenue is €42.

Firm produces three units of output

Let us examine what would happen if our firm decided to produce three units of output. How many units should be sold in each market? If we sell all three units at home, our total revenue is €117 (3 units at €39 each). If we sell all three units abroad, our total revenue is €96 (3 units at €32 each). If we sell two units at home and one abroad, our total revenue is €132 (2 at €45 each and 1 at €42). If we sell one unit at home and two abroad, our total revenue is €126 (1 unit at €50 and 2 at €38 each). To maximise our revenue, therefore, we should sell two units at home and one abroad.

Let us now look at marginal revenue on both markets to see if we can arrive at the same conclusion. If the firm is already selling one unit at home and one unit abroad, and is uncertain about where to sell the third unit, a quick look at *Tables 14.1* and *14.2* will solve the problem.

By selling the extra unit on the home market, marginal revenue would be €40. This is because this third unit of output produced would be the second unit sold on this market. Alternatively, if this extra unit were sold abroad, marginal revenue would be €34. This is because this third unit of output produced would be the second unit of output sold on this market. By continuing this process we can find out, for any level of output, the optimum market allocation of that output, and consequently, the maximum revenue attainable from the sale of that level of output. *Table 14.3* below is based on the revenue information contained in *Tables 14.1* and *14.2*. It shows the optimum allocation of output between the two markets, and the maximum revenue attainable, for outputs in the range one to eight units. We are now in a position to make the following statement concerning the allocation of output between two markets by a price-discriminating monopolist.

Total output produced	Optimum allocation of output	Maximum revenue attainable (€)
1	1 home 0 foreign	50
2	1 home 1 foreign	92
3	2 home 1 foreign	132
4	2 home 2 foreign	166
5	3 home 2 foreign	193
6	4 home 2 foreign	216
7	4 home 3 foreign	236
8	4 home 4 foreign	252

Table 14.3 Allocation of output between markets and maximum revenue attainable (based on revenue conditions shown in *Tables 14.1* and *14.2*)

As long as marginal revenue in the first market is greater than marginal revenue in the second market, it would be possible to increase total revenue by switching sales from the second market to the first market.

Therefore, a condition for revenue maximisation is that marginal revenue in both markets must be equal.

All our attention so far has been focused on revenue. We have said nothing about cost. For profit maximisation (in any type of market) we have already seen that the firm should produce that quantity where marginal revenue equals marginal cost. Our basic rule for profit maximisation for a price-discriminating monopolist can now be finalised as follows.

A price-discriminating monopolist, in order to earn maximum profit, must produce that quantity where marginal cost equals marginal revenue in the home market equals marginal revenue in the foreign market. Therefore, $MC = MR_h = MR_f$.

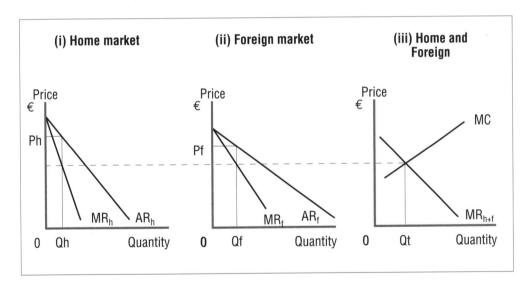

Fig. 14.1 Equilibrium for a price-discriminating monopolist

This equilibrium position of a price-discriminating monopolist is depicted in *Figure 14.1*. We have shown our revenue information for the home market and the foreign market separately.

AR_h = average revenue in home market
MR_h = marginal revenue in home market
AR_f = average revenue in foreign market
MR_f = marginal revenue in foreign market
P_h = price on home market
Q_h = quantity on home market
P_f = price on foreign market
Q_f = quantity on foreign market
Q_t = quantity on home and foreign market combined

Notice that we have drawn the home demand curve as a steeper graph than the foreign one. This is usually the case since the firm's demand is more likely to be inelastic at home due to fewer competitors. This is why price charged on the home market is higher than that charged abroad. However, marginal revenue on the home market is the same as marginal revenue on the foreign market at the equilibrium position. *Figure 14.1 (iii)* shows the overall equilibrium position for the price-discriminating monopolist where MC = MR. Profit maximisation occurs at the level of output Q_t, where $Q_t = Q_h + Q_f$.

15

Imperfect Competition

Imperfect competition is the name given to that form of market structure which lies between the two extremes of perfect competition and monopoly. We have seen in *Chapter 12* above that the assumptions underlying perfect competition are such that very few industries correspond to this type of market structure. Similarly, monopolies because of their potential to exploit the market are restricted very much by government control. It follows that imperfect competition is the market structure which most closely mirrors the conditions under which the vast majority of firms operate in a modern economy.

CHARACTERISTICS OF IMPERFECT COMPETITION

The following are the characteristics, or underlying assumptions, of imperfect competition:

1. There is a large number of firms in the industry, each of which acts independently.
2. There are many buyers of the goods produced by firms in the industry.
3. Product differentiation exists. This means firms produce similar (but not identical) products. Unlike perfect competition, the consumer can distinguish the product of one firm from that of another. This is possible because 'branding' of goods and 'competitive advertising' take place under imperfect competition.
4. Freedom of entry and exit exists. New firms may enter and existing firms leave the industry without any difficulty.
5. There is widespread knowledge concerning profit levels being earned in the industry.
6. Each firm tries to maximise its profits.

Implications of these assumptions

A close examination of the above assumptions will enable us to compare and contrast imperfect competition with the other market structures already considered in previous chapters.

Like perfect competition, the industry is characterised by many buyers and sellers, none of whose actions is likely to influence others. Also there is widespread knowledge of profit levels within the industry, so we can expect an influx of new firms if supernormal profits are being earned in the industry. Similarly, because we are making the assumption that firms aim to maximise their profits, we can predict that unprofitable firms will be forced out of the business.

Let us now turn our attention to assumption (3) above. Unlike perfect competition, the products of different firms are not homogeneous. Even if the products of competing firms appear very similar, consumers are still able to tell one firm's product from all other products because of the existence of distinctive brand names and packaging (e.g. Benson and Hedges, Carrolls, and Dunhill in the tobacco industry).

Indeed it can be argued that the whole purpose of competitive advertising by a firm is to enable consumers to differentiate one product from another, with a view to encouraging as many customers as possible to switch from consuming goods produced by rival firms to consuming goods produced by the firm in question.

It should be obvious that the firm under imperfect competition is not a price taker. Each firm is faced with a downward sloping demand curve for its product as was the case under monopoly. If it wants to sell more, it must lower its price.

SHORT-RUN EQUILIBRIUM OF A FIRM IN IMPERFECT COMPETITION

Figure 15.1 shows the situation facing an imperfectly competitive firm in the short run.

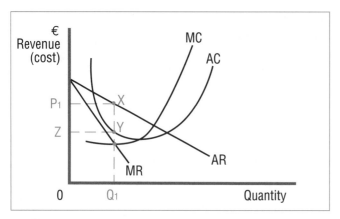

Fig. 15.1 Short-run equilibrium position of a firm under imperfect competition

Note:

1. The demand curve (i.e. average revenue) slopes downwards from left to right.

2. When average revenue is falling, marginal revenue will be below average revenue. (See *Table 13.1* to clarify this point.)

3. Average cost, as usual, is drawn as a U-shaped curve (see *Chapter 10*).

4. As is always the case, marginal cost cuts average cost at the lowest point on the average cost curve.

5. The basic rule for profit maximisation (under any form of market structure) is – 'produce that level of output where marginal cost equals marginal revenue'.

The firm depicted in *Figure 15.1* should therefore produce quantity Q_1 at a price P_1, if it wishes to maximise its profits. In this situation it will earn supernormal profits.

Supernormal profit per unit = AR – AC = XY
Total supernormal profit = (AR – AC) x Q_1 = rectangle $XYZP_1$

If the above analysis seems familiar, it is because the short-run equilibrium position of the firm under imperfect competition is exactly the same as the short- (and long-) run equilibrium position of the monopolist. The only difference is that the imperfectly competitive firm will have a flatter demand curve than the monopolist. The monopolist has a relatively inelastic demand for his product, since no substitutes are available. The imperfectly competitive firm has a relatively elastic demand curve for its product since there are many substitutes available. A quick glimpse at *Figure 13.3* will confirm this.

However, the imperfectly competitive firm will have to face extra competition from new firms which are attracted into the industry by the presence of supernormal profits. While the monopolist can hold onto supernormal profits in the long run, the firm in imperfect competition will be faced with a drop in its demand curve (i.e. its average revenue curve) in the long run as new firms enter the industry.

As a result of the entry of new firms, total supply increases so that there is a reduction in the level of the demand for the individual firm, as shown in *Figure 15.2*.

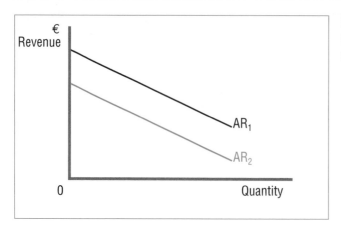

Fig. 15.2 Entry of new firms to the market shifts the AR curve to the left

LONG-RUN EQUILIBRIUM OF A FIRM IN IMPERFECT COMPETITION

This process will continue as long as supernormal profits are being earned in the industry. New firms will enter (attracted by high profits), while some existing firms will leave the industry if price (average revenue) is forced down so much that they cannot earn even normal profit. This would occur if the firm's costs were such that all points on the average cost curve lie above the average revenue curve. This is shown in *Figure 15.3*.

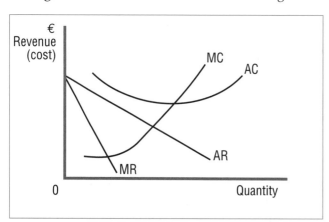

Fig. 15.3 A firm in imperfect competition which is faced with closure

It can clearly be seen that there is no level of output at which this firm can continue to earn normal profit, and thus it is forced to cease production.

The long-run equilibrium position of the imperfectly competitive firm is shown in *Figure 15.4*. The firm will produce quantity Q_2 at price P_2, since this level of output fulfils the profit-maximising condition, MC = MR. At price P_2, the AR line is tangential to the AC curve, i.e. AC = AR. There is no SNP since SNP = AR − AC.

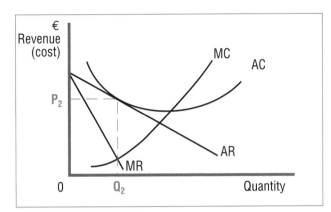

Fig. 15.4 Long-run equilibrium of a firm in imperfect competition

From a comparison of *Figures 15.1* and *15.4*, it should be clear that the entry of new firms, in shifting the AR curve to the left, has also shifted the MR curve to the left.

Other things being equal, the entry of new firms does not alter the cost structure of the firm in question. Therefore, the profit-maximising output will be lower in the long run than the short run. We have already seen that the profit-maximising price (AR) will be lower in the long run than the short run. That is:

$$P_2 \text{ (in } Fig. \text{ 15.4)} < P_1 \text{ (in } Fig. \text{ 15.1)}$$
$$\text{and } Q_2 \text{ (in } Fig. \text{ 15.4)} < Q_1 \text{ (in } Fig. \text{ 15.1)}$$

SUMMARY AND EVALUATION OF IMPERFECT COMPETITION

1. Unlike perfect competition, in the long run the firm does not produce the level of output corresponding to the lowest point on the average cost curve. This is because AR cannot be tangential to AC at the lowest point of AC (since AR is downward sloping). Therefore, the imperfectly competitive firm does not produce at the lowest possible average cost.

2. Because of the firm's inability to operate at the lowest possible point on the average cost curve, imperfect competition is said to be inefficient and wasteful of resources. There are two reasons for this:

   (a) *Excess capacity.* Firms in imperfect competition will generally be producing too small an output to exploit economies of scale to the full. The difference between actual output and the output required to achieve full economies of scale is called the excess capacity of the firm.

(b) *Competitive advertising.* This is defined as any advertising that stresses the qualities of one firm's product over the goods produced by all competing firms (i.e. 'our product is better than all the others!'). It must be distinguished from informative advertising, which simply makes the public aware of the existence of the good and its qualities, and thus increases consumers' knowledge. Competitive advertising is not a feature of perfect competition, as was already explained, since the products are homogenous. Similarly, there is no competitive advertising undertaken by a monopolist, since there are no close substitutes.

Therefore competitive advertising is essentially a feature of imperfect competition, as many firms producing similar goods compete for the consumer's attention (and his/her income!).

Opponents of competitive advertising argue that it imposes additional costs on firms, which, in most cases, are passed on to consumers in the form of higher prices. It can also act as a barrier to entry by discouraging new firms entering the market (i.e. if the advertising costs involved are prohibitive).

Those in favour of advertising argue that it gives employment directly in the advertising industry and indirectly through larger sales. They also point out that profits earned from extra sales, achieved as a result of the advertising, often are sufficiently large to cover the costs of the advertising. A further advantage of advertising concerns sponsorship. Advertising by firms, undertaken in association with sports and cultural events, often ensures the very survival of such events in the absence of alternative sources of funding.

3. In long-run equilibrium under imperfect competition, MC = MR and AC = AR. This is not the same as long-run equilibrium in perfect competition where MC = MR = AC = AR (see *Fig. 12.6*). It is also different from long-run equilibrium in monopoly where MC = MR and AR > AC (see *Fig. 13.3*).

4. The firm in imperfect competition can earn SNP in the short run but this is eliminated in the long run by the entry of new firms. This characteristic is also a feature of perfect competition but not of monopoly.

5. The firm in imperfect competition faces a downward sloping demand curve for its product. This characteristic is also a feature of monopoly but not of perfect competition.

6. In the long-run profit-maximising position, both price and output will be lower than was the case in the short-run profit-maximising position.

7. In defence of imperfect competition, it can be said that customers usually desire product differentiation and brand names, even if this means higher prices. Sometimes people want low-priced homogeneous products, but most of the time we demand a wide variety of goods and services both in terms of quality and price. The higher price we must pay can be seen as the cost of providing us with this choice.

Bakeries may not demand more than one type of wheat, but shoppers want the freedom to choose from over 20 types of bread, as you see by visiting any large supermarket today. If consumers were to be offered only one generic style of product in place of the many varied styles currently available, then the overall standard of living would definitely decline.

In this regard it is perhaps unfortunate to call the demand for homogenous goods 'perfect' and the demand for heterogeneous goods (i.e. with brand names) 'imperfect'.

8. Product innovation is encouraged under imperfect competition. This means that firms are constantly striving to introduce new or better products to the market so as to gain a competitive edge over their rivals, even if such an advantage is only a temporary one.

9. The theory of imperfect competition developed in this chapter is based on competition between large numbers of firms producing similar but not identical products. However, many industries in a modern economy are characterised by a small number of large firms operating in close competition with each other. Such firms operate in the market structure called oligopoly, which is the subject of the next chapter.

CHAPTER 16

Oligopoly

In the last chapter we considered the market structure of imperfect competition. We assumed that imperfectly competitive markets were characterised by many firms supplying similar products which are close but not perfect substitutes for each other. However, if we examine the markets for certain goods and services, such as petrol, cigarettes, beer, motor cars, retail banking services, washing powders and detergents, we can see that such markets are not characterised by many sellers acting independently. On the contrary, a small number of large firms supply similar products, and each firm is conscious that any action on its part is likely to result in other firms responding to that action. The market for such goods is thus not composed of many firms acting independently. It contains only a few firms whose actions are interdependent. Such a market is known as oligopoly.

MAIN FEATURES OF OLIGOPOLY

1. The market is dominated by a few large suppliers, who have the power to influence the selling price of the good or service. An industry is said to have a high *concentration ratio* if a small number of firms account for a very large part of the total output. Oligopolistic industries generally have high concentration ratios. For example in 2002, the general insurance market in Ireland had five companies (Hibernian, Allianz, Royal SunAlliance, AXA and Eagle Star) with about 80 per cent of the market.

2. Firms are *interdependent*. This means that firms in an oligopolistic market do not operate in isolation. Every decision a firm takes (for example, a decision to change the price of its good) will be based on the likely reaction of its rivals to that decision.

3. Product *differentiation* exists. A firm will spend large sums of money emphasising the differences (real or imaginary) between its product and those of its rivals. Products may be very similar in certain industries (e.g. petrol) so the scope for advertising in this manner may be limited.

4. Because of the intense competition between firms which is a feature of oligopoly, firms may be reluctant to engage in *price competition*. If one firm lowers its price to gain extra sales, other firms will do likewise, and the resulting price war could mean less profits for all. For this reason, firms in oligopoly often resort to *non-price competition* in an effort to take sales from rival firms. This is defined as any action undertaken by a firm to increase its sales at the expense of rival firms, other than the lowering of price.

   Examples of non-price competition are free gifts, special promotional offers, introductory offers to new customers, coupons, 'money off next purchase' schemes, quantity discounts, sponsorship of major events, etc. Such promotional schemes are a noted feature of oligopoly because they offer the firm the chance of extra sales without the danger of a full-scale price war.

5. There are usually some *barriers to entry*. The most common are:
   (a) The high cost of starting up in the industry. For example, vast expenditure on plant and machinery would be required in the motor car industry.
   (b) The absolute cost advantages of existing firms. These are the advantages that existing firms have over potential new entrants to the industry, e.g. patents, customer goodwill, an established network of sales outlets, and a highly trained workforce.
   (c) Economies of scale in advertising may be significant (see *Chapter 3*).
   (d) *Brand proliferation* may be practised by existing firms. This is where each existing firm produces and advertises several brands thus limiting the market available to a potential new entrant. This is practised successfully by tobacco firms and breweries, but perhaps the most celebrated example is in the detergent industry where two firms, Proctor and Gamble (producing *Daz, Tide, Bold, Ariel, Dreft* and *Fairy* among others) and Lever Brothers (whose products include *Surf, Persil, Omo* and *Lux*) have managed to create virtual duopoly. By producing and advertising a range of different washing powders, these companies have made it very difficult for other firms to get established in the market.

6. Prices tend to be more 'sticky' in oligopoly than in other forms of market structure. There tends to be a long period of price stability, occasionally interruped by intense price competition. Possible explanations for this will be examined later.

7. There may be scope for *collusion* in oligopoly. Two or more firms may agree to restrict competition between themselves with the aim of increasing total profit.
8. There may be objectives of the firm other than profit maximisation. We will consider some of these alternative objectives later.

It should be clear from the above list of features that, unlike other market structures we have examined, there is no one theory of oligopoly which will provide us with a unique price/output combination at which the firm will be in equilibrium. Therefore, we are unable to predict precisely the behaviour of firms, as was done in previous chapters for the other types of markets. The behaviour of any firm depends on the industry concerned and how it perceives its relationship with the other firms in that industry. We will now consider a number of cases that have been developed to explain certain aspects of oligopolistic markets.

EXPLANATION FOR STICKY PRICES – THE KINKED DEMAND CURVE

One possible explanation for sticky prices was put forward in the 1930s by Paul Sweezy. This became known as the kinked demand curve and is shown in *Figure 16.1.*

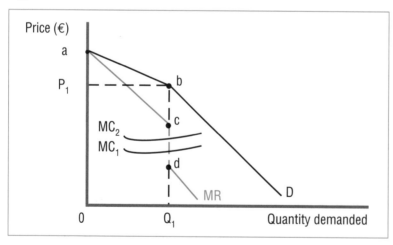

Fig. 16.1 The kinked demand curve

Sweezy argued that a firm will not wish to raise its price above the original price, P_1, because it assumes that other firms will not respond by raising their prices. The firm will therefore assume that demand is relatively elastic for a price rise. In other words, if it increases price, demand will fall by a proportionately greater amount. The firm's market share and its total revenue would fall in such circumstances. When demand is elastic, a rise in price will cause a fall in total revenue. (See *Table 9.2* for relationship between price elasticity of demand and total revenue.)

If the firm were to lower its price below the original price, P_1, other firms will do the same so that its share of the market will not rise by as much as the price fall. Demand is therefore inelastic below the original price, P_1. When demand is inelastic, a fall in price will lead to a fall in total revenue. (See *Table 9.2* to confirm this fact.)

Any change in price away from the original price (i.e. a price rise or a price fall) will result in a fall in total revenue. The firm will, in such circumstances, be extremely reluctant to change its price. This is known as *price rigidity*. The black line, abD, in *Figure 16.1*, represents the firm's idea of its demand curve. The corresponding marginal revenue curve is the discontinuous curve, acdMR.

A rise in marginal cost, say from MC_1 to MC_2, will obviously not alter equilibrium output or price. Remember that equilibrium for the firm is where MC = MR. We can see, therefore, that changes in cost will not always result in a price change. By responding to every increase in cost by increasing price, a firm will generate even further cost increases. Price lists and catalogues will have to be altered, computer programs storing price information will have to be changed, advertising campaigns might be affected, and there might be a loss of customer goodwill. Also there is the possibility that the initial cost increase may be only temporary. For these reasons firms will also be reluctant to alter prices. This is known as *price constancy*.

While Sweezy's model may have been an accurate explanation in the 1930s (when there was a depression and most firms had spare capacity), it did not stand up well in the 1970s and 1980s. Many oligopolistic firms raised their prices in the 1970s because of high inflation, increases in wages and high oil prices. In the 1980s and again in the 1990s many firms raised prices because of the strength of consumer demand.

A further problem with the kinked demand curve model of oligopoly is that it does not explain how the initial equilibrium price is set. In those industries where it is difficult for firms to raise prices without experiencing declining revenue, there is a great incentive to engage in collusion. It is to the case of collusion by oligopolistic firms that we now turn.

COLLUSION

We can define collusion as any action undertaken by separate and rival companies to restrict competition between them with a view to increasing their total profits.

Because of the features of oligopoly discussed above, firms can gain important advantages by colluding with rival firms. Such collusion can be explicit or implicit. *Explicit collusion* occurs when separate companies jointly decide on a specific course of action in an arrangement known as a *cartel*. Such collusion might include:

---

1. A fixed price which applies to all firms in the cartel.
2. A refusal to supply their products to retailers who also buy from firms not in the cartel.
3. A quota system which limits production to certain agreed amounts (in order to keep price at the highest possible level).
4. An agreement to divide sales territories into different smaller markets, with only one firm supplying each market.

Implicit (or tacit) collusion occurs when there is no formal agreement between firms, but each firm recognises that joint profits will be higher if firms collectively behave as if they were branches of a single monopolistic firm. A firm will not provoke its rivals by cutting prices since such a move would lead to a price war with less profits for all firms. Instead a firm may attempt to gain a greater market share by the use of non-price competition (e.g. a more aggressive advertising campaign). Firms which engage in collusion in this manner are said to be following a policy of *joint profit maximisation*. The oligopolistic firm wants to co-operate with its competitors to maximise the total profits of the industry; but it also wants as large a share of these profits as possible. It is because of these conflicting aims that cartels generally are of a temporary nature. For example, once a high price has been achieved (by restricting supply), the individual firm will be tempted to raise its supply to make extra profits.

Examples of cartels are OPEC (Organisation of Petroleum Exporting Countries) and IATA (International Air Transport Association). OPEC, founded in 1960 and consisting of 11 petroleum producing (and exporting) countries, set petroleum quotas for its members in an effort to keep oil prices high. Initially very successful, in the early 1970s OPEC accounted for 90 per cent of total world exports of crude oil. OPEC was able to successfully increase price on many occasions in the past because the demand for oil is highly inelastic. However, high prices led to the substitution of oil by other fuels, energy conservation programmes, and expansion of oil output by non-OPEC members. There were also disputes within OPEC concerning adherence to quotas. Consequently, by 1999 OPEC accounted for only 40 per cent of world oil exports. OPEC is now dependent on the co-operation of non-member countries in its efforts to secure price rises.

IATA tries to prevent competition between airlines forcing the prices of scheduled services too low. A fall in prices would lead to some airlines going out of business or cutting their costs (which might lead to a fall in safety standards). However the growth in the number of chartered flights and the policy of deregulation has made its job extremely difficult.

PRICE LEADERSHIP

An alternative theory of oligopoly to the kinked demand curve model is one which assumes the existence of *price leadership*. In this model, one firm is assumed to be in a dominant position, either because of its large size or its early entry to the market. This firm, known as the price leader, may set its prices independently of other firms in the industry. If this firm raises prices, other firms will follow because they feel a price war would be self-defeating in the long run. If the price leader lowers price, the other firms follow with price reductions, since otherwise they would lose customers to the price leader.

The motor industry and the travel agency/tour company business are often cited as examples of industries where price leadership exists. For example, Budget Travel has for many years been the leading travel company operating package holidays from Ireland. If Budget Travel raises the price of a holiday to a particular destination, rival companies will feel free to do likewise. Similarly, if Budget Travel lowers price, the other companies may feel they have no option but to follow suit. The following extract from Budget Travel's website (*Figure 16.2*) shows that the company sees itself as a price leader for the industry.

BUDGET TRAVEL PRICE GUARANTEE

We are so confident that our prices are lower than ANYBODY else, we offer you the following guarantee: If within 14 days after booking with Budget, you find an identical holiday in another Irish tour operator's first edition brochure available at a cheaper price; tell us, and if it is genuinely identical, we'll reduce our price to match it or refund you the money paid.

Fig. 16.2 Extract from Budget Travel website

OBJECTIVES OTHER THAN PROFIT MAXIMISATION

It has been assumed in all cases considered so far, that the firm has the basic aim of maximising its profits. Although this seems perfectly reasonable, a number of alternative explanations of firms' behaviour will now be considered. While profit maximisation is the basic aim of the vast majority of firms in the market place, a number of firms may put other objectives ahead of maximum profits in deciding on its price/output combination.

1. A firm may fear that very large supernormal profits might cause the government to investigate its activities. This could lead to the imposition of restrictions on price or the encouragement of more competition. Consequently, the firm may opt for a level of output other than the one which maximises profit.

2. A firm may fear that the existence of large supernormal profits might attract new entrants to the industry, with a consequent price war and loss in sales. The firm might, therefore, engage in *limit pricing*, i.e. setting the price so low that potential new firms are discouraged from entering the industry. The firm is willing to accept less than maximum profits now, because by doing so, it will make greater gains in the long run.

3. In the case of a small family business, the owner may be satisfied with an adequate level of profit which will enable him/her to provide a reasonable standard of living for his/her family. He/she may not strive for profit maximisation, since this usually implies a greater workload, increased stress, less leisure time, etc.

4. In companies where managers are not shareholders (e.g. semi-state bodies) profit maximisation might not be pursued, since the salary of the manager is fixed, regardless of the profit earned.

5. Another theory concerning the behaviour of the firm is the sales maximisation theory, first explained by Professor William Baumol. He argued that some firms will prefer sales maximisation rather than profit maximisation, once a certain minimum target level of profits has been reached. The target level of profits will be the minimum level required to keep shareholders satisfied; once this has been reached, the firm can concentrate on other objectives, e.g. maximising sales, control of a certain percentage of the market, etc. This is shown in *Figure 16.3* below.

The curve, PP, represents the level of profits the firm could earn at various levels of output. The horizontal red line, PT, represents the target level of profits the firm has set itself. If the firm pursues the normal objective of profit maximisation, it will produce Q_2 units of output.

If the firm goes for sales maximisation once the target level of profits has been reached, as suggested by Baumol, then it will produce Q_3 units of output. A third possibility is that the firm will be satisfied once the target level of profits has been reached, and will not be concerned with sales maximisation. In this case the firm would be willing to produce any level of output between Q_1 and Q_3. Q_1 is the minimum output required to achieve the target level of profits.

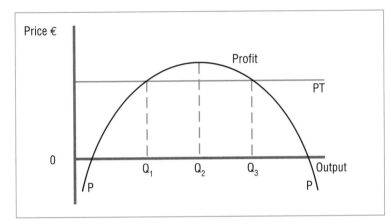

Fig. 16.3 Baumol model of sales maximisation (once a target level of profit is reached)

The example of a mobile phone cartel operating in Ireland is taken from the *Sunday Business Post*, 4 November 2001.

Mobile phone cartel in Ireland, says IBEC

By Adrian Weckler

Are you overpaying for a basic service because of the actions of a mobile phone cartel? IBEC thinks so. Its telecomms unit last week released a survey showing that two-thirds of companies thought service was poor and too dear.

It is backed up by the latest OECD report which showed Ireland as '17th cheapest' in mobile phone costs. What none of the statistics reveal, though, is the tightly-controlled nature of the mobile phone business in Ireland.

Understanding this gives a better insight as to why costs are kept so high. The key battleground in controlling the mobile market is contribution. Eircell and Digifone each owns about 100 stores, the lion's share of the market.

The two have gone on an acquisition spree over the last five years, buying out Let's Talk Phones, Talk to Me, P2P and Let's Go (all now Eircell shops) and O'Hagan Communications, Access, Eire Communications, Fones Direct and Cellular World (all Digifone).

The biggest independent competitor, Carphone Warehouse, has only 29 outlets (with a further 13 in Northern Ireland). Even so, can't the independent mobile shops compete by undercutting the big two on price?

Not really. Both Eircell and Digifone demand that independents buy models pre-chosen by them from distributors they choose (in Eircell's case from one half-owned by it).

So if mobile sellers see a nice model not being sold in Ireland and want to introduce it to the Irish market, they can forget about it. The big two won't connect the model to their network.

Then there's location. Ever wonder why there has only been two mobile phone shops in Grafton Street? (A third, Carphone Warehouse has just opened.) Or why there's rarely more than one in a busy shopping centre? This is because landlords charge more for mobile phone tenants. And shopping centres. It charges a premium over and above other retail units in the centre

on the understanding that no other mobile seller will be allowed. This is called 'key money' (not a phenomenon exclusive to the mobile phone business).

It was a major bar to Meteor establishing a presence in Grafton Street or Stephen's Green shopping centre (instead it had to settle for St Stephen's Green). And what of Meteor's promise to break the deadlock?

Its stated customer target (deliberately conservative) since its February launch is 100,000 subscribers by next January. According to CEO Dave Sims, the company was due to pass the 70,000 mark last Thursday. It sells phones in 400 locations around the country, but only owns 10 shops.

It seems to be trying, but suffers because of its incomplete network (though its metropolitan networks are now up and running). It has also had mixed success with its flat pricing strategy – a fact reflected by Sims' admission last week that the company might change this after Christmas. Until then, it's carry on cartel.

17
The Markets for Factors of Production

In *Chapter 2* we saw that the supply of goods and services to consumers depended on the supply of four factors of production to firms – land, labour, capital and enterprise. A certain minimum quantity of each of these factors is required for the provision of any good or service. The contribution of each factor to the productive process, together with the corresponding income or reward earned by the factor, is summarised in *Table 17.1*.

Factor	Explanation	Income (reward)
Land	Anything supplied by nature which is used to produce goods and services	Rent
Labour	Human effort which is used to produce goods and services	Wages
Capital	Anything man-made which is used to produce goods and services	Interest
Enterprise	The factor that combines land, labour and capital, and bears the risks involved in production	Profit

Table 17.1 The factors of production

This chapter examines the ways in which the rewards to the factors of production are determined. The next four chapters will deal with specific aspects of the demand and supply of each factor of production.

The markets for factors of production function in exactly the same way as the markets for goods and services. The price of a factor is determined by the interaction of demand and supply. The demand for factors of production comes from entrepreneurs who wish to use the factors to produce goods and services.

The supply of factors comes from the owners of factors who wish to make them available to others in return for a payment or income.

> The income of any one person depends on:
> (a) The amount of factors of production which he/she is able to provide, and
> (b) The price of the factors.

The ownership of factors of production is the basic determinant of the distribution of income (and wealth) in society. If a person is able to supply a resource which is required by others, he/she can expect to receive a reward in the form of factor income.

THE DEMAND FOR FACTORS OF PRODUCTION

1. Derived demand

The demand for a factor of production is said to be a derived demand. This means that the factor is not wanted for its own sake, but only because it is useful in the production of goods and services that people want. If there is an increase in the demand for a finished good, there will be a rise in the demand for the factors which are needed to make it. This is shown in *Figure 17.1*.

2. Profitability to firm

The demand for a factor of production depends on its profitability to the firm. We have already stated that the basic aim of the firm is to maximise profits. It follows that the firm will only demand additional units of a factor of production if it is profitable to do so. The willingness of a firm to employ a unit of a factor of production depends, therefore, on the extra output that would be produced if that unit were employed, and on the revenue that can be earned from the sale of that output.

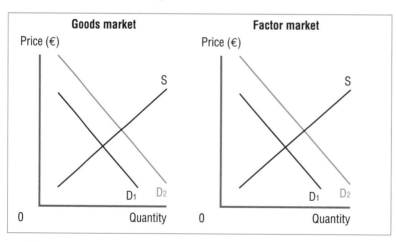

Fig. 17.1 An increase in demand for a good will lead to an increase in demand for factors of production required to make that good

MARGINAL PHYSICAL PRODUCTIVITY

The marginal physical product (MPP) of a factor of production is the extra output produced as a result of the employment of an extra unit of that factor. If a firm has five machines, and has estimated that the employment of a sixth machine would increase output by 1000 units, then the MPP of the sixth unit of capital in this firm is 1000 units. *Table 17.2* shows the total output that can be produced by employing various quantities of labour in a particular factory. If only one worker is employed, total output will be 40 units per week. The addition of a second worker brings total output to 100 units per week, i.e. the MPP of the second worker is 60 units per week.

No. of workers	Total output	Marginal physical product (MPP)
1	40	–
2	100	60
3	180	80
4	280	100
5	350	70
6	400	50
7	430	30
8	440	10

Table 17.2 The marginal physical product (MPP) of labour

Similarly, the employment of a third worker will bring total output up to 180 units per week. Therefore, the MPP of the third worker is 80 units, and so on. It can be seen that MPP may rise at low levels of output. There are increasing returns to labour. This is because the employment of extra workers allows specialisation and the division of labour to take place. However, the MPP will eventually decline because of the Law of Diminishing Returns. *Figure 17.2* shows the MPP of labour based on the data in *Table 17.2*.

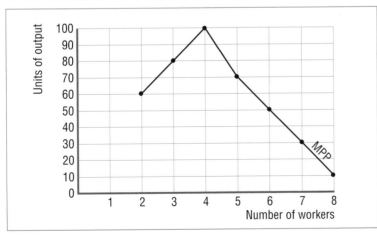

Fig. 17.2 The marginal physical product of labour (based on data in *Table 17.2*)

MARGINAL REVENUE PRODUCTIVITY

Closely allied to the concept of marginal physical productivity is marginal revenue productivity. The marginal revenue product (MRP) of a factor of production is the extra revenue earned by the firm as a result of the employment of an extra unit of that factor.

Marginal revenue product in perfectly competitive market

Let us assume that our firm is operating in a perfectly competitive market and that the price of its product is fixed at €10 per unit. The marginal revenue product of labour in this firm is given in Column 6 of *Table 17.3*.

1 No. of workers	2 Total output (units per week)	3 Marginal physical product (MPP)	4 Price (€)	5 Total revenue (€)	6 Marginal revenue product (€)
1	40	–	10	400	–
2	100	60	10	1,000	600
3	180	80	10	1,800	800
4	280	100	10	2,800	1,000
5	350	70	10	3,500	700
6	400	50	10	4,000	500
7	430	30	10	4,300	300
8	440	10	10	4,400	100

Table 17.3 MPP and MRP of labour in a firm under perfect competition (MRP = MPP x price)

Under perfect competition, marginal revenue product is equal to marginal physical product multiplied by price. That is, MRP = MPP x price. This is because the firm in perfect competition is a price taker. It does not have to

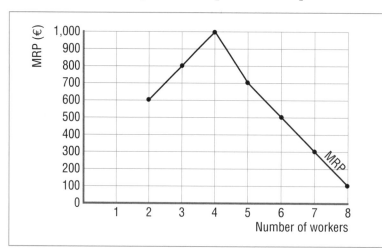

Fig. 17.3 The marginal revenue product of labour (based on data in *Table 17.3*)

lower price in order to sell additional units of the good. Therefore, when we draw the graph for the marginal revenue product of labour, we get a graph which is identical in shape to the graph for the marginal physical product of labour. This is shown in *Figure 17.3*.

Marginal revenue product in monopoly or imperfect competition

As we have seen in *Chapters 13* and *15*, firms operating in conditions of monopoly or imperfect competition are faced with downward sloping demand curves. If they want to sell extra units of output, they must lower price. Under such market conditions, marginal revenue product will not equal marginal physical product multiplied by price. To understand this, we will assume that our firm is not able to sell output at a fixed price per unit. Columns 1, 2 and 3 are the same as before, but price must now be reduced if additional units of the good are to be sold. Let us suppose that the price reductions are as shown in Column 4 of *Table 17.4*. Total revenue (TR) and marginal revenue product (MRP) are then as shown in Columns 5 and 6.

1 No. of workers	2 Total output (units per week)	3 Marginal physical product (MPP)	4 Price (€)	5 Total revenue (€)	6 Marginal revenue product (€)
1	40	–	10.00	400	–
2	100	60	9.50	950	550
3	180	80	9.00	1,620	670
4	280	100	8.50	2,380	760
5	350	70	8.00	2,800	420
6	400	50	7.50	3,000	200
7	430	30	7.00	3,010	10
8	440	10	6.50	2,860	–150

Table 17.4 MPP and MRP of labour in a firm in imperfect competition or monopoly (MRP ≠ MPP x price)

Figure 17.4 (overleaf) shows the MRP curve drawn from the data in *Table 17.4*. Three observations can be made. First, MRP is not equal to MPP x price. In fact, MRP is less than MPP x price. Second, it is possible to have a negative value for MRP. If the firm employs seven workers, total revenue is €3,010 (430 units at €7). If the firm takes on an extra worker, total revenue falls to €2,860. Therefore, MRP = – €150. We can see that the employment of the extra man added 10 units to total output, each of which can be sold for €6.50. So €65 is added to total revenue. However, 430 units per week have now to be sold at €6.50 instead of €7.00. So €215 is taken from total revenue. The net effect of the employment of the eighth worker is a fall in revenue of €150 (i.e. + €65 – €215).

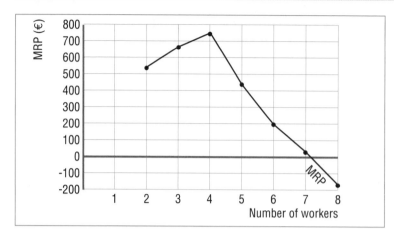

Fig. 17.4 The marginal revenue product of labour (based on data in *Table 17.4*)

Third, the MRP curve of a firm in imperfect competition or monopoly will slope downwards at a faster rate than would the MRP curve of a similar firm in perfect competition. We can explain this as follows.

> For the firm in imperfect competition or monopoly, there are two reasons why the MRP curve slopes downwards:
>
> (a) MPP slopes downwards because of the operation of the Law of Diminishing Returns. MRP depends on MPP.
>
> (b) Because the firm faces a downward sloping demand curve for its product, it must lower price to sell extra units of output.

However, for the firm in perfect competition, only point (a) above applies.

The above analysis has been carried out in relation to the MPP and MRP of labour. It must be stressed that it is equally applicable to the other factors of production.

> The MRP is a very important concept in economics. This is because the firm's MRP curve represents the firm's demand curve for that factor.

If we put the wage rate on the vertical axis in *Figure 17.4*, the MRP curve tells us what quantity of labour the firm will be willing to employ at each wage rate. The firm will not be willing to employ a worker if the cost of that worker (i.e. the wage rate) is higher than the extra revenue which he brings into the firm. Our firm would not be willing to employ the sixth worker if the wage rate was more than €200 per week. The MRP curve usually slopes downwards. Thus we can say that the higher the wage rate, the fewer workers the firm is willing to employ.

Let us compare *Figures 17.3* and *17.4*. *Figure 17.3* relates to a firm in perfect competition, while *Figure 17.4* depicts a firm in monopoly or imperfect competition. We have already noted that the MRP curve for the firm in monopoly or imperfect competition slopes downwards at a faster rate than the MRP curve for a firm in perfect competition.

The downward sloping part of the MRP curve is the demand curve for the factor of production. Therefore, we can now say that if other costs are constant, the demand for labour will be higher in a perfectly competitive firm than in a monopoly or an imperfectly competitive firm.

We have already said that a firm will not employ a worker if his wage exceeds his MRP. One possible exception to this is known as *labour hoarding*. This is where the firm is unwilling to let workers go even if the wage rate exceeds the MRP. A firm may see a fall in the volume of its sales as temporary. It may prefer to keep workers on the payroll, rather than have to make redundancy payments and then incur further hiring and training costs at a later stage.

MRP AND PRICE OF FACTOR OF PRODUCTION

Sometimes marginal revenue productivity is seen as a suitable basis for setting the price of a factor of production. However, there are several problems associated with this practice. First, it is not always possible to separate the MPP of labour from the MPP of capital. An increase in output may have been achieved by the use of more labour and more capital. It is sometimes very difficult to state how much of the increased output is due to labour and how much to capital. If the MPP of a factor is difficult to estimate, measuring MRP will also be a problem.

Second, there are many jobs where it is difficult, if not impossible, to measure MPP. A manufacturing firm can easily calculate the MPP of a worker, because physical goods are being produced. It is fairly easy to base wage rates on the MRP of the worker in such cases. However, in the case of service industries, there are no tangible end products that can be measured. One cannot pay teachers on the basis of the number of students they teach, nurses on the number of patients they look after, or gardaí on the number of criminals they apprehend. In these instances, MRP is not an appropriate method of setting wage rates. The wage rates set for such workers depend on other factors, such as tradition, relativity with other jobs, shortages of trained personnel, trade union strength and society's opinion of the value of the contribution made by such workers. We shall return to these factors in *Chapter 19*.

ECONOMIC RENT AND TRANSFER EARNINGS

The transfer earnings of a factor of production is defined as the minimum payment necessary to keep that factor in its present use and discourage its movement to another employment. Economic rent is thus defined as any surplus earned by a factor of production over and above its transfer earnings.

Payment to a factor − transfer earnings = economic rent

For example, let us take a professional footballer who is currently earning €1,000,000 a year as a player with his club. If his next most highly paid employment would have been as a salesman on €100,000 a year, he is said to be currently earning an economic rent of €900,000 a year. His transfer earnings are €100,000.

Similarly, we can apply these concepts to the other factors of production. Suppose I own a piece of land, which I am willing to lease to a local farmer for €10,000 a year. If demand for land in the area rises, such that this farmer pays me €15,000 a year, I am said to be earning an economic rent of €5,000.

The concept of economic rent is a very important one. In general, an economic rent is earned where an increase in the supply of a factor of production is difficult or impossible. A worker with a skill which is in short supply will be able to earn economic rent. Similarly, a monopoly supplier is in a position to earn economic rent. He can fix price at a high level, safe in the knowledge that no one can undercut him. The owners of land in areas where there is a housing shortage can earn economic rents. On the other hand, no economic rent is earned in a perfectly competitive market. This is because firms operate at minimum average cost so no payments are made to factors other than those necessary to keep them in their present use. We must now distinguish between specific factors and non-specific factors of production.

Specific factor of production

A specific factor of production is one which can be used for only one purpose. For example, a worker may have a skill which is only needed in one job. Therefore, he cannot transfer to another job. Similarly, a machine may have been developed for a particular purpose such that it is not suitable for anything else, e.g. machines for car assembly. Land can be specific if it has no alternative use, e.g. a bog is only suitable for turf production.

Non-specific factor of production

A non-specific factor is one which can be transferred from one use to another. Most factors of production are non-specific. Most workers can transfer from one type of job to another, most land and capital can be put to different uses.

We can make the following two points concerning economic rent:

(a) The more inelastic the supply of a factor of production, the more likely it is to earn economic rent.

(b) The more specific the factor of production, the more economic rent it will earn.

In the case of (a), if the supply of a factor is such that it cannot be increased in response to an increase in demand, then that factor is likely to earn high economic rent. For example, when computers became widely available in industry, there was a big increase in the demand for programmers, systems analysts, etc. while the supply of people with such skills was limited. Consequently, competition between firms forced wages of such workers to a high level, so that they earned economic rents. Such economic rents are sometimes termed quasi-rents because they are of a temporary nature. When the supply of such factors is eventually increased in response to the increased demand, the payments to the factors fall and quasi-rents are eliminated.

In the case of (b), if a factor is specific, then it has no alternative use. Therefore, it has no transfer earnings. The supply is totally inelastic in relation to price. The entire payment to such a factor is economic rent.

THE CONTROL OF ECONOMIC RENT

Because economic rent can be seen as a surplus payment to a factor of production which is not necessary to keep it in its present use, it is often suggested that such economic rent should be taxed or controlled in some way. Three methods of controlling economic rent can be suggested.

1. Maximum price imposed

A maximum price can be imposed on the factor. This is usually done by government but it may sometimes be attempted by private organisations. However, market forces usually make any attempts to curb the rewards to high-earning individuals extremely difficult. For example, attempts were made to put upper limits on the transfer fees of football players in England, and efforts were made to get rid of appearance money for professional golfers on the European tour. However, these efforts were unsuccessful. Highly skilled individuals with rare talents are generally able to continue to earn high economic rents as long as their services are in demand.

2. Economic rent taxed

Economic rent can be taxed. The main advantage of taxing economic rent is that such a tax will not affect the use to which factors are put. In other words, it will not affect resource allocation. It is easier to tax land in this manner than the other factors. This is because the other factors are mobile while land is not. Labour, capital and enterprise can move from high-tax countries to low-tax countries. Formula One racing drivers and top-earning tennis players move from their own countries to tax havens such as Monaco and Jersey to avoid the taxation of their economic rents. The same can be said of certain entrepreneurs and owners of capital.

Fig. 17.5 Monaco – a tax haven

3. Economic rent reduced or eliminated by government

The government can take measures to increase the supply of the factor so that economic rents can be reduced or eliminated. For example, if economic rents are earned in a particular profession by a policy of restricted entry to that profession, or as a result of excess demand for the services of that profession, the government may intervene in an effort to increase supply. This might involve the provision of more college places, the granting of licences to competitors, etc. Similarly, by increasing the supply of land zoned for building purposes, the government can reduce economic rents accruing to landowners in areas of high demand for housing.

Highly skilled and talented soccer players can earn high economic rents as shown in the following article from *Business & Finance* on 15 November 2001.

Players' high pitch

By Eoghan Corry

Bonuses of £2m [€2.5m] and more are already being mentioned for the Irish soccer stars should we survive the second leg of our nerve-wrecking World Cup play-off in Tehran.

But whether such a bonus, representing a quarter of the FAI's turnover and equivalent to the income generated by five home qualifiers, manifests itself or not, the past week has been a lesson in how important soccer is to the economics of Irish sport in general.

According to economist Chris Gratton and sociologist Alan Tomlinson, in Dublin for a sports development conference recently, television has turned Britain from a multi-sport society, with soccer now overwhelming cricket, rugby union and everything else in terms of its economic power.

The same phenomenon may be happening in Ireland. With the country's anticipated qualification for the World Cup, no other sporting occasion can generate the equivalent commercial spin-offs ranging from cheap posters to supermarket FMCGs (Fast Moving Consumer Goods). In other words, an industry expected to generate in excess of £5m [€6.3m]. And players will participate to a greater or lesser degree in this commercial carnival.

There are some who believe that failing to qualify for Euro 1996 and 2000 and France '98 may have helped steady disproportionate financial demands from Ireland's premiership soccer stars.

In 1990 an inexperienced FAI negotiated too good a deal with their players, and Ireland ended up paying bonuses which were higher than their English or German counterparts. That was at least one of the reasons why Irish soccer emerged from the most profitable years in its history with so few financial assets to show for it.

How the Irish players will be rewarded for anticipated qualification for Japan and Korea is almost certain to fall below, rather than above, the European norm despite the fact that England's player bonuses have jumped substantially.

The potential earnings from spin-off sponsorship may be another story. The dominant position soccer players commanded in the public appearance and product endorsement market from 1988 until 1994 caused a knock-on effect on other sports. During Jack Charlton's era, sports personalities were favoured for public appearances, representing the new competitive and assertive Ireland, performing on the world stage and setting a lead for the business community.

When the soccer and rugby teams' achievements plummeted, businessmen were less likely to sit up and pay attention, so it was back to the round of US management gurus to brighten up after-dinner speeches.

"When we qualify for the World Cup, the scramble starts once more for soccer stars," a sports agent claims, "when we don't qualify companies tend not to focus on the sports market at all."

But the question of the likely bonus levels for Irish soccer players is minor compared with the wages crisis, which has befallen English Premiership soccer.

Clubs, which used to treat their stars simply as exploitable assets on the balance sheet, have found that changed transfer rules, dwindling loyalty and increased rewards elsewhere have forced them to pay the market price for the footballing services they rent from their staff.

Throughout the 1990s, wages inceased at a compound annual rate of 25.8%, five per cent higher than turnover.

Complaints about greed sound hollow to players who have seen everybody else get rich on their backs. Club revenues rose above £1 bn [€1.27bn] in 1999–2000. With new television money coming on stream, income is set to exceed £1.7 bn [€2.16bn] this season.

That is what triggered the threat of a strike. Since the issue arose in 1909, England's soccer players, individualists endowed with rare skills, have been unsure how to use their industrial relations muscle. That is how, when baseball

star Babe Ruth met the greatest goal scorer of all time, Dixie Dean of Everton in 1930, their respective wages were £300 [€381] a week and £8 [€10] a week.

Despite exploitation of players the PFA never organised a strike through-out that period of maximum exploitation of footballers; only now when many players are earning £1m [€1.27m] a year and more, have they chosen to do so.

This may be because they have a clearly identifiable target for the first time. Rupert Murdoch's "battering ram" has made him the principal player in English TV, his potential fortune increasing with every satellite dish sold on the back of live interactive soccer.

Today's football investors too are a different breed to the sheepskin-coated benefactors of old, chasing quick results to cash in on their shares.

Support for the players is non-existent among the fans and public opinion will count for somethng if the players are to win this battle. In America where sportsmen have always been better paid, the howls of discontent about player

salaries began earlier and continued until a series of strikes created an atmosphere in which the clubs introduced salary caps.

One important pressure group has already opted for an early bath. Big wage demands have all but killed off the interest from the financial community that offered football such a bright future only 10 years ago. Now trading in football shares is a dismal business, while analysts call out for financial discipline and some sort of cap on wages. Before a ball was kicked in the current season, parallels were being drawn with the mobile phone auctions for third-generation licences.

Football is not alone in this respect. Investment banks have faced similar pay explosions. High profit margins in industries based on human physical or intellectual capital are almost impossible to achieve in the long term. And if you are an organisation like the FAI, and don't have a profit to begin with, a shopping list from increasingly deman-ding footballers, is exactly what you don't want right now.

CHAPTER 18

Land and Rent

In *Chapter 2* we defined land as 'anything supplied by nature which is used in the production of goods and services'. Because of the scope of this definition, the term 'natural resources' might be a more accurate one to describe these gifts of nature, which are essential for production to take place.

COMPONENTS OF LAND

Land as a factor of production includes the following:

1. *Agricultural land.* The most widespread use of land is for the production of foodstuffs – the growing of cereal crops, fruit and vegetables and the provision of pasture for animals.

2. The *rivers, lakes and seas* of the world must also be counted as natural resources. As the population of the world increases, the importance of fishing and fish-farming will grow, as will the need to develop the other resources of the seas. Hydroelectric power is a very important source of energy while water itself is a vital raw material in the production of many goods.

3. The *mineral wealth* and *natural resources* of the earth are part of the factor of production, land. Such resources are useful as raw materials in their own right while some are also valuable as sources of energy (e.g. oil, coal, natural gas and turf).

4. The *forests* of the world supply the timber required for the construction industry, furniture making, and the paper, printing and packaging industries.

159

5. The *atmosphere, weather and climate* are natural resources which are included in our definition of 'land'. Adequate rainfall and sunshine are essential for the growth of crops. A suitable climate is required for the operation of a successful tourist industry in many countries, for example, adequate sunshine in Greece, Portugal and Spain, and snow in Switzerland and Austria.

6. No production could take place without the availability of a certain minimum quantity of *land itself.* Sites are required for factories, offices and shops, etc.

The components of land as a factor of production can also be classified as renewable or non-renewable resources. Renewable resources are those resources the supply of which can be replenished or added to, e.g. water, forests, fish, etc. Non-renewable resources are those resources which cannot be replenished, so that an increase in their present consumption means less being available in future. Examples of such resources are coal, oil, mineral wealth, etc. We have already pointed out that the over-exploitation of renewable resources (or their improper use) can cause them to become non-renewable. We will now concentrate on the narrow definition of land so that we can examine how its price is determined.

ECONOMIC CHARACTERISTICS OF LAND

Land has two economic characteristics:

1. Fixed in supply

The supply of land cannot be increased in response to an increase in demand. Land is thus said to be *fixed in supply*. Because it is fixed in supply, a rise in demand will cause a large increase in price. This can be seen in *Figure 18.1*. An increase in the demand for land from D_1 to D_2 causes price to increase by a large amount (from P_1 to P_2). This is because the supply curve is a vertical straight line. A similar increase in the demand for any of the other factors of production would cause the price to rise by a smaller amount (from P_3 to P_4). This is because the supply curves for such factors are upward sloping. Since the supply of land is fixed, the price of land is influenced solely by demand.

2. No cost of production

Land has *no cost of production*. Unlike the other factors of production, it cost nothing to put it there. However, there is a cost of use. Land requires the addition of labour and capital for output to be produced and, therefore, costs are involved in using land. Similarly, it has a cost of production as far as the individual user is

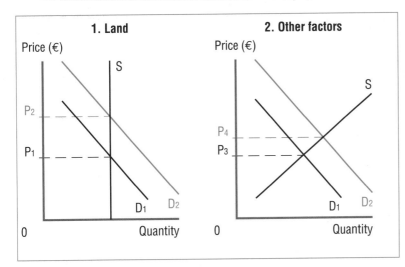

Fig. 18.1 (1) An increase in the demand for land causes a large increase in the price of land, and (2) an increase in the demand for the other factors causes a smaller rise in price

concerned. Those who wish to use land for any purpose must purchase or rent it. Since land has no cost of production, the entire payment for the use of land can be considered as an economic rent, from the point of view of society as a whole. However, the individual user of land regards the entire payment as necessary since if he/she did not pay it, he/she could not use the land.

DEMAND FOR LAND

Like all factors of production, the demand for land depends on its marginal revenue product. A farmer will only be willing to pay €1,000 a year to rent a piece of land if the additional revenue he earns by doing so exceeds €1,000. In most cases, the MPP will be subject to the Law of Diminishing Returns. Therefore, the MRP will depend mainly on the price of the goods produced on the land. It is important to realise that the price of the finished good determines the price paid for land and not vice versa. In the case of agricultural land, it is the price of food items that determines the price that can be paid for land. In the case of land for housing, it is the selling price of houses that determines the price the builder is prepared to pay for building land.

LAND AND ITS MOST PROFITABLE USE

Most land is non-specific. It can be transferred easily from one use to another. Because of this, land will be devoted to its most profitable use. If there is no interference by government in the buying and selling of land, the forces of competition will ensure that the land is bought by the highest bidder, who will use it to earn the maximum profit. This is the reason why city centre locations have high rents. Shops, offices and banks can afford to pay the high prices needed to acquire such scarce sites. Private houses are generally built in the suburbs where land prices are not quite so high.

MARKET INTERVENTION BY GOVERNMENT

It is generally agreed that, because land is a scarce resource, its use should be carefully controlled. The government can intervene in the market for land and restrict its use for particular purposes. This is one of the functions of local government. Each local authority is responsible for land use within its own area. It has the power to 'zone' land for particular purposes. Land can be zoned as agricultural, residential, industrial and commercial, or recreational (amenity). These powers have been given to local authorities for the following reasons:

1. To ensure that development takes place in an orderly manner.
2. To ensure the preservation of open space (or 'green belts'), especially near large urban centres.
3. To ensure an adequate supply of suitable sites for industrial and commercial use.
4. To ensure that areas of special beauty or historical interest are not lost to the citizens of the country.

The rezoning of land from one use to another can alter the value of the land. This is because land will be more profitable in one use than in another. A piece of land worth €5,000 an acre as agricultural land might be worth ten times as much if rezoned as building land.

TRENDS IN IRISH HOUSING MARKET

The years 1996–2001 saw an unprecedented increase in the price of housing in Ireland, as a severe mismatch between the demand for new housing and the available supply emerged. Over these years the average price of a house in Ireland has more than doubled, despite the fact that the number of new houses completed reached record levels. *Table 18.1* shows the number of house completions in Ireland for 1996–2001, while *Table 18.2* shows the trend in prices of new and second-hand houses over the same period.

Year	Total
1996	33,725
1997	38,842
1998	42,349
1999	46,512
2000	49,812
2001	47,750
Source: Department of the Environment and Local Government	

Table 18.1 New house completions in Ireland, 1996–2001

Year	New (€)	Second-hand (€)
1996	87,202	85,629
1997	102,222	102,712
1998	125,302	134,529
1999	148,521	163,316
2000	169,191	190,550
2001	177,763	203,158

Source: Department of the Environment and Local Government

Table 18.2 Average house prices in Ireland, 1996–2001

Factors leading to rising house prices

1. Ireland has the largest proportion of its population under 25 in the EU (see *Chapter 32*). The average age of a first-time house buyer is now 27, so the demand for new housing is likely to remain strong in the coming years. It is estimated that at least 55,000 new housing units per annum are needed to cater for the demand.

2. The change in the urban–rural profile has led to an increase in house prices. Over one-third of the country's population now resides in the Dublin area. There has also been significant growth in other major urban centres. The supply of land for building is limited, so there is strong upward pressure on prices.

3. The strong growth in the Irish economy in recent years has also fuelled demand for housing. Employment and disposable incomes have increased, while unemployment has fallen dramatically.

4. Net inward migration has been a major feature in the Irish economy in recent years. Labour shortages have led to sizeable movements of people into the country, most of whom are in the 25–44 age bracket.

5. Falling average household size and the impact of divorce and separation have also contributed to the demand for housing.

6. Strong demand in the private rented sector has seen an increase in the number of people purchasing houses as an investment.

7. Low interest rates have reduced the real cost of borrowing and have stimulated the demand for housing.

8. In the National Development Plan 2000–2006, the shortage of affordable housing is identified as a major capacity constraint on the economy. The shortage of housing is seen as being due to a shortage of serviced building land which can be tackled by investment in water and sewage

services. Following the publication of the third Bacon Report on the Irish housing market in June 2000 the Government introduced a range of measures to achieve its housing policy which it identified as follows:

- To maximise output to meet strong demand
- To curb short-term speculative demand
- To strengthen the position of first-time buyers in the market
- To increase the supply of social and affordable housing
- To provide the required infrastructure for housing.

Fig. 18.2 The shortage of affordable housing is a constraint on the economy

Labour and Wages

In *Chapter 2* we defined labour as the human effort which goes into the production of goods and services. The reward for the factor of production, labour, is wages.

DEMAND FOR LABOUR

In *Chapter 17* we saw that a firm's demand for any factor of production is determined by the MRP of that factor. In the case of labour, the demand curve is given by the MRP curve of labour. This curve is downward sloping from left to right. Thus, we can say that the higher the wage rate, the lower the demand for labour (other things being equal). This is depicted in *Figure 19.1*.

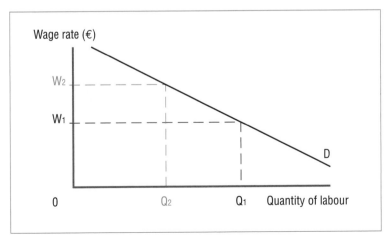

Fig. 19.1 The demand curve for labour

An increase in wage rates lessens the profitability to an employer of taking on additional workers. So if the wage rate increases from W_1 to W_2, the quantity of labour demanded falls from Q_1 to Q_2. We can summarise this as follows:

As wages rise, the demand for labour falls.
As wages fall, the demand for labour rises.

SUPPLY OF LABOUR

The supply of labour in a country depends on the following three factors; the population of the country, the number of hours worked by each member of the work force, length of holidays, etc. and the participation rate.

1. Population of country

The greater the population of a country, the greater the number of people who will be in the labour force.

The labour force in an economy is defined as the total number of people at work or looking for work, that is: Labour force = total at work + total unemployed

The total at work is sometimes called the work force. *Table 19.1* gives figures for the Irish labour force for the years 1993–2000. The strong performance of the Irish economy in these years is reflected in the fact that the numbers at work grew by over 40 per cent during this time while unemployment fell to historically low levels. The labour force grew by 24 per cent over the same period – due to a natural increase in the working age population, higher participation rates and increased inward migration.

Year	At work	Unemployed	Labour force
1993	1,183.1	220.1	1,403.2
1994	1,220.6	211.0	1,431.6
1995	1,281.7	177.4	1,459.2
1996	1,328.5	179.0	1,507.5
1997	1,379.9	159.0	1,539.0
1998	1,494.5	126.6	1,621.1
1999	1,591.1	96.9	1,688.1
2000	1,670.7	74.9	1,745.6

All figures in thousands
International Labour Organisation (ILO) labour force classification used
Source: Central Statistics Office (CSO)

Table 19.1 Total number of persons at work, unemployed and in labour force, 1993–2000

2. Number of hours worked, length of holidays, etc.

The greater the length of the working week, the greater will be the supply of labour in a country. There are major variations in the length of the working week from country to country. Recent EU figures show that Irish workers have one of the longest working weeks in the EU, one of the shortest legal holiday entitlements, and relatively few public holidays compared to other member countries. Also statutory paid maternity leave is 18 weeks in Ireland, while in most other EU states it is 26 weeks (see *Tables 19.2, 19.3* and *19.4*).

Ranking	Country	Average weekly working hours	Ranking	Country	Average weekly working hours
1	Greece	42.37	9	Sweden	38.00
2	Portugal	41.49	10	Belgium	37.92
3	Finland	40.52	11	Germany	37.37
4	**Ireland**	**40.42**	12	UK	37.10
5	Spain	40.37	13	Denmark	36.07
6	Luxembourg	39.80	14	France	35.00
7	Austria	39.51	15	Netherlands	32.90
8	Italy	38.96			
Source: EU					

Table 19.2 Average length of working week in EU countries in 2000

Self-employed people are more likely to be able to vary the length of their working week than 'employees' (i.e. those working for an employer). Many employees are required to work a standard week, with voluntary overtime as an option. In the UK, minimum holiday entitlements are covered by collective agreements.

Ranking	Country	Minimum holidays	Ranking	Country	Minimum holidays
1	Spain	30	9	Portugal	21
2	Austria	25	10	Denmark	20
	Finland	25		Italy	20
	France	25		Netherlands	20
	Luxembourg	25	13	Germany	18
	Sweden	25	**14**	**Ireland**	**15**
7	Belgium	24			
	Greece	24			
Source: EU					

Table 19.3 Minimum legal holiday entitlements in EU countries in 2000

Ranking	Country	Public holidays	Ranking	Country	Public holidays
1	Finland	14	9	Denmark	10
	Germany	14		France	10
3	Austria	13		Italy	10
4	Belgium	12		Spain	10
	Luxembourg	12	**13**	**Ireland**	**9**
	Portugal	12		Netherlands	9
7	Greece	11	15	UK	8
	Sweden	11			
Source: EU					

Table 19.4 Number of public holidays in EU countries in 2000

3. Participation rate

The participation rate is the proportion of the population who are in the labour force. The higher the participation rate, the greater the supply of labour available in a country. Participation rates vary considerably from one age cohort to another. There are also major differences between male and female participation rates. Participation rates will be depend on the following factors:

- School-leaving age

- Age of retirement

- Opportunities for married women to work outside the home

- Numbers in full-time third-level education

- Demand for labour in the economy – an increase in the demand for labour may entice those who had left the labour force to rejoin, if only on a part-time basis, e.g. older people, married women, etc.

Table 19.5 gives details of the participation rates in Ireland. While male participation rates have remained relatively static, there has been a huge increase in female rates in recent years. In the age group 35–44, 63.1 per cent of women were in the labour force in 2000 compared to only 38.7 per cent 10 years earlier. This rapid acceleration in female participation has led to the serious shortage of childcare facilities evident in recent years.

Age group	Male (%)	Female (%)
15-19	34.1	26.2
20-24	79.0	67.6
25-34	94.0	77.2
35-44	93.4	63.1
45-54	88.0	52.2
55-59	73.9	35.0
60-64	53.7	19.5
65 and over	14.7	2.9
Total	**71.0**	**47.2**

Source: Statistical Yearbook of Ireland 2001, Central Statistics Office

Table 19.5 Labour force participation rates in Ireland, 2000

USUAL SUPPLY CURVE OF LABOUR

The supply curve of labour is usually upward sloping from left to right. This is because there is a positive relationship between the wage rate and the supply of labour. This can be expressed more precisely in the following way:

As wages rise, the supply of labour rises.
As wages fall, the supply of labour falls.

There are two reasons for this occurring.
1. An increase in wages will encourage more people to join the labour force, that is, the participation rate will rise.
2. An increase in wages will usually lead to those already in the work force supplying an increased quantity of labour. That is, an increase in the hourly rate of pay will usually cause a worker to increase the number of hours he/she works.

The supply curve of labour is, therefore, usually drawn as an upward sloping curve, as shown in *Figure 19.2 (overleaf)*. An increase in the wage rate from W_1 to W_2 will cause the quantity of labour supplied to increase from Q_1 to Q_2.

BACKWARD BENDING SUPPLY CURVE OF LABOUR

There are some workers who will supply less labour as the wage rate increases. Such workers prefer additional leisure to additional income and have a backward bending supply curve of labour, as shown in *Figure 19.3 (overleaf)*.

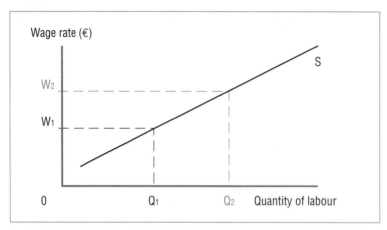

Fig. 19.2 The usual supply curve of labour

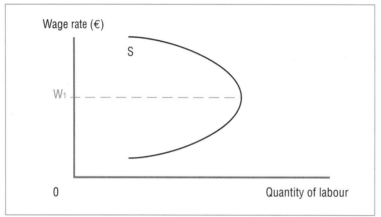

Fig. 19.3 A backward bending supply curve of labour

At wage rates up to W_1, these workers increase their supply of labour as the wage rate rises. However, if the wage rate goes above W_1, these workers actually reduce their supply of labour and choose more leisure time. At high wage rates, they prefer more leisure to more income. This feature has been observed for high-income earners, where high marginal tax rates may provide a further disincentive to working longer hours.

Another example might be a music group. When the group is unknown, it has to work as many nights as possible at small venues, often for little or no pay, in order to establish a reputation. Once it is successful, there will not be the same need for live appearances, so it may only do a few shows in the year.

HOW WAGES ARE DETERMINED

Determination of wages in free markets

By a free market, we mean a market where there are no restrictions on either the demand or supply of labour. This would be the situation if:

(a) Trade unions did not restrict the supply of labour
(b) Employers did not restrict the demand for labour
(c) The government did not impose a minimum (or maximum) wage.

In this situation, the demand and supply curves of labour would be as shown in *Figure 19.4*. The equilibrium wage rate is W_1, and the equilibrium quantity of labour is Q_1. If the wage rate were higher than W_1, there would be excess supply of labour. This would force wages down. If the wage rate were below W_1, there would be excess demand for labour. This would force wages up. Only at W_1 is the quantity of labour demanded equal to the quantity supplied.

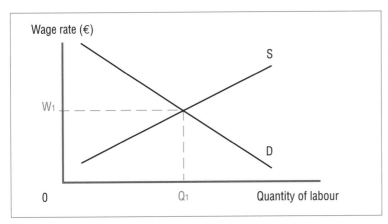

Fig. 19.4 How the wage rate is determined in a free market

Determination of wages in markets where trade unions exist

1. SETTING A MINIMUM WAGE

The basic function of a trade union is to safeguard wages and working conditions for its members. This may involve the setting of a minimum wage rate for a particular type of job, below which no labour will be supplied. Its ability to do this depends on it having a monopoly of the supply of labour for that job.

In *Figure 19.5* (*overleaf*) W_1 represents the minimum wage fixed by the trade union. Q_1 is the quantity of labour that employers are willing to employ at this wage rate. However, Q_2 is the quantity of labour that workers would be willing to supply at this wage rate. Therefore, there would be unemployment, represented by Q_2-Q_1. The problem faced by the trade union is the same as that faced by the monopolist. It can decide on the price or quantity, but not both.

2. RESTRICTING SUPPLY OF WORKERS

Sometimes a trade union will limit the supply of labour to an occupation in an effort to keep wages high. In this case the trade union is deciding the quantity and is letting the market set the price. The methods chosen to restrict supply

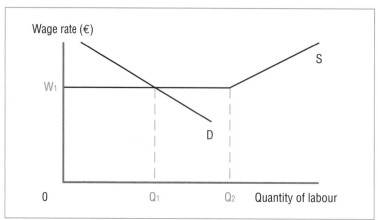

Fig. 19.5 The setting of a minimum wage by a trade union

include lengthy (and costly) training periods, more difficult exams, restricted openings for trainees, etc. The effect of such restrictions is to shift the supply curve to the left, as shown in *Figure 19.6*. If W_1 was the original wage rate, W_2 represents the new wage rate once supply has been limited. This policy of restricted entry has one advantage to the trade union which is not present if the union sets a minimum wage. There is no unemployment.

In *Figure 19.6* at W_2 the quantity of labour demanded (Q_2) is equal to the quantity of labour supplied, whereas in *Figure 19.5* at W_1, quantity of labour supplied is Q_2 but only Q_1 is demanded. When a minimum wage is set, therefore, there may be a pool of unemployed workers who would be willing to work at this wage (or even at a lower wage) but are prevented from doing so.

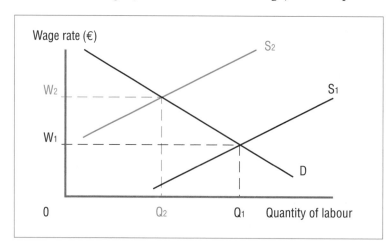

Fig. 19.6 Restricting entry to an occupation causes the supply curve of labour to shift to the left

3. Trade Unions Unwilling to Accept Wage Reductions

In most countries where trade unions exist, wages tend to be mobile in one direction only, that is, upwards. If there is an increase in the demand for labour, wages will be forced upwards. Firms will compete against each other for the available pool of workers, and wages will rise. If demand is sufficiently strong wages may even rise above the rate negotiated by employers and unions. This is referred to as *wage drift*. On the other hand, if there is a reduction in the demand for labour, trade unions will generally be unwilling to accept a cut in wages. Consequently, unemployment will rise.

4. GOVERNMENT RESTRICTIONS ON WAGES

Sometimes in an effort to control inflation, the government may impose a temporary wage freeze. This means that for a specified length of time, employers are prevented from granting wage increases to their workers. Alternatively, a small wage increase may be granted. If the demand for labour remains high, employers will compete against each other by offering overtime, special bonuses and commissions in order to retain their existing workers and attract 'the best of the rest'.

DIFFERENT WAGE RATES FOR DIFFERENT JOBS

In our analysis of labour so far, we have talked about changes in 'the wage rate'. It should be obvious that there is no such thing as a single wage rate. Different jobs pay different wages. Even workers in the same job can earn different wages if they have been in the job for different lengths of time. We will now examine the reasons why such *wage differentials* exist – why workers in some jobs get paid more than those in other jobs.

1. Differences in productivity

We have already seen that the marginal revenue product of a worker is the addition to the total revenue of the firm as a result of the employment of that worker. Thus a worker's marginal revenue product reflects the profitability to the firm of employing him/her. If a worker in one firm adds €800 a week to the revenue of the firm, while a worker in another firm adds only €600, then it is reasonable to expect that the first worker will command a higher wage. A worker's MRP can be influenced by factors over which he/she has no control. Such factors include:

• Price of the good he/she produces
• Availability of suitable capital
• His/her natural ability
• Employer's managerial ability.

A worker's MRP can be influenced by factors over which he/she has control. Such factors include:

• His/her commitment to the job

- His/her willingness to undergo on-the-job training
- His/her skill
- His/her ability to work satisfactorily with others.

A worker's MRP sets an upper limit to his/her wages. No matter how powerful a trade union is, it cannot negotiate a wage rate which is above the MRP of labour. To do so would force a firm to pay more to the worker than the worker earns for the firm. The firm will be unwilling to employ the worker in such circumstances.

2. Tradition and views of the public

Traditionally, some jobs are highly paid, while others are poorly paid. The wage rate for a particular job can be seen as society's estimate of the worth of such a job. This is particularly true in 'service' type jobs, where the MRP of labour is difficult, if not impossible, to calculate. Once the pay for a job has been at a certain level relative to other jobs, it is very difficult for a trade union to establish a new wage relativity with those other jobs.

3. Length of training and cost

Some jobs require a lengthy period of training and/or an apprenticeship. From the point of view of the employer, training makes the worker more productive and so increases his/her MRP. Therefore, it justifies the payment of higher wages. From the point of view of the worker, training involves costs, both direct (e.g. fees) and indirect (e.g. loss of earnings during the period of training). Therefore, higher wages are needed to compensate for such costs. Jobs that require lengthy and costly periods of training will usually pay higher wages.

4. Monetary benefits other than pay

Some jobs have monetary benefits other than pay. The existence of such benefits can mean that employers do not have to pay as high a wage as would otherwise be required. Examples of such monetary benefits are low interest loans for bank employees and pension rights in the public service.

5. Non-monetary benefits

As with monetary benefits, the existence of non-monetary benefits can mean the acceptance by workers of lower wages. Examples of non-monetary benefits are long holidays (teachers), opportunities to travel (airline staff, holiday tour company reps), good social infrastructure (those working in large cities), etc.

6. Working conditions

Some jobs by their nature are difficult or unpleasant. In Britain, miners' leaders have always stressed this aspect of their job when looking for wage rises. Similarly, bar staff justify higher wages on the grounds that their hours of work are unsocial. Generally workers whose jobs involve night work receive higher pay in compensation.

7. Nature of job

Whether a job is permanent or temporary may affect the wage rate paid. However, the precise relationship between the rate of pay and the nature of the employment is not the same for all industries. In some jobs, a higher hourly rate of pay applies to part-time or temporary workers, presumably as compensation for the absence of job security. In other jobs, most notably where workers are very young or not unionised, rates of pay of part-time or temporary workers are lower than those of permanent workers.

8. Different wage rates for males and females

Women are still earning as much as 40 per cent less than men in the EU, despite recent advances in equal pay and the fact that more women are scaling the top of the executive ladder. In Ireland in 2000, gross hourly earnings for male industrial workers averaged €11.64, compared with €8.56 for women.

9. Different wage rates for private and public sector workers

Traditionally public sector employment offered greater job security than the private sector. Greater job security and state pension rights were seen by some as justifying lower rates of pay. However, the increasing use of fixed-term contracts in parts of the public service means that greater job security no longer applies. Also significant differences between public sector and private sector pay could lead to the loss of skilled personnel from the public to the private sector, which could affect the quality of service delivered.

Under the terms of its *Programme for Prosperity and Fairness (PPF)*, the government set up a Benchmarking Body to compare public service jobs and pay rates with jobs and pay rates across the economy. Its report was issued in June 2002.

The growth in the Irish economy in the period 1995–2000 led to serious labour shortages in certain sectors. It also led to changes in the way employers looked at the whole question of workers' pay. Some of these changes are outlined in the following article from the *Sunday Independent*, 18 November 2001.

Show me the money

By Dick O'Brien

For the past number of years the job market in Ireland has been moving at breakneck speed. Less than a decade ago many workers were simply glad to have jobs. The period experienced a huge transformation, so much so that skilled workers were in desperately short supply. As a result, wage bills went through the roof and stories abounded of the extravagant packages that were being offered in some sectors. However, the past number of months has brought about further changes. The US economy has slowed down dramatically and with our economy so closely tied to it, the effects have begun to be felt on this side of the Atlantic.

"We've detected a much more realistic sense in the marketplace in recent times," according to Michael McDonnell, director of the Chartered Institute of Personnel and Development (CIPD). "Over the last two years, logic was jettisoned. It became an employee's market and employers were throwing money at people," he said. "In many cases, the money that was on offer bore no relation to the value of the job. Nowadays, there's a far more cautious approach. While many would see it as beginning in the aftermath of the September 11th attacks, we'd say it started a couple of months previously, when the US economy began to slow down."

Yet this slowdown in the job market hasn't meant a reversion to old practices. The fact is that Ireland's period of unprecedented economic growth has wrought considerable changes upon the remuneration system.

"There has been a dramatic shift in the culture underpinning the reward system," said McDonnell.

"Traditionally, the private sector relied on incremental salary scales. This has virtually vanished, although it is still significant in the public sector."

According to McDonnell, external relativities are not as important as they used to be in the private sector. Instead, there has been a shift to individual reward structures. Employers are now asking themselves what added value a particular individual is bringing to an organisation. Performance-related remuneration is now a widespread practice and individual contracts that are renewed on a yearly basis are now becoming the norm. McDonnell noted that this trend has developed further in recent times and that team-based reward is now coming into play.

Another noticeable development is the wider range of benefits available within individual organisations. "Employers are now recognising that they don't have a homogenous workforce," said McDonnell. "You have everyone from young, single people to older, married people with the responsibilities of children and homeownership. A successful remuneration system ought to be relevant to everybody, no matter what point they're at in their careers."

This has resulted in the introduction of what's known as the 'cafeteria system'. All employees will receive the same basic rewards such as salary and pension. In addition to this, a whole range of benefits is also on offer and these extras are tailored to the individual's needs. For example, in the case of health insurance, a young person may be interested in something that caters for accidents or sports-related injuries, while someone older may be more interested in life assurance. In tandem with this, there has also been an increased recognition of the role of training. "The concept of life-long learning has been embraced by employers and we're finding that there's more of a trade-off between pay and development opportunities," said McDonnell.

Of course, at the height of the economic boom, much of the attention was focused on share option schemes. At the time, it was a very attractive benefit, so much so that many saw share options as an opportunity to become wealthy overnight. However, the tumble in stock market prices has greatly lessened people's expectations and it remains to be seen whether stock options will still feature prominently in remuneration packages. According to McDonnell, more traditional profit sharing schemes will probably re-emerge in their place.

One of McDonnell's chief areas of concern is what he perceives as a slowdown of reform in the public sector. "Unfortunately, there is still no significant reward for merit," he said. "Reform will be very difficult now that we're heading into more uncertain times. We now run the risk of serious public expenditure problems which could put enormous pressure on our economy."

Problem of Unemployment

Traditionally in Ireland, unemployment was seen as the greatest social and economic problem facing the country. Persistently high levels of unemployment were an ever-present feature of our economy since the foundation of the state and would have been even worse without the 'safety valve' of large-scale emigration.

Year	Unemployment rate (%)
1996	11.9
1997	10.3
1998	7.8
1999	5.7
2000	4.3
2001*	3.8

*Estimated
International Labour Organisation (ILO) labour force classification used
Source: CSO

Table 19.6 Unemployment rates in Ireland, 1996–2001

The level of unemployment in Ireland is measured by the Quarterly National Household Survey (QNHS) which was introduced in September 1997 and has now replaced the Labour Force Survey (see *Table 19.6* above). The primary classification used for the QNHS is the International Labour Organisation (ILO) labour force classification. This classification is used to facilitate international comparisons. It distinguishes three main sub-groups of the population aged 15 and over.

1. 'In Employment'

(a) Persons who worked in the week before the survey for one hour or more for payment or profit (including work on the family farm or in the family business).

(b) All persons who had a job but were not at work because of illness or holidays in the week before the survey.

2. 'Unemployed'

Persons, who in the week before the survey, were without work but available for work, and had taken specific steps, in the preceding four weeks to find employment.

3. 'Economically Inactive'

All other persons.

The Live Register

The Live Register is a list of those persons under 65 years of age who are claiming Unemployment Benefit (UB) and Unemployment Assistance (UA) as well as applicants for certain social welfare contributions. It is not designed to measure unemployment. It includes part-time, seasonal and casual workers who are entitled to Unemployment Assistance or Benefit. *Table 19.7* shows the annual average of persons on the Live Register for the years 1995–2001.

Year	Number of persons on Live Register
1995	277,767
1996	279,235
1997	254,379
1998	227,096
1999	193,237
2000	155,398
2001	142,258
Source: Central Statistics Office	

Table 19.7 Annual average number of persons on the Live Register, 1995–2001

CAUSES OF UNEMPLOYMENT

1. Insufficient demand for goods and services

When a recession occurs in an economy, people spend less money on goods and services. Therefore, companies have less need for workers to supply these goods and services, and unemployment occurs. This is probably the most serious type of unemployment because it tends to affect all industries at the same time. This type of unemployment is called *cyclical unemployment* (because it occurs in cycles).

2. Frictional unemployment

This type of unemployment is unavoidable and occurs even when the economy is doing well. It arises when (a) people are unemployed between jobs – i.e. if there is a time lag between people leaving their old jobs and taking up new jobs, and (b) when the skills of the unemployed do not match the skills required in the jobs that are vacant.

3. Seasonal unemployment

Certain industries require more workers at one time of the year than at other times. For example, during the summer months, more building work is carried on and also more agricultural workers are required. The tourist industry is also busier during the summer, so hotels and restaurants will employ more people.

4. Structural unemployment

This type of unemployment occurs in two ways.

(A) CHANGE IN PATTERN OF DEMAND IN ECONOMY

Industries that previously were major employers have now gone into decline. For example, the shipbuilding industry employed tens of thousands of workers in Britain at a time when international air transport for passengers was only in its infancy. With a change in the pattern of demand, there was no longer a need for such large numbers of workers. Other examples of structural unemployment arising from changing demand are the European iron and steel industry, where over-capacity exists, and the UK coal industry, where rising production costs and the availability of cheap oil have reduced demand.

(B) NEW IMPROVED TECHNOLOGY REDUCES NEED FOR WORKERS

This has been a feature of the agricultural industry in Europe. Output was never higher than at present, yet employment in agriculture has fallen steadily as new and better machines do the work previously done by labour. Structural unemployment may result in the relocation of workers in areas where jobs are available, and/or their retraining in the skills that are demanded today.

5. Institutional unemployment

This refers to unemployment which arises due to obstacles to the mobility of labour or the removal of the incentive to work. It can occur in the following situations:

- When there is a shortage of housing in areas where jobs are available
- When immigration regulations in other countries prevent people taking up jobs there
- Where a 'closed shop' arrangement exists, that is, where membership of a trade union is required for certain jobs
- When the gap between unemployment benefit and take-home pay in available jobs is so small that there is no incentive for the worker to take up employment.

6. Underemployment

A worker is described as being 'underemployed' if he/she is not working to full capacity. This could happen if:

- The worker is employed for only a part of the week (e.g. three days)
- The worker is employed on a week-on and week-off basis
- The worker is employed for the full working week but his/her addition to total output (i.e. MPP) is very low. This would be the case if a student leaving school goes to work in the family business, but total output does not increase as a result. In other words, the work is divided out among a greater number of people.

THE MOBILITY OF LABOUR

Labour mobility refers to the ease of movement of workers from one job to another (occupational mobility), or from one area to another (geographical mobility). The greater the mobility of labour, the lower the level of unemployment. Certain features of an economy can restrict the mobility of labour and thereby contribute to unemployment. Such restrictions on the mobility of labour include:

- Trade union barriers, such as the closed shop practices mentioned earlier
- Lack of knowledge about available job opportunities on the part of workers
- Lack of housing or a high cost of housing in areas where vacancies exist
- The need for a high level of skill, or natural ability for certain jobs
- Language and cultural barriers may restrict labour mobility internationally
- Non-monetary considerations, for example, a reluctance to leave the place of one's birth, reluctance to disturb children's education, etc.
- Government actions and policies, for example, immigration regulations, work permit rules, etc.

Upskilling and training of workers – the role of FÁS

When the government agency FÁS was set up in 1988, its main focus was finding jobs for the large numbers of people unemployed at the time. In recent years as the country has headed in the direction of full employment FÁS has switched its focus to attracting workers from abroad (in areas where Ireland has skill shortages), and providing the opportunity for those currently employed to engage in further training. FÁS is now engaged in upskilling the current workforce, apprentices and trainees to increase productivity and improve their promotional opportunities. FÁS introduced the 'Excellence Through People' programme which is Ireland's national standard for human resource development (*Figure 19.7*). This accreditation programme acknowledges the quality of staff training in certain companies, which are then awarded the 'Excellence Through People' mark.

Fig. 19.7 FÁS 'Excellence Through People' programme

Capital and Interest Rates

In *Chapter 2* we defined capital as anything made by man which is used in the production of goods and services. It includes plant and machinery, factory buildings, transport equipment, computers, and stocks of finished and partly finished goods. All of these assist in the production of goods. Offices, shops, schools, hospitals, cinemas and leisure centres are also capital since they are used in the production of services.

We have already identified three types of capital. *Fixed capital* is the name given to stocks of fixed assets, such as factory buildings, equipment, machinery, etc. *Working capital* includes stocks of man-made raw materials, partly finished goods and finished goods. Finally, *social capital* refers to the capital which is owned by society in general, for example, roads, schools, hospitals, etc.

> The process of adding to the stock of capital is called investment (or capital formation).

Gross investment is defined as the total amount of capital created in the economy during the year. However, some of this is merely replacing capital which has worn out or become obsolete during the year (*depreciation*), and does not represent an increase in the productive capacity of the economy.

Net investment (gross investment minus depreciation) shows us how much extra capital the economy has created during the year. The greater the volume of net investment in a country, the greater is that country's ability to produce the goods and services that its citizens want.

ESSENTIAL FEATURES OF CAPITAL

1. Capital makes labour more productive

The more capital that is at the disposal of a worker, the greater will be the output that he/she is capable of producing. To understand this, think of the development of new technology that has occurred in the last 20 years. The introduction of new and better machines has led to a huge increase in the output per worker in most factories. On farms, the same is true. Agricultural output is now higher than ever before, yet fewer people are employed in agriculture. Therefore, output per worker is higher. In offices, the introduction of computers, fax machines, photocopiers, etc. has led to a huge increase in the volume of transactions that each worker can handle. So we can say that those who supply capital are helping to improve society as a whole by allowing more goods and services to be produced.

2. Creation of capital involves opportunity cost

In *Chapter 1* we defined opportunity cost as the cost of one thing in terms of the alternatives that must be done without. Because the resources of a country are limited, the more capital goods that are created in any period of time, the less resources that can be devoted to consumer goods. Investment, therefore involves a reduction in current consumption so that future consumption can be higher.

To see this consider two countries, A and B, both of which have enough resources to produce €5,000m worth of goods this year. Country A decides to devote €1,000m this year to investment by building factories, improving roads, harbours, airports, etc. Country B devotes all its resources this year to the production of consumer goods. There is no doubt that Country B will enjoy a higher standard of living this year than Country A. However, in future years Country A will be able to produce more goods and services as a result of its investment this year. Country B will find its standard of living will fall next year not only because of its failure to create any new capital, but also because it didn't set aside any resources to replace its worn out capital.

Investment, therefore, involves the giving up of the opportunity to consume now in order to be able to consume more in future. In other words, investment requires saving. The more saving that takes place, the more funds available for investment. One of the problems of poor countries is that incomes are so low that saving cannot take place. All income is spent. Consequently, no funds are available within the country to allow investment to take place, so these countries rely heavily on outside aid.

3. Savers provide funds for investors

Those who save provide funds for those wishing to invest. It is very important to be absolutely clear on what we mean by the terms, 'saving' and 'investment'.

Saving refers to that part of income which is not spent, i.e.
saving = income − consumption

> Investment is the process of adding to the stock of capital.

It will simplify matters if we consider saving to be undertaken by one category of people, and investment by another. Although this is not always true, it will allow us to see the relationship between saving and investing more clearly. Saving is usually undertaken by: (a) those whose incomes exceed their current needs, and (b) those who decide to forego present consumption in favour of future consumption.

In either case, the saver is entitled to a return for making funds available for others who wish to invest. This return is called the *rate of interest.* Investment is undertaken by those who create additional capital goods. Such capital goods can be paid for by the use of the investors' own funds or else by borrowing.

We can now see that one of the main functions of the financial institutions is to bring together savers and investors. Savers will be compensated for allowing others to use their funds. Savers are the 'owners of capital' who receive a reward (in the form of interest). Investors are the 'users of capital', who make payments (in the form of interest) for the privilege of using the capital of others. The rate of interest paid to the saver is lower than the rate charged to the borrower. The difference represents the fee charged by the financial institution for its role in bringing saver and borrower (i.e. investor) together.

REASONS FOR SAVING

Savings can be undertaken by:
1. Individuals, when they do not spend all of their incomes (personal savings).
2. Companies, when they do not distribute all of their profits as dividends to shareholders (corporate savings or retained earnings).
3. The government, when its revenue exceeds its expenditure (current budget surplus).

The following are the main reasons why savings are undertaken.
(a) To purchase goods and services at a future date.
(b) As a precaution against unplanned expenditure, for example, illness or repairs to car, etc.
(c) To provide an income in retirement or in the event of redundancy.
(d) To be in a position to purchase an asset if it is expected to increase in value or generate a future stream of income.
(e) To build up a credit rating with a financial institution. For example, a bank or building society will insist that a prospective house buyer must save a certain proportion of the purchase price of the house before a loan will be considered.

FACTORS AFFECTING LEVEL OF SAVING

1. Level of income

An individual with a small income will find that most (if not all) of that income will be required to provide for present consumption. A high income earner, on the other hand, even though his level of spending will be much higher, will be able to save part of his income for any of the five reasons outlined above. Therefore in general we can say that the higher the level of income, the greater the amount of saving.

2. Rate of interest

The higher the rate of interest, the greater the amount of saving. We have seen that the rate of interest can be considered the reward to the saver for foregoing present consumption. Accordingly, the higher the rate of interest, the greater the incentive to save.

3. Level of social security benefits

In former years, individuals accumulated savings during their working lives in order to supplement fairly small pensions. Because of the growth of state-financed retirement benefits (contributory and non-contributory old age pensions), the need for such saving may not be as obvious to some people.

4. Effect of tax system and government policy on savings

(a) If the government increases the tax payable on interest earned (DIRT), while leaving unchanged (or reducing) the rates of VAT on goods and services bought, this will act as a disincentive to saving.

(b) The granting of tax relief on personal pension plans encourages saving in such schemes.

(c) In February 2001 the government introduced a major initiative to increase the level of savings in Ireland. Under this scheme anyone over the age of 18 was eligible to open a Special Savings Incentive Account (SSIA), lodging a minimum of €12.50 and a maximum of €254.00 every month for five years. In addition to the rate of interest given by the financial institution the government agreed to top up the amount saved by 25 per cent at the end of the five-year period. The scheme was designed to encourage people to get into the habit of regular saving after the massive spending spree of the previous five years and to reduce excess demand in the economy which might lead to inflation.

The following article from *The Irish Times* on 1 March 2002 argues that with a personal savings ratio of about 10 per cent, Ireland already has the savings habit.

Savings data undermine SSIA rationale

By Dan McLaughlin

In May 2001, the Government introduced an extraordinary measure designed to encourage savings. It involved the Exchequer adding £1 to every £4 [€1 to every €4] saved by individuals under the scheme.

Since then, a plethora of special savings incentive accounts (SSIAs) have been introduced by financial institutions in order to encourage households to avail of the unprecedented act of fiscal generosity - Irish taxpayers have never before subsidised Irish savers.

The Minister for Finance, when announcing the incentive, spoke of the Government's keenness to foster the savings culture, and noted that "the habit of savings by individuals has been neglected in recent times".

Yet the evidence available, albeit incomplete, argues that the savings habit is alive and well, and that household savings in the Republic have actually risen in recent years, contrary to popular belief.

The standard approach to the measurement of household savings at the aggregate level is the personal savings ratio, which simply defines savings as that percentage of household disposable income not spent on personal consumption. If my after-tax income is €100 for example, and I spend €90, my savings are €10 and my saving ratio 10 per cent.

This construct allows us to compare savings through time and across economies and, in truth, the ratio varies enormously across the globe.

In the US, for example, the savings ratio is currently around zero (i.e. Americans spend all their income), while in Korea it is more than 20 per cent. Indeed the US ratio was for a time in negative territory, implying that the desire to live for today extended to paying for it out of tomorrow's income.

Definitional inconsistencies may partly account for this huge disparity in saving ratios, but economic analysis does throw up some other reasons why the desire to save varies so much across the globe and why it varies through time in specific countries.

One factor is age: an ageing population will tend to save for retirement and states differ in the generosity of publicly funded pensions. Uncertainty is another: savings would tend to rise in periods of weak growth and rising unemployment, as individuals become less confident about job security and prospects for future income.

Inflation, too, is likely to affect spending and savings, in that individuals will probably save more if inflation is expected to rise, in order to protect the real purchasing power of a nest-egg. Finally, interest rates and the tax treatment of savings will play a part as they affect the reason for abstaining from spending today in order to spend tomorrow.

On that basis, one might have expected the Irish saving ratio to have fallen steadily in recent years. After all, interest rates are very low by historical standards, and are actually negative on many deposit accounts when one adjusts for inflation. Similarly, unemployment fell steadily through the 1990s, which might have encouraged more spending at the expense of thrift.

In fact, the data show the reverse: the saving ratio has risen steadily since 1996, when it measured 8.7 per cent. The ratio rose to 9.7 per cent in 1997, to 9.9 per cent in 1998 and to 10.5 per cent in 1999, the last year for which we have official data. The ratio may well have fallen marginally in 2000 (to 10.3 per cent) but probably rose again last year to around 11 per cent, as personal consumption growth did not appear to keep pace with the rise in disposable income.

Clearly then, there is little here to support the view that individuals of the Republic have abandoned thrift for a hedonistic binge. We may be all Americans now in a cultural sense but, in the savings habit at least, the Republic has retained its identity.

www.ireland.com

5. Rate of inflation affects savings

If the rate of inflation is higher than the rate of interest, then the *real rate of interest* is said to be negative. A saver loses in this situation. Suppose I save €1,000 for one year at a rate of interest of 8 per cent. If during this year, the rate of inflation was 10 per cent, then I am worse off (by €20) as a result of saving. I will receive €1,080 at the end of the year, but I require €1,100 to have the same purchasing power as I had at the start of the year. The higher the rate of inflation, therefore, the less the incentive to save.

How Rate of Interest is Determined

Loanable funds theory of interest rates

This is the name given to the theory of interest rates put forward by the 19th century Classical economists. Loanable funds referred to money which was available for lending on financial markets. The supply of such funds was seen as being upward sloping, indicating that the higher the rate of interest, the greater the supply of such funds. The demand curve for loanable funds was seen as downward sloping indicating that the higher the rate of interest (i.e. the price of capital), the lower the amount of such funds that would be demanded. The rate of interest would thus adjust until the demand for loanable funds equalled the supply of such funds. This is shown in *Figure 20.1*.

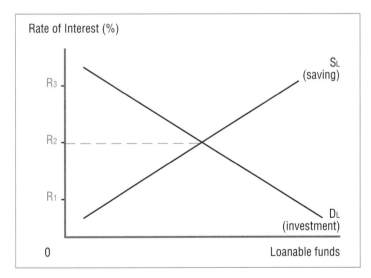

Fig. 20.1 The loanable funds theory of interest rate determination

The demand for loanable funds comes from borrowers (i.e. investors), while the supply of loanable funds comes from savers. If the rate of interest was R_1, then the demand for funds exceeds the supply, so there would be upward pressure on the interest rate. If the rate of interest was R_3, the supply of loanable funds would exceed the demand, so there would be downward pressure on the interest rate. At R_2, the demand for loanable funds equals the supply, so this is the equilibrium rate of interest.

Summary of loanable funds theory

$$S_L = f(\text{r of i})$$
$$D_L = f(\text{r of i})$$
If $S_L > D_L$, r of i falls.
If $S_L < D_L$, r of i rises.
Rate of interest changes until $S_L = D_L$ where:
$$S_L = \text{supply of loanable funds}$$
$$D_L = \text{demand for loanable funds}$$
$$\text{r of i} = \text{rate of interest}$$

The Loanable Funds Theory is now recognised as being too simple an explanation of how interest rates are determined. The interest rate is not the most important thing affecting the demand for funds by investors. The expected rate of return will be much more important. Similarly the level of income is more important than the interest rate in determining the level of saving (i.e. the supply of loanable funds). Also, the fact that banks can create credit complicates the picture. An alternative explanation can be found in the writings of John Maynard Keynes (see also *Chapter 33*).

THEORY OF LIQUIDITY PREFERENCE

This theory, which was developed in the 1930s by the English economist, John Maynard Keynes, concentrates on the demand and supply of money rather than the demand and supply of loanable funds to explain how interest rates are determined. The supply of money was taken as fixed. It was a policy decision of the Central Bank, in accordance with the wishes of the government. It did not depend on the rate of interest. Therefore in *Figure 20.2*, we draw the money supply curve (S_M) as a vertical straight line.

The fact that the money supply does not depend on the rate of interest can be expressed more concisely as:

$$S_M \neq f(\text{r of i})$$

By the demand for money, Keynes meant the desire of individuals to hold their wealth in *liquid* form, that is, as notes, coins or current account bank balances. This desire on the part of individuals was called *liquidity preference*. Keynes identified three reasons or motives why people preferred to hold their wealth in liquid form.

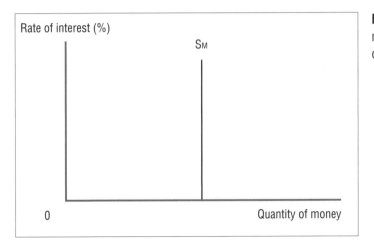

Rate of interest (%)

S_M

0   Quantity of money

Fig. 20.2 The supply of money does not depend on the rate of interest

1. The transactions motive (D_t)

This simply means that people need to have cash for day-to-day spending. The amount that people need for this purpose depends on how much they spend, which in turn depends on their income. The higher the level of income, the greater the transactions demand for money. The rate of interest has no effect on the amount that people keep for transactions purposes, so in *Figure 20.3*, the transactions demand for money is shown as a vertical straight line.

SUMMARY

$$D_t = f(Y)$$

where Y = the level of income

If Y rises, D_t rises.

If Y falls, D_t falls.

$$D_t \neq f(r \text{ of } i)$$

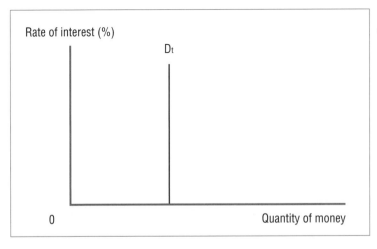

Rate of interest (%)

D_t

0   Quantity of money

Fig. 20.3 The transactions demand for money does not depend on the rate of interest

2. The precautionary motive (D$_p$)

The precautionary demand for money refers to money held by individuals in case of emergencies, for example, illness, breakage of household appliances, car repairs, etc. Such expenses inevitably arise, but the individual does not know precisely when or how they will arise.

The precautionary demand for money depends on the level of income. The higher the level of income, the greater the precautionary demand for money. It will also depend to a certain extent on the rate of interest. The higher the rate of interest the less money that will be held for precautionary purposes. I may be willing to keep €1,000 as cash in case of emergencies that may arise if the rate of interest is only 3 per cent. However, I am unlikely to do this if the rate of interest is 20 per cent, since I would be at the loss of €200 a year interest by doing so. *Figure 20.4* shows this relationship between the rate of interest and the precautionary demand for money.

> **SUMMARY**
> $$D_p = f(Y)$$
> More precisely:
> If Y rises, D$_p$ rises.
> If Y falls, D$_p$ falls.
> $$D_p = f(r \text{ of } i)$$
> More precisely:
> If r of i rises, D$_p$ falls.
> If r of i falls, D$_p$ rises.

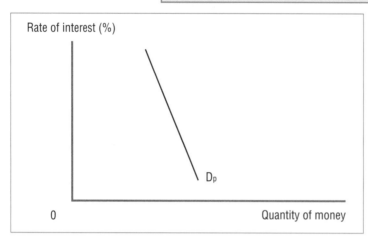

Fig. 20.4 The precautionary demand for money is influenced by the rate of interest

3. The speculative motive (D$_s$)

This refers to the money held by individuals to take advantage of a profit-making opportunity that might arise. People will want to have cash to purchase an asset that is expected to increase in value in the future. This asset could be a piece of capital, a unit of stock (i.e. shares in a company) or a government bond.

Let us concentrate on the government bond. When the government wishes to borrow from the public on a long-term basis it does so by issuing long-term government bonds. A bond is really an IOU from the government to the person who buys the bond. In return for his €100, a buyer of a government bond gets a piece of paper which guarantees him a certain amount of money every year (say €10), together with the return of his €100 at a specified future date (called the redemption date or repayment date). This may be in 10 years time. The amount he gets every year is fixed and is based on interest rates at the time when the bond is first issued. If the bond holder wishes, he may sell his bond on the stock exchange at any time.

There is no risk of a loss to the bond holder if he keeps the bond until the redemption date. However, if he decides to sell it before the redemption date, he could make a loss. This would happen if interest rates rose in the meantime. Suppose our bondholder decides to sell his bond after one year. If the rate of interest had risen to 13 per cent by then, he would not get €100 for the bond. Anyone with €100 to spend would buy a new bond which would yield a return of €13 a year. The market value of his bond can be found by using the following formula:

$$\text{market price of bond} = \frac{\text{original price of bond} \times \text{original rate of interest}}{\text{new rate of interest}}$$

$$= \frac{€100 \times 10}{13}$$

$$= €77$$

Similarly, if the market rate of interest had fallen to 7 per cent, the value of his bond would be:

$$= \frac{€100 \times 10}{7}$$

$$= €143$$

Thus we can see that there is an inverse relation between the rate of interest and the market value of existing bonds. When the rate of interest rises, the market value of existing bonds falls. When the rate of interest falls, the market value of existing bonds rises.

When rates of interest are low, people expect them to rise. Consequently, they expect the value of bonds to fall. In such circumstances they will prefer to hold their wealth as cash. So when interest rates are low, the speculative demand for money will be high. When rates of interest are high, people will expect them to fall. Consequently, they expect bond prices to rise. In such circumstances they will prefer to buy bonds. So when interest rates are high, the speculative demand for money will be low. This inverse relationship between the rate of interest and the speculative demand for money is shown in *Figure 20.5*. The relationship can be summarised as follows:

SUMMARY

$D_s = f(r \text{ of } i)$
More precisely:
If r or i rises, D_s falls.
If r or i falls, D_s rises.

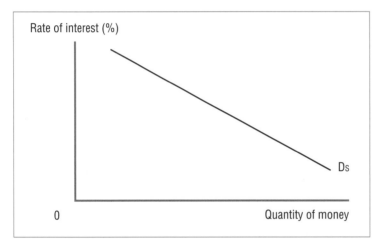

Fig. 20.5 The speculative demand for money is greatly influenced by the rate of interest

This line of analysis can also be applied to the demand by individuals for other assets, e.g. shares, property, etc. When interest rates are high (say 15%), the speculative demand for money will be low. People will prefer to put their money into fixed-interest earning accounts where there is little or no risk. So the amount they hold as cash for a profit-making opportunity will be small. Very few profit-making opportunities can guarantee a return of 15 per cent. On the other hand, when interest rates are low (say 5%), the speculative demand for money will be high. People will prefer to hold onto cash in the hope of finding a profit-making opportunity that will yield a return greater than 5 per cent.

The total or aggregate demand for money (D_M) is simply the sum of the transactions, precautionary and speculative demands. It is shown in *Figure 20.6*. According to Keynes, the rate of interest (R_1) will be determined by the intersection of this curve with the vertical money supply curve (S_M), as shown in *Figure 20.6*.

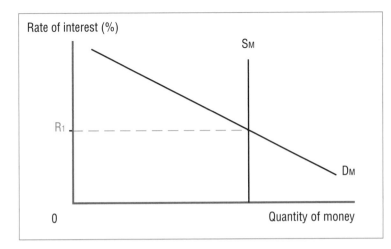

Fig. 20.6 The total (or aggregate) demand for money (D_M) and the money supply (S_M)

CHANGES IN DEMAND AND SUPPLY OF MONEY

1. Increase in money supply, demand unchanged – interest rates fall

An increase in the money supply, while demand remains unchanged, will cause the interest rate to fall. This encourages investment but discourages saving. In *Figure 20.7*, if the Central Bank raises the money supply from SM_1 to SM_2, the interest rate will fall from R_1 to R_2. However, the interest rate may be so low that everyone expects it to rise. No one will want to buy bonds (since their market value will fall if interest rates rise). Everyone will want to hold cash. If the government increases the money supply in this situation, the interest rate will not fall. This is known as a liquidity trap, and it may result in a rise in inflation and/or increased imports. This situation is shown in *Figure 20.8*. An increase in the money supply from SM_1 to SM_2 will not cause the interest rate to fall below R_1.

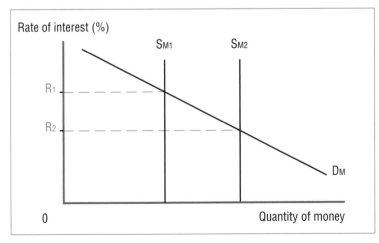

Fig. 20.7 A change in the money supply (with demand unchanged) will cause the interest rate to change

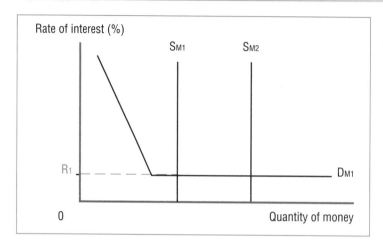

Fig. 20.8 The liquidity trap

2. Decrease in money supply, demand unchanged – interest rates rise

A decrease in the money supply, while demand remains unchanged, will cause interest rates to rise. This discourages investment but encourages saving. In *Figure 20.7*, if the Central Bank reduces the money supply from SM_2 to SM_1, the interest rate will rise from R_2 to R_1.

3. Increase in money demand, supply unchanged – interest rates rise

An increase in the demand for money, while the supply remains unchanged, will cause interest rates to rise. This discourages investment but encourages saving. In *Figure 20.9*, if the demand for money rises from D_{M1} to D_{M2}, the interest rate will rise from R_1 to R_2.

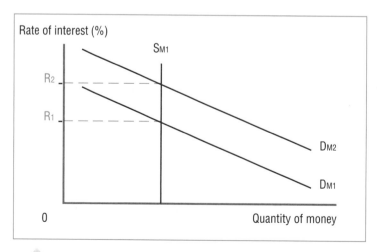

Fig. 20.9 A change in the demand for money (with supply unchanged) will cause the interest rate to change

4. Decrease in money demand, supply unchanged – interest rates fall

A decrease in the demand for money, while the supply remains unchanged, will cause interest rates to fall. This encourages investment but discourages saving. In *Figure 20.9*, if the demand for money falls from D_{M2} to D_{M1}, the rate of interest will fall from R_2 to R_1.

FACTORS AFFECTING RATE OF INTEREST

1. Rate charged by ESCB

The rate charged by the European System of Central Banks to credit institutions when it supplies them with liquidity will affect all other interest rates. This rate is set in accordance with the EU's monetary policy at the time. If this rate is increased, other interest rates will increase. If this rate is reduced other rates of interest will fall. The work of the ESCB in relation to interest rates will be examined further in *Chapter 22*.

2. Degree of risk to lender

In general, the greater the degree of risk to the lender, the higher the rate of return that he/she will expect. The degree of risk depends on (a) the borrower and (b) the purpose for which the money is borrowed. In the case of (a) the government and local authorities are seen to pose less of a risk of non-payment than a personal borrower, and so pay a lower rate of interest. In the case of (b), if the money is borrowed for a purpose which is seen as worthwhile and one which is likely to generate a reasonable return, then the rate of interest will be fairly low (e.g. a company with a good record of profits seeking a loan for further expansion). If the money is borrowed for something which is seen as less worthwhile or more risky, the rate of interest charged will be higher.

3. Degree of liquidity of loan

There are two aspects to the degree of liquidity of the loan:

(a) The longer the period of the loan, the greater the period of time the lender has to do without his/her money, and therefore, the higher the rate of interest charged.

(b) The longer the notice of withdrawal given by a saver (i.e. the lender), the higher the rate of interest he/she will expect. For example, suppose Mr Murphy and Mr O'Brien both deposit €1,000 in the same bank on the same day. Mr Murphy wants to be able to withdraw his money 'on demand', i.e. whenever he likes. Mr O'Brien informs the bank that he will give six months notice of withdrawal. Even if both men leave their money with the bank for the same length of time, Mr O'Brien will receive a higher rate of interest than Mr Murphy.

4. Rate of inflation

The higher the rate of inflation, the higher the rate of interest that a lender will require. If the lender is happy with a 7 per cent real return on his money, and if the rate of inflation is 4 per cent, he will require a rate of interest of at least 11 per cent before parting with his money.

Similarly, the higher the rate of inflation, the higher the rate of interest which a borrower is willing to pay. If I borrow €1,000 for one year at a rate of interest of 5 per cent, when the annual inflation rate is 10 per cent, then the real rate of interest to me is –5 per cent. I can buy something for €1,000 which will cost €1,100 in a year's time, but I will only have to pay back €1,050. Therefore, we can say that in general, the higher the rate of inflation, the higher the rate of interest. A negative real interest rate arises when the rate of inflation exceeds the rate of interest.

5. Demand for loans

The greater the demand for loans, the higher will be the rate of interest. Borrowers compete against each other for available funds. Just as the price of any good will be high when demand is strong, lenders will be able to charge higher rates of interest when there are many would-be borrowers.

FACTORS AFFECTING LEVEL OF INVESTMENT

1. Rate of interest

We have already seen that the higher the rate of interest, the lower will be the willingness of business people to invest. This is because the rate of interest is the cost of borrowing. Even a fairly modest rise in interest rates may cause some firms to postpone or cancel investment plans.

2. Expectations of future demand

The expectations of business people concerning future demand is more important than the rate of interest in deciding the level of investment. If business people are optimistic about the economy in general or their own sector in particular, then they will be more likely to invest. If they have pessimistic expectations either of their own sector or of the economy in general, they will be less likely to invest. *Figure 20.10* shows the findings of a survey of chief executives in Irish publicly quoted, semi-state and large private companies carried out by the *Sunday Business Post* in 2002.

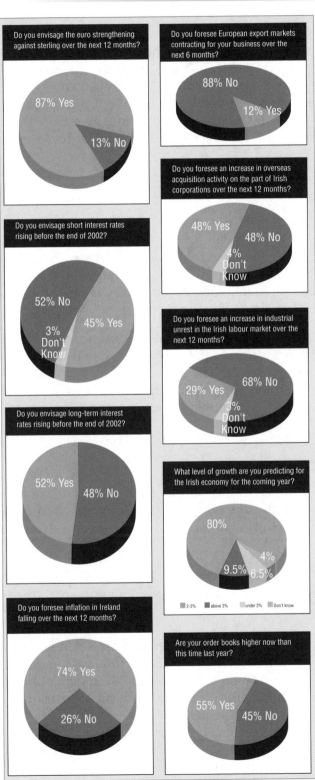

Fig. 20.10 Results of *Sunday Business Post* poll of Irish business leaders on prospects for 2002 (Source: *Sunday Business Post*, 13 January 2002)

3. Cost of capital

The profitability of investment will obviously depend on the cost of capital goods. The *marginal efficiency of capital* (MEC) is the extra profit earned as a result of the employment of an extra unit of capital. The marginal efficiency of capital is the MRP of capital minus its cost. For example, if an additional machine costs €200,000, but adds €600,000 to total revenue, then its MEC is €400,000. In general, the greater the cost of capital, the lower the level of investment.

4. Government policy

Government policy will affect the level of investment. Government policies designed to increase the level of investment include state grants to industry, administered by the Industrial Development Authority (IDA), reduced tax rates on company profits, generous depreciation allowances on capital equipment, the provision of an adequate infrastructure, tax reliefs on loans taken out by companies for the purchase of equipment, etc.

From 1 January 2003, the corporation tax rate for all trading profits arising from Irish trade is 12.5 per cent, regardless of the industrial sector in which the profits are generated. This rate which has been approved by the EU Commission is very low by international standards and will ensure that Ireland will remain a major recipient of foreign direct investment, even if a downturn in economic activity occurs.

5. The state of technology

As the state of technology improves, the output from a unit of capital employed will increase. Consequently, the purchase of new capital goods will become more worthwhile (i.e. more profitable).

6. International economic climate

An economy like Ireland's depends very much on foreign investment. If there is a recession abroad, this will mean that foreign investment in Ireland will be affected in two ways:
(a) An international recession implies a fall in the demand on world markets for the goods produced by companies. Most of the foreign companies operating in Ireland produce for the export market. A fall in demand will mean a fall in production and, therefore, a fall in the level of investment required by companies already operating here.
(b) A recession may lead to the postponement of investment by companies thinking of setting up here. The opposite applies to a situation where there is a high level of demand in international markets.

7. Availability of skilled and educated labour force

The availability of a well-educated and highly skilled labour force has been a critical factor in the investment decisions of many foreign companies in recent years. Many multinational companies locating in Ireland have put this factor at the top of their list of reasons for locating here (see newspaper article at the end of this chapter). A skilled work force will achieve high productivity and will thus ensure that companies will earn high rates of return on their investment.

CAPITAL WIDENING AND CAPITAL DEEPENING

Capital widening is defined as an increase in the use of capital which leaves the ratio of capital to labour unchanged.

For example, suppose a factory has 100 workers and 10 machines. As a result of an increase in the demand for its good, the firm takes on 30 more workers and an extra three machines. This firm is said to be engaged in capital widening. The ratio of capital to labour does not change.

Capital deepening is defined as an increase in the use of capital which increases the ratio of capital to labour.

For example, if the factory above had responded to the increase in demand by employing an extra five machines and only 10 extra workers, it would be engaged in capital deepening. In other words, its production would be more capital intensive. The higher the wage rate is, relative to the cost of capital, the more likely the firm is to engage in capital deepening.

THE INVESTMENT RATIO

The investment ratio is defined as gross investment as a percentage of GNP.

The investment ratio shows the fraction of a country's income which it devotes to investment. The higher the investment ratio, the greater the future productive capacity of the country. *Table 20.1* shows GNP, gross investment and the investment ratio for Ireland from 1995 to 2000. It can be seen that the ratio increased steadily over this period as increasing business confidence led to an increased volume of investment.

Year	GNP (€m)	Gross investment	Investment ratio (%) (€m)
1995	46,748	8,986	19.2
1996	51,523	10,819	21.0
1997	58,978	13,540	23.0
1998	67,728	17,027	25.1
1999	75,811	20,952	27.6
2000	87,122	24,448	28.0

Source: Statistical Yearbook of Ireland, 2001, Central Statistics Office

Table 20.1 GNP, gross investment and the investment ratio in Ireland, 1995–2000

Why Ireland became an attractive location for US multinationals is outlined in the following article from *The Irish Times*, 2 March 2001.

US Multinationals – The Irish Connection

By Conor O'Clery

"The first question for any company looking to put an operation in Europe is why not Ireland?" according to Ms Deborah Lange, senior vice-president of Oracle Corporation. "Because most senior executives have heard such good stories about Ireland, you almost have to get over the Irish hump if you want to go somewhere else."

Such pro-Irish sentiments are not uncommon among executives in US technology and pharmaceutical companies interviewed last week about why they chose the Republic for investment. But when asked about future direct US investment, especially in a period of a slowing US economy, they also identified downsides in the Republic, including skills shortages, house prices and traffic congestion as problems for investors.

More than 600 US companies have invested in Ireland and exports sent back across the Atlantic have put the US on a par with the UK as an overseas market.... Almost all the leading US companies are in Ireland, including household names like IBM, Dell, EMC, Hewlett-Packard, Apple and Compaq in the technology sector, and Pfizer, American Home Products, Schering-Plough, and Johnson & Johnson among pharmaceutical firms.

Microsoft, the world's biggest software provider, was among the first to arrive 15 years ago. Its positive experiences helped persuade similar companies, such as Oracle, the biggest software company in Silicon Valley, to take the same route.

"They were able to show us that the infrastructure was in place," said Ms Lange.... Oracle also looked at Scotland, Switzerland and the Netherlands before deciding in 1991 to establish a centre in Ireland, which now employs more than 750 people. What swung it for the Republic was the calibre of employees, according to Ms Lange. This was a "critical issue", and on education "you were ahead of the pack"....

The fact that the Republic had the lowest corporate tax rate in Europe – 10 per cent until the end of 2000 and 12.5 per cent until 2025 – was not decisive, she said.

On the other hand, prices have gone up, she added. "It's now quite costly, especially if you move people to Ireland. Then there is traffic congestion"...

Another concern was the high demand for qualified workers... and some firms felt they just became training grounds for rival companies. The lack of direct air flights from San Jose or San Francisco is also a serious irritant for Silicon Valley executives.

For Xerox, the low Irish corporate tax rate was "the cream on the cake rather than the cake itself," said Mr Bill Goode, deputy managing director of Xerox in Europe. The world-famous copying company, which employs 1,600 in Dundalk and 1,000 in Dublin, chose Ireland in 1998.... Scotland and the Netherlands were in the running, but Ireland topped a checklist of language, demographics, education and infrastructure.

What tilted the decision was the people.... "There are more people in the 18-28 age group than in many other countries," he said. There was also the Republic's "incredible education system", with Dundalk Institute of Technology prepared to tailor technical courses to Xerox's needs. Like other companies Xerox found the turnover rate of employees quite high "because there's a massive pool of employers all vying for the same population".

Technology giant Hewlett-Packard chose the Republic six years ago over Puerto Rico, Spain, San Diego and Oregon.... "What was decisive was the availability of a technically skilled workforce," said Ms Una Halligan, the company's Irish public affairs manager.... Hewlett-Packard found that Irish trainees performed extremely well, and showed enthusiasm and innovation, and that the Irish government was prepared to be reactive to its needs....

www.ireland.com

201

21

Enterprise and Profit

In *Chapter 2* we defined enterprise as the factor of production which takes the initiative in organising land, labour and capital, and which bears the risks involved in production. Even though plentiful supplies of land, labour and capital may be present in an economy, no production will take place unless people come forward who are willing to combine these factors in an appropriate way.

The person who takes the risks involved in production is willing to put some of his/her money into a business, with the aim of making a profit. He/she decides what goods or services are to be supplied, and how they are to be produced, that is, what combination of land, labour and capital will be used. He/she must also decide the price to charge for the goods or services. The price must be sufficiently high to cover the costs of production and provide a return to the person who puts in the money. The person who makes such decisions is called the *entrepreneur*. The return to the entrepreneur is called *profit*. Even though it is possible to consider the entrepreneur as a specialised form of labour, his/her role is so unique and so important that enterprise is considered as a separate factor of production.

Although the entrepreneur hopes to make a profit, there is the possibility of a loss. In a free market economy, consumers are free to decide whether to purchase the goods and services offered by the entrepreneur or do without them. The entrepreneur undertakes production in anticipation of demand. He/she may undertake market research prior to going into production to find out the size of the market and the strength of demand on the part of potential customers. However, such activities, while they may reduce the risks involved in production, cannot eliminate them entirely. Risk is an ever-present feature of a free market system.

Risks faced by entrepreneurs

The risks faced by the entrepreneur can be classified as insurable and non-insurable.

INSURABLE RISKS

Insurable risks include the following:

(a) Damage to factory buildings, e.g. fire, storm, etc.

(b) Accidents to workers or members of the public

(c) Theft

(d) Dishonesty by employees

(e) Non-payment for goods supplied (in foreign trade only).

NON-INSURABLE RISKS

Non-insurable risks include the following:

(a) Strikes

(b) Loss of profits due to increased costs of production

(c) A movement in taste away from the goods produced by the firm

(d) Entry of rival firms

(e) Adverse effects of new legislation or new trading agreements.

WHO IS THE ENTREPRENEUR?

In a free market economy such as ours, the factor of production, enterprise, is supplied by private individuals. The sole trader in a shop or farm, the partners in a partnership, and the ordinary shareholders in a limited company are all entrepreneurs, since they bear the risks involved in production. In the case of a semi-state body, the taxpayers of the country can be considered entrepreneurs, since any losses made by the company must ultimately be borne by them in the form of tax payments to the exchequer. Some manufacturing firms faced with closure have been bought out by the workers, who have used their redundancy money to keep the business open. In such a business (known as a workers' co-operative), the workers themselves take the risks and are classified as entrepreneurs.

It is important to realise that the management and risk-taking functions are separated in many forms of business today. If a company appoints a manager who is paid a salary and who does not own shares in the company, then this person is not really an entrepreneur but a supplier of labour. He/she does not bear the risks, since a salary will be received irrespective of whether the company makes a profit or a loss.

ENTREPRENEUR IN CENTRALLY PLANNED ECONOMY

In *Chapter 2* we defined a centrally planned economy as one where the state owns the means of production. In such an economy, the state carries out the entrepreneurial role. It organises the production and distribution of goods and services. A state agency decides what goods and services are to be produced, and what prices are to be charged.

While the idea of planning from the centre might at first appear an attractive idea, the system has proved to be a failure in many countries where it was tried, most notably in the countries that made up the former Soviet Union (USSR), and the states of Eastern Europe. The absence of the profit motive proved to be too great a burden for the system to bear. Since there were no private entrepreneurs, there was no incentive for an individual to work harder to make profits. There was no reason for companies to introduce new methods of production to gain an advantage over their rivals, since in reality there was no competition.

While the system did eliminate a lot of waste (e.g. money spent on advertising), it created more waste by requiring a huge state bureaucracy to make production decisions, administer prices, etc. Also it did not fulfil the most basic function of a market system – it did not provide consumers with the goods and services they wanted. This was because consumers had no part in the decision-making process in such countries. The cost of incorrect planning on the part of the state falls on consumers in a centrally planned economy. In a free market economy, the cost of incorrect planning falls on the entrepreneur.

Any advantages of such a centrally planned system are heavily outweighed by the disadvantages, a fact borne out by the efforts of the Eastern European states to introduce a free market economic system in their countries, once democracy had been achieved.

ROLE OF PROFITS IN FREE MARKET ECONOMIC SYSTEM

The above discussion of the flaws in the centrally planned system serves to highlight the crucial role which profits play in a free market economy.

1. Profits encourage risk-taking

If there were no extra reward for supplying enterprise or bearing the risk, then no one would be willing to put money into companies. Everyone would put their money into safe interest-bearing accounts, where a modest return is guaranteed. It is the prospect of making large profits that encourages people to put their money into companies, and provides the framework within which such companies can grow and prosper.

2. Profits act as guide to correct use of resources

Profits act as a guide to the correct use of the resources in an economy. If factors of production are employed in a company making goods which consumers want, then profits will be made by that company. On the other hand, if a company is producing goods and services which consumers do not want, losses will be made. The earning of profits by a company is a signal to producers as to what goods and services the public want. On the other hand, if a company is making losses, this is a sign that it is unable to provide goods and services at prices people are willing to pay. In the long term, such companies will be forced to close down. Therefore, profits act as a mechanism whereby resources are directed to those entrepreneurs who can make best use of them.

3. Profits ensure best use of investors' funds

Profits ensure that investors' funds are put to the best uses. Profitable firms will find it easy to acquire the funds needed for expansion. Banks will be more willing to grant loans to companies with a good record of profit. Similarly, the shares of profit-making companies will be the most sought-after on the stock exchange, thus providing such companies with another source of funds.

4. Profits as a sign of efficiency

In highly competitive industries, profits are a sign of efficiency. This is because the firms that earn most profits in such markets are the ones that can keep costs to a minimum.

5. Profits as criterion for continuing in business

The earning of normal profits (at least) is the criterion by which companies decide whether to continue in business. See *Chapter 10*.

ECONOMIC CHARACTERISTICS OF PROFIT

1. Unlike the payments to the other factors of production, the payment to the entrepreneur is a *residual*. That is, profit is what is left over after all the other expenses of the business have been met. Rent, wages and

interest are contractual payments. They are agreed in advance with the suppliers of land, labour and capital.

2. The entrepreneur is the only factor of production that can receive a *'negative'* reward.

3. The return to the entrepreneur tends to fluctuate more than the payments to the other factors of production. While the wages, interest and rent payable will probably increase over time, the return to the entrepreneur may increase or decrease, in accordance with the changing fortunes of the company in the market place.

THE ENTREPRENEUR IN IRELAND

It has been long accepted that the factor of production in shortest supply in Ireland is enterprise. Possibly because of historical and geographical factors, there is not a strong tradition in Ireland of people starting their own business. We have relied heavily on outside investment as a means of increasing our output and providing employment. In 2002, there were 1,200 multinational companies operating in Ireland employing over 140,000 people. While such firms are a vital part of the industrial scene in Ireland, there has been a growing realisation in recent years that small Irish owned businesses need to be encouraged, and that advisory and support services for the entrepreneurs of such firms need to be put in place.

In the government's *National Development Plan 2000–2006 (Figure 21.1)*, there is a commitment to promoting entrepreneurial and management capability, particularly in the case of small and medium-sized enterprises. This would help improve productivity in indigenous (Irish-owned) companies, where gross output per worker is about 45 per cent of that for workers in foreign owned firms.

Efforts to encourage and develop entreprenurship in Ireland in 1999 are described in *The Irish Times* (6 December 1999).

Fig. 21.1 National Development Plan 2000–2006

NEW CHALLENGE TO ROLE OF ENTREPRENEURS

By Rory Kelleher

In today's economy, the entrepreneur has become a central figure behind our economic growth. Traditional views of entrepreneurialism are that it is essentially a money-making exercise in which developing a business to bring a product to the market is the central aim, with eventual success embodied in a listing on the stock exchange.

The concept is, however, being challenged, with political, artistic, community and social innovators included as part of a new club soon to be set up in Ireland to encourage the development of entrepreneurs, not just in the business and commercial world but across the whole range of society.

One of the people behind the idea, Mr Billy Glennon, managing director of Vision Consulting, says entrepreneurs are people who spot an anomaly in the world and feel that it is something worth exploring, while also possessing the passion and tenacity to find a solution for it.

Mr Glennon points to non-business people who are successful entrepreneurs in organisations such as 'Mothers Against Drink Driving' in the United States. The originators of this idea, having seen and experienced the effect drink driving has had on their own and other people's lives, started a campaign against it.

The group, starting from a very small base, almost single-handedly managed to change the whole culture of drink driving and transformed the attitudes towards the issue.

Can the skills of the entrepreneurship be learned? Not all people are suited to it or are capable of success, as the uncertainty and risk which are bywords for entrepreneurs require drive and self-belief.

The entrepreneurs club, which initially will take in around 50 members, hopes to provide guidance to members by developing the core practices of entrepreneurs and providing a forum for exchange of ideas and methods.

"You can't point to any one source. The sources expected to provide entrepreneurs, like MBAs and business schools, are not doing it, and the traditional educational systems have failed to produce them," says Glennon.

With the social structures of Ireland breaking down, resulting in more and more uncertainty in people's lives, the entrepreneurial spirit is being increasingly brought out in Irish people.

Prof Deirdre Hunt, the director of the masters in entrepreneurship at University College, Cork, says that parents can "still play a huge role in creating a climate of entrepreneurship as, after investing in their children's education, they don't want to see those same children facing bankruptcy a few years later".

Increasingly, smaller businesses are coming to dominate economies as big companies downsize and outsource, leading to a myriad of small suppliers.

"It is not incredible to think of becoming an entrepreneur in Ireland, but until the mammies start putting a career in self-employment or setting up your own business next to a job as a bank manager or as a civil servant, the climate will be slow to change."

Many people think success equates only with large companies, but in most European countries the majority of GNP is from companies employing 100 people or less.

Prof Hunt firmly believes the skills of entrepreneurship can be learned. She thinks they are mainly about persuading and encouraging creativity in people, as well as placing trust in young people in both intangible and tangible ways.

"Contemporary business is about brokerage, and Ireland has an enormous cultural asset in that it traditionally has been in the position of brokering between large competing groups, which is integral to modern business," she says.

The masters degree is attracting a lot of mid-career people from large companies (like Beamish and Coca Cola) that are having to deal with more and more suppliers, while the entrepreneurialism and new ventures option as part of the commerce faculty has developed from a course of four or five people a few years ago to being one of the most popular courses in the faculty today.

"Big businesses are now being seen as organisations which are inefficient users of resources, with IKEA, the international furniture suppliers, basically a management company for a conglomeration of over 100,000 small businesses around Europe, a perfect example of the new era," Prof Hunt says.

www.ireland.com

The Banking System

INTRODUCTION

Economic activity in a modern society depends on the ability of individuals to supply factors of production (land, labour, capital and enterprise) and receive income in return. This income is then used to purchase goods and services produced by firms. Such transactions involve exchange, and require a method by which payment can be made (and received). Money is used for this purpose.

In primitive societies, individuals supply their own needs, e.g. food, clothing and shelter. Such societies have little need for a system of money because there is very little exchange of goods and services. Any exchange that does occur is conducted on a system of barter.

> Barter is the direct exchange of goods and services for other goods and services.

Barter is an extremely cumbersome method of exchange for a number of reasons. First, it depends on a *double coincidence of wants*. If I wish to exchange one good for another good, not only must I find a person with the good that I am looking for, but he/she must also want the good that I have.

Second, even if I am lucky enough to find such a person, how are we going to decide on a rate of exchange? How many units of one good should exchange for one unit of the other good? Third, goods are not of uniform quality. If it is accepted that one table equals three chairs, there will be differences in the quality of chairs. Some chairs will be better than others. Finally, there is the problem of divisibility. Someone with a valuable item to trade who only wants a small item will encounter great difficulty.

The above disadvantages of barter should convince you that such a system cannot provide the basis on which goods and services can be traded in a modern economy. Some form of money is required.

Functions of Money

Money is defined as anything which is generally accepted by individuals in payment for goods and services.

The functions of money are as follows:

1. Medium of exchange

Money acts as a medium of exchange. This is the primary function of money. Goods and services can be bought and sold without the disadvantages of barter. We can exchange our goods and services (including labour) for money, and then use this money to buy the goods and services that we require.

2. Unit of account

Money acts as a unit of account. By using money, we should be able to measure exactly how much something is worth. Money provides us with a framework by which we can relate the value of one item to the value of others.

3. Store of value

Money also acts as a store of value. This means that people can accumulate wealth, knowing that it will be equally acceptable as payment for goods and services at some future date. High inflation rates will undermine this function of money. Other assets, e.g. land, houses, jewellery, works of art, etc. can provide a better store of value in such circumstances.

4. Standard for deferred payment

Money acts as a standard for deferred payment. Money allows goods and services to be bought and sold on credit. The buyer receives the goods now but pays at some future date. A system of credit increases the total volume of sales as many potential buyers will not have enough money to purchase the goods outright. Also contracts can be made to supply goods and services on a specified future date at a price agreed now.

In addition to the above four functions, money should possess the following characteristics:

1. It must be generally acceptable. If people lose confidence in the value of money, it will no longer be accepted in payment for goods and services.

2. It should be easily recognisable as genuine. It is for this reason that the watermark and the metal strip are used in paper currency.

3. It should be portable, i.e. easy to carry.

4. It should be durable or long lasting.

5. It should be divisible, i.e. it must come in many different denominations so that the purchase of both large and small items is facilitated.

6. It should be relatively scarce. If money is too plentiful, it would quickly lose its value. This is one of the reasons why a government cannot solve the financial problems of a country simply by printing more money.

THE ORIGINS OF MONEY AND BANKING

The commodities which have been used as money down through the ages include cattle in ancient Ireland, cocoa beans in Africa, salt in ancient Rome, tobacco in the United States, and sugar in the West Indies, etc.

Fig. 22.1 Cattle were used by the Celts as money

Precious metals

Precious metals, such as gold and silver, however, had most of the qualities listed above as desirable for money. They were easily recognisable, scarce, acceptable, and they could be subdivided into very small units. Before the invention of coins, precious metals had to be weighed out carefully when transactions were taking place.

The development of coins did away with the need to weigh the metal at each transaction. The monarch or government weighed the metal, and made coins with an official seal which guaranteed the amount of precious metal contained in them. This was more convenient than the old system of individual weighing but it did give rise to a number of abuses.

First, the practice of '*clipping*' emerged. This was where people clipped a small piece from the coin, yet still passed the coin on at its face value. The market value of the clipped metal was then clear profit to such unscrupulous persons. To overcome this problem, the rough edges on coins were introduced.

Second, the practice of '*sweating*' of coins developed. This involved placing a large number of coins in a bag, and shaking the bag vigorously. Again, the coins would be passed on at face value, while the amount of dust collected represented the profit this time.

Third, rulers themselves were guilty of dishonest practices. When they were short of money, they '*debased*' the currency. They would use a suitable occasion (e.g. a marriage, a peace treaty, an anniversary, etc.) to order their subjects to bring in their coins, so that they could be re-minted with a new seal. Unknown to the subjects, some of the gold would be taken out and a cheaper metal used instead. Eventually when this became widely known, inflation resulted. Traders would put up their prices to be sure of receiving the same amount of precious metal as before.

This situation led to the observation by Sir Thomas Gresham (1519–1579), financial advisor to Queen Elizabeth I, that '*bad money drives out the good money*'. In other words, if two types of coin are in circulation, with the same face value, but one is debased, then people will pass around the debased one in everyday transactions. They will melt down the full value coins to make profits. This became known as *Gresham's Law*. Today we use the term '*token money*' to mean coins whose intrinsic (i.e. metallic) value is less than their face value.

> Token money is the term used to describe coins whose intrinsic (metallic) value is less than their face value.

Paper currency

The origins of our modern paper currency are to be found in the receipts issued by goldsmiths. These were craftsmen who worked with gold, and who kept very secure safes in which to store it. People who possessed large amounts of gold were naturally worried about its safety, so they handed the gold over to goldsmiths for safekeeping. The goldsmiths charged a fee for this service, and issued receipts to the owners of gold so that they could withdraw it whenever they wished to make purchases.

Suppose Mr A had £100 (i.e. one hundred pounds) worth of gold stored with a goldsmith for safekeeping. He owed Mr B £100 and wanted to pay him. He could go to the goldsmith, hand in his receipt, withdraw his £100 worth of gold and give it to Mr B, who might then deposit it with the same goldsmith. It would make much more sense if Mr A simply handed his receipt to Mr B who could then withdraw the gold whenever he liked. Eventually people realised that it was much more convenient to use pieces of paper (i.e. the receipts) rather than the gold itself when buying and selling goods.

The very first paper money to be used was, therefore, a promise by goldsmiths to pay so much gold on demand. The receipts were acceptable because people knew that they were fully backed by gold. Some goldsmiths gave up their craft to become full-time dealers in money. These goldsmiths were the first bankers. This stage in the evolution of money occurred in the 17th century. Such goldsmiths then began to issue receipts for fixed small amounts to facilitate trade. A person who deposited £100 worth of gold might get 100 receipts for one pound each, rather than one receipt for £100.

During the 18th century such goldsmiths found a new way of increasing their profits. They had, at this stage, noticed that most people were perfectly happy to use the receipts as money in their day-to-day dealings. It was very unlikely that all those who had gold deposited with them would seek to withdraw it at the same time. Perhaps as little as 20 per cent of a goldsmith's stock of gold was demanded at any one time. So the goldsmiths found that they could write receipts for a sum in excess of what was deposited with them. In doing so, they became the first bankers. They issued receipts to those who had no gold deposited, that is, they gave loans. Of course, a goldsmith who did this was taking a risk. If all those with receipts tried to convert them into gold at the same time, the goldsmith (banker) would be unable to meet his liabilities. This happened to some greedy bankers who gave out far too many receipts.

So the early banks took in gold and gave out pieces of paper which promised to pay that gold on demand. These notes were the first bank notes. When a country's money can be converted on demand into gold, the country is said to be 'on the Gold Standard'. This situation applied in Britain right down to the outbreak of the First World War in 1914. Gold coins were in circulation, and bank notes were fully convertible into gold.

When the banks issued more receipts than the amount of gold held in their vaults, they were able to make interest-earning loans. In this situation, the currency was said to be *fractionally backed by* the reserves.

As time passed the government began to regulate the issue of notes by the banks. In Britain the Bank Charter Act of 1844 limited the issue of such notes by ordinary banks, but allowed the Bank of England to issue £14 million more in notes than it had in gold. This £14 million was known as the *fiduciary issue* (derived from the Latin word for trust, *fiducia*). The fiduciary limit has been successively raised, and the Bank is now free to alter the note issue as it wishes. In most countries, the note issue is entirely fiduciary. Such money is sometimes called *fiat money* – it is based on trust.

When banks amalgamated, their note issue was taken over by the Bank of England. Many amalgamations took place in the 19th century, so that as time passed, the Bank of England became the sole issuer of notes. A further development took place at this stage in that banks allowed borrowers to withdraw loans in cash form, or transfer money from one account to another by means of a cheque.

As already stated, notes were fully convertible into gold until 1914. The outbreak of the First World War forced the suspension of this system, and Britain was 'off the Gold Standard' from 1914 to 1925. From 1925 to 1931, a 'Gold Bullion Standard' operated. There were no gold coins, and the Bank of England would only exchange 400 oz gold bars for £1,700. The Gold Standard finally collapsed in 1931, but people continued to accept bank notes and coins because they had confidence in them. Bank notes now are only fractionally backed. Coins today contain no precious metals. Yet people are prepared to accept them because they are legal tender.

> Legal tender is money that must be accepted if offered as payment for a purchase or in settlement of a debt.

Fig. 22.2 Gold bullion

Fig. 22.3 Notes and coins are the standard legal tender in countries throughout the world

Irish legal tender

In Ireland legal tender consists of euro coins and notes. Cheques are not legal tender, even though they are now widely used as money.

Following the establishment of the Irish Free State in 1922, the Coinage Act was passed to allow the Irish Minister for Finance to issue new Irish coins. A commission recommended that an Irish pound, backed 100 per cent by sterling and gold reserves, be created. This was done in 1927 by the Currency Act, which established a one-to-one exchange rate with sterling, and set up the Currency Commission to administer the new legal tender. These notes and coins were used until 1971, when a new currency was issued following decimalisation.

The one-to-one parity of the Irish pound with sterling was maintained until 1979, when this country entered the European Monetary System (see *Chapter 29*). This was an attempt by member countries of the EU to limit exchange rate movements between their currencies so as to eliminate some of the risks associated with international trade and borrowing. It was widely viewed as a forerunner to a much more ambitious plan – to have a common currency among the member states of the EU (see *Chapter 30*).

On 1 January 2002, this plan became a reality – the euro became the common currency of 12 of the 15 member states of the EU (Denmark, Sweden and the UK retained their national currencies). These 12 countries are referred to as the eurozone. It is widely expected within the eurozone that a single currency will bring many benefits. The euro will be examined more fully later in this chapter and in *Chapter 30*.

The article below from *The Irish Times* of 28 December 2001 captures the sense of anticipation felt in the eurozone countries in the final days leading to the introduction of the new currency.

Final countdown to a new currency

By Siobhan Creaton

E-day is almost upon us. In just four days, euro notes and coins will replace national currencies in 12 of the 15 EU member-states marking the realisation of one of the greatest political dreams in history. ...

The euro will become the single currency of Ireland, Germany, France, Spain, Austria, Belgium, Finland, Greece, Italy, Luxembourg, the Netherlands and Portugal, with expectations that Britain, Denmark and Sweden will join some time in the future. ...

Coordinating the switch to the euro has been a monumental logistical exercise. In the biggest movement of cash in peacetime, some 50 billion coins and 14.5 billion banknotes are entering circulation.

One billion bank accounts will automatically be converted into euros on January 1st. Around seven million vending machines, 140,000 cash machines and four million tills, will be filled with the new currency.

Businesses and the international money markets are well versed in the new currency having switched to the euro on January 1st, 1999, when it was first introduced on the world currency markets.

But for most Europeans the euro will only become a reality on E-Day when they begin to pay for groceries and services in euro notes and coins. ...

Euro bank notes in each of the 12 member-states will be indistinguishable but the coins will be unique. ... All coins will be accepted throughout the euro zone.

In the words of EU Commissioner for monetary affairs, Mr Pedro Solbes: "Citizens will hold a piece of Europe in their hands every day." ...

European Central Bank (ECB) president Mr Wim Duisenberg believes the circulation of the euro will truly mark European integration. "It will, I believe, help to change the way in which we think about one another as Europeans. The euro is more than just a currency. It is a symbol of European integration in every sense of the word," he said.

In the past two years the 12 member-states have surrendered the two most important controls over their economies – the right to devalue money and set interest rates – to facilitate the introduction of the single currency. ...

A key challenge will be for the ECB to reassure the international markets that its management of the euro-zone economies will be effective. The greatest reservation centres on whether a uniform economic policy will be appropriate for each of the 12 member-states that are facing different economic problems.

The single currency by itself will not break down the barriers that are still impeding the completion of a single EU market. There are still huge price differentials between goods and services in the various states and it will take many years before these are dissolved.

The introduction of the new currency has also triggered a massive spending boom across Europe as billions of francs, deutschmarks, pesetas, pounds and schillings have been emptied out of jam jars and from under mattresses. ...

A lot of this money has never been declared for income tax and many people have decided the best way to regularise it is to spend it. Most of this money has gone into luxury goods and property.

Those travelling to any of the participating EU member-states will immediately see the benefits of a single currency, in terms of convenience and price transparency.

Within the euro zone, consumers will be able to compare the price of a cup of coffee, a car or a house, from Galway to Andalusia.

A major concern for consumers is that the euro's introduction will trigger a surge in prices as retailers round up prices. It is up to consumers to be vigilant and the Director of Consumer Affairs will also be maintaining a watching brief. But sadly there are no sanctions that can be applied other than the naming and shaming of those taking advantage of the transition.

www.ireland.com

OTHER FORMS OF MONEY

'Near money' is the term used to describe those assets which fulfil some of the functions of money but not all four of them.

1. Cheques

A bank deposit can be created in two ways. First, a person may lodge cash to a bank. Second, the bank creates a deposit for a customer when it gives that customer a loan. In the case of the loan, the bank normally credits the amount of the loan to the current account of the borrower, who can then withdraw the money in cash or else write cheques.

A cheque itself is not legal tender, nor is it part of the money supply. The claim on the bank deposit is money, and the cheque merely transfers ownership of the claim from one individual to another. The creation of bank deposits (both current accounts and deposit accounts) allows banks to create money, long after the right to print notes has been taken from them. The banks themselves seek to increase the use of cheques as methods of payment. This is done by issuing cheque cards (also called banker's cards) to customers. Such cards guarantee that the bank will honour the cheque, once certain conditions (stated on the back of the card) are fulfilled.

2. Plastic money

In recent years an increasing number of transactions are being carried out by means of plastic money. This is the term used to describe charge cards, credit cards, ATM cards and debit cards, and is seen as evidence of a move to a cashless society (*Figures 22.4* and *22.5*).

- *Charge cards* (e.g. American Express and Diners Club) allow the cardholder credit facilities in over one million outlets, e.g. shops, airports, hotels, garages, etc. worldwide. The account must be settled in full once a statement has been issued, which is usually at the end of each month.

- *Credit cards* (e.g. Access and Visa) are mainly issued through the banks. These cards provide free credit for one month, enable the holder to spread the cost of purchases over a period of months, and also provide cash withdrawal facilities.

- *ATM* (*Automated Teller Machine*) *cards* marked a further stage in the evolution of banking services. Cardholders can withdraw cash from or lodge cash to their current accounts, and transfer money between accounts.

- *Debit cards* are payment cards which allow the user to pay for goods and services electronically instead of using cash, cheques or a credit card. When making payment the buyer's card is swiped through a machine by the retailer. The buyer's account is electronically debited by the amount of the purchase while the retailer's account is credited.

Further developments in banking

In recent years the pace of change in banking services for both personal and business customers has increased steadily. Telephone banking is well established and online banking is available from most commercial banks. Customers can access their details over the phone or on personal computers, and make payments from or lodgements to their accounts. *Figure 22.6* gives a summary of the stages in the evolution of money and banking.

Fig. 22.4 Automatic teller machine

Fig. 22.5 Plastic money

Fig. 22.6 The evolution of money and banking

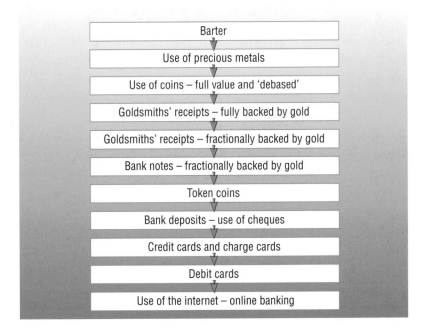

Barter
↓
Use of precious metals
↓
Use of coins – full value and 'debased'
↓
Goldsmiths' receipts – fully backed by gold
↓
Goldsmiths' receipts – fractionally backed by gold
↓
Bank notes – fractionally backed by gold
↓
Token coins
↓
Bank deposits – use of cheques
↓
Credit cards and charge cards
↓
Debit cards
↓
Use of the internet – online banking

THE IRISH FINANCIAL INSTITUTIONS

Under the Central Bank Acts 1942–1998, the Central Bank of Ireland is responsible for the licensing and supervision of all credit institutions operating in the State. As of 31 December 2000, 47 credit institutions were authorised to carry on banking business in the State under Irish legislation. These institutions had banking licences issued by the Central Bank. In addition, a further 168 credit institutions authorised in another member state of the European Union were operating in Ireland, 28 of them on a branch basis and the remainder providing deposit taking and other services on a cross border basis.

The Central Bank

This is the foremost monetary authority in the country. It regulates most of the other financial institutions. Its role will be examined in detail later in this chapter.

The Clearing Banks

These are Ireland's five biggest banks (AIB Bank, Bank of Ireland, National Irish Bank, Permanent TSB Bank and Ulster Bank). They are also called commercial banks or retail banks. These banks are privately owned and the profits they make are distributed to their shareholders. They have a virtual monopoly of current account services in Ireland. With over 900 branches nationwide, their money transmission system handles over one million transactions a day. The money transmission system includes cash payments, cheques, ATMs, credit transfers, etc. It also includes Electronic Funds Transfer Services (EFTS), which allows payment by electronic means rather than by cash and cheque. This is now used by many employers to pay wages directly into employees' bank accounts.

The main functions of the Clearing Banks are deposit taking, and lending to personal borrowers and businesses. They also provide a wide range of other services, including foreign exchange, night safe facilities, travellers' cheques, tax consultancy, advice for business, acting as trustees and executors in wills, providing credit cards and mortgages, etc.

Merchant Banks and other commercial banks

MERCHANT BANKS

The merchant banks deal with the business sector rather than with the personal borrower or saver. Because of this, they are sometimes called wholesale banks. Their activities include:

- Accepting and discounting bills of exchange. A bill of exchange is an unconditional promise by the drawer to pay a sum of money to the drawee at a specified future date, usually three months from the date of issue. The drawee may have this bill discounted at a merchant bank. In other words, he/she may cash it in before the maturity date for an amount less than its face value. The difference between the discounted value and the face value is profit to the merchant bank.
- Underwriting new issues of shares.
- Providing advice on mergers and takeovers.
- Providing financial advice for companies.
- Portfolio management, i.e. managing shares and investments.

NORTH AMERICAN BANKS

These banks bid for deposits and also give out loans. They are active borrowers and lenders on the Dublin money market. They provide advice to business, and, because of their international links, most of their dealings are with foreign companies who have manufacturing interests in Ireland.

OTHER BANKS

These include some European banks, e.g. ABN-AMRO, Banque Nationale de Paris, etc. They provide some of the services of the merchant banks and the North American banks.

Industrial Banks

These banks specialise in providing *instalment credit* to personal borrowers and companies. Personal instalment credit is used for the purchase of cars, furniture, foreign holidays, etc. They also arrange leasing (i.e. renting) of machinery and vehicles for companies.

Building Societies

These were originally set up as mutual societies. A mutual society is a company without issued capital, owned by those members that do business with it, and whose profits are shared out among members. Their sole concern was the acceptance of deposits from savers and the provision of finance for house purchase. The Building Societies Act of 1989 brought them under the control of the Central Bank for the first time. As a result of this Act, they are now able to operate current accounts, provide ATMs, give loans for purposes other than house purchase, provide foreign exchange and issue credit cards.

During the 1990s many building societies gave up their mutual status and became public limited companies (plc). As of 31 December 2000, only three

Building Societies were authorised to raise funds under the Building Societies Act, 1989 – the EBS, the ICS and Irish Nationwide.

Post Office Savings Bank

Entirely government owned, its deposits are lent to the government. It is purely a savings medium, where deposits are state guaranteed. An Post has 1,400 branches and is open six days a week.

To the above list of financial institutions can be added:

Insurance Companies

During the 1990s, life assurance companies, both Irish owned and foreign, have increased their share of the savings market. They now account for over 50 per cent of the overall domestic savings market. They mostly provide long-term life cover, but compete directly with the banks in providing a wide range of short-term savings-related schemes.

Credit Unions

These are small locally based organisations which take deposits and give loans. They are non-profit-making co-operatives set up in a locality or within a workplace or trade union. In 2002 there were more than 500 credit unions operating in Ireland, with over 2 million members who had savings of €3,600 million.

Fig. 22.7 Sandymount Credit Union, Dublin

THE INTERNATIONAL FINANCIAL SERVICES CENTRE

The International Financial Services Centre (IFSC) was established in 1987. This Centre which was built on a 27-acre site at the Customs House Docks in Dublin, was designed to accommodate both Irish-owned and foreign companies involved in financial services (*Figure 22.8*). By September 1999 there were over 485 international institutions directly operating from Dublin employing over 6,500 people directly.

Fig. 22.8 The International Financial Services Centre, Dublin

The IFSC now ranks as one of the leading locations worldwide for international banking, investment funds, corporate treasury and insurance activities. A corporation tax rate of 10 per cent will continue until 2005 for operations in existence by 1994. The Central Bank is the regulator for all financial services activities in the IFSC except for insurance activities, which are regulated by the Department of Enterprise, Trade and Employment. The Centre now extends to 39 acres and employs 11,000 people. The National College of Ireland campus was opened on the site in 2001. Presently the IFSC is the second largest funds administration and custody centre in the world with managed funds in excess of €150 billion. More than 25 of the top 50 banks in the world have operations in the IFSC.

HOW BANKS CREATE MONEY

The term commercial banks covers all those privately owned banks who operate current accounts, accept deposits, take in and pay out notes and coins and give out loans.

Commercial banks can create money by giving loans. They are able to do this because other people deposit cash with them. The banks can give out loans to a multiple of the cash deposited with them. Like the early goldsmiths, they know from experience that only a fraction (about 10%) of their depositors will wish to withdraw their money in cash form.

Let us look at how this process works. For the sake of simplicity, we will assume that there is just one bank in the country (called the Monopoly Bank), and one depositor.

Liabilities	€	Assets	€
Deposit (Mr Smith)	10,000	Cash	10,000
	10,000		10,000

Table 22.1 Balance sheet of the Monopoly Bank (initial position)

Suppose that Mr Smith lodges €10,000 cash in the bank. The balance sheet of the bank is shown in *Table 22.1*. The bank has one asset (€10,000 in cash) and one liability (the deposit of €10,000 which it owes to Mr Smith).

The bank is aware that, in other countries, only 10 per cent of the total deposits are demanded in cash. It has €10,000 in cash, so it calculates that this is enough to support total deposits of €100,000. The bank can create another €90,000 in deposits. It does this by giving out loans to a total value of €90,000. We will assume that the bank gave a loan of €10,000 each to nine people. It must be pointed out that these loans are not given in cash (since the bank has only got €10,000 in cash). They are given by opening accounts for the borrowers.

The bank calculates that only 10 per cent of its total deposits will be demanded in cash (either by Mr Smith or by some of the borrowers). So €10,000 cash is sufficient for this purpose. The new balance sheet of the bank is shown in *Table 22.2*. The bank has two assets, the cash of €10,000 and the loans which it has made, totalling €90,000. Its liabilities are made up of the claim of €10,000 which Mr Smith has on the bank, and the claims of the nine borrowers on the bank. Mr Smith and the borrowers can write cheques up to a total value of €100,000 on the bank.

Liabilities	€	Assets	€
Deposit (Mr Smith)	10,000	Cash	10,000
Deposit (others)	90,000	Loans made	90,000
		9 @£10,000 ea.	
	100,000		100,000

Table 22.2 Balance sheet of the monopoly Bank (after loans were made)

The position is exactly the same if there are a number of banks in the economy. In practice, the amount of loans the bank can give out will be determined by the Central Bank, which can increase or decrease the percentage of total deposits which must be held as cash.

> The percentage of a bank's total deposit liabilities that it must hold in cash form is called the reserve ratio (or primary liquidity ratio or cash ratio).

It can be expressed as follows:

$$\text{Reserve ratio} = \frac{\text{Cash}}{\text{Total deposits}} \times 100$$

An increase in the amount of cash deposited with a bank will allow an increase in the amount of loans granted. This is what we mean when we say that 'the commercial banks have the power to create money', or that 'the commercial banks can increase the money supply'. The increase in the money supply as a result of the actions of commercial banks can be expressed in the following equation:

Increase in money supply =
$$(\text{Increase in cash reserves} \times \frac{1}{\text{Reserve ratio}}) - \text{Increase in cash reserves}$$

In the case of our example above:

$$\text{The increase in cash reserves} = €10,000$$
$$\text{The reserve ratio} = 10\% \text{ or } 0.1$$
$$\frac{1}{\text{reserve ratio}} = 10$$

So, the increase in the money supply is:
$$(€10,000 \times 10) - €10,000 = €90,000$$

MEASURING THE MONEY SUPPLY

There are three measures of the money supply (or monetary aggregates) used by the Central Bank (see *Table 22.3*).

M1	M2	M3
Irish contribution to narrow money supply	Irish contribution to intermediate money supply	Irish contribution to broad money supply
€21,036	€92,404	€115,832
Source: Central Bank		

Table 22.3 Monetary aggregates on 28 September 2001

Irish contribution to narrow money supply (or M1)

This is currency in the hands of the public plus current accounts held at the state offices of all credit institutions by Irish and other monetary union resident private sector entities. By private sector entities is meant, Irish and other monetary union resident entities other than credit institutions, the Central Bank and the Central Government.

Irish contribution to intermediate money supply (or M2)

This is M1 plus deposits with an agreed maturity of up to two years or a period of notice of up to three months held at the state offices of all credit institutions and the Post Office Savings Bank by Irish and other monetary union private sector entities.

Irish contribution to broad money supply (or M3)

This is M2 plus debt securities with a maturity of up to two years issued by the state offices of all credit institutions to Irish and other monetary union private sector entities.

THE INTER-BANK MARKET

This is the name given to the money market in which banks can borrow or lend among themselves for fixed periods. Banks which have surplus funds can lend to banks which have short-term liquidity problems. The lending can be for as short a period as one day. The inter-bank market is a major source of day-to-day liquidity for the banking system.

Interest rates are the prices paid for money. This price increases or decreases as changes occur in the demand for and supply of money. A shortage of liquidity on the inter-bank market causes interest rates to rise. A surplus of liquidity on the inter-bank market causes interest rates to fall.

Inter-bank market interest rates are therefore a form of wholesale interest rate. The Dublin inter-bank offer rate (DIBOR) is the most widely known wholesale rate. Inter-bank rates, together with competition between the banks, largely determine the retail interest rates which banks charge to borrowers, in much the same way as the prices for goods in shops are determined by what the wholesaler charges the retailer.

STRUCTURE OF A BANK'S ASSETS

A bank wishes to be as profitable as possible, yet it must retain sufficient cash to satisfy its customers' needs. Thus it is faced with a conflict between its desire for profitability and its need for liquidity.

The profitable (earning) assets of the bank are:

* *Term loans* (one to seven years) and overdrafts (payable on demand)
* *Government stock* (one to 15 years), bought on the stock exchange. These are known as gilt-edged securities and earn a fixed rate of interest, with a fixed maturity date.

The liquid assets of the bank are those assets which can be turned into cash quickly. They comprise:

* *Exchequer Bills and Bills of Exchange.* Bills of Exchange relate to the private sector and have already been explained. Exchequer Bills are instruments for short-term borrowing by the government. They are promissory notes to pay the bearer the face value of the bill in 91 days plus interest.
* *Money at call and short notice.* This is money loaned on the inter-bank market on a very short-term basis. It includes overnight loans and loans for up to 14 days. These loans are regarded as part of the liquid assets of the bank because they can be turned into cash very quickly.
* *Cash.* This is the most liquid of all assets.

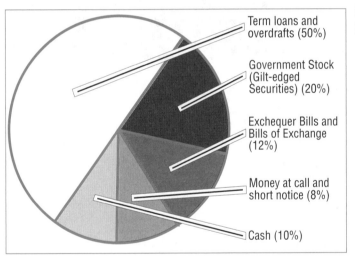

Term loans and overdrafts (50%)

Government Stock (Gilt-edged Securities) (20%)

Exchequer Bills and Bills of Exchange (12%)

Money at call and short notice (8%)

Cash (10%)

Fig. 22.9 The structure of a bank's assets

Figure 22.9 gives an example of the way a bank might structure its assets. The figure in brackets refers to the percentage of total assets which might be accounted for by that item.

THE CENTRAL BANK

The Central Bank of Ireland was established in 1943 (*Figure 22.10*). It was a national bank which operated in the public interest, unlike the other banks whose primary responsibility is to their shareholders. Its duty was 'the safeguarding of the integrity of the currency'. This means it had responsibility for protecting the value of the currency. Traditionally it was also responsible for implementing *monetary policy* in Ireland. By monetary policy we mean the government's economic policy in relation to:

- The rate of interest
- The money supply
- The availability of credit
- The value of the currency.

Fig. 22.10 The Central Bank of Ireland on Dame Street, Dublin

With the establishment of Economic and Monetary Union on 1 January 1999, member states could no longer pursue their own independent monetary policies. The role of the Central Bank of Ireland has thus changed significantly in recent years, and it now is a member of the European System of Central Banks (ECSB), whose main objective is the maintenance of price stability in the eurozone.

European System of Central Banks

The European System of Central Banks (ESCB) includes:
- The European Central Bank
- The National Central Banks (NCBs) of member states (including the Central Bank of Ireland).

European Central Bank

The European Central Bank was established in June 1998, and in January 1999 it became responsible for formulating and implementing monetary policy in the euro area. It has three decision-making bodies as follows:

1. The Executive Board, comprising the President, vice-President and four other appointees.

2. The General Council, comprising the Executive Board and the governors of the Central Banks of all 15 EU member states.

3. The Governing Council, comprising the Executive Board and the governors of the Central Banks of the 12 eurozone countries.

The Governing Council formulates monetary policy in the eurozone. Each member has one vote so each country's governor has an equal say in decision-making. The Executive Board implements monetary policy and gives the necessary instructions to the national central banks.

Fig. 22.11 The European Central Bank located in Frankfurt, Germany

Functions of European System of Central Banks

1. To define and implement monetary policy in the eurozone.
2. To hold and manage official external reserves.
3. To carry out foreign exchange operations.
4. To promote the smooth operation of the payments system.
5. To contribute to the supervision of credit institutions in member states and the stability of the financial system.

The main monetary policy instruments of the Eurosystem are:

1. *Main refinancing operations* (MROs). These are open market operations with credit institutions carried out on a weekly basis (by repurchase agreements) to provide liquidity. This liquidity is provided on a tender basis and the rate charged will affect interest rates throughout the zone.

2. *Standing facilities.* These are made up of:
   - *The marginal lending facility* which allows credit institutions to draw down overnight liquidity from the ECB (and provides a ceiling for the overnight market interest rate), and
   - *The deposit facility* which allows credit institutions to make overnight deposits with the Bank (and provides a floor for the overnight market interest rate).

3. *Minimum reserve requirements.* Credit institutions in the eurozone are required to hold minimum deposits with their respective national central banks. The purpose of this is to stabilise money market interest rates by dealing with daily liquidity fluctuations.

In Ireland these monetary policy instruments are carried out by the Central Bank of Ireland, which is also charged with responsibility for the maintenance of price stability under the Central Bank Act of 1998.

Functions of Central Bank of Ireland – following economic and monetary union

1. As outlined above, the Central Bank is responsible for implementing the monetary policy of the ECB within Ireland, using the instruments described above.

2. Section 6(1) of the Central Bank Act, 1998 states that 'in discharging its functions as part of the European System of Central Banks, the primary objective of the Bank shall be to maintain price stability'.

3. The Bank exercises supervisory functions over a range of financial entities. These include credit institutions, both in terms of banks and building societies, International Financial Services Centre (IFSC) operations, stock exchange member firms, investment intermediaries and insurance intermediaries. The objectives of such supervision are to protect the stability of the banking system and to provide a degree of protection to depositors and investors. It is illegal to take deposits in Ireland without authorisation from the Central Bank. An appendix to its annual report each year includes a list of those credit institutions authorised to carry on banking business in the State.

4. The Bank is responsible for supplying the currency needs of Ireland and produces the Irish euro notes and coins. At its currency centre in Sandyford,

Co Dublin, the Central Bank started the minting of its euro coins in September 1999, while the printing of its euro banknotes started in June 2000. By 1 January 2002, the date for the introduction of the euro notes and coins into circulation, the Central Bank had minted over 1 billion coins and printed over 300 million banknotes.

Fig. 22.12 Euro notes and coins came into circulation on 1 January 2002

5. The Central Bank holds and manages the *official external reserves*. These are the country's official holdings of gold, foreign currencies and other reserves held as security against the issue of the euro. *Table 22.4* shows the official external reserves of the Central Bank in September 2001.

In addition to these reserves the Bank also had €2,070 million of euro-denominated assets (arising from its holdings of EMU currencies, prior to January 1999). The board of the Bank determines how these reserves are managed. It must decide the currency composition of non-euro reserves, the choice of investment instruments for these reserves and the overall degree of risk appropriate for its investment activities.

Gold (€m)	SDRs (€m)	Reserve position In IMF (€m)	Foreign Exchange (€m)	Total (€m)
57	51	344	5,355	5,807
Source: Central Bank				

Table 22.4 Official external reserves, September 2001

6. The Central Bank carries out economic research relevant to the Bank, the ECB, the ECSB and the Irish economy as a whole. This research helps to determine overall monetary policy in the eurozone and is also useful to the Irish government. Its Annual Report gives a detailed account of its activities in the past year while its Quarterly Bulletins provide a range of articles and statistics on monetary matters in Ireland and abroad.

7. The Central Bank acts as agent for and banker to the government. All government revenues (e.g. taxes) are paid into the Central Bank, while all payments made by the government are drawn on its account at the Central Bank.

8. The Central Bank is accountable to the Dáil and Seanad for its activities each year. Its accounts are audited by an independent firm of auditors. Its Governor is required to attend meetings of joint Oireachtas committees, if requested to do so. In 2000 the Bank's net profit was €520 million of which €451 million was paid to the Exchequer.

23

The Measurement of National Income

Aperson's income is the wealth he/she receives for producing something.

National income is the total income earned by the residents of a country in one year.

Just as a person's income reflects the value of the goods or services he/she produces in a year, national income reflects the total value of all goods and services produced by the residents of a country during the year. There are three ways in which the total wealth produced in a country can be measured:

1. We can add up all the incomes received in the country during the year. This is known as the **income method**.
2. We can add up the value of the goods and services produced in the country during the year. This is known as the **output method**.
3. We can add the total amount of money spent on goods and services in the country during the year, adding on the value of exports and subtracting the value of imports. This is known as the **expenditure method**.

It is important to note that: National Income = National Output = National Expenditure

To see this clearly, we will examine the relationship between income, output and expenditure at the level of the individual. Suppose a wood turner who specialises in making table lamps can produce 10 lamps a week which he sells for €100 each. His weekly income is €1000. If he works 46 weeks in a year his annual income is €46,000. The value of the output he produces is €46,000 during the year. Similarly, the total expenditure (by others) on the goods produced by this man during the year is €46,000. So income equals output, which equals expenditure.

Since national income, national output and national expenditure are the same, the Central Statistics Office uses all three methods to ensure a more reliable measure of the total amount of goods and services produced in the country during the year. We will now examine each of these methods in turn.

THE INCOME METHOD

Table 23.1 shows the National Income of Ireland in 2000, as measured by the income method. The figures here are mainly based on the annual returns made for income tax purposes. People earn incomes by supplying land, labour, capital and enterprise. In return they receive rent, wages, interest and profits.

	€m	€m
1. Income from agriculture, forestry and fishing		2,976
2. Non-agricultural income:		
(a) Company profits, trading profits and professional earnings	36,932	
(b) Wages and salaries	41,410	
(c) Rent (actual and imputed)	5,051	
		83,393
3. Adjustments:		
(a) Stock appreciation	−841	
(b) Financial services	−4,312	
		−5,153
4. Net domestic product at factor cost		81,216
5. Net factor income from rest of world		−16,348
6. Net national product at factor cost (= national income)		64,868
Source: National Income and Expenditure, 2000, CSO		

Table 23.1 The income method, 2000

Explanation

1. The total incomes earned by farmers, farm workers, forestry workers and fishermen. It includes income in kind, e.g. farm output which is consumed on the farm.
2. (a) This includes company profits, incomes of self-employed people, etc.
   (b) This is the biggest item. It includes wages, salaries, overtime, commission and income in kind (e.g. use of a company car).
   (c) Actual rent is rent received from the ownership of property. If you own the house you live in, you are assumed to be receiving an income equal to the amount you could get if you let it. This is known as imputed rent.

3. (a) If the value of the stock of goods owned by companies and farms rises, then this overstates the actual profits made from production. A figure equal to the rise in the value of stocks must be deducted. Similarly, if the value of the stocks falls, then profits from actual production are understated. A figure equal to the fall in the value of the stocks must be added on. In 2000 the value of stocks rose. Therefore, the amount of the rise must be deducted.

   (b) This is the excess of interest and dividends received by financial institutions over payments of interest to depositors. The reason for making this adjustment is that interest and dividends received by the banks less the interest paid to depositors is taken to be the cost of providing the services to customers. As such, it should not be included in profits.

4. This is the total of Items 1, 2 and 3 above.

5. This is income earned by Irish individuals and companies abroad less the income earned by foreign individuals and companies in Ireland. This has been a minus figure since the mid 1970s, mainly because of the huge amount of profits, which foreign companies operating in Ireland send back to their parent companies abroad. Such profits are termed *repatriated profits*.

6. This is Item 4 + Item 5.

Net national product at factor cost is equal to net domestic product at factor cost plus net factor income from the rest of the world. It is also called national income.

When using the income method, the following two points should be noted:

- *Incomes in kind* must be included.

Incomes in kind are incomes received in a non-monetary form.

Examples of such incomes are:

   (a) A farmer who consumes part of the output from his farm. If the farmer sold produce worth €50,000 and his family consumed another €10,000 worth of produce, then his income is €60,000 (since his output is €60,000).

   (b) A salesperson, who has the use of a company car, has an income in kind.

- *Transfer payments* must be excluded.

Transfer payments are payments made to individuals, for which no factor of production is supplied in return.

Examples of transfer payments are children's allowances, student grants, non-contributory old age pensions, pocket money and charity payments. Because no output is produced in return for these payments they cannot be considered income. They are 'received' but not 'earned'.

THE OUTPUT METHOD

Table 23.2 shows the National Income of Ireland in 2000, as measured by the output method.

		€m	€m
1.	Agriculture, forestry and fishing		2,979
2.	Industry		36,361
3.	Distribution, transport and communication		13,678
4.	Public administration and defence		3,124
5.	Other services (including rent)		30,227
6.	Adjustments:		
	(a) Stock appreciation	−841	
	(b) Financial services	−4,312	
			−5,153
7.	Net domestic product at factor cost		81,216
8.	Plus depreciation		10,093
9.	Gross domestic product at factor cost		91,309
10.	Plus taxes on expenditure		14,445
11.	Less subsidies		−2,283
12.	Gross domestic product at current market prices		103,471
13.	Net factor income from rest of world		−16,348
14.	Gross national product at current market prices		87,123
Source: National Income and Expenditure, 2000, CSO			

Table 23.2 The output method, 2000

Explanation

1. The total value of output produced in farming, forestry and fishing.
2. The total value of output produced by industrial and building firms.
3. The total value of services provided by those involved in distribution, transport and communication.
4. The total value of services provided by those in central and local government, the army, and gardaí.
5. The total earnings of all those employed in the professions, financial and insurance companies, health services, personal services, hotels, entertainment and sport.
6. See under 'The Income Method'.
7. The sum of Items 1 to 6.
8. The value of capital goods which were used up during the year. Since gross

output minus depreciation equals net output, net output plus depreciation equals gross output.

9. *Gross domestic product* (GDP) at factor cost is equal to net domestic product at factor cost plus depreciation.

GDP at factor cost measures the total amount of goods and services produced in the economy during the year, valued at the cost of production, that is, in terms of the incomes paid to the factors of production.

10. These are taxes on goods and services, e.g. VAT, customs and excise duties, etc. They raise the selling price of goods and services, and must be added to GDP at factor cost to get GDP at current market prices.

11. These are the opposite of indirect taxes.

Subsidies are payments by the government to producers to enable them to sell their products at a lower price.

They reduce the selling price of goods and services, and must be deducted from GDP at factor cost to get GDP at current market prices.

12. In *Table 23.2*: Item 12 = Item 9 + Item 10 – Item 11.

GDP at current market prices is equal to gross domestic product at factor cost plus taxes on expenditure minus subsidies.

13. See under 'The Income Method'.

14. In *Table 23.2*, Item 14 = Item 12 + Item 13.

Gross national product (GNP) at current market prices is equal to gross domestic product (DGP) at current market prices, plus net factor income from abroad.

To get the figure for net national product at factor cost (i.e. national income), we must continue as shown in *Table 23.3*.

	€m
1. Gross national product at current market prices	87,123
2. Less taxes on expenditure	−14,445
Plus subsidies	2,283
3. Gross national product at factor cost	74,961
4. Less depreciation	−10,093
5. Net national product at factor cost (= national income)	64,868

Table 23.3 The output method (continued)

Using the output method

When using the output method, great care must be taken to avoid '*double counting*'. If a carpenter buys a piece of wood for €200 and makes a table worth

€500, his output is €300, not €500. The value of output of a firm is, therefore, the selling price of its goods less the cost of raw materials used in production. This is known as the *value added* of the firm.

THE EXPENDITURE METHOD

Table 23.4 shows the National Income of Ireland in 2000, as measured by the expenditure method.

	€m
1. Personal consumption of goods and services	50,685
2. Net expenditure by central and local government on current goods and services	12,573
3. Gross domestic fixed capital formation	24,449
4. Value of physical changes in stocks	1,083
5. Exports of goods and services	98,165
6. Less imports of goods and services	−83,484
7. Gross domestic product at current market prices	103,471
8. Net factor income from rest of world	−16,348
9. Gross national product at current market prices	87,123
Source: National Income and Expenditure, 2000, CSO	

Table 23.4 The expenditure method

Explanation

1. This is all the money spent by people on food, clothing, entertainment, household goods, cars, etc.
2. Money spent by central and local government on items which are used up during the year, e.g. wages, salaries, goods, services, materials, etc.
3. This is investment by both private companies and government, e.g. factories, roads, harbours, machinery, transport equipment, airports, etc.
4. This is the estimated value of changes in 'stocks'. These stocks include livestock, stocks of raw materials and finished goods, and work in progress. If stocks increase, the amount of the increase is added to the other items of expenditure. If stocks decrease, the amount of the decrease is deducted from the other items of expenditure.
5. Goods and services produced in Ireland and sold abroad. Exports earn income for those who produced them and so are added to the other items of expenditure.
6. Goods and services produced abroad which are bought by Irish people. Money spent on imports does not earn income for Irish people. Therefore, imports are subtracted from the other items of expenditure.

7. This is derived by adding Items 1 to 5 and subtracting Item 6.
8. See under 'The Income Method'.
9. This is derived by adding Items 7 and 8: Item 9 = Item 7 + Item 8.

As was the case when using the output method, to get the figure for net national product at factor cost (i.e. national income), we must continue as shown in *Table 23.5*.

	€m
1. Gross national product at current market prices	87,123
2. Less taxes on expenditure	−14,445
Plus subsidies	2,283
3. Gross national product at factor cost	74,961
4. Less depreciation	−10,093
5. Net national product at factor cost (= national income)	64,868

Table 23.5 The expenditure method (continued)

GLOSSARY OF TERMS

National income (net national product at factor cost)	Total of all incomes earned by the permanent residents of a country (whether earned in that country or abroad).
Net domestic product at factor cost	Total income earned from the production of goods and services within the state.
Gross domestic product at factor cost	Net domestic product at factor cost plus depreciation.
Gross national product at factor cost	Net national product at factor cost (i.e. national income) plus depreciation.
Gross national product at current market prices	Gross national product at factor cost plus taxes on expenditure minus subsidies.
Gross national product at factor cost	Plus/minus net factor income from abroad equals gross domestic product at factor cost.

CURRENT AND CONSTANT PRICES

If I earned €40,000 in 2002 and €44,000 in 2003, it might appear that I am 10 per cent 'better off' in 2003 than I was in 2002. However, this may not be the case. If prices had increased by 6 per cent over the year, then I will need €42,400 in 2003 to purchase the same goods and services that I bought in 2002. In this situation, an increase in my salary to €44,000 represents an increase in my standard of living of 4 per cent (i.e. 1,600 / 40,000). So I am only 4 per cent better off.

The same applies to the national income figures. Very often, what appears to be a large rise in GDP may really be a much smaller rise (or perhaps even a fall) when we 'allow for inflation'. This is because GDP in the *Tables* above was measured at current market prices, i.e. at the prices prevailing in the market at the time.

To overcome this problem, we can measure GDP at constant prices. This is very simple. We measure GDP in the second year at the prices prevailing in the first year. A short example will illustrate this.

Example: Suppose a country produces two goods, wheat and beef.

2002 output at 2002 prices

Wheat: 1,000 tonnes at €200 per tonne	=	€200,000
Beef: 500 tonnes at €400 per tonne	=	€200,000
Gross domestic product at current market prices	=	€400,000

2003 output at 2003 prices

Wheat: 1,200 tonnes at €240 per tonne	=	€288,000
Beef: 624 tonnes at €500 per tonne	=	€312,000
GDP at current market prices	=	€600,000

There has been a 50 per cent increase in GDP at current market prices. Does this mean the country is 50 per cent better off in 2003? The calculation of GDP at constant prices shows that it is not 50 per cent better off in 2003.

2003 output at 2002 prices

Wheat: 1200 tonnes at €200 per tonne	=	€240,000
Beef: 624 tonnes at €400 per tonne	=	€249,600
		€489,600

GDP at constant prices has risen by 22.4 per cent between 2002 and 2003 (i.e. 89,600 / 400,000). Another way of saying this is that the annual rate of growth of real GDP was 22.4 per cent. *Table 23.6* shows GDP at current market prices and GDP at constant (1995) prices for Ireland for the period 1995–2000.

Year	GDP at current market prices (€m)	GDP at constant (1995) prices (€m)
1995	41,502	41,502
1996	45,725	44,719
1997	52,781	49,564
1998	60,729	53,830
1999	70,116	59,671
2000	81,489	66,511
Source: National Income and Expenditure, 2000, CSO		

Table 23.6 GDP at current and constant (1995) prices for period 1995–2000

USES AND LIMITATIONS OF NATIONAL INCOME STATISTICS

Gross domestic product (GDP) at current market prices is the most commonly used indicator of the economic performance of a country. It measures the goods and services produced within the country during the year, and values them at the prices at which they were sold.

GDP is used for three basic purposes:
1. To see if the income (output) of a country is rising from one year to the next.
2. To make international comparisons, i.e. to see how our income (output) compares with other countries.
3. To assist the government in choosing the correct policies for the country. For example, if output fell, additional government spending might be required.

However, GDP as a measure of a country's economic performance is not perfect. Care needs to be taken when using the figures. The main points to be considered are discussed below.

1. Constant prices

To see if output rose from one year to the next, GDP must be expressed in constant prices, as explained already.

2. The larger the population, the larger the GDP

The USA, with a population of 274 million, had a GDP in 1998 of $8,011 billion. In the same year, Ireland, with a population of 3.7 million, had a GDP of €77.1

billion. In order to make meaningful statements about the standard of living in both countries, two things need to be done.

Firstly, we must express GDP in both countries in the *same currency*. The US dollar is generally chosen for this purpose. So, for Ireland in 1998, we can say that GDP was $69.23 billion. Second, we must find out GDP *per capita* (i.e. per person). This is done by dividing total GDP by the population of the country. The USA has, therefore, a GDP per person of $29,240, while the figure for Ireland is $18,710. This is how the figures in *Table 31.1* are derived.

3. Distribution of income

Unfortunately, GDP per person does not tell us anything about the distribution of income. A high GDP per person may hide very large inequalities in the distribution of income. A simple example will illustrate this.

Suppose there are two countries, X and Y, both of which have 10 inhabitants. The incomes of the inhabitants are as follows:

Country X: 10 people, each earning 20,000 a year.

Total income (GDP)	=	200,000
GDP per person	=	20,000

Country Y: 10 people, nine who earn 10,000 a year each. The tenth person earns 110,000 a year.

Total income (GDP)	=	200,000
GDP per person	=	20,000

An examination of total GDP and GDP per person would lead one to the conclusion that both countries enjoy the same standard of living. Yet the distribution of income is such that 'the average person' in Country X enjoys a much higher standard of living than in Country Y.

4. Non-market economic activities

GDP figures do not include '*non-market economic activities*'. These are the goods and services produced in a country which are *not recorded.* In most countries, there are people who understate their income in order to avoid paying tax. Also, some people may be registered as unemployed and yet produce goods and services. Their output is not recorded and so does not appear in the GDP figures.

The more *market-oriented* the economy, the greater the level of GDP. By market-oriented, we mean an economy where a high proportion of goods and services produced are paid for and recorded. In many of the poorest countries of the world, a man may provide food, clothing and shelter for himself. Since little or no payment is made, these productive activities do not show up in the national accounts, so the GDP figures understate the real level of output of such countries.

5. Standard of living

A rising GDP per person may be as a result of a longer working week, or shorter holidays. Therefore, it might be the case that the standard of living of the people has been reduced, rather than increased.

6. Nature of goods produced

GDP figures do not take into account the nature of the goods produced. This is particularly true in the case of government spending. Country A might have a total GDP of €10 billion, half of which is devoted to the production of military equipment. Country B might have the same total GDP, with only a small fraction devoted to the production of military expenditure, and the balance of government spending devoted to schools, factories, hospitals, roads, etc. It is obvious that the inhabitants of Country B enjoy a higher standard of living.

7. Government involvement

In comparing the GDP of different countries, another point to bear in mind is the extent to which the government provides goods and services. In some countries, the extent of government involvement in the provision of goods and services is quite high (e.g. in centrally planned economies and in countries with many state-sponsored bodies). In others, such as the USA, the vast majority of goods and services are provided by private individuals and companies, with little or no state involvement. The output produced by the private sector is valued at selling price. However, many of the goods and services supplied by the state are provided free (or at a reduced price), for example, education, health care, etc. If services are provided free, they must be valued at cost price (since there is no selling price). If services are supplied at a low price, the country will record a lower GDP than that of other countries with the same standard of living. Therefore, we can make the following statement.

> The greater the extent to which the state provides goods and services, the lower the figure for GDP that will be recorded in the national accounts.

In a list of countries ranked by GDP per person, (such as *Table 31.1*), such countries will appear *poorer* than they really are.

241

8. Rent paid and imputed

We have already seen above that both rent paid and imputed rent are included as income in the national accounts. If Ms Smith rents her house for €1000 per month, then a figure of €12,000 appears as income to the landlord (in Item 2(c) in *Table 23.1*). If Ms Jones, who lives next door, owns her own house, then a figure for imputed rent (say, €6,000 per annum) is included as part of her income in the accounts. Imputed rents will be lower than actual rents. Therefore we can make the following statement.

> The greater the number of people who own their own houses, the lower the figure for GDP that will appear in the national accounts.

9. Rate of exchange

We have already seen that in order to make international comparisons of income per person, we had to express GDP per person in a single currency. In order to do this, the official rate of exchange is normally used. However, the official rate of exchange is very much influenced by international trade. The greater the volume of exports of a country, the greater is the value of its currency.

Suppose two countries, A and B, produce exactly the same amount of goods and services. Country A does not engage very much in international trade. Most of what it produces is used within the country, so its exports are small. Consequently, the value of its currency will be low. Country B produces exactly the same amount of goods and services but much of its output is exported. Therefore, the value of its currency will be high. Even though both countries produce the same output, Country B will appear to be a wealthier country when international comparisons are made. We can now make the following statement:

> The greater the percentage of a country's output which is traded internationally, the greater is the figure for its GDP, when converted to a common currency (to facilitate international comparisons). Therefore, countries which are relatively self-sufficient will have their GDP understated in international comparisons.

10. GDP shows income of country only

We have already pointed out that increased income does not mean *increased welfare*. GDP figures only show one aspect of a country's welfare, namely, income.

The United Nations have devised a Human Development Index that is published annually, and which ranks countries according to their citizens' quality of life rather than just on income figures alone (see *Tables 23.7* and *23.8*). The criteria for calculating rankings include:

- Life expectancy
- Adult literacy
- Whether average income is sufficient to meet basic needs
- School enrolment
- Educational attainment
- Per capita GDP.

Most Liveable Countries, 2001			
1	Norway	14	United Kingdom
2	Australia	15	Denmark
3	Canada	16	Austria
4	Sweden	17	Germany
5	Belgium	18	Ireland
6	United States	19	New Zealand
7	Iceland	20	Italy
8	Netherlands	21	Spain
9	Japan	22	Israel
10	Finland	23	Greece
11	Switzerland	24	Cyprus
12	Luxembourg	25	Singapore
13	France		
Source: Human Development Report, 2001, United Nations			

Table 23.7 Most liveable countries, 2001

Least Liveable Countries, 2001			
1	Sierra Leone	14	Gambia
2	Niger	15	Eritrea
3	Burundi	16	Benin
4	Burkina Faso	17	Angola
5	Ethiopia	18	Senegal
6	Mozambique	19	Côte d'Ivoire
7	Guinea-Bissau	20	Zambia
8	Chad	21	Congo, Dem. Rep. of
9	Central African Republic	22	Uganda
10	Mali	23	Tanzania
11	Rwanda	24	Mauritania
12	Malawi	25	Sudan
13	Guinea		
Source: Human Development Report, 2001, United Nations			

Table 23.8 Least liveable countries, 2001

Fig. 23.1 Norway – the most liveable country in 2001

24

Factors Affecting Size of National Income

In the previous chapter, we defined national income as the sum total of all incomes earned by the residents of a country in a year. We then examined the three methods of measuring national income. We noted that the size of national income varied enormously from one country to another. The purpose of this chapter is to analyse those factors which affect the size of national income, so that we can understand why such differences exist. We will see how income spent by one person creates income for others. We will then examine the role of the government in influencing the size of national income.

WHAT DETERMINES SIZE OF NATIONAL INCOME?

To answer the question what determines size of national income in a country, we must distinguish between the potential level of national income and the actual level of national income.

The potential level of national income is the maximum level of output the economy is capable of producing, given its resources.

This depends, not only on the quantity of land, labour, capital and enterprise available in the country, but also on the quality of such factors of production. Agricultural output depends not only on the quantity of land in use, but on its fertility, its correct use and the presence of an adequate system of irrigation. In the case of labour, the volume of output depends not only on the size of the labour force, but also on its level of skill and adaptability, the length of the working week, length of holidays, etc. In the case of capital, the more advanced the technology available in a country, the higher the potential level of output.

Finally, we must remember that the presence of plentiful supplies of land, labour and capital does not guarantee a high level of national income. Entrepreneurial talent is also required. Those countries which promote enterprise and risk-taking, by giving generous rewards to people with such abilities, will be able to achieve a higher level of national income.

Two further points need to be made. First, the potential level of national income is not constant. As the stock of factors of production increases over time, the ability of the economy to produce more goods and services also increases. Second, if all the resources in the economy are not being fully utilised at present, then the actual level of national income will be less than the potential level.

The actual level of national income (Y) in an economy depends on the following five factors:

1. Consumption (C)
2. Investment (I)
3. Government expenditure (G)
4. Exports (X)
5. Imports (M)

The first four of these create income within the country, while imports create income in other countries.

$$Y = C + I + G + X - M$$

Consumption

When people receive income, they spend most of it and save part of it. So we can say, income (Y) equals consumption (C) plus savings (S).

$$Y = C + S$$

Consumption depends on many things – availability of credit facilities, the rate of interest, etc. However, the most important factor affecting consumption, according to the great English economist JM Keynes (see *Chapter 33*), was the level of income itself. So we can say that consumption (C) depends on income (Y).

$$C = f(Y)$$
If Y rises, C rises.
If Y falls, C falls.

When people get an increase in income, they spend more on consumer goods. If their incomes fall, people spend less on consumer goods. Keynes said that as incomes rise, people increase their consumption, but not by as much as the increase in income. The marginal propensity to consume (MPC) is greater than 0, but less than 1.

> **The marginal propensity to consume (MPC) is the fraction of extra income which is consumed.**

Suppose I spend €18,000 out of my income of €20,000. Then I receive an increase in income of €1,000. If I now spend a total of €18,800, then my MPC is 0.8. Out of my extra income of €1,000, I spent €800. We can express MPC as follows:

$$MPC = \frac{\Delta C}{\Delta Y}$$
where ΔC = change in consumption
ΔY = change in income

The *average propensity to consume* (APC) is simply the fraction of income spent, that is:

$$APC = \frac{C}{Y}$$

> **The marginal propensity to save (MPS) is the fraction of extra income which is saved.**

Returning to the example above, when I got an increase in income of €1,000, I spent an extra €800, so I saved an extra €200. Therefore, my MPS was 0.2. We can express the marginal propensity to save as follows:

$$MPS = \frac{\Delta S}{\Delta Y}$$

Note that MPC + MPS = 1.

The average propensity to save is simply the fraction of income saved, that is:

$$APS = \frac{S}{Y}$$

Investment

Investment is another form of spending. It is spending by business people on capital equipment – machines, plant and equipment, new factory buildings, etc. When business people undertake investment, they do so in the hope of making profit. The level of investment (I) depends mainly on two factors: the expectations of business people (E) and the rate of interest (r).

If business people expect an increase in the demand for the goods they produce, then they will be willing to undertake additional investment. If the rate of interest rises, the cost of borrowing increases. Therefore, we can say that the higher the rate of interest, the less investment that will be undertaken. We can express the factors affecting investment as follows:

$$I = f(E, r)$$

Investment is said to be independent of the level of income.

Government spending

The size of government spending will depend on the decisions of government, as laid out in the annual budget. It is independent of the level of income.

Exports

The size of exports depends on the strength of demand abroad for the goods and services we produce. This is something which is largely outside our control. Exports are independent of the level of income.

Imports

The size of imports depends directly on income. As incomes in an economy increase, the level of imports will increase. There are two reasons for this. First, when their incomes rise people spend more. It is only to be expected that some of this increased spending will go on imports. Second, increasing incomes in an economy reflect increasing output. To achieve additional output, extra raw materials will be required. Some of these raw materials will have to be imported. Therefore, we can say that imports (M) depend on income (Y), that is:

$$M = f(Y)$$
If Y rises, M rises.
If Y falls, M falls.

The marginal propensity to import (MPM) is the fraction of extra income in an economy which is spent on imports.

$$MPM = \frac{\Delta M}{\Delta Y}$$

Similarly, the *average propensity to import* (APM) is the fraction of income spent on imports.

$$APM = \frac{M}{Y}$$

THE CIRCULAR FLOW OF INCOME

This is the name given to a simple model which shows the workings of an economy. It shows the movement of resources from firms to households, and from households to firms.

Step 1

As a starting point, we will look at a closed economy, that is, where there are no imports and exports. We will assume that all income is spent (i.e. there are no savings). We will also ignore the government sector. *Figure 24.1* shows the circular flow of income in such an economy.

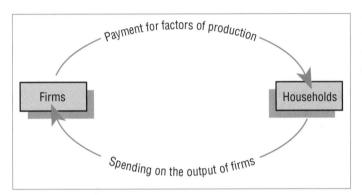

Fig. 24.1 The circular flow of income in a closed economy, with no savings and no government sector

Firms, in order to produce output, require land, labour, capital and enterprise. Households supply these factors. Households receive income in return, in the form of rent, wages, interest and profit. With these incomes, households are able to purchase the output of firms.

Step 2

We have already seen that not all of income is consumed. People save part of their incomes. They may deposit such savings in banks and other financial institutions, as shown in *Figure 24.2*. Consequently, not all of the income received by households is returned by them to firms. This causes firms to cut back on production. There is no point in producing goods if people are not prepared to buy them. Therefore, the effect of savings is to reduce the circular flow of income. This may seem surprising at first. However, remember that many firms close down due to a fall in demand for the goods and services they produce. In other words, there is not enough spending by households to keep them in business.

Saving is said to be a withdrawal (or leakage) from the circular flow of income.

A withdrawal or leakage is something which reduces the flow of income in the economy.

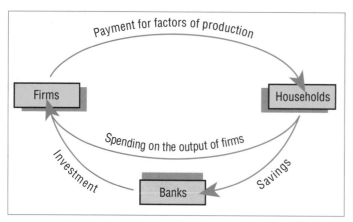

Fig. 24.2 The circular flow of income with savings and investment in a closed economy, with no government sector

The greater the fraction of income which is saved, the smaller the flow of income throughout the economy.

However, things are not as bad as they seem. The money which households save is deposited in banks and other financial institutions. It is available to business people who wish to borrow for investment purposes. In fact, the banks can give out more in loans than is deposited with them. Investment represents an injection into the circular flow of income, since firms need more factors of production in order to expand output.

An injection is something which causes the flow of income in the economy to increase.

NET EFFECT OF SAVING (S) AND INVESTMENT (I) ON CIRCULAR FLOW OF INCOME

1. If investment is greater than saving, the circular flow of income will rise. There is said to be 'an increase in the level of economic activity'.
2. If investment is less than saving, the circular flow of income will fall. There is said to be a 'reduction in the level of economic activity'.
3. If investment is equal to saving, the circular flow of income does not change.

We can express this more concisely as follows:

$$\text{If } I > S, \text{ then Y rises}$$
$$\text{If } I < S, \text{ then Y falls}$$
$$\text{If } I = S, \text{ then Y remains unchanged}$$

Step 3

Figure 24.3 shows the effect of international trade on the circular flow of income. When households spend part of their incomes on imports, there is a withdrawal from the circular flow of income. Incomes are created in other countries as a result of such expenditure. On the other hand, exports constitute an injection into the circular flow of income since money spent abroad on our exports creates income here. Exports represent a demand abroad for the goods produced by home firms. This in turn will lead to an increase in the demand for factors of production to make these goods. So the payments to the factors of production will increase.

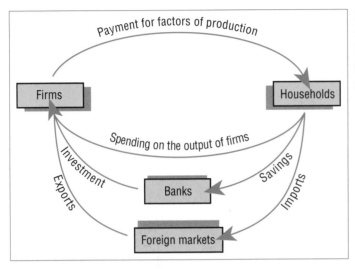

Fig. 24.3 The circular flow of income with savings, investment and international trade, but no government sector

---

NET EFFECT OF INTERNATIONAL TRADE ON CIRCULAR FLOW OF INCOME

1. If exports (X) are greater than imports (M), the circular flow of income will rise, i.e. there will be an increase in the level of economic activity.
2. If exports are less than imports, the circular flow of income will fall, i.e. there will be a reduction in the level of economic activity.
3. If exports are equal to imports, there is no change in the level of economic activity.

We can express this more concisely as follows:

If $X > M$, then Y rises
If $X < M$, then Y falls
If $X = M$, then Y remains unchanged

Step 4

Figure 24.4 represents the full circular flow of income model. It shows the effect of government on the circular flow of income. Government reduces the circular flow of income by imposing taxation. Taxation of incomes reduces the disposable income of households, and consequently reduces the amount of goods and services that households can purchase. Indirect taxes (i.e. on goods and services) have the same effect. Similarly, taxation of company profits reduces the ability of firms to purchase additional factors of production and so reduces the level of economic activity. On the other hand, the government increases the circular flow of income when it undertakes expenditure.

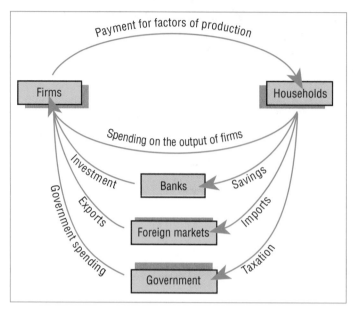

Fig. 24.4 The complete circular flow of income, with a banking sector, foreign markets and a government sector

Government spending can be on the output of goods and services of firms, the payment of social welfare, etc. or the payment of wages to state employees. The effect of each of these forms of spending is to increase the level of economic activity in the state. (Note in *Figure 24.4* we showed taxation as levied only on households, and government spending as only going to firms. This was done solely to keep the diagram simple.)

NET EFFECT OF GOVERNMENT ON CIRCULAR FLOW OF INCOME

1. If government spending (G) exceeds taxation (T), the circular flow of income will rise, i.e. there will be an increase in the level of economic activity.
2. If government spending is less than taxation, the circular flow of income will fall, i.e. there will be a reduction in the level of economic activity.
3. If government spending equals taxation, the circular flow of income is unchanged.

We can express this more concisely as follows:

If G > T, then Y rises

If G < T, then Y falls

If G = T, then Y remains unchanged

Summary of circular flow of income

The circular flow of income represents the flow of resources between the different sectors of the economy. Anything which causes the circular flow of income to increase is called an injection. Anything which causes the circular flow of income to fall is called a withdrawal (or leakage).

Injections	Withdrawals (or leakages)
1. Investment (I)	1. Savings (S)
2. Exports (X)	2. Imports (M)
3. Government spending (G)	3. Taxation (T)

MULTIPLIER IN CLOSED ECONOMY WITH NO GOVERNMENT SECTOR

We have seen above that injections increase the level of income in the economy and withdrawals reduce it. To understand how this works, we will return to the type of economy depicted in *Figure 24.2*. There is only one form of injection (i.e. investment), and only one form of withdrawal (i.e. saving).

Let us assume that firms in the economy decide to invest €100m. All of this will be spent on the output of goods and services produced by other firms in the economy (builders, builders' providers, hardware shops, architects, engineers, etc.). Let us assume that the marginal propensity to consume in this economy is 0.8. In other words, people spend 0.8 or 80 per cent of any extra income they receive.

The €100m spent on investment is income to other firms and individuals of €100m
Those who receive this €100m will spend 80% of it, so others receive income of €80m
Those who receive the €80m will spend 80% of this, so others receive an income of.. €64m
Those who receive the €64m will spend 80% of this, so others receive €51m
...and so on.

If we continued this process, we would find that as a result of an initial investment of €100m, additional income of €500m had been created. The multiplier is 5.

The multiplier is defined as the number of times an injection results in an increase in income.

Suppose in the above example the MPC had been 0.5, and not 0.8. In other words, people spend half of any increase in income they receive. Then the position would be as follows:

The initial investment of €100m created income for others of €100m
Those who receive this €100m spend 50% of it, so this represents
income to others of.. €50m
Those who receive this €50 million spend 50% of it, so others receive
income of €25m
...and so on.

If we continue the process this time, we find that the initial injection of €100m
has created additional income of €200m. We can now make the following
statements:

1. The bigger the MPC, the bigger the multiplier.

2. There is a precise mathematical relationship between the injection and the
   increase in income, which we can state as follows:

$$\text{Increase in income} = \frac{1}{1 - MPC} \times \text{injection, where } \frac{1}{1 - MPC} \text{ is the multiplier}$$

Let us look again at our examples above. When the MPC was 0.8 and the injection was €100m:

$$\text{Increase in income} = \frac{1}{1 - 0.8} \times €100m$$

$$= \frac{1}{0.2} \times €100m$$

$$= 5 \times €100m$$

$$= €500m$$

When the MPC was 0.5 and the injection was €100m:

$$\text{Increase in income} = \frac{1}{1 - 0.5} \times €100m$$

$$= \frac{1}{0.5} \times €100m$$

$$= 2 \times €100m$$

$$= €200m$$

You will recall that MPS = 1 − MPC. Therefore, we can write the multiplier as: $\frac{1}{MPS}$

MULTIPLIER IN OPEN ECONOMY WITH NO GOVERNMENT SECTOR

We will now examine how the multiplier works in an economy where foreign trade takes place. An increase in exports represents an injection, and so can create income in exactly the same way as the increase in investment described above. What about imports? Imports represent a withdrawal from the circular flow of income. They create income abroad. Since any money spent on imports is not passed on to other people within the economy, imports will make the multiplier smaller.

Let us look at the original example again. The injection was €100m and the MPC was 0.8. Suppose the MPM is 0.3. People spend 30 per cent of any extra income they receive on imports. The position now is as follows.

The initial investment of €100 created additional income for
others of €100m
Of this €100m, €80m is spent on consumer goods
but €30 of these are imported, so Irish people receive income of €50m
Of this €50m, €40m is spent on consumer goods but €15m
of these are imported, so Irish people receive income of €25m
.... and so on.

If the process is continued, you will find that the initial injection of €100m has led to an increase in income of €200m. Because of the MPM of 0.3, the multiplier fell from 5 to 2. Our formula now is:

Increase in income $\quad = \quad \dfrac{1}{MPS + MPM} \quad$ x injection

$\qquad\qquad\qquad = \quad \dfrac{1}{0.2 + 0.3} \quad$ x €100m

$\qquad\qquad\qquad = \quad \dfrac{1}{0.5} \quad$ x €100m

$\qquad\qquad\qquad = \quad$ €200m

$\dfrac{1}{MPS + MPM} \qquad$ is called the foreign trade multiplier

MULTIPLIER IN OPEN ECONOMY WITH GOVERNMENT SECTOR

An increase in government spending represents an injection, and so can create income in exactly the same way as the increase in investment described above. What about taxation? Taxation is a withdrawal from the circular flow of income and will make the multiplier smaller.

The marginal propensity to pay tax is the fraction of additional income which is paid in tax.

$$MPT = \frac{\Delta T}{\Delta Y}$$

Our full multiplier formula can be expressed as follows:

$$\frac{1}{MPS + MPM + MPT} \times \text{injection}$$

Sample question 1

Given that MPC = 0.9, MPM = 0.25, and MPT = 0.2, find as a result of an injection of €200m:

1. The increase in income
2. The increase in savings
3. The increase in imports
4. The increase in tax.

ANSWERS

1. If MPC = 0.9, then MPS = 0.1

   Increase in income $= \frac{1}{MPS + MPM + MPT} \times \text{injection}$

   Increase in income $= \frac{1}{0.1 + 0.25 + 0.2} \times €200m$

   $= \frac{1}{0.55} \times €200m$

   $= 1.8 \times €200m$

   $= €360m$

2.   Increase in savings = increase in income x MPS
                                = €360m x 0.1
                                = €36m

3.   Increase in imports = increase in income x MPM
                                = €360m x 0.25
                                = €90m

4.   Increase in tax   = increase in income x MPT
                                = €360m x 0.2
                                = €72m

Sample question 2

	Income (€)	Consumption (€)	Investment (€)	Exports (€)	Imports (€)
Year 1	7,800	6,500	1,550	1,200	1,450
Year 2	8,400	6,950	1,650	1,400	?

Table 24.1 Sample question details

1. From the above details in *Table 24.1*, calculate:
   (a) The level of imports in Year 2
   (b) The multiplier
   (c) The level of demand for domestically produced goods and services in Year 2
   (d) The savings in Year 2.

2. If the level of investment remains unchanged at €1,650, at what level of income would the balance of payments be at equilibrium?

ANSWERS

1. (a) Y = C + I + G + X − M
   No government sector, therefore:
       Y = C + I + X − M
   8,400 = 6950 + 1650 + 1400 − M
   8,400 = 10,000 − M
      M = 1600

   (b) MPC = $\frac{\Delta C}{\Delta Y}$ = $\frac{450}{600}$ = 0.75
      MPS = 1 − MPC
      MPS = 0.25
      MPM = $\frac{\Delta M}{\Delta Y}$ = $\frac{150}{600}$ = 0.25

$$\text{Multiplier} = \frac{1}{\text{MPS} + \text{MPM}}$$

$$= \frac{1}{0.25 + 0.25}$$

$$= \frac{1}{0.5}$$

$$= 2$$

(c) The level of demand for domestically produced goods in Year 2 is the income in Year 2.
Answer = 8,400

(d)
$$Y = C + S$$
$$Y = 8,400$$
$$C = 6,950$$
Therefore, S = 1,450

2.
$$\text{MPM} = 0.25$$
Multiplier = 2
Let ΔX = increase in exports

No other injection, therefore:
$$\Delta Y = 2 \times \Delta X$$
$$X + \Delta X = M + \Delta M$$
But $\Delta M = 0.25\ (\Delta Y)$
Therefore, $\Delta M = 0.25\ (2 \times \Delta X)$
$$X + \Delta X = M + 0.25\ (2 \times \Delta X)$$
$$1,400 + \Delta X = 1,600 + 0.25\ (2 \times \Delta X)$$

Multiplying across by 4, we get:
$$5,600 + 4(\Delta X) = 6,400 + (2 \times \Delta X)$$
$$4(\Delta X) - 2(\Delta X) = 6,400 - 5,600$$
$$2\ (\Delta X) = 800$$
Therefore, $\Delta X = 400$
Therefore, $\Delta Y = 800$
Therefore, Y = 9,200

DETERMINATION OF NATIONAL INCOME – A GRAPHICAL APPROACH

The theory of the determination of national income was largely the work of JM Keynes (see *Chapter 33*), who was writing at the time of the Great Depression of the 1930s. The earlier Classical economists believed the economy would be at equilibrium at full employment, so that there could be no long-term unemployment. By the early 1930s, it was clear that this was obviously not the case. An alternative explanation was required. Keynes argued that the economy could settle at a level of output where there is unemployment.

Keynes' theory can be briefly stated as follows:

1. The level of employment depends on the level of output.
2. The level of output depends on the level of demand.
3. The level of demand depends on the level of income, that is, D = f(Y).
4. Government could intervene in the economy to influence the level of income.

Consumption

In *Figure 24.5* income is measured on the horizontal axis and consumption on the vertical axis. The line Y represents the situation shown in *Figure 24.1*, where all the income received by households is spent on the output of firms. Since this line bisects the origin, it is called the 45° line. At any point on this line, income = output = expenditure. Each point on this line represents an equilibrium level of income, since the entire output produced by firms is purchased by households. We have already stated that consumption depends on income. This is called the consumption function. The higher the level of income, the higher the consumption.

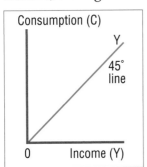

Fig. 24.5 The 45° line – equilibrium levels of income

We express this as follows:

C = f(Y)
If Y rises, C rises.
If Y falls, C falls.

The *consumption function* can be expressed in the following way:

$$C = a + bY$$

where a = that part of consumption which is independent of income
and b = the marginal propensity to consume

The part of consumption which is independent of income is called *autonomous expenditure*. Even if income is zero, people must consume. They will borrow, use up previous savings, etc. An example is useful at this stage. Suppose the consumption function for the economy as a whole is:

C = €2000m + 0.8Y	
if Y = 0	C = €2,000m
if Y = €2,000m	C = €3,600m
if Y = €4,000m	C = €5,200m
if Y = €6,000	C = €6,800m
if Y = €8,000	C = €8,400m
if Y = €10,000	C = €10,000m
if Y = €12,000	C = €11,600m

This consumption function is shown in *Figure 24.6* by the red line C. Where the consumption function crosses the 45° line, represents the equilibrium level of income. At this point C = €10,000m and Y = €10,000m.

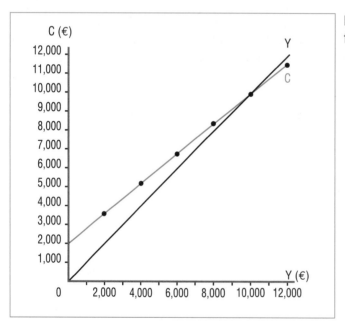

Fig. 24.6 Consumption function C = €2,000m + 0.8Y

Investment

Investment is independent of the level of income. It depends on the expectations of business people and on the rate of interest. Suppose investment is €1,000m. Then total spending in the economy is given by the red line C + I in *Figure 24.7*. The equilibrium level of income now is €15,000m. We can check this as follows:

If Y = €15,000m
C = €2,000m + 0.8Y
= €14,000m
I = €1,000m
Therefore C + I = €15,000m

An injection of €1,000m increases the equilibrium level of income by €5,000m. The multiplier is 5.

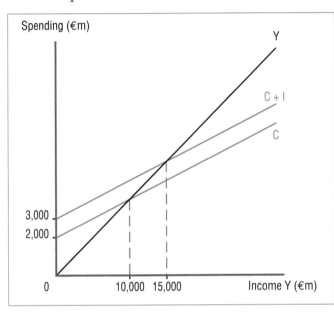

Fig. 24.7 Consumption and investment combined – the equilibrium level of income

Government spending

Government spending is independent of the level of income. It depends on the policy decisions of government as laid out in the annual budget. Suppose government spending is €1,500m. The total spending is now given by the red line C + I + G as shown in *Figure 24.8*. Since the multiplier is 5, the injection of €1,500m raises the equilibrium level of income by €7,500m. The new equilibrium level of income is therefore €22,500m.

We can check this as follows:
If Y = €22,500m
C = €2,000m + 0.8 (€22,500)
= €20,000m
I = €1,000m
G = €1,500m
Therefore C + I + G = €22,500m

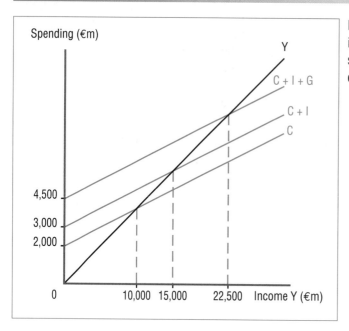

Fig. 24.8 Consumption, investment and government spending combined – the equilibrium level of income

International trade (if exports exceed imports)

If exports exceed imports, there will be a net injection into the economy which will increase the equilibrium level of income. Suppose net exports (X – M) are €500m, then the equilibrium level of income will rise by €2,500, since the multiplier is 5. The new equilibrium level of income is €25,000m. This situation is shown in *Figure 24.9*.

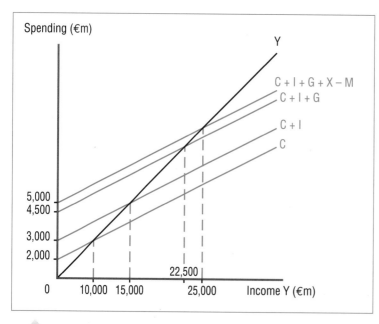

Fig. 24.9 The equilibrium level of income when exports exceed imports

International trade (if imports exceed exports)

If imports exceed exports, there will be a net withdrawal from the economy which will reduce the equilibrium level of income. Suppose imports exceed exports by €500m. Net exports (X – M) are then – €500m. The equilibrium level of income will fall by €2,500m to €20,000m, as shown in *Figure 24.10*.

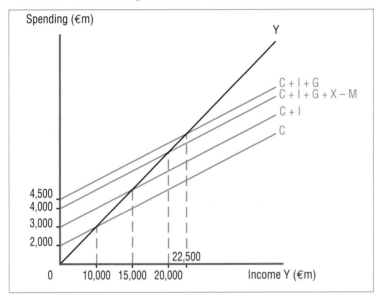

Fig. 24.10 The equilibrium level of income when imports exceed exports

A deflationary gap

If the equilibrium level of income is less than the level required to have full employment of resources, then there is said to be a deflationary gap. For

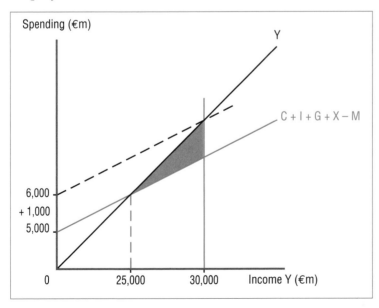

Fig. 24.11 A deflationary gap

example, suppose the full employment level of income was €30,000m and the equilibrium level of income is €25,000m. Then, if the multiplier is 5, there is a deflationary gap of €1,000m, as shown in *Figure 24.11*. This is the amount by which spending in the economy would have to increase in order to achieve the full employment level of income.

An inflationary gap

If the equilibrium level of income is higher than that required to bring about full employment, then there is said to be an inflationary gap.

Such a situation will cause prices to rise, since total demand in the economy (i.e. C + I + G + X – M) exceeds the economy's ability to produce goods and services. The inflationary gap is the reduction in spending required to bring the equilibrium level of income back to the full employment level. Suppose the multiplier is 5, and the full employment level of income is €20,000. If the equilibrium level of income is €23,000m, as shown in *Figure 24.12*, then there is an inflationary gap of €600m.

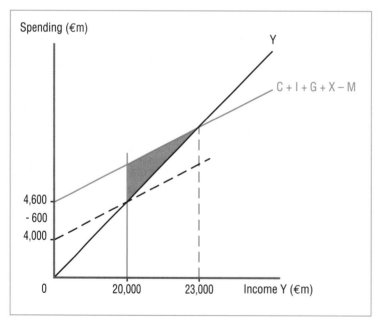

Fig. 24.12 An inflationary gap

The Price Level

Inflation is a steady and persistent increase in the general level of prices. When the prices of goods and services are rising, there is a fall in the value of money. By this we mean that a given quantity of money will purchase less goods and services when inflation occurs. The control of inflation is one of the principal economic objectives of governments in all countries. In this chapter, we will examine why prices of goods and services rise (i.e. the causes of inflation) and the economic consequences of inflation. We will initially examine how changes in the prices of goods and services are measured.

> Inflation is defined as a steady and persistent increase in the general level of prices.

HOW CHANGES IN PRICES ARE MEASURED

A simple price index

Changes in the price of a single good can be measured by means of a simple price index, which shows the percentage change in the price of that good over a period of time. There are three steps involved in constructing a simple price index for a good.

1. **Choose a base year.** The base year is the reference date or starting point from which the change in the price of the good is measured. If we are examining the change in the price of a good over a number of years, it is usual to take the first year as the base year.

2. **Find price of good**. Find out the price of the good in each of the years being examined.
3. **Express as a percentage.** Express the price of the good in each year as a percentage of the price of the good in the base year.

EXAMPLE

Suppose I wish to find out how the price of digital cameras has changed over the period 2001–2005.

1. **Choose a base year**. Because 2001 is the first year of my price study, I will take it as the base year.
2. **Find price of good**. Find out the price of the good in each of the years. Suppose the price of a digital camera in each year was as shown in *Table 25.1*.

Year	2001	2002	2003	2004	2005
Price (€)	300	200	250	350	400

Table 25.1 Price of digital cameras over the period 2001–2005

3. **Express as a percentage.** Express the price of the good in each year as a percentage of the price of the good in the base year. For each year, we put price that year over price in the base year and multiply by 100. Thus, we get:

2001: $\dfrac{300}{300} \times 100 = 100.0$

2002: $\dfrac{200}{300} \times 100 = 66.7$

2003: $\dfrac{250}{300} \times 100 = 83.3$

2004: $\dfrac{350}{300} \times 100 = 116.7$

2005: $\dfrac{400}{300} \times 100 = 133.3$

The index number for each year is: $\dfrac{\text{new price} \times 100}{\text{base year price}}$

The simple price index for digital cameras can be put in tabular form as shown in *Table 25.2*.

Year	2001	2002	2003	2004	2005
Index number	100	66.7	83.3	116.7	133.3

Table 25.2 Simple price index for digital cameras for the years 2001–2005 (with 2001 as base year)

Note: The base year will always have an index number of 100. By constructing a simple price index, we can find out the percentage change in the price of an item between two points in time. For example, from the above simple index, we can say that the price of digital cameras fell by 16.7 per cent between 2001 and 2003 or rose by 33.3 per cent between 2001 and 2005.

If we are measuring changes in the prices of a number of items we can do so by constructing a simple price index. Such an index does not take into account the fraction of income spent on each item, and is called an unweighted index. Because a simple price index attaches equal importance to each product, it cannot accurately reflect changes in the cost of living.

A composite (or weighted) price index

By constructing simple price indices for the goods I buy, I can see what has happened to the prices of these goods over a period of time. However, I will not be able to make any statement about the change in my cost of living over that period of time. This is because I do not spend the same amount of my income on each good.

Suppose my income is spent on three goods, A, B, and C. If the price of A rises by 10 per cent, B by 20 per cent and C by 30 per cent between the base year and this year, I cannot say that the increase in my cost of living is 20 per cent. This is because I do not spend the same amount of income on each of the three goods. If I spend most of my income on Good A, my cost of living will have risen by less than 20 per cent. Alternatively, if I spend most of my income on Good C, my cost of living will have risen by more than 20 per cent. In order to make meaningful statements about the change in the cost of living, a composite price index is needed.

> A composite price index is one which does not give equal importance to each good. Each good is given a 'weight' which reflects the percentage of income which is spent on it.

By attaching such a weight to each good, it is possible to make accurate statements about how changes in the price of a good affect the overall cost of living. A composite price index is a weighed price index, while a simple price index is an unweighted price index. The steps in constructing a composite price index are as follows:

1. **Choose a base year.**

2. **Decide which goods to include in the index.** The greater the number of goods included, the more accurate the index will be, as a measurement of changes in the cost of living.

3. **Find price of goods.** Find out the price of each good in the base year and in each of the subsequent years being studied.

4. **Calculate a simple price index for each good.**

5. **Find the weights.** Find out the percentage of income spent on each good, that is, find out the weights.

6. **Multiply each index number by its weight.** For each year, multiply each simple index number by its weight, add the results together and divide the answer by 100.

EXAMPLE

Suppose that the inhabitants of a certain country spend their income on four goods, A, B, C and D. We wish to measure changes in the cost of living for this country over the period 2001–2004.

1. **Choose a base year.** We will pick 2001 as the base year because it is the first year being studied.

2. **Decide which goods to include.** We will include all four goods.

3. **Find price of goods.** Find out the prices of the goods in the base year and in the subsequent years. Suppose the prices of the four goods in the four years were as shown in *Table 25.3*.

Year	Good A (€)	Good B (€)	Good C (€)	Good D (€)
2001	20	15	30	40
2002	23	18	25	50
2003	25	12	30	55
2004	26	10	35	58

Table 25.3 Prices of goods A, B, C and D, 2001–2004

4. **Calculate a simple price index for each good.** We assign a value of 100 to each good in the base year. We then express the price of the good in each year as a percentage of the price of that good in the base year. For example,

the index number for Good A in 2001 is 100. The index number for Good A in 2002 is:

$$\frac{23}{20} \times 100 = 115$$

The simple indices for the four goods are given in *Table 25.4*.

Year	Good A	Good B	Good C	Good D
2001	100	100	100	100
2002	115	120	83	125
2003	125	80	100	138
2004	130	67	117	145

Table 25.4 Simple price indices for goods A, B, C and D, 2001–2004.

5. **Find out the percentage of income spent on each good (i.e. the weights).** This is done by means of a Household Budget Survey. A Household Budget Survey is a survey carried out by the Central Statistics Office to find out the percentage of income which people (on average) spend on various goods and services. Let us assume that the percentage of income spent on each of the four goods is as shown in *Table 25.5*.

Weight of A (%)	Weight of B (%)	Weight of C (%)	Weight of D (%)
40	25	15	20

Table 25.5 Percentage of income spent on goods A, B, C and D

6. **Multiply each index number by its weight.** This is done in *Table 25.6*. Now we add the results for each year and divide by 100. This is done in *Table 25.7* and gives us our composite price index.

Year	Good A (index no. x weight)	Good B (index no. x weight)	Good C (index no. x weight)	Good D (index no. x weight)
2001	4,000	2,500	1,500	2,000
2002	4,600	3,000	1,245	2,500
2003	5,000	2,000	1,500	2,760
2004	5,200	1,675	1,755	2,900

Table 25.6 Index number multiplied by weight for goods A, B, C and D, 2001–2004

Year	Total (from Table 25.6)	Composite price index
2001	10,000	100.00
2002	11,345	113.45
2003	11,260	112.60
2004	11,530	115.30

Table 25.7 Composite price index for goods A, B, C and D, 2001–2004

We can now make precise statements concerning changes in the cost of living in this country between 2001 and 2004. We can say that the cost of living rose by 13.45 per cent between 2001 and 2002. A basket of goods costing €100 in 2001 cost €113.45 in 2002. We can also see that the cost of living fell between 2002 and 2003.

THE CONSUMER PRICE INDEX

This is the most important and commonly used composite price index in Ireland.

> The Consumer Price Index (CPI) measures the change in the average level of prices paid for consumer goods and services by all private households in the country.

Since January 1997 it is compiled on a monthly basis, taking November 1996 as the base (i.e. = 100). It covers 985 items, which are classified into 10 major commodity groups. On the second Tuesday of each month, over 45,000 prices are collected for a representative basket of the 985 items in a fixed panel of retail and service outlets in 82 locations throughout the country.

A Household Budget Survey is taken (usually every seven years, but more recently five years) to find out the fraction of income spent on each item. The most recent Household Budget Survey was taken between June 1999 and July 2000. The Survey is of a representative random sample of all private households in the state. The aim is to find out in detail the current pattern of household spending so that the weights used in the CPI can be updated. Households surveyed must keep a detailed diary of household spending over a two-week period.

Table 25.8 shows the weights for the major commodity groups according to the 1999–2000 Household Budget Survey, in which 7,644 households participated. The weight for each commodity group is the fraction of average household income spent on all the items included in that commodity group.

Commodity group	Weight (i.e. % of income spent)
Food	22.850
Alcoholic drink	12.630
Tobacco	4.824
Clothing and footwear	6.131
Fuel and light	4.904
Housing	8.038
Durable household goods	3.579
Other goods	6.381
Transport	13.940
Services & related expenditure	16.723
Total	**100.00**

Source: Household Budget Survey 1999–2000, Central Statistics Office

Table 25.8 Percentage of average household expenditure on each of the 10 major commodity groups

Is Consumer Price Index an accurate measure of price change?

The Consumer Price Index is the best available method of assessing changes in the general level of prices. However, it does suffer from a number of limitations which must be borne in mind when using it.

1. CPI BASED ON AVERAGE PATTERNS OF SPENDING

As previously stated, the CPI is based on average patterns of spending. Thus it may not accurately reflect changes in the cost of living of certain individuals and groups in society. For example, tobacco and alcohol jointly account for almost 17.5 per cent of average household spending in Ireland and thus have a 17.5 per cent weighting in the CPI. A rise in the prices of these goods will, thus, have a significant effect on the CPI but absolutely no effect on the cost of living of a person who does not drink or smoke.

2. WEIGHTS USED IN CPI APPLY IN BASE YEAR ONLY

It is unrealistic to assume that the fraction of income spent on each item will remain the same from year to year. However, this is precisely what is implied when we calculate the CPI for different years, using the weights derived from a Household Budget Survey taken in the base year. The problem in relation to the use of weights is as follows:

- If we want to accurately measure the cost of living this year, we should be using this year's weights.
- If we want to compare the cost of living this year with the cost of living in the base year, we have no option but to use the weights which applied in the base year.

3. Changes in Quality of Goods not Measured

It is not possible to allow for changes in the quality of goods. For example, suppose a particular model of car cost €20,000 in 2002 and €22,000 in 2003. This represents a 10 per cent increase in price. However, if the 2003 model includes a number of features not present on the 2002 model (e.g. air conditioning, electric sunroof, CD player, alloy wheels, etc.), then the cost of the car may be reduced in real terms. The 10 per cent increase in price is what is recorded in the CPI, with no allowance for the 'quality changes'.

4. New Products on Market not Included

Because it is based on expenditure patterns as revealed in the Household Budget Survey, the CPI does not take into account new products which have arrived on the market since the survey was taken. Any new products introduced to the Irish market since 2000 will have to wait until 2005 before they can be included in the weights. For example, prior to the 1999 Household Budget Survey the huge range of microwaveable ready meals were not included. Neither was ciabatta bread nor Red Bull drink. If these products are widely used and have replaced cheaper products, then the CPI will understate the increase in the cost of living.

5. Switch to Cheaper Brands not Measured

The CPI does not measure the extent to which people may switch to cheaper brands of the same good when prices are rising.

Despite these shortcomings, the CPI is the most accurate measure available to us of changes in the price of goods, and has many uses.

Uses of Consumer Price Index

To measure rate of inflation

The change in the CPI from one year to the next is the means by which the country's inflation rate is measured. For example, taking 1996 as the base year, the following were the CPI figures for the years 1996–2001.

Year	CPI
1996	100.0
1997	100.7
1998	103.1
1999	104.8
2000	110.7
2001	116.1

The rate of inflation for the year 1996–1997 is 0.7 per cent. We can work out the rate of inflation for any year by subtracting the index number for that year from the index number for the previous year and then expressing this figure as a percentage of the index number for the previous year. For example, the inflation rate for the year 2000–2001 can be derived as follows:

$$\frac{116.1 - 110.7}{110.7} \times 100 = 4.9\%$$

Wage negotiations

Workers will use the rise in the CPI as justification for seeking a compensatory wage rise. Trade unions will want to secure a rise in money wages which is at least equal to the increase in the cost of living. Otherwise the real income of their members will be reduced.

Widening tax bands

Changes in the CPI may be used by the government as the yardstick by which tax bands are widened in the annual budget. Unless tax bands are widened in accordance with the rise in inflation, taxpayers will pay more, even if the government does not increase the rates of income tax.

Maintaining the real value of social welfare payments

The government attempts to ensure that the real value of social welfare payments is maintained in times of inflation. This is achieved if the increase in social welfare is at least equal to the rate of inflation as measured by changes in the CPI.

Maintaining the real value of savings

Some savings schemes have 'index-linked' returns. This means that a saver can be sure that the real value of his savings will not fall. He is guaranteed a rate of interest that is at least equal to the rate of inflation.

Indexation of investments

The CPI is the basis on which an individual can increase his insurance cover on his personal possessions so as to avoid the danger of under-insurance. Many house insurance policies are index-linked so that the increase in the value of the house is reflected in the policy. The same applies to pension plans, life assurance policies, etc. where the individual is given the option to increase his contribution in line with inflation so as to maintain the real value of his investment.

Measure of international competitiveness

A comparison of our inflation rate with those of our trading partners indicates whether our international competitiveness is improving or worsening. If our inflation rate is higher than those of our trading partners we will lose competitiveness. If our inflation rate is lower, our competitiveness will improve.

Other composite price indices

- *The Constant Tax Price Index* measures changes in the prices of goods, but excludes price changes which are caused by changes in indirect taxes. When used with the CPI, it shows how much of the overall price change in any period is due to indirect taxes and how much is due to all other factors.
- *The EU Harmonised Index of Consumer Prices (HICP)* is calculated in each member state of the EU to allow comparison of consumer price trends in the various member states. It excludes mortgage interest but includes personal expenditure of tourists within each country.
- *The Agricultural Output Price Index* measures changes in the prices of agricultural output.
- *The Agricultural Input Price Index* measures changes in the price of agricultural inputs (i.e. feeding stuffs, fertilisers, seeds, etc.)
- *Import Price Index* measures changes in the price of our imports.
- *Export Price Index* measures changes in the price of our exports.

CAUSES OF INFLATION

We have already defined inflation as a steady and persistent increase in the general level of prices. To be able to deal effectively with the problems caused by inflation, a government must first be able to identify the causes (or sources) of inflation.

Demand-pull inflation

> **Demand-pull inflation occurs when the economy cannot produce enough goods and services to meet the demands of its citizens.**

There is 'too much money chasing too few goods'. Aggregate demand exceeds aggregate supply. Producers will be unable to meet the demand for goods and services at existing prices. They will see the opportunity to increase their profits by raising prices. In a small open economy like Ireland's, excess demand, if it exists at all, tends to be met by an increased volume of imports. However, in the case of personal services and housing, where imports are not an option, excess demand will usually lead to higher prices.

Cost-push inflation

Cost-push inflation occurs when the selling prices of goods and services are increased to compensate the producer for an increase in the costs of production.

Such increases in the cost of production can arise in any of the following ways:

- **An increase in the price of an imported raw material**. Inflation caused in this way is referred to as imported inflation and is seen as largely unavoidable. This is a major source of inflation in a country such as Ireland, where in 2000, 61 per cent of our imports were classified as 'materials for further production'.

- **An increase in the cost of labour.** If firms concede wage increases to their workers this puts pressure on profits. In such circumstances, firms may be forced to increase the selling prices of the goods they produce in order to remain viable. Cost-push inflation could also arise in the case of labour if wage drift occurs. If there is a high demand for labour, a firm may find itself granting a wage rise in excess of the negotiated rate in order to retain its workforce. It may then attempt to recoup the cost of this by raising the selling of its goods.

- **An increase in the price of home-produced raw materials**. This may also cause firms to increase the selling prices of finished goods.

Government-induced inflation

Even though governments will usually regard the control of inflation as one of their principal aims, the government itself may be partly responsible for inflation. This can happen in the following ways:

- If the government raises indirect taxes, it is contributing to inflation in three ways. First, it is adding directly to the CPI the amount of the tax increase. Second, since workers base their wage claims on real take-home pay, any increase in prices will set in motion a *'wage-price spiral'*. Workers will seek wage increases to compensate for price increases and a further impetus is given to cost-push inflation. Third, if the indirect tax is placed on materials which are used as inputs by firms, then there will be higher costs to the manufacturer. He will then try to pass these costs on to the consumer in the form of higher prices.

- If the government increases expenditure in the economy too much, then it can cause demand-pull inflation.

- If the government allows the banks to give out too many loans to personal borrowers, then it can also contribute to demand-pull inflation.

Methods to fix prices contributes to inflation

The methods sellers use to fix prices may contribute to inflation. Some contractors operate on a 'cost-plus system of pricing'. This means they charge the consumer the cost of the goods to themselves plus a fixed percentage of the selling price. This is often done when it is difficult to estimate in advance what costs will be. In this situation, not only is there no incentive for the seller to keep costs down, but he actually gains by allowing costs to rise.

A similar system is used in retailing as a method of setting prices. In this case the retailer will respond to a rise in his costs (e.g. an increase in tax) by raising price again, so as *to maintain the same percentage profit margin*. For example, suppose the price of a pint of beer is broken down as follows:

Publican	€0.90	(25%)
Brewery	€0.90	(25%)
Government	€1.80	(50%)
Total price	€3.60	(100%)

If the government increases the tax on beer by 40c, the position now is as follows:

Publican	€0.90	(22.5%)
Brewery	€0.90	(22.5%)
Government	€2.20	(55.0%)
Total price	€4.00	(100%)

If the publican and the brewery both have the aim of maintaining their share of the selling price at 25 per cent, then they each must add a further 20c to the price of the pint. This gives a new position as follows:

Publican	€1.10	(25%)
Brewery	€1.10	(25%)
Government	€2.20	(50%)
Total	€4.40	(100%)

In other words the initial tax increase has contributed to two further price rises as both publican and brewery try to maintain their relative share of the overall selling price.

ECONOMIC EFFECTS OF INFLATION

1. Production encouraged

Production may be encouraged. We have already seen that the higher the price, the greater the quantity that will be supplied. In a period of inflation, two conflicting trends affect the producer.

- He may be in a position to increase the selling price of his good. This will encourage him to produce more.
- His costs of production may have risen. This will encourage him to produce less.

If the increase in the selling price exceeds the rise in his costs of production, then production is encouraged.

2. Consumption encouraged

Consumption may be encouraged. This occurs if consumers develop 'inflation psychology', that is, if they expect inflation to continue. In such circumstances consumers may purchase goods now rather than wait because they expect prices to be even higher in future.

3. People on fixed incomes lose out

People on fixed incomes tend to lose. This category includes employees, social welfare recipients and pensioners. These people are not in a position to increase their incomes to compensate for inflation. In the case of employees, they must await the outcome of wage negotiations. In the case of social welfare recipients and those on state pensions, they must await the introduction of the annual budget. Those on private pensions would appear to be most vulnerable in times of inflation.

4. Gains made by self-employed

Self-employed people gain during periods of inflation if they are able to increase the price they charge for their services by more than the general increase in prices.

5. Borrowers gain and lenders lose

Borrowers gain and lenders lose if the rate of inflation is greater than the rate of interest. In the case of the borrower, the amount he must repay is less in real terms. In the case of the lender (i.e. the saver) the purchasing power of his savings falls if the rate of inflation exceeds the rate of interest. In such a situation, the real interest rate is negative.

6. Speculation encouraged

Inflation encourages speculators to transfer their wealth out of cash (the value of which is falling) and into land, property, antiques, precious metals, works of art, etc. The increase in the demand for such assets during times of inflation causes an increase in their value which exceeds the rate of inflation. Thus, large gains can be made by those who can afford to buy them.

Fig. 25.1 Buying works of art is one way speculators transfer their money during inflationary times

7. Loss of international competitiveness

There will be a loss of international competitiveness if our inflation rate exceeds that of our trading partners.

8. Benefits to government

The government can benefit from inflation in two ways.

- The government is a borrower. If the rate of inflation exceeds the rates of interest on government borrowing (i.e. the national debt), then the amount the government has to pay back is falling (in real terms).

- The government gains as a result of more people paying income tax at higher marginal rates of tax. Without altering the rates of tax, the government can collect more in income tax during a period of inflation. As money incomes rise, people will move from a low tax bracket to a high tax bracket.

9. Hyperinflation

Very rapid growth in the rate of inflation in which money loses its value to the point where alternative methods of exchange are used (such as barter or foreign currency) may completely undermine public confidence in the currency and cause major instability. Such inflation is referred to as *hyperinflation*.

INFLATION IN IRELAND

Table 25.9 shows the rate of inflation in Ireland in recent years. Our low inflation rate in the mid-1990s is usually accepted as one of the reasons why Ireland's export performance has been so strong in recent years. However as the growth in the economy soared and we got closer to full employment, significant inflationary pressures built up, especially in those areas of the economy such as services which are not open to foreign competition. The EU issued a formal reprimand to Ireland in 2000 and urged the government to take steps to curtail the level of demand in the economy.

Year	Inflation rate (%)
1996	1.6
1997	1.5
1998	2.4
1999	1.6
2000	5.6
2001	4.9
Source: Central Statistics Office	

Table 25.9 Irish inflation rates, 1996–2001

Table 25.10 shows the inflation rates of EU member states in 2000, with OECD and Central Bank estimates of rates for 2001 and 2002. It can be seen that Ireland currently has one of the highest inflation rates in the EU.

Country	2000 (%)	2001 (%)	2002 (%)
Austria	1.5	2.6	1.8
Belgium	2.2	2.4	1.2
Denmark	3.1	2.1	1.7
Finland	3.5	2.6	1.7
France	1.2	1.7	1.4
Germany	1.4	1.9	1.0
Greece	3.1	3.3	2.6
Ireland	5.6	4.8	3.2
Italy	2.9	2.8	1.7
Luxembourg	2.9	2.6	2.5
Netherlands	2.8	4.6	2.4
Portugal	2.9	4.3	3.5
Spain	3.2	3.7	2.5
Sweden	0.9	2.6	3.0
UK	3.1	2.1	1.7
Sources: Central Bank of Ireland and OECD			

Table 25.10 EU inflation rates, 2000–2002

Fig. 25.2 In 2001 households drank an average of €3.06 worth of wine at home each week, compared with €1.26 in 1995.

The Household Budget Survey in 2001 showed a major change in lifestyle for most people since 1995, according to the *Sunday Business Post* on 18 November 2001.

THE YEARS OF LIVING CHABLIS

By Aine Coffey

We are spending our money on steak and shirts, pasta and peppers, wine, videos and parking fines, according to the latest Household Budget Survey.

We spend far more on our clothes – albeit with such interesting exceptions as men's socks and vests. And over five years since the previous survey, we also kitted our homes out in comfort, according to research carried out by the Central Statistics Office last year and forming the basis of the new study.

We own more televisions (49% of households had two or more), microwaves (71.5% of households, up from 46.6%), videos (85%, from 60.9%), stereos (66.2%, from 51.7%), home PCs (29.2%, from 16%), clothes dryers (42%, from 26.3%) and dishwashers (32%, from 18.7%). Over 24% of households own two or more cars. Over 83% have full central heating, up from 68% in 1995.

Our spending spree has come as average gross weekly household income rose by 53% to £525.06 [€666.69]. ...

Back in 1994/1995, households spent an average of £70.75 [€89.83] per week on food, but over five years increased by 31% to £92.67 [€117.67]. We lay out about £4 [€5.08] more a week on hotel and restaurant meals. And when eating in our tastes have become more European: pasta and pizza didn't feature in the 1995 survey, but now cost us over £1 [€1.27] weekly....

We may spend 46% more on sport and 'recreational goods', but it hasn't all been a health kick.... Households drink an average of £2.41 [€3.06] worth of wine at home every week, compared with 99p [€1.26] in 1995.... The average household spends £19.88 [€25.24] a week on alcohol consumed outside the home, a nearly 64% increase. We are spending nearly £2 [€2.54] more on cigarettes....

Our reading tastes have changed. We spend...less on comics and get our fantastical diversions elsewhere, with growth areas including computer games and videos....

Some life basics are costing us dearly with weekly transport spend up from £44.72 to £74.76 [€56.78 to €94.93]. In as new categories are court fines, parking fines and the driving test, costing us 3p [4c] weekly apiece. After health insurance refunds, we spend £6.91 [€8.77] on medical expenses.... Fuel and light cost us 11% more and total weekly housing spend, including decoration and repair, has soared by nearly 43%....

Gaps have widened between the poorest and the wealthiest, between those in a position to take advantage of the explosion in employment opportunities and those who were not. The disposable income of households with gross weekly income of more than £800.86 [€1,016.63] rose by more than 61% over five years, but increased by just 37% for the lowest earners, with gross weekly income of less than £168.90 [€214.46].

The rich have got richer.

26

The Economic Objectives
of Government

INTRODUCTION

In most countries, the 20th century brought a huge increase in the level of government involvement in economic affairs. Today we take for granted that the government should give social welfare payments to disadvantaged people, unemployment benefits to those who cannot find work, pensions to those who are unable to provide for themselves in old age, etc. We also regard as normal, direct state involvement in the provision of goods and services through state-sponsored companies (i.e. semi-state bodies). State funding of training schemes for workers and state grants to firms are two further areas of government involvement, which we accept as desirable and appropriate.

However, in the 19th century, there was widespread acceptance of the doctrine of *laissez faire*. Underlying this doctrine was the belief that the state should not involve itself in economic matters unless absolutely necessary. The wealth of the country would be maximised if business people were allowed to trade with little or no interference or regulation by government. The role of the state was seen as being confined to areas such as national security, justice and the provision of a framework within which private enterprise could flourish.

Attitudes to state involvement in economic matters began to change in the early years of the 20th century. Laws were passed in many countries improving working conditions and laying down maximum hours of work. Trade unions were given greater powers. The foundations of a social welfare system were put in place. Public acceptance of a greater role for government increased with the outbreak of the First World War in 1914. It was considered appropriate for the government to have greater control over the means of production in a time of national emergency.

The Great Depression in the 1930s gave a further impetus to state involvement.

If traditional theories had failed to come up with answers to the problem of mass unemployment, then a fresh approach was needed. The writings of JM Keynes advocated a role for government in the creation of a level of demand in the economy sufficient to generate full employment. The Second World War (1939–1945) again led to a greater level of state control over the means of production in many countries, and was followed by the introduction of social welfare schemes. Political parties in most countries began to accept that the state had a role in creating employment and in looking after the weaker members of society.

As economic prosperity increased in the 1960s, there was widespread public acceptance of the concept of a *welfare state*, that is, one where the benefits of economic growth would be distributed fairly. The range of social welfare services provided by the state increased significantly, and it was considered fair that those in employment should pay higher taxes to fund such services. A policy of *nationalisation* of key industries was pursued in some countries, including Britain.

> Nationalisation means the takeover by the state of private sector firms in an industry so as to increase public control in that industry.

Many of these industries have since been privatised, i.e. put back into private ownership.

The 1980s saw a questioning of the extent of the role of the state in many countries. In Britain, the Conservative Party was in power continuously from 1979 to 1997 and committed itself to 'rolling back the frontiers of the state'. A policy of privatisation of state enterprises was pursued. In Eastern Europe, the changes have been even more profound. In 1990 and 1991, the communist governments in East Germany, Poland, Czechoslovakia, Hungary, Romania and Bulgaria collapsed. The Soviet Union fragmented into its 15 constituent republics, each of which became an independent state. These countries embarked on the process of transition from a centrally planned economic system to a free enterprise system.

Despite these changes, we can say that governments in all countries have a very important role to play in economic affairs. Governments everywhere share certain key economic objectives or aims. We will now consider these economic objectives.

THE ECONOMIC AIMS OF GOVERNMENT

1. Provision of adequate infrastructure

There are certain supports which industry requires before it can function properly. Good roads, airports, sewage and water systems, railways, harbours, telephone, e-mail and other communication systems are all required (*Figures 26.1* and *26.2*).

Fig. 26.1 Dublin Airport

Fig. 26.2 Rosslare Ferryport

These services are usually provided by government rather than by private companies because:

- Large-scale expenditure is required

- Provision of such facilities needs to be co-ordinated on a national basis, and

- The private sector may be unwilling to get involved if the service is not a profit-making one.

A feature of some countries in recent years is joint private and public sector infrastructure projects. From the point of view of government, such projects have the advantage of providing additional funds and technical expertise as well as reducing the need for borrowing.

In Ireland a private company, National Toll Roads plc, was responsible for the construction of the East Link Toll Bridge and the West Link Toll Bridge (see *Figures 26.3* and *26.4*).

Fig. 26.3 The M50 spanning the River Liffey at the Strawberry Beds in Dublin

Fig. 26.4 The East Link Bridge on the River Liffey in Dublin

The Irish Government's *National Development Plan 2000–2006* promotes the use of *Public Private Partnerships* (PPPs) for the provision of economic infrastructure, with a total of €2.35 billion earmarked for projects such as national roads, water supply, public transport (including LUAS) and waste management.

> Public private partnerships are defined as partnerships between public sector organisations and private sector investors and businesses for the purposes of designing, planning, financing, constructing and/or operating infrastructure projects.

2. Achievement of full employment

> Full employment is defined as a situation in which jobs are available for all those willing to work at existing wage levels.

Full employment does not mean zero unemployment. We have already seen (in *Chapter 19*) that in any economy there will always be people who are moving from one job to another, who will be unemployed for a while. However, since the foundation of the State, Ireland has had persistently high levels of unemployment. As recently as 1993, almost one sixth of the labour force was out of work. Since then strong economic growth has seen the unemployment rate fall to below 4 per cent in 2001. An unemployment rate of 4 per cent or less was usually regarded as corresponding to full employment because job losses in declining sectors would require people to move to other growing sectors, which could not occur immediately.

In the *National Development Plan 2000–2006*, the Irish Government sets out its employment objectives as follows:

• To provide employment for all those who want employment

• To address skills shortages

• To set a new target of 5 per cent unemployment and 2 per cent long-term unemployment.

3. Control of inflation (i.e. price stability)

We have examined in detail the economic consequences of inflation in *Chapter 25*, so there is no need to repeat them here. The main problem with inflation, as far as the Irish Government is concerned, is the danger of a loss of competitiveness on international markets. Ireland relies more heavily on exports than most other countries. A rise in Irish prices will therefore lead to a rise in the cost of our exports on foreign markets.

A loss of competitiveness can be defined as a situation where our goods abroad are less attractive to foreign buyers.

This happens if our inflation rate is higher than those of our competitors, i.e. our goods have become relatively more expensive. Inflation is also undesirable in that it redistributes income from one sector of society (those on fixed incomes) to another.

4. Achievement of economic growth

By economic growth we mean an *increase in output per person in the economy.* An increase in economic growth is the means by which the standard of living of a country's inhabitants improves. An increase in output per person implies an increase in income per person. This will allow more goods and services to be consumed and is generally seen as a desirable objective. However, it must be realised that economic growth has costs as well as benefits.

Fig. 26.5 Traffic congestion

Pollution, waste, traffic congestion, destruction of the environment, crime, social problems and inequality are all problems which have appeared in those countries where the rates of economic growth have been most impressive. Nevertheless, the achievement of economic growth is a major economic objective of most governments. The benefits of such growth are considered to far outweigh the disadvantages. Rates of growth are measured by changes in the volume of output (GNP) of a country from one year to the next. If the volume of output rises by 5 per cent, the country is said to have a growth rate of 5 per cent.

5. Achievement of equilibrium on balance of payments

Equilibrium on the balance of payments means having imports and exports roughly equal.

If imports are continuously bigger than exports, then the country is living beyond its means. In such a situation, we would be spending more on foreign goods and services than foreigners are spending on our goods and services. There would be downward pressure on the value of our currency.

What would happen if exports were continuously bigger than imports? In this case foreigners would spend more on our goods and services than we spend on their goods and services. There would be upward pressure on the value of our currency. This may not seem like much of a problem but the revenues received from the sale of exports may cause inflation in the economy.

For these reasons, governments are happy with a situation where exports and imports are roughly equal. In fact, in recent years, the ability of governments to influence this objective appears to have been diminished. The signing of international trade agreements, the lowering of trade barriers and membership of trade blocs (such as the EU) have all contributed to a situation where governments have less power to reduce imports. Furthermore, government efforts to encourage citizens to spend more on home-produced goods may be seen as discriminatory and may invite retaliation. Also, government efforts to increase exports (e.g. by granting subsidies) may be seen as giving producers from that country an unfair advantage on international markets.

6. Control of government expenditure

This objective relates to government finances. In many countries, including Ireland, governments have sought to stimulate the level of economic activity (and thereby increase employment) by increasing the level of government spending. Governments have resorted to *budget deficits*, where government current revenue is less than government current spending. The extra money needed is borrowed, and thus contributes to the National Debt. 'Servicing' the National Debt (i.e. paying interest on the money borrowed) can eat up a large part of government revenue in subsequent years, thus limiting the scope of the government to spend this money as it would like. For this reason, the government may have as one of its economic objectives, the control of government spending. This aim can be set out in a number of ways:

(a) A limit may be set on the amount of government spending (or on the size of government borrowing).

(b) An upper limit may be set on the Debt/GNP ratio.

This is $\dfrac{\text{National Debt} \times 100}{\text{GNP}}$

The greater this ratio is, the greater is the burden of government debt.

(c) The government may commit itself to a balanced budget (i.e. where revenue equals expenditure).

7. Achievement of just social policy

The government's social policy refers to its efforts to treat all its citizens fairly regardless of their economic status. It covers the provision of such services as healthcare, education, housing, and social welfare. The government tries to ensure that everyone receives a certain minimum quantity of these essential goods and services (known as *merit wants*), regardless of their ability to pay for them. Thus, free second-level education is available to all (and compulsory up to 16 years of age). Third-level fees were abolished in 1995. Grants are available to third-level students whose family income might not be sufficient to pay for books and accommodation, etc.

Social welfare benefits are available to those who need them (i.e. the unemployed, the disabled, old age pensioners, etc.). Free hospital treatment, drugs and medical care are provided for those whose income is below a specified figure. In relation to housing, the government's stated objective is to ensure that 'every household has a dwelling suitable to its needs, located in an acceptable environment, at a rent or price it can afford'. While political parties differ on the extent to which such services should be made freely available, it is generally agreed that a certain minimum quantity should be available to all.

Another aspect of social policy is in the area of income distribution. The government will try to ensure that the benefits of economic growth do not remain in the hands of a small section of the population, but are spread widely. This aim is usually expressed as 'the achievement of a fair distribution of income and wealth'.

8. Achievement of balanced regional development

Governments in many countries are faced with the problems of unbalanced development. Some regions may lag behind the rest of the country in terms of economic development. This could be due to their peripheral location, declining population, poor infrastructure or a shortage of natural resources.

Such regions are called disadvantaged (or depressed) areas. Governments seek to spread the benefits of growth across the country and will, therefore, positively discriminate in favour of such disadvantaged areas.

INSTRUMENTS OF GOVERNMENT ECONOMIC POLICY

The methods used by governments to achieve their aims are known as the instruments (or tools) of economic policy. There are six instruments.

1. Fiscal policy

This relates to government revenue and government expenditure. Fiscal policy is carried out by (a) increasing or decreasing tax; and (b) increasing or decreasing government spending.

2. Monetary policy

This is carried out by the Central Bank. It is implemented by (a) increasing or decreasing the money supply; (b) increasing or decreasing rates of interest; and (c) making it easier or more difficult to get loans.

3. Exchange rate policy

This relates to the value of a currency in terms of other currencies. It is implemented by (a) devaluation, i.e. making a currency worth less in terms of other currencies; and (b) revaluation, i.e. making a currency worth more in terms of other currencies.

4. Direct intervention

This is where the government intervenes directly in the economy to achieve its aims. It can be implemented by (a) the setting up of state companies to supply goods and services which the private sector is not willing or able to provide; and (b) the passing of laws of the Oireachtas.

5. Prices and income policy

This is a policy to restrain prices and incomes so as to control inflation. It can be implemented by (a) imposing a wage freeze or else imposing strict limits on wage increases; (b) strict price control, possibly involving the setting of maximum prices for certain essential items; and (c) insisting that companies get government approval before raising their prices.

6. Economic planning

This involves consultation with the social partners (employers, trade unions, farmers, etc.) with a view to setting realistic targets for the immediate future on a wide range of economic issues. It is implemented by holding discussions with the social partners and agreeing a range of measures which have general support and which are capable of being carried through.

LINKING AIMS AND INSTRUMENTS

Various ways of achieving the government's economic aims are now considered. It must be stressed that these do not cover all the possible options available to a government.

1. Provision of adequate infrastructure

Fiscal policy	Increase government expenditure.
Direct intervention	Give more resources to state companies involved in the provision of infrastructure.
Economic planning	Promote public private partnerships.

2. Achievement of full employment

Fiscal policy	(a) Increase government spending on job creation. (b) Reduce income tax to increase disposable income and encourage more spending. (c) Reduce indirect tax to encourage more spending.
Monetary policy	(a) Increase the availability of loans. (b) Lower interest rates. (c) Increase the money supply.
Exchange rate policy	Devalue currency to increase exports (and therefore increase employment).
Direct intervention	(a) Increase employment in the public sector. (b) Give more resources to the IDA. (c) Introduce wage subsidies to companies to encourage them to recruit more workers. (d) Increase the mobility of labour by retraining and resettlement allowances.

Prices and incomes policy	Encourage wage restraint.
Economic planning	Conduct discussions with social partners to identify the labour requirements in various sectors.

3. Control of inflation

Fiscal policy	(a) Reduce government spending. (b) Increase direct tax to reduce consumer spending. (c) Reduce indirect tax, thereby lowering prices.
Monetary policy	(a) Reduce the money supply. (b) Increase interest rates. (c) Make loans more difficult to get.
Prices and incomes policy	(a) Impose a wage freeze. (b) Impose strict price control.
Economic planning	Conduct talks with the social partners with a view to achieving a modest set of wage increases.

4. Achievement of economic growth

Fiscal policy	(a) Increase government expenditure. (b) Reduce taxation on company profits (to encourage more investment).
Monetary policy	Provide low-interest loans to companies.
Direct intervention	Set up state companies to supply goods and services that the private sector is unwilling to provide.
Economic planning	Conduct talks with the social partners to set realistic targets for the different sectors of the economy

5. Achievement of equilibrium on balance of payments

Fiscal policy	Increase direct tax (to reduce spending on imports).
Monetary policy	(a) Reduce bank lending to personal borrowers. (b) Increase interest rates.
Exchange rate policy	Devalue the currency to make exports cheaper abroad (and imports more expensive at home).

6. Control of government expenditure

Fiscal policy	Reduce government spending (and borrowing).

7. Achievement of just social policy

Fiscal policy
(a) Increase income tax rates for high-income earners.
(b) Reduce VAT on essential items.
(c) Increase spending on social welfare, etc.

8. Achieve balanced regional development

Fiscal policy
Pay higher grants to firms willing to locate in disadvantaged regions.

POSSIBLE CONFLICTS BETWEEN GOVERNMENT ECONOMIC OBJECTIVES

It should be obvious from the above that policies designed to further one aim of government may make the achievement of another aim more difficult. Examples of such conflicts are:

1. Full employment versus the control of inflation

Policies designed to increase employment usually involve increased government expenditure, thus making it harder to control inflation. Policies designed to reduce inflation usually involve the control of spending. Such policies may make it harder to increase employment.

2. Full employment versus balance of payments equilibrium

Policies designed to increase employment usually involve more spending (by both the government and the private sector). Some of this spending will be on imports and may widen the gap between imports and exports.

3. Economic growth versus just social policy

To achieve a more equal distribution of wealth in society, the government may impose high taxes on high-income earners and use this money to increase social welfare payments. However the high-income earners may be the creators of wealth in the country. By taxing them highly, the government may force them out of business, or cause them to transfer their operations to countries with lower tax rates.

4. Control of government spending versus full employment

Policies designed to increase the level of employment may involve increased government expenditure. Budget deficits may result, adding to the National

Debt. The increased cost of servicing this debt makes it more difficult to control government spending in subsequent years.

Just how much an economy can be subsidised was detailed by *Business & Finance* on 4 March 1999.

Subsidising the Economy

By Brendan Menton

Ireland has a long history of using tax reliefs and subsidies to assist economic activity. Nearly every substantive segment of economic life in Ireland is subsidised to a greater or lesser extent, either directly through subsidies or indirectly through tax exemptions and reliefs. This includes agriculture, housing, industry, tourism, construction and the IFSC. Further elements of Government influence on activity and consumption are free provision of public goods, such as water, parking and, in some areas, refuse disposal, and heavy regulation of certain segments of economic activity.

Subsidies and tax reliefs distort the pattern of economic activity, either internally or across international boundaries, depending on their nature. Whatever validity subsidies may have had in the past, there is little justification for them in today's economic environment. Ireland's

economy is approaching full capacity and the focus must change from promoting increased activity to preventing excess activity leading to bootlenecks and inflationary pressures.

In addition, the basic philosophy of the European Union is to remove distortions to economic activity. By signing up to Economic and Monetary Union, Ireland signalled its agreement to compete on a level playing field with the other members of the system. The EU has a philosophy of minimising incentives and charging the economic price for public goods. This contrasts sharply with current practice in Ireland.

Irish enterprise has grown up on a diet of subsidies and tax reliefs. Despite having a lower level of public expenditure, as a percentage of GNP, than many other European countries, the Irish Government's involvement in and direction of the economy is probably higher than in most economies.

The full impact of subsidies on activity and the pattern of demand is seldom fully realised. The focus is on the direct impact, which may not be the most important one, and secondary impacts are generally ignored. Frequently the subsidy or relief is over generous and this results in an unnecessary loss of resources to the Exchequer. In addition, many subsidies are sustained past their sell-by date.

The housing market is a topical and typical example. Currently there are two main elements of Government intervention – mortgage interest relief and grant assistance for first time buyers. Both act to increase demand. At a time of excess demand and inadequate supply most of the benefits of these interventions go to the builders of the houses in increased profits or impact through cost inflation. It is nonsensical that there continues to be calls for additional subsidies as a solution to the current housing crisis. They would increase the demand for housing and given that the problem is the inability of the supply side to react, any additional subsidies would simply translate into higher prices.

A basic first year economics lesson is that the benefit of a subsidy (impact of a tax) gets divided between the demand and the supply side depending on their responsiveness to react. In today's housing market, extra subsidies will bring new purchasers to the market but will have little impact on the supply of housing. Hence the result is inflationary.

The IFSC is attracting many international financial firms to operate from the old docklands in Dubin. They are attracted by the very low, currently 10%, tax rate applying and by the additional subsidies of double rent relief and rates allowances. Their effective tax rate is well below 10%. The incentive is undoubtedly more than is required to make a success of the IFSC. When these incentives were criticised by our fellow members of the EU for diverting economic activity to Ireland, the Government's solution was to annnouce a phasing in of a univeral 12.5% corporate tax regime by 2003. This will be well below comparable rates in other EU countries.

With the liberalisation of world trade, Ireland has moved from using import duties and export subsidies to the tax regime to influence economic activity in her favour.

When the Irish economy was less developed, there was some justification for using subsidies and the tax system to encourage economic activity in specific areas. However, the need for these incentives is seldom reviewed. In addition there are always interest groups who benefit by their retention. Nearly every budget submission presented to the Minister for Finance contains requests for the retention of subsidies and tax reliefs or the introduction of new ones.

Subsidies and tax reliefs are justified in situations of exceptional economic or social need. However, they should be the exception and not the norm. As Ireland's funding, both structural and agricultural, from Europe declines, we will have to fund a much greater proportion of development from our own resources. Thus a fundamental review of how we allocate resources in the economy is required. ...

With the development of the economy, the focus of policy has shifted from encouraging economic activity to avoiding bottlenecks. The economy is now supply constrained whereas just six years ago it was severely demand constrained. Resources must be shifted from encouraging additional economic activity to providing additional infrastructure and skilled labour. In a supply constrained economy operating at full capacity, taxes and charges are a legitimate way of controlling demand. ...

The Irish economy historically has a high level of regulation in certain activities. The limited deregulation that has been introduced to date has been successful. The telecommunications area is the dramatic example. Deregulation was accelerated and the result has been competition to the previous state monopoly, improved service and lower prices. This has been an important factor in attracting foreign investment in teleservices and some high technology industries. Energy and transport are the next areas where deregulation should be accelerated. ...

The Irish economy is now mature. Intervention must focus on infrastructure provision, education, long term structural requirements, such as serviced land and energy, and health and social inclusion measures. Many current incentives should be abandoned.

The Government and the Economy – Fiscal Policy

In the last chapter we examined the economic objectives of government, and the instruments (or tools) used to achieve those objectives. One of the most powerful instruments at the disposal of a government is fiscal policy.

> Fiscal policy can be defined as any action by the government which affects the size or composition of government revenue and expenditure.

Fiscal policy is carried out by the central government. In Ireland, the central government is known as the Oireachtas and consists of the President, the Seanad and the Dáil. The effective power of central government is exercised by the Dáil. The responsibility for the implementation of the government's fiscal policy rests with the Minister for Finance. The Budget or financial statement presented to the Dáil each year by the Minister for Finance is the means by which the government's fiscal policy is pursued.

In this chapter we shall examine the procedures involved in the preparation of the annual budget, and the composition of government revenue and expenditure. We shall also examine the other components of the public sector – local authorities and semi-state bodies.

GOVERNMENT PLANNING OF RECEIPTS AND EXPENDITURE

The central government is composed of the following departments, each of which is under the control of a Minister appointed by the Taoiseach.

1. Agriculture and Food	8. Foreign Affairs
2. Arts, Heritage, Gaeltacht and the Islands	9. Health and Children
	10. Justice, Equality and Law Reform
3. Defence	11. The Marine and Natural Resources
4. Education and Science	
5. Enterprise, Trade and Employment	12. Public Enterprise
	13. Social, Community and Family Affairs
6. Environment and Local Government	
	14. The Taoiseach
7. Finance	15. Tourism, Sport and Recreation

Towards the end of the year, each of these departments prepares its spending plan for the coming year and submits it to the Department of Finance. The Department of Finance examines these spending plans carefully. If some are considered too large they may be altered after discussions with the Department concerned. Once the spending plans of the Departments have been agreed, they are published in the *Book of Estimates* in mid-November.

In early December a White Paper entitled *Estimates of Receipts and Expenditure* is published. In addition to the estimates of spending for the coming year, this also contains estimates of the revenue that would be collected by the government if the rates of tax were not changed. The publication of this information before the budget allows us to see if the Minister for Finance will have sufficient revenue to meet total planned expenditure for the year. If there is a shortage of revenue, then we know that some increase in taxation is likely, or else additional government borrowing is required.

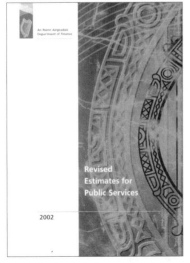

Fig. 27.1 Every year a new Book of Estimates (left) and Budget (right) are published

About a week later the Minister for Finance presents the budget to the Dáil. In the budget speech, the Minister reviews the country's economic performance during the past year, and considers its prospects for the year ahead. Any changes in taxation and expenditure for the year ahead are then announced. The Dáil then debates the budget and eventually two Acts are passed. *The Finance Act* gives the government permission to make the changes in taxation contained in the budget, while *The Appropriation Act* allows the government to spend its money in accordance with the provisions of the budget.

Fig. 27.2 Minister for Finance, Mr Charlie McCreevy, TD delivers the 2002 Budget

At the end of the year each government Department sends its accounts to the *Comptroller and Auditor General*, showing the money it received during the year and how it was spent. The Comptroller and Auditor General is the government's accountant. He/she checks to make sure that all calculations are correct, that the amount received was authorised and that all money spent was as laid out in the budget. The completed audit, known as the *Report of the Comptroller and Auditor General* is presented to the Dáil. Here a *Public Accounts Committee*, composed of TDs from all the major parties, examines the Comptroller's Report. The Committee issues its own report, which highlights any unauthorised expenditure or any waste of public money.

THE CURRENT BUDGET AND THE CAPITAL BUDGET

The annual budget is a statement of the government's planned income and expenditure for the coming year. It is divided into two parts – the *current budget* and the *capital budget*.

The current budget consists of *current expenditure* and *current revenue*.

Current expenditure is government spending on items which are used up during the year, e.g. wages and salaries of state employees, stationery and supplies for the civil service, social welfare payments, heating, lighting and maintenance of state buildings, etc.

Current revenue is the money received by the government in direct and indirect tax, and other income received during the year.

The capital budget contains expenditure by the government on items which are not used up during the year, but which increase the productive capacity of the country in future years. In other words, capital expenditure is investment by the government in roads, schools, hospitals, advance factories, airports, telecommunications, etc. The money to pay for capital expenditure is usually borrowed by the government.

Why is a distinction made between current expenditure and capital expenditure? The distinction is made because government borrowing to pay for capital expenditure was considered justified, while it was seen as essential to pay for current items out of tax received during the year. Current items are used up within the year so they should be financed by money taken in during that year. Borrowing to pay for capital items is, however, justified because such items have a lifespan of many years and so will generate future income for the country.

Two points need to be made concerning this distinction. First, the government may plan to have current spending higher than current revenue in order to increase the level of aggregate demand in the economy. This was discussed in *Chapter 24*. Second, not all capital spending is on worthwhile items which will improve the economy in future years.

THE CURRENT BUDGET

Table 27.1 (overleaf) gives details of the 2002 current budget.

Explanation of revenue items

Item 1. This is the estimate of total tax receipts for the year, from all forms of taxation, before the changes made in the budget. *Figure 27.3* provides detailed estimates of the receipts from the various taxes.

Item 2. This is the estimate of total government receipts for the year from sources other than taxation. It includes the proceeds from the National Lottery, interest and dividends on exchequer advances (i.e. government loans to local authorities and semi-state bodies), surplus income of the Central Bank, court and land registry fees, etc.

	Revenue	€m	€m		Expenditure	€m	€m
1	Pre-budget tax revenue		29,080	1	Central Fund Services		3,424
2	Non-tax revenue		832	2	Supply Services		22,247
3	Deduct income tax reliefs	−508		3	Social Welfare improvements		638
	Deduct stamp duty measures	−20	−528	4	*Other measures:*		
4	Add VAT measures	194			Health	215	
	Add corporation tax measures	780			Education and Science	88	
	Add excise measures	255	1229		Others	242	545
5	Net effect on tax revenue of tax and spending changes		538	5	Estimated departmental balances		−28
6	Add euro changeover receipts		610	6	Post-budget current expenditure		26,826
7	Add Social Insurance Fund transfer		635	7	Current budget surplus		5,570
8	Post-budget current revenue		32,396				32,396
Source: Budget 2002, Dept of Finance							

Table 27.1 Table explanatory of current budget, 2002

Item 3. These are the changes made in the budget which will cause the amount of tax collected by the government to fall during the year.

Item 4. These are the changes made in the budget which will cause the amount of tax collected by the government to increase during the year.

Item 5. This figure represents the estimated extra taxation the government will receive as a result of the *revenue buoyancy* effects of the budget. These revenue buoyancy effects include the increase in income tax revenue as a result of people moving into a higher tax bracket, and the increase in indirect tax revenue as a result of consumer spending being higher than expected.

Item 6. This was the amount taken by the Minister for Finance from the Central Bank. It represents profits from the minting of coins and the surplus arising from lost or misplaced bank notes arising from the changeover to the euro.

Item 7. This is money taken by the Minister for Finance from the Social Insurance Fund.

Explanation of expenditure items

Item 1. *Central Fund Services.* These are the items of current expenditure that are outside the discretion of the government. No vote is taken in the Dáil on Central Fund Services, because such expenditure is authorised by Acts of the Oireachtas. The main components of Central Fund Services are:
- The cost of servicing the national debt (i.e. interest and sinking fund contributions)
- Salaries of the President, judges, and the Comptroller and Auditor General
- Pensions of former ministers and judges

- Allowances for expenses to the leaders of the political parties
- Ireland's contribution to the EU budget.

Item 2. *Supply Services.* These are the services run by the government depart-ments listed above. The main items included here include:
- Salaries of civil servants, teachers, the gardaí, army, etc.
- The day-to-day running costs of all state offices (i.e. heating, lighting, cleaning, etc.)
- The cost of running the health service
- Social welfare payments.

Item 3. This is the extra spending on social welfare as a result of the changes in this year's budget.

Item 4. This is the extra spending on health, education and other items.

Item 5. Money previously set aside but not spent in various government departments.

Item 6. The total of expenditure items 1 to 5 above.

Item 7. Post-budget current revenue exceeds post-budget current expenditure by €5,570m. Therefore, there is current budget surplus of this amount.

THE CAPITAL BUDGET

Table 27.2 gives a summary of the 2002 current and capital budgets.

	2002 Post-budget estimate	€m	€m
1	*Current Budget* Expenditure (a) Central Fund Services (b) Supply Services	3,424 23,402	
			26,826
2	Revenue (a) Tax (b) Non-tax	30,319 2,077	
			32,396
3	Current budget surplus (Current budget surplus as % of GNP)		5,570 (5.4%)
4	*Capital Budget* Capital Expenditure	6,674	
5	Capital Resources	1,274	
6	Exchequer Borrowing Requirement for capital purposes		5,400
7	Exchequer balance		170
Source: Budget 2002, Dept of Finance			

Table 27.2 Summary of current and capital budgets, 2002

Explanation of items

Item 1(a). See explanation above.

Item 1(b). See explanation above.

Item 2. See explanation above.

Item 2(b). This comprises revenue Items 2, 6 and 7 from *Table 27.1*.

Item 3. See explanation above.

Item 4. This is the total amount of money spent by the government on capital items. Included here is investment in infrastructure, energy, telecommunications, housing, hospitals, schools, etc. Also included is 1 per cent of GNP that goes annually to the pre-funding of future pensions.

Item 5. This is the total amount of resources available to the government to fund capital expenditure. Included in the 2002 figure above are receipts of €322m from the sale of the state-owned ICC Bank and €408m from the sale of TSB.

Item 6. This is the difference between total capital spending and resources (i.e. Item 4 – Item 5). In 2002, the government planned to spend €6,674m on capital items, while it had resources at its disposal of only €1,274m. Therefore, the exchequer borrowing requirement for capital purposes was €5,400m.

Item 7.

> The exchequer balance is the sum of the current and capital budgets.

In 2002 the current budget surplus of €5,570 exceeded the exchequer borrowing requirement for capital purposes of €5,400 so there is an exchequer balance of €170m.

What happens if there is a deficit on the current account?

In that case the current budget deficit is added to the exchequer borrowing requirement for capital purposes to give the total exchequer borrowing requirement (TEBR). The TEBR is then given as a percentage of GNP. This is the measure used to evaluate the burden of government borrowing in any year. Just as an individual can measure his/her indebtedness by relating his/her borrowings to his/her current income, the government can measure its indebtedness by relating this year's borrowing to the country's income this year. *Figure 27.3* shows where the money came from and where the money went in the 2002 budget.

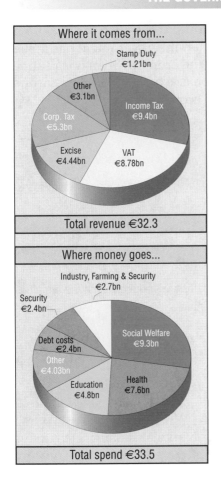

Fig. 27.3 Budget 2002: Where the money came from and where the money went (*Source:* Budget 2002)

DEFICIT, SURPLUS AND NEUTRAL BUDGETS

The term *budget deficit* refers to the current budget.

> A current budget deficit arises if government current expenditure exceeds government current revenue.

In other words, a current budget deficit occurs when day-to-day government spending exceeds what the government is collecting in tax and non-tax revenue. When the government has a budget deficit, it is putting more money into circulation than it is withdrawing, so there is an increase in the level of economic activity. Therefore, a budget deficit will have an inflationary effect on the economy.

> A current budget surplus arises if government current revenue exceeds government current expenditure.

In other words, day-to-day government spending is less than the tax and non-tax revenue collected by the government. When the government has a budget surplus, it is withdrawing more money from the economy than it is putting in, so there is a decrease in the level of economic activity. Therefore, a budget surplus will have a deflationary effect on the economy.

> If government current revenue is equal to government current expenditure there is said to be a balanced budget.

> If the overall effect of the budget is neither inflationary nor deflationary, it is called a neutral budget.

THE NATIONAL DEBT

> The National Debt is the total amount of money borrowed by the government which is still 'outstanding' (i.e. not yet paid back).

The national debt is composed of domestic debt and foreign debt.

Domestic debt

Domestic debt is that part of the national debt which is owed to Irish individuals and Irish financial institutions. When Irish people purchase government stock (e.g. Exchequer Bonds, National Loans, etc.), Savings Certificates, Prize Bonds, National Instalment Savings, etc., they are giving loans to the government.

Foreign debt

Foreign debt is that part of the national debt which is owed to individuals and financial institutions outside the country.

Year	Domestic debt (€m)	Foreign debt* (€m)	Total national debt (€m)
1995	24,945	13,413	38,358
1996	26,911	11,070	37,981
1997	28,442	10,524	38,966
1998	28,144	9,366	37,510
1999	31,446	8,404	39,850
2000	34,400	2,112	36,512
2001	34,080	2,106	36,186

*The debt shown under foreign debt after 1998 represents all non-euro debt
Source: NTMA

Table 27.3 Ireland's National Debt, 1995–2001

The National Treasury Management Agency (NTMA) was established in 1990 to borrow money for the Exchequer and to manage national debt for the Department of Finance. In 2001 its functions were widened to include the management of the National Pensions Reserve Fund, set up to fund part of the cost of rising social welfare and public service pensions from 2025 onwards. One per cent of GNP is now set aside each year in the budget for this purpose.

Table 27.3 shows Ireland's national debt in recent years, and its domestic and foreign components. If the government relies heavily on domestic borrowing, it is competing with the private sector for scarce funds. This will put upward pressure on interest rates. There is a danger that the private companies will be unable to finance their investment plans, either because funds are not available or interest rates are too high. The government is said to be *crowding out* the private sector in this case.

On the other hand, if the government relies heavily on foreign borrowing, then substantial funds are transferred out of the country in interest payments to foreign individuals and banks.

Therefore, the government will divide its borrowings between domestic and foreign debt, in such a way that private sector firms have access to adequate funds, while at the same time a large-scale transfer of interest payments out of the country is avoided.

Is National Debt a burden?

1. SELF-LIQUIDATING PROJECTS

If the government uses the borrowed money on projects which will increase the future productive capacity of the country, then the national debt does not constitute a burden. Such projects are said to be *self-liquidating*, that is they will eventually create sufficient income to repay the borrowed money and the interest charged.

If, however, the borrowed money is spent on loss-making projects or on items which yield little long-term benefit to the country, then such debt is known as *deadweight debt* and does constitute a burden to the state.

2. INFRASTRUCTURE

Productive infrastructure refers to state investment in those things which will directly increase output, e.g. roads, airports, energy sources, etc. Such expenditure is self-liquidating, since better transport facilities and energy supplies will increase the profitability of firms, resulting in increased tax revenue to the state.

Social infrastructure refers to the provision of services such as health, education, housing, etc. Such expenditure is not self-liquidating directly, since no additional tax revenue accrues to the state. However, there is an indirect benefit, since the workforce is better educated and healthier, and consequently is likely to be more productive. Borrowing to provide an improved social infrastructure does not, therefore, constitute a burden to the state.

3. PRIVATE SECTOR BORROWING

If the government borrows funds which are not required by the private sector, then this does not represent a burden. If, however, the government borrows funds which could have been put to better use by the private sector, then this constitutes a burden on the state. Output (and income) could have been higher in the absence of such government borrowing.

4. INTEREST

The greater the amount of national debt which is borrowed abroad, the greater the financial burden on the government. In the case of domestic borrowing, any interest received by Irish individuals is income and so is liable to taxation. In this way, the government recoups some of its interest payments. However, interest paid abroad is not subject to taxation in Ireland, so no part of the interest payment on foreign debt can be reclaimed by the government.

5. BORROWING FOR CURRENT PURPOSES

Borrowing for current purposes does not always represent a burden. If such borrowing is undertaken to stimulate an economic recovery by increasing aggregate demand, then it may be worthwhile. However, it must be remembered that all such borrowing allows current consumption to be increased at the expense of future consumption.

The following article from the *Irish Independent*, 30 December 2000, shows the improvement in Ireland's national debt in recent years following the strong performance of the economy.

NATIONAL DEBT NOW DOWN TO A RECORD LOW

By Pat Boyle

Ireland is going into 2001 with the National Debt at its lowest level ever.

The booming economy and low interest rates have made the country the envy of Europe. Only tiny wealthy Luxembourg owes less.

End-of-year figures show the biggest cut in the National Debt – down by almost nine per cent, or £2.7bn [€3.43bn].

The amount of money owed by the country now stands at £28.68bn [€36.42bn], leaving us with the second lowest debt, as a percentage of GDP, in the EU.

Figures from the National Treasury Management Agency, published yesterday, show the cost of servicing the national debt has fallen by almost three quarters over the last decade.

In 1990 almost 28pc of the money collected in tax revenues went towards paying the interest bill on the National Debt. Last year the figure was just 7.6pc and forecasts suggest it will fall again in the coming year to just 7.1pc.

This huge improvement means that now only 7p [9c] in every pound collected in taxes will go towards servicing the National Debt, instead of 28p [35c], as it was 10 years ago.

Last year the National Debt fell from 50pc to 39pc of our Gross Domestic Product – a measure of national output.

Michael Somers, the head of the NTMA, said yesterday this figure should continue to fall in the coming year to 33pc and to 24pc by the end of 2003.

This dramatic improvement in the state of the nation's finances has enabled Finance Minister Charlie McCreevy to set up a National Pensions Reserve Fund which will help cushion the National Exchequer against the rising cost of providing pensions in future years.

This new fund currently has more than £5bn [€6.3bn] in its coffers and its management will be overseen by a new commission to be appointed in the new year.

Mr Somers said yesterday a large portion of the fund should be invested in equities, the portion of the investment market which gives the largest return over the long term.

Mr McCreevy has already said that one per cent of the National GDP will be set aside to be invested in the fund each year up to 2025. At the moment that one per cent would result in an additional £678m [€861bn] being added to the fund each year, while further returns can be expected once the fund is properly invested.

Mr Somers said the agency was currently seeking legal advice as to whether management of the fund would have to be put out to tender. However, the new commission would have ultimate discretion as to how any fund managers invested the funds.

The £5bn [€6.35n] already in the fund represents most of the proceeds of the sale of Eircom plus accumulated interest of almost £200m [€253.95bn].

Under legislation passed last year the NTMA is to be given responsibility for the management of all compensation claims against the state.

The largest proportion of these – more than 50pc – relate to claims from the security services, including the army deafness claims.

The claims agency established by the NTMA will be recruiting a small team of experienced claims and risk management staff and will provide risk management services to State authorities with a view to reducing the level of claims.

It is envisaged that some claims which are currently at an early stage of litigation will also be handled by it. The NTMA will also assume responsibility for funds lying in dormant savings accounts – those which have not been touched by customers for 15 years. If account owners cannot be traced, the funds will be handed over for charitable purposes.

TAXATION

The principal source of government revenue is taxation. Over 93 per cent of Ireland's current budget in 2002 was financed through taxation (see *Table 27.3*). We will examine the main forms of taxation and assess their economic significance. First, however, it is necessary to refer to the characteristics that a good tax system should possess.

CHARACTERISTICS OF A GOOD TAX SYSTEM

In 1776 Adam Smith published *The Wealth of Nations* (see *Chapter 33*). In this book, he set out four canons (or rules) of taxation. These canons still form the basis on which tax systems are judged. The four canons of taxation are:

1. Equity

Each person should pay tax according to his/her ability to pay. The more a person earns, the more tax he /she should pay.

2. Certainty

Each taxpayer should be aware of his/her tax liability.

3. Convenience

The payment of taxes should be convenient for the taxpayer. In this regard, the PAYE system is more convenient than a system which required a lump sum payment at the end of the year.

4. Economy

The cost of collecting the tax should use up only a small part of the amount collected.

In addition to these rules, a good tax system should have the following additional features:

5. Redistribution

Taxation should enable the government to redistribute income from the rich to the poor. This is done through a system of progressive taxes.

A progressive tax is a tax that takes a higher percentage of income from the high-income earner than from the low-income earner.

In other words, an increasing proportion of income is taken in tax as income rises. Our income tax system is an example of a progressive tax.

Following the tax changes in Budget 2002, the rates of income tax for a single person are as follows: 20 per cent on the standard rate tax band of €28,000, and 42 per cent on the balance of income. A tax credit of €1,520 applies to a single person while an additional tax credit of €660 applies to PAYE taxpayers.

Let us take the case of two PAYE taxpayers, Ms A and Ms B both of whom are employees and therefore pay tax by PAYE. Ms A has a gross income of €30,000 while Ms B earns €60,000. For the sake of simplicity we will ignore PRSI and other tax credits that might apply. Their tax liabilities are, therefore, as follows:

EXAMPLE 1: MS A

Gross pay = €30,000

Tax liability:
€28,000 @ 20% = €5,600
€2,000 @ 42% = €840
€6,440

Less tax credits:
PAYE = €660
Personal = €1,520
€2,180

Tax payable = €4,260
(or 14.2% of gross pay)

EXAMPLE 2: MS B

Gross pay = €60,000

Tax liability:
€28,000 @ 20% = €5,600
€32,000 @ 42% = €13,440
€19,040

Less tax credits:
PAYE = €660
Personal = €1,520
= €2,180

Tax payable = €16,860
(or 28.1% of gross pay)

It can be seen that the above system is progressive. The high-income earner pays a higher proportion of her income than the low-income earner.

A regressive tax is a tax that takes a higher percentage of income from the low-income earner than from the high-income earner.

Examples of regressive taxes are TV licences, VAT on necessities, etc. A TV licence costing €95 represents 16.5 per cent of one week's gross pay for Ms A, but only 8.25 per cent of one week's gross pay for Ms B.

A proportional tax is one which takes the same percentage in tax from everyone.

An example of such a tax would be an income tax system where there is only one rate of tax, e.g. 35 per cent, regardless of income.

6. Not discourage work

A good tax system should not be a disincentive to work. If marginal rates of income tax are too high, they may discourage workers from accepting promotion, overtime or extra responsibilities. Similarly, high tax rates, together with high levels of unemployment payments, may discourage the unemployed from actively seeking work.

7. Not discourage investment

A good tax system should not discourage investment. Capital is very mobile internationally. If rates of tax on company profits are too high, then investors will transfer their operations to other low-tax countries.

8. Consistent with other objectives

A good tax system should work in harmony with the government's other objectives. If, for example, the government is pursuing an anti-inflation policy, then it should not impose additional VAT on goods and services. Similarly, if the government wishes to encourage additional investment by the private sector, then it could structure the tax system so that profits distributed to shareholders are taxed at a higher rate than profits retained and re-invested in the company.

9. Adjustability

A good tax system should be adjustable upwards or downwards to suit the prevailing economic conditions.

10. Act as automatic stabiliser

A good tax system should have a stabilising effect on national income. When incomes are rising, the amount collected in taxes will also rise, so the increase in demand in the economy is curtailed. This will lessen inflationary pressures in the economy. Similarly, when incomes are falling, the amount collected in taxes also falls, so the decrease in demand in the economy is not as great as it would otherwise be. Taxes are thus said to be *automatic stabilisers* in the economy. They prevent incomes rising too fast in times of high demand. They prevent incomes falling too low in times of low demand.

TYPES OF TAXES

Taxes can be classified as direct or indirect.

Direct taxes

Direct taxes are taxes on income or wealth.

They can be levied on individuals or on companies. The main types of direct taxes in Ireland are:

1. INCOME TAX

Every individual who is employed is liable for income tax. In 2002 the standard rate of tax is 20 per cent (applicable on the standard tax band of €28,000) and the high rate is 42 per cent (applicable to the balance of income). A system of tax credits has replaced the old tax-free allowance system. This ensures that any tax concession will benefit low-income workers to the same extent as those on high incomes. A tax credit of €1,520 applies to single taxpayers and a credit of €3,040 applies to married couples.

2. CORPORATION TAX

This is tax on company profits. From 2003 the standard rate of tax on trading profits is 12.5 per cent. A special low rate of 10 per cent applies to manufacturing firms up to 2010.

3. CAPITAL GAINS TAX

This is a tax levied on an individual if he/she sells an asset at a price higher than he/she purchased it. A standard rate of 20 per cent applies. The first €1,270 capital gain in any year is tax free.

4. CAPITAL ACQUISITIONS TAX

This is a tax on gifts or inheritances. A single rate of 20 per cent applies. There is a series of thresholds, below which tax is not liable. This depends on the relationship of the taxpayer to the donor.

Indirect taxes

Indirect taxes are taxes levied on goods and services.

The following are the main types of indirect tax in Ireland.

1. Value-Added Tax (VAT)

This is a tax levied at each point of exchange of goods or services from primary production to final consumption. In 2002 there is a zero rate on certain food items, medicines, books, children's clothes and footwear; a 12.5 per cent rate on heating fuel, electricity, restaurant meals, hotel and B&B lettings, and newspapers; and a 21 per cent rate (the standard rate) on telephone charges, cars, petrol, soft drinks and alcohol, and adult clothing and footwear.

2. Excise Duties

These are taxes levied on goods which are produced for home consumption, e.g. Irish beer and cigarettes.

3. Customs Duties

These are taxes on goods which are imported into the country, e.g. cars, machinery and foreign beers and spirits.

4. Stamp Duties

This is a form of taxation which involves the fixing of pre-paid stamps to legal and commercial documents. For example, stamp duties ranging from 3 per cent to 9 per cent are payable when purchasing a house.

Advantages of Direct Taxation

- Direct taxation conforms to the principle of equity. It is related to a person's ability to pay, since it is based on income or wealth.
- Direct taxation conforms to the principle of certainty. The amount of tax for which a person is liable can be easily worked out, by referring to the rates of taxes, the tax bands and the tax credits, etc.
- The cost of collection is low relative to the yield. This is because employers are obliged to make tax returns for their employees, while self-employed people are now taxed on the basis of self-assessment.
- Direct taxation is convenient for the taxpayer. In the case of employees, the PAYE system ensures regular deductions from wages and salaries, while self-employed people are now able to pay in instalments.
- Direct taxes are automatic stabilisers. As incomes rise in the economy, the yield from direct taxation increases, while a decline in incomes will lead to a reduction in the amount of direct tax collected. Therefore, they automatically take more out of the economy during a boom and less during a depression.

DISADVANTAGES OF DIRECT TAXATION

- High marginal rates of direct tax discourage workers from accepting promotion, doing overtime, etc.
- High marginal rates of direct tax lessen the costs of absenteeism to the worker. This is because the worker loses less if he/she misses work.
- High marginal rates of direct tax encourage tax avoidance and tax evasion. Tax avoidance involves finding legal loopholes to avoid paying tax. Tax evasion is the illegal non-payment of tax.
- High rates of direct tax discourage investment. This happens in two ways. First, high rates of corporation tax discourage enterprise and risk-taking. Second, high rates of income tax reduce savings, thereby reducing the pool of funds available for investment.
- High rates of direct tax penalise the most efficient companies. Corporation tax is levied on profits. The most efficient companies are usually the most profitable ones. These are the companies whose tax liability is highest.

ADVANTAGES OF INDIRECT TAXATION

- The cost of collection is low. This is because shops and retail outlets collect the taxes involved.
- Indirect taxes are hidden in the sense that the taxpayer is often unaware of the tax component in the price of a good. This means that it is often easier to extract indirect taxes than direct taxes.
- It is more difficult to evade indirect tax than direct tax. A person's income may be understated to avoid paying direct tax. However, the higher a person's income is, the more goods and services he/she will buy and so the more indirect tax he/she will pay.
- Indirect taxes do not discourage work.
- Indirect taxes can be used by the government to encourage or discourage consumption of certain goods and services. High taxes may be placed on socially undesirable goods, e.g. cigarettes, while low taxes may be placed on home-produced goods.
- Indirect tax acts as an automatic stabiliser.
- Payment of indirect taxes is convenient for the taxpayer.

DISADVANTAGES OF INDIRECT TAXATION

- Indirect taxes are inflationary. They increase the prices of goods and so add to the cost of living.
- If indirect taxes are levied on goods and services consumed in equal

quantities by rich and poor, then they are regressive. This is why the government has a zero VAT rate on essential food items.

- Indirect taxes may prevent consumers spending their incomes on the goods and services they prefer. Consumers may reduce their spending on highly taxed goods and services, and increase their spending on goods and services which are taxed lightly.

- Indirect taxes do not conform to the principle of equity. A man who earns €50,000 but does not smoke, drink or drive a car will pay a lot less tax than a man who also earns €50,000 but does consume such goods.

- It is not possible for the government to predict accurately the yield from indirect taxation. This is because an increase in indirect tax on certain goods and services may cause consumers to refrain from consumption or switch to alternative goods.

THE IMPACT AND INCIDENCE OF A TAX

The impact of a tax refers to the individual, company, good or service on which the tax was initially levied. The incidence of a tax refers to the individual, company, good or service on which the tax eventually rests. Therefore, the incidence of a tax refers to the burden of the tax.

Generally, in the case of direct taxation, the impact and incidence are the same. However, in the case of indirect taxation, if a tax is placed on a good or service, it may be possible for the producer/supplier to shift the burden onto the consumer. The more inelastic the demand for a good or service, the more likely the producer is to be able to shift the incidence of a tax from the producer/supplier to the consumer.

SEMI-STATE BODIES

Semi-state bodies are state-owned companies which are involved in the provision of a wide range of goods and services to the public.

In a small economy, such as Ireland's, semi-state bodies can fill the gap left by the reluctance of private firms to get involved in the provision of certain goods and services. Despite the recent trend towards privatisation in many European countries, the commercial semi-state bodies continue to play a very significant role in the Irish economy. They are represented in nearly every sector – transport (Aer Lingus, CIE, Aer Rianta), energy (ESB, Bord Gáis, Bord na Móna, INPC), communication (RTÉ, An Post), and industry (IDA, Forbairt), etc.

Merits of semi-state bodies

- Some goods and services are too important to be left in the control of private companies. This is particularly true in the case of transport and communications, since these facilities form part of the infrastructure of the economy.

- In a small open economy such as Ireland's the provision of services involving large amounts of capital by two or more private companies would involve wasteful duplication of facilities.
- Some essential services are not profitable, and would not be provided at all by private firms. This applies particularly to transport in sparsely populated areas.
- Semi-state bodies have access to funds not available to private sector firms, e.g. the World Bank. Consequently, they may have a greater chance of success.
- Semi-state bodies were seen as having the potential to develop into large-scale indigenous companies capable of exploiting the Single European Market.

Problems faced by semi-state bodies

- The Boards of such companies may contain people with little knowledge of what is required to successfully run a large-scale business.
- In some cases, the profit motive is absent. In *Chapter 21* we saw that profit acted as the signal to entrepreneurs as to which goods and services consumers wanted, and as the reward for risk taking.
- The salaries of top management in semi-state bodies are not dependent on the commercial performance of the company.
- Because they are answerable to the taxpayer, the directors of semi-state bodies may be reluctant to take risks and introduce new methods of production.
- In many cases, semi-state bodies were monopolies and did not have to face competition from any quarter. With the arrival of the Single European Market, this has now changed. There is a free market in the provision of goods and services across national frontiers, so semi-state bodies now have to face the full rigours of the market place.
- Direct government interference in the day-to-day running of the company may occur.
- Semi-state bodies may be more open to pressure groups than private sector firms, because public money is involved.
- In *Chapter 13* we saw that a feature of monopolies was the likelihood that firms would tackle losses by raising prices rather than reducing costs.

PRIVATISATION

Privatisation is the sale of a government-owned company to private investors. It became quite common in Europe during the 1980s, most notably in Britain, where it was a major feature of the Conservative Party's policy of reducing state involvement in industry.

In the 1990s a limited programme of privatisation started in Ireland. Irish Sugar was privatised in April 1991, and is now known as Greencore. In July 1991 the insurance company, Irish Life, was privatised. In December 1991 the sale of the state-owned shipping company, B&I Line, to Irish Ferries was concluded. Telecom Éireann, the state-owned telecommunications company, was privatised in 1998. The state-owned bank, ICC Bank plc was sold to Bank of Scotland in February 2001. In April 2001, TSB Bank was sold to Irish Life and Permanent plc. In December 2001, ACC Bank plc was sold to the Dutch Rabobank group for €206m. Following the impact of the terrorist attacks on America on 11 September 2001 on aviation, Aer Lingus has completed a survival plan which sees a 25 per cent reduction in its scale of operation. The government has said that it will facilitate private sector interests making investments in Aer Lingus.

Fig. 27.4 Irish Ferries fleet in 2002

Advantages of privatisation

* The sale of state companies to the private sector would raise money for the government, thereby reducing the borrowing requirement in future years.
* Many state-sponsored bodies require large injections of capital on a regular basis. If sold to the private sector, the state would no longer be responsible for such funding.
* As private companies, such firms would be answerable to their shareholders and would be judged on their trading performance and ability to make profits. Loss-making activities would cease.
* Companies would have the opportunity to expand and compete for business in foreign markets. As a state company, Irish Life was not permitted access to some foreign markets, most notably, the profitable US market.

- Government will be unable to keep funding companies at the rate it did in the past. If the companies are to survive they must have access to new sources of finance. As private companies they have access to such finance by the sale of additional shares on the stock exchange.

- Privatisation provides Irish people with the opportunity to invest in major Irish companies. The British government's policy of privatisation was characterised by discriminating in favour of the investor seeking a small number of shares, and against large institutional investors. In this way, a wider spread of ownership was achieved. This made privatisation more politically acceptable.

- The state can still exercise control even though ownership is in private hands. Maximum prices can be set, company activities can be regulated, etc.

- From an employee perspective many workers feared privatisation because of worries over job security. However, a feature of recent privatisations has been part ownership by employees. In return for agreeing to transformation and flexibility agreements, workers in former state companies were given part ownership of the new company through an Employee Share Ownership Trust (ESOT). For example, the 590 employees of ACC Bank got shares of €49,100 each in the company, equivalent to a 14.9 per cent stake in the company.

Disadvantages of privatisation

- Some state-owned companies are profitable while others are loss-makers. If a policy of privatisation were pursued, the government would only succeed in selling the profitable companies, while it would be left with the unprofitable ones.

- Control of the companies could fall into foreign hands, and decisions could be taken which would be against the national interest.

- Some services which are socially desirable but unprofitable, e.g. transport services to sparsely populated areas, may be discontinued since the sole objective of a private company would be profit maximisation.

- Unemployment could increase. Traditionally, trade unions have been opposed to privatisation since state companies were seen as providing greater job security. Private firms may seek cost-cutting measures such as reductions in employee numbers. Some observers see this as an advantage of privatisation – employees will work harder in the absence of job security.

- If the firm in question has a monopoly in the provision of a good or service, it could seek to increase profits by raising prices. This disadvantage could be overcome to some extent if the state were to retain a supervisory role in the area of pricing policy.

The trend towards privatisation is likely to continue in this country. Aer Lingus, Coillte and Bord Gáis are just some of the state companies where privatisation is considered feasible.

Fig. 27.5 Coillte, the Irish Forestry Board, manages public forests and related commercial activities

LOCAL AUTHORITIES

Local Authorities comprise County Councils, County Boroughs, Corporations, Urban District Councils, Health Boards, VECs and County Committees of Agriculture. The financial procedures of local authorities are similar to those of central government. Revenue and expenditure are classified as current or capital. The main items under each heading are given below.

Current revenue

- Rates (on commercial property only)
- Rents received on local authority houses and flats
- Grants from central government
- Interest received on housing loans
- Other receipts – domestic service charges (for refuse collection, water supply, etc.), library charges, parking discs and meters, parking fines, etc.

Current expenditure

- Housing subsidies and payments to the agricultural sector by County Committees of Agriculture
- Interest on money borrowed

- Wages and salaries
- Day-to-day running costs. Expenditure on items used up during the year, e.g. heating, lighting, stationery, maintenance costs, etc.
- Transfer payments, e.g. maintenance allowances, third-level education grants, etc.

Capital revenue

- Grants from central government
- Repayment of housing loans (principal)
- Loans from central government
- Other loans.

Capital expenditure

- Gross physical capital formation (i.e. investment). Expenditure on house building, roads, hospitals, harbours, water supplies, etc.
- Loans to persons for house purchase
- Repayment of loans received from central government and other sources (principal)
- Grants for local improvement schemes, etc.

THE PUBLIC SECTOR BORROWING REQUIREMENT (PSBR)

Refer again to *Table 27.2*. We had a surplus on the current account, that is, government current expenditure was less than government current revenue. Let us assume that there is a current budget deficit. This arises if government current expenditure exceeds government current revenue. This deficit must be financed in some way.

In the current budget:

Current Budget Deficit = Current Expenditure – Current Revenue

In the capital budget:

Exchequer Borrowing Requirement for Capital Purposes =
Capital Expenditure – Capital Resources

Combining the current and capital budgets:

Total Exchequer Borrowing Requirement (TEBR) =
Current Budget Deficit + Exchequer Borrowing Requirement for Capital Purposes

317

The Public Sector Borrowing Requirement (PSBR) is derived by adding to the Total Exchequer Borrowing Requirement (TEBR), the borrowing undertaken by state-sponsored bodies and local authorities. The PSBR is the overall amount of borrowing undertaken during the year by all elements of the public sector – central government, state-sponsored bodies and local authorities. That is:

> Public Sector Borrowing Requirement (PSBR) =
> Total Exchequer Borrowing Requirement +
> Borrowing by State-Sponsored Bodies and Local Authorities

Where is this money obtained? The PSBR can be financed by non-monetary means or monetary means.

Non-monetary financing of the PSBR

This is the financing of the PSBR which does not result in an increase in the supply of money in the economy. In other words, the government is simply using other people's money. Non-monetary financing of the PSBR occurs if:

* The governments uses 'small savings', i.e. money deposited with the Post Office Savings Bank, and
* The government sells government stock to Irish residents.

Monetary financing of the PSBR

This is the financing of the PSBR which does result in an increase in the supply of money in the economy. The domestic money supply increases if:

* The government borrows from Irish banks
* The government borrows from foreign banks, and
* The government sells government stock abroad.

We saw in *Chapter 22* that the commercial banks can increase the supply of money by the granting of loans. We now see that the government can increase the money supply by monetary financing of the PSBR. Therefore:

> Domestic Credit Expansion (DCE) =
> Monetary Financing of the PSBR + Increase in Bank Lending to Private Sector

CHAPTER 28

International Trade

In *Chapter 22* we saw that before the introduction of money as a medium of exchange, people used a system of barter to get rid of their surplus goods and acquire the things they most wanted. In exchanging goods in this way, they recognised the advantages of specialisation. Instead of trying to be completely self-sufficient and provide all his/her own needs, the individual worker today devotes his/her energy to one job, at which he/she acquires a reasonable degree of proficiency. He/she is then able to purchase his/her other needs from people who are relatively efficient at providing those goods and services. Such *specialisation* is the hallmark of an advanced economy.

The advantages of specialisation can be just as easily applied to countries. A country can increase its standard of living by engaging in international trade. For centuries, merchants have seen the benefits of trade between countries, and the opening up of new lands led to a huge increase in the range of goods available. In the 19th century, business people advocated a policy of *laissez faire*, that is, the minimum government interference in international trade. In the 20th century, the volume of international trade increased enormously with improvements in transport and better storage and handling facilities. Also, since the end of the Second World War, there has been an increase in awareness of the benefits of less restricted international trade, with the emergence of the World Trade Organisation (WTO) and the European Union (EU).

ADVANTAGES OF INTERNATIONAL TRADE

1. Wider choice of goods

By engaging in international trade, a country can consume products which it cannot produce. For example, Ireland is able to enjoy fruit, vegetables and cereal crops from countries which have climates very different from ours. Also, natural resources are not distributed evenly across the earth. Some countries have abundant supplies of mineral wealth, while others have none.

2. Competition increased

International trade increases competition. This leads to more efficient methods of production and lower prices for the consumer.

3. Productivity increased

Some goods, for example cars, must be produced in vast quantities if firms are to be profitable. Even in large countries, the demand from domestic customers alone would not be sufficient to make production worthwhile.

4. Market for excess output

International trade provides a market for a country's excess output. Goods that cannot be sold at home can be disposed of abroad.

5. Better international relations

International trade increases contact and leads to better relations between countries.

6. Higher standard of living

Just as the individual worker gains by the specialisation of labour, a country is able to enjoy a higher standard of living by concentrating on the production of those goods and services at which it is relatively efficient, and obtaining its other requirements through international trade.

BASIS OF INTERNATIONAL TRADE – ABSOLUTE ADVANTAGE

A country has an absolute advantage in the production of a good if it can produce that good more cheaply than other countries. Another way of saying this is that a country has an absolute advantage in the production of a good if less resources are required to make a unit of that good than is the case in other countries.

Example 1

Let us consider the case of two countries, Spain and Portugal. For the sake of simplicity, we will assume that both countries produce only two goods (oranges and wine), and that there are only two workers in each country. *Table 28.1* shows the output that a worker in each country can produce per year.

Output per worker per year	Oranges (boxes)	Wine (litres)
Spain	1,000	2,000
Portugal	500	3,000

Table 28.1 Spain has an absolute advantage in the production of oranges, while Portugal has an absolute advantage in the production of wine

A worker in Spain can produce 1,000 boxes of oranges or 2,000 litres of wine in a year. A worker in Portugal can produce 500 boxes of oranges or 3,000 litres of wine in a year.

With no Trade

If the two countries supply their own needs and do not engage in trade, Spain will have one worker producing oranges and one producing wine; and Portugal will have one worker producing oranges and one producing wine. Spain will produce 1,000 boxes of oranges and 2,000 litres of wine; and Portugal will produce 500 boxes of oranges and 3,000 litres of wine. The total output of oranges will be 1,500 boxes. The total output of wine will be 5,000 litres.

With Trade

Spain is better at producing oranges. Portugal is better at producing wine. If Spain specialises in oranges and Portugal in wine, Spain's two workers will produce 2,000 boxes of oranges; and Portugal's two workers will produce 6,000 litres of wine.

The benefits of trade are obvious. If trade takes place, total output of oranges will increase from 1,500 to 2,000 boxes. Total output of wine will increase from 5,000 to 6,000 litres.

By specialising and engaging in international trade both countries can enjoy a higher standard of living by sharing the increased output between them. Spain is said to have an absolute advantage in the production of oranges, while Portugal has an absolute advantage in the production of wine.

The Law of Absolute Advantage states that each country should specialise in the production of that good in which it has an absolute advantage.

BASIS OF INTERNATIONAL TRADE – COMPARATIVE ADVANTAGE

Suppose one country is relatively more efficient in the production of both products. Will specialisation and trade still benefit both countries?

Example 2

Let us consider the case of two countries, Denmark and France. In order to make the explanation easier, we will again assume that each country produces only two goods (beer and bread), and that each country has only two workers. *Table 28.2* shows the output that a worker in each country can produce per year.

Output per worker per year	Beer (units)	Bread (units)
Denmark	100	80
France	50	75

Table 28.2 Denmark has an absolute advantage in the production of both goods

A worker in Denmark can produce 100 units of beer or 80 units of bread in a year. A worker in France can produce 50 units of beer or 75 units of bread in a year.

WITH NO TRADE

If the two countries supply their own needs and do not engage in trade, Denmark will have one worker producing beer and one producing bread; and France will have one worker producing beer and one producing bread. Denmark will produce 100 units of beer and 80 units of bread; and France will produce 50 units of beer and 75 units of bread. The total output of beer will be 150 units. The total output of bread will be 155 units.

WITH TRADE

- A Danish worker is twice as good as a French worker at producing beer (100:50 = 2:1).
- A Danish worker is only 1.07 times as good as a French worker at producing bread (80:75 = 1.07:1).
- Denmark is said to have a comparative advantage in the production of beer. That is, Denmark is better at producing beer than producing bread.
- A French worker can produce only half the output of beer of a Danish worker (50/100 = 1/2).
- A French worker can produce 94 per cent of the output of bread of a Danish worker (75/80 = 0.94).

- France is said to have a comparative advantage in the production of bread. That is, France is better at producing bread than producing beer.

The Law of Comparative Advantage states that a country should specialise in the production of those goods at which it is relatively most efficient, and obtain its other requirements through international trade.

In this case, Denmark should concentrate on beer and France on bread. If Denmark specialises in beer and France in bread, Denmark's two workers will produce 200 units of beer; and France's two workers will produce 150 units of bread.

The benefits of trade are obvious. If trade takes place, total output of beer rises from 150 units to 200 units. Total output of bread falls from 155 to 150. The rise of 33.3 per cent in beer production more than compensates for the fall of 3.2 per cent in bread production.

LIMITS TO THE RATE OF EXCHANGE

We have just seen that total output is higher if specialisation and trade takes place. We will now turn our attention to the rate of exchange. How many units of beer will be exchanged for a unit of bread?

- In Denmark a worker can produce 80 units of bread or 100 units of beer. Therefore, producing one unit of bread requires the same amount of effort as producing 100/80 (i.e. 1.25) units of beer. This means that Denmark will not be willing to pay more than 1.25 units of beer for one unit of bread.

- In France a worker can produce 50 units of beer or 75 units of bread. Therefore, producing one unit of beer requires the same amount of effort as producing 75/50 (i.e. 1.5) units of bread. This means that France will not be willing to pay more than 1.5 units of bread for one unit of beer.

- In Denmark a worker can produce 100 units of beer or 80 units of bread. Therefore, producing one unit of beer requires the same amount of effort as producing 80/100 (i.e. 0.8) units of bread. This means that Denmark will not be willing to accept less than 0.8 units of bread for one unit of beer.

- In France a worker can produce 75 units of bread or 50 units of beer. Therefore, producing one unit of bread requires the same amount of effort as producing 50/75 (i.e. 0.67) units of beer. This means that France will not be willing to accept less than 0.67 units of beer for one unit of bread.

The price of bread in terms of beer

- France is not willing to accept less than 0.67 units of beer for one unit of bread.

- Denmark is not willing to pay more than 1.25 units of beer for one unit of bread.

Therefore, the price of one unit of bread will be somewhere between 0.67 units of beer and 1.25 units of beer.

The price of beer in terms of bread

- Denmark is not willing to accept less than 0.8 units of bread for one unit of beer.

- France is not willing to pay more than 1.5 units of bread for one unit of beer.

Therefore, the price of one unit of beer will be somewhere between 0.8 units of bread and 1.5 units of bread.

The price of one product in terms of the other is known as the rate of exchange. Just as was the case in 'haggling' between two individuals (see *Chapter 5*), the precise amount of one product which exchanges for one unit of the other product will depend on the relative bargaining strengths of the two countries.

HOW VALID IS LAW OF COMPARATIVE ADVANTAGE?

The Law of Comparative Advantage shows us that international trade could be mutually beneficial to both countries, even if one was better at producing both products. However, it suffers from a number of limitations which we will now consider.

1. Transport costs ignored

The Law of Comparative Advantage completely ignores transport costs. Transport costs can be so high that the gains from trade are removed. For example, the cost of producing Danish beer and transporting it to France might be greater than the cost of producing beer in France.

2. Assumption of constant returns to scale

The Law assumes that there are constant returns to scale. This is unrealistic. Even though one worker in Denmark can produce 100 units of beer a year, we cannot be sure that two workers will produce 200 units. In fact, there will (probably!) be diminishing returns.

3. Assumption that workers are occupationally mobile

The Law also assumes that workers are occupationally mobile. It assumes that workers can switch easily from producing one good to producing another. In our example, we assumed that the French brewer could switch to making bread, and that the Danish baker could switch to making beer. However, workers are not completely mobile. They may require lengthy periods of training before they can switch from one type of work to another.

4. Strategic reasons for avoiding specialisation ignored

The Law ignores strategic reasons for avoiding complete specialisation. Governments today recognise the dangers of complete specialisation. By specialising in the production of a narrow range of goods, countries face the risk of shortage if some interruption to supply occurs. In our example, a transport strike in France which disrupts the supply of Danish beer will cause many people in France to question the merits of comparative advantage.

5. Assumption that free trade exists

The Law assumes that free trade exists between countries. It assumes that governments do not interfere with the gains from trade. In reality, governments interfere with free international trade in a number of different ways and for a variety of reasons, which we will examine now.

WHY DO GOVERNMENTS INTERVENE IN FREE INTERNATIONAL TRADE?

At the beginning of the chapter, we listed the advantages of free international trade. We then considered how total output could be increased by countries concentrating their resources on the production of the goods at which they are most efficient, and obtaining their other needs through international trade. If these advantages are so obvious, why is it that governments do not allow completely free trade between countries?

1. To protect from competition by low-wage countries

Protecting home firms from competition by 'low-wage' countries is one of the most common arguments used to justify protection.

However, it has very little validity, as we shall now see. Workers in industries which are under pressure from cheap foreign goods sometimes demand government protection from these foreign rivals. The workers argue that, because wages are significantly lower in these other countries, competition is somehow 'unfair'. However, even though wages may be lower, we must remember that wages are only a part of the total cost of production. If foreign firms can purchase raw materials, pay wages to their workers, pay the transport costs to bring the goods to this country and still sell their products here at a price lower than similar Irish goods, then we must conclude that they are better at producing such products than the Irish firms. The foreign firms have a comparative advantage in the production of such goods. Providing Irish firms with protection in such circumstances denies Irish consumers the opportunity of buying at the lowest price.

2. To protect an infant industry

The argument here is as follows. A newly established Irish firm will produce a small quantity, and so will not be able to achieve economies of scale. Therefore, the average cost of producing a unit of output is high. Consequently, it must charge a high price for its good. Longer-established foreign firms, which are producing similar goods, have reached a size where average cost is low, so they can afford to sell their goods at low prices. If the Irish firm is to grow, it will require protection from the cheaper foreign goods. It will then be able to expand to a size where its unit cost of production is the same as that of foreign firms. At this stage, protection will no longer be necessary.

This argument calls for protection on a temporary basis only. Experience has shown that many infant industries become so dependent on protection that once it is removed they are unable to survive.

3. To prevent dumping

Strictly speaking, dumping is defined as the sale of goods on foreign markets at a price which is less than the cost of producing those goods. However, many people consider dumping to exist if goods are sold abroad at a lower price than at home. How could it be profitable for a firm to sell goods abroad below cost price?

Consider the following situation. An Irish firm made 20,000 T-shirts for the Irish market last year. It cost €8 to make each one, and each was sold for €10. The firm's position was as follows:

```
Total revenue =  20,000 x €10  =   €200,000
Total costs    =  20,000 x €8   =   €160,000
Total profit                    =    €40,000
```

The firm calculates that if it could expand output to 30,000 units a year, the average cost of production would fall to €6. However, there is no possibility of increasing sales at home. The extra 10,000 T-shirts must be sold abroad. The firm decides to increase production to 30,000 and 'dump' the extra 10,000 T-shirts abroad at €5.00 each. The firm's position is now as follows:

```
Total revenue = €200,000 + €50,000  = €250,000
Total costs    = 30,000 x €6          = €180,000
Total profit                          =   €70,000
```

Even though it sold 10,000 items below cost price, the firm's profit increased by €30,000 (i.e. from €40,000 to €70,000).

A country may ban dumping of foreign goods on its home market if the government sees such dumping as a threat to domestic producers.

4. To protect employment at home

If a reduction in demand takes place, a country may respond by restricting the imports of those goods which could be produced at home. In this way, the government hopes to maintain employment in domestic firms. It tries to ensure that the losses associated with falling demand are borne by foreign producers. If this policy is pursued by one country, it may cause retaliation by other countries. A major international recession could be the outcome.

5. To allow 'phasing out' of an industry

In the case of an industry which is seen as having no long-term future, the government may wish to avoid a sudden increase in the numbers of unemployed, so that alternative jobs can be found. In this case, tariffs may be imposed on imported goods, to allow the phasing out of the industry over a period of time.

6. To encourage domestic production of vital goods

A country may impose restrictions on the import of certain goods to reduce its dependence on foreign supplies of such goods. For example, even though wheat may be much cheaper to import than to produce domestically, the government may impose tariffs on imported wheat to allow the home producer to compete with the foreign producer. This is done to ensure regular supplies of wheat, in the event of a scarcity abroad or interrupted supplies (e.g. a war). No government wants to be dependent exclusively on foreign countries for supplies of important goods like food, fuel and transport equipment.

7. To achieve political aims

The six points listed above are economic reasons for interfering with international trade, and involve measures designed to reduce imports. Sometimes governments interfere in trade to achieve political aims. This may involve the restriction of both imports and exports. Such measures are called *economic sanctions*. Examples include:

- The USA has a complete ban on trade with Cuba because of its opposition to the communist government there.
- The UN imposed sanctions on trade with Iraq following the Gulf War. These sanctions are still in force after 10 years.

- In April 1999, the EU imposed an export ban on oil sales to Serbia following that country's military intervention in Kosovo.

Summary of reasons for government intervention in international trade

1. To protect home firms from competition by 'low-wage' countries.
2. To protect 'infant industries'.
3. To prevent dumping.
4. To safeguard employment at home.
5. To allow a declining industry to be phased out.
6. To ensure the domestic production of vital goods.
7. To achieve political aims.

HOW DOES A GOVERNMENT INTERVENE IN INTERNATIONAL TRADE?

There are six methods of intervention in international trade available to a government.

1. Tariffs

A tariff is a tax on imports.

A tariff can be:

- *ad valorem*, that is, a percentage of the selling price of the good, or
- *Specific*, i.e. a specified amount per item.

From the government's point of view, an *ad valorem* tariff has the advantage that an increase in the selling price of the good will lead to an increase in its revenue. Tariffs are also called import taxes, import levies or customs duties.

THE EFFECTS OF TARIFFS

- Tariffs earn revenue for the government.
- Tariffs reduce the amount of imports. The extent of the reduction in imports depends on the elasticity of demand for the good. The more elastic the demand for imports, the greater the reduction in imports following the imposition of tariffs.

- Tariffs should increase the demand for the output of domestic firms since the price of home produced goods is now lower, relative to the price of imports.
- Tariffs increase the price of imports and are thus inflationary.

2. Quotas

A quota is a physical limit placed by the government on the amount of a good which can be imported, e.g. 200,000 pairs of shoes, 10,000 TVs, etc.

THE EFFECTS OF QUOTAS

- A quota is more certain in its effects than a tariff. A quota is certain to restrict imports of a good to a specified amount. A tariff may be ineffective if the demand for the imported good is inelastic, i.e. people may continue to buy the same amount of the imported good at the higher price.
- A quota raises no revenue for the government.
- Domestic producers have a guaranteed share of the total market. They may exploit this position by raising their prices.
- Quotas are operated through the issue of licences to a limited number of importers. Once a licence has been granted it is difficult to justify its removal. Accordingly, it is very difficult for new firms to acquire such licences. Also new sources of supply abroad may not be explored since importers will tend to continue doing business with their existing suppliers.
- Importers are aware that there will be unsatisfied demand for the imported good. They may exploit this situation by raising their prices.

3. Exchange control

Exchange control is a system whereby imports from a particular country are limited to a certain money value.

Whereas a quota is a restriction on imports expressed in terms of the number of units of the good which can be brought into the country, exchange control is a quota system expressed in terms of the amount of foreign currency that can be spent on imports.

EFFECTS OF EXCHANGE CONTROL

- Imports are restricted to a specific value (expressed in foreign currency).
- It should be possible for the government to restrict the size of a balance of payments deficit.

- It is possible for the government to discriminate in favour of certain goods and against others.
- It is possible for the government to discriminate in favour of certain countries (by allocating a high quota to the currency of that country) and against others.
- By controlling the amount of foreign currency that can be legally acquired, a government can safeguard its own currency against speculation.

4. Embargoes

An embargo is a complete ban on the importation of certain goods.

A trade embargo imposed against a particular country could involve the total banning of all foreign trade (exports and imports) with that country. It is very rare since it would almost certainly provoke retaliation and lead to a worsening of international relations between countries. An embargo is used for the following reasons:

- Political reasons (see above). The UN Security Council imposes economic sanctions to enforce international law.
- Health reasons, e.g. certain food items may not meet required hygiene regulations.
- Safety reasons, e.g. certain electrical goods may not meet minimum safety standards.

5. Administrative barriers

Administrative barriers (or 'red tape') are those obstacles which the government place in the path of importers in order to reduce the amount of imports into the country.

Such administrative measures may include:
- Excessive documentation (i.e. a lot of paperwork)
- Lengthy delays at ports of entry for customs clearance
- Exacting quality standards, which are expensive to meet
- Detailed safety features and/or technical requirements.

While there has been a reduction in tariff barriers in recent years, there has been an increase in administrative barriers.

6. Subsidies

The previous five methods of intervention are designed to reduce imports, whereas subsidies are intended to raise exports. The government may encourage exports by providing a range of services to domestic firms which reduce their costs and/or increase their revenue. Such services need not be in the form of direct payments, as can be seen from the following examples.

- The government can provide wage subsidies to exporting firms.

- Low-interest loans may be available to exporters.

- The government is authorised to underwrite export credit insurance and provide export guarantees.

- The government may subsidise certain exports directly, by making a payment to the producer for each item exported.

- Enterprise Ireland provides a range of services for exporters, especially in the marketing area.

IRELAND'S INTERNATIONAL TRADE

Ireland's international trade has been the most successful aspect of our economic performance in recent years. As a small open economy Ireland relies heavily on foreign markets, both as a source of imports and as destination for our exports. Total exports in 2000 amounted to almost €83 billion or 80 per cent of GDP. In the same year total imports amounted to over €55 billion or 53 per cent of GDP. *Table 28.3* shows a summary of Ireland's external trade for the period 1991–2000. *Table 28.4* shows the source of our imports, while *Table 28.5* shows the destination of our exports. *Table 28.6* shows the sectoral origin of our exports, while *Table 28.7* shows imports classified by main use.

Year	Imports (€)	Exports (€)	Trade surplus (€)
1991	16,317.2	19,070.1	2,752.9
1992	16,754.0	21,260.2	4,506.2
1993	18,900.0	25,178.5	6,278.5
1994	21,945.4	28,890.9	6,945.5
1995	26,180.9	35,330.1	9,149.2
1996	28,479.5	38,609.0	10,129.5
1997	32,863.5	44,868.0	12,004.5
1998	39,715.0	57,321.8	17,606.8
1999	44,327.0	66,956.2	22,629.2
2000	55,052.5	82,980.3	27,927.8
Source: CSO			

Table 28.3 Value of Irish exports and imports, 1991–2000

Country	Percentage (%)
Great Britain	29.2
Northern Ireland	2.1
Germany	5.8
France	4.7
Other EU countries	12.8
USA	16.6
Japan	4.8
Rest of the world	24.0
Total	100.0
Source: CSO	

Table 28.4 Source of Irish imports, 2000

Country	Percentage (%)
Great Britain	19.8
Northern Ireland	2.0
Germany	11.3
France	7.6
Other EU countries	20.9
USA	17.2
Japan	3.8
Rest of the world	17.4
Total	100.0
Source: CSO	

Table 28.5 Destination of Irish exports, 2000

Industrial origin	€m	Percentage (%)
Agricultural produce	4,003.9	4.8
Forestry and fishing produce	385.5	0.5
Industrial produce	76,910.0	92.7
Unclassified exports	1,680.9	2.0
Total exports	82,980.3	100.0
Source: Statistical Yearbook of Ireland 2001, CSO		

Table 28.6 Irish exports in 2000 classified by industrial origin

Main use	€m	Percentage (%)
Producers' capital goods ready for use	7,891.7	14.3
Consumption goods ready for use:	11,362.5	20.6
Food, drink & tobacco	2,454.5	4.4
Other	8,908.0	16.2
Materials for further production:	33,635.1	61.1
Agriculture	891.5	1.6
Other	32,743.6	59.5
Unclassified	2,163.0	4.0
Total imports	55,052.5	100.0
Source: Statistical Yearbook of Ireland 2001, CSO		

Table 28.7 Distribution of imports in 2000 according to main use

THE TERMS OF TRADE

The ratio of export prices to import prices is known as the *terms of trade*. It is obtained by using the following formula:

$$\text{Terms of trade} = \frac{\text{Index of export prices} \times 100}{\text{Index of import prices}}$$

The export price index and the import price index are composite price indices, and are constructed in exactly the same way as the consumer price index (see *Chapter 25*). Like any composite price index, they involve the use of 'weights'. In the export price index, the weight given to an item is the fraction of total exports which that item makes up. In the import price index, the weight given to an item is the fraction of total imports which that item makes up. The terms of trade show us which is rising faster – export prices or import prices. A simple example will help to explain terms of trade.

Example

Suppose Ireland's only export is beef and Britain's only export is coal. We will also assume that the two countries trade only with each other. The prices of beef and coal for 2001–2003 are given in *Table 28.8*. In 2001, every tonne of beef Ireland exports can pay for 5 tonnes of coal (800:160). In 2002, every tonne of beef we export will only pay for 3 tonnes of coal (960:320). The price of our imports rose faster than the price of our exports in 2002. We can say that Ireland's terms of trade worsened in 2002. This is known as *'an unfavourable movement in our terms of trade'*.

Year	Price per tonne of beef (€)	Price per tonne of coal (€)
2001	800	160
2002	960	320
2003	1,360	340

Table 28.8 Beef and coal prices, 2001–2003

In 2003, every tonne of beef Ireland exports will pay for 4 tonnes of coal (1,360:340). Export prices rose faster than import prices in 2003. Therefore, Ireland's terms of trade improved in 2003. This is known as *'a favourable movement in our terms of trade'*.

Two separate price indices are now constructed, taking 2001 as the base year. The index number for exports is taken as 100 in the base year, and the price of exports in 2002 and 2003 is then expressed as a percentage of the price in the base year.

Year	Index of export prices	Index of import prices
2001	100	100.0
2002	120	200.0
2003	170	212.5

Table 28.9 Export and import price indices, based on data in *Table 28.8* (2001 = base year)

The index number for imports is taken as 100 in the base year, and the price of imports in 2002 and 2003 is then expressed as a percentage of the price in the base year. The index numbers for Ireland's exports and imports would then be as shown in *Table 28.9*. To find the terms of trade for each year, we use the formula given below.

$$\text{Terms of trade} = \frac{\text{Index of export prices}}{\text{Index of import prices}} \times 100$$

$$2001 = \frac{100 \times 100}{100} = 100$$

$$2002 = \frac{120 \times 100}{200} = 60$$

$$1993 = \frac{170 \times 100}{212.5} = 80$$

What the figures tell us

A rise in the figure from one year to the next tells us that our terms of trade have improved. This means that for a given quantity of exports, we will now receive a greater quantity of imports. This would happen if the following occurred:

- Price of exports rose faster than the price of imports, or
- Price of exports rose while import prices remained the same, or
- Price of exports remained the same, while the price of imports fell, or
- Percentage fall in export prices was less than the percentage fall in import prices.

A fall in the figure from one year to the next tells us that our terms of trade have worsened. This means that we must give a greater quantity of exports to receive the same quantity of imports as before. This would happen if the following occurred:

- Price of imports rose faster than the price of exports, or
- Price of imports rose while export prices remained the same, or
- Price of imports remained the same while the price of exports fell, or
- Percentage fall in import prices was less than the percentage fall in export prices.

Table 28.10 shows Ireland's terms of trade from 1990 to 2000.

Year	Index of export prices	Index of import prices	Terms of trade
1990	100.0	100.0	100.0
1991	99.3	102.3	97.0
1992	96.6	100.2	96.4
1993	103.9	105.4	98.6
1994	103.8	108.1	96.0
1995	105.7	112.7	93.7
1996	105.1	111.4	94.3
1997	106.3	112.0	94.9
1998	109.1	114.6	95.2
1999	109.5	118.0	92.8
2000	n/a	n/a	n/a
Source: CSO			

Table 28.10 Ireland's terms of trade, 1990–2000 (1990 = base year)

The terms of trade of less developed countries tend to be low. This is because many of these countries are heavily dependent on the export of one product (usually a primary product such as tea, coffee, rubber, copper, tin, etc.). The prices of these products have fallen on world markets in recent years while the prices of the goods they import (oil, machinery and vehicles) have risen sharply (see *Figure 28.1*). Consequently, the terms of trade of these poorer countries have worsened.

Fig. 28.1 The terms of trade of less developed countries tend to be low (*Source:* Congood)

The Balance of Payments – Foreign Exchange

The Balance of Payments is a record of a country's financial transactions with the rest of the world. It records all flows of money into and out of the country. It can be divided into two parts, the Current Account and the Capital Account.

THE CURRENT ACCOUNT

The current account section of the balance of payments includes all those flows of money arising from the purchase or sale of goods and services. It can be subdivided into two parts; the visible balance and the invisible balance.

1. The Visible Balance

The visible balance is also called the balance of trade. It relates to goods only. It is derived as follows:

Balance of trade = Exports of goods – Imports of goods
(visible balance)

EXAMPLES

Exports of goods (i.e. visible exports)

*   Kerrygold butter

*   Guinness stout

*   Baileys Irish Cream.

Imports of goods (i.e. visible imports)

- Toyota cars
- Pioneer Hi-fi systems
- Texaco oil.

Fig. 29.1 The Toyota Corolla is one of the most popular imported cars in Ireland

Ireland's balance of trade (or visible balance) has been in surplus since 1985. The surplus has grown steadily in subsequent years reaching a record level of almost €19 billion in 2000 (see *Table 29.1*). This reflects the strong performance of Irish manufacturing companies in overseas markets in recent years.

	1995 (€m)	1996 (€m)	1997 (€m)	1998 (€m)
Exports of goods	35,169	39,010	46,364	57,852
Imports of goods	25,698	27,892	32,307	38,972
Balance of trade (visible balance)	+9,471	+11,118	+14,057	+18,880
Source: CSO				

Table 29.1 Ireland's balance of trade (visible balance), 1995–1998

2. The Invisible Balance

The invisible balance relates to *services only*. It is derived as follows:

> Invisible balance = Exports of services − Imports of services

EXAMPLES

Exports of services (i.e. invisible exports)

- Aer Lingus and Ryanair earnings from carrying foreign passengers
- Earnings of Irish hotels and guesthouses from foreign tourists
- Receipts of Irish firms for services provided abroad, such as consultancy work, construction, electricity generation, etc.
- Earnings of Irish bands, such as U2, The Cranberries, Westlife, etc. from foreign concerts
- Emigrants' remittances
- All interest, dividends, profits and royalties earned by Irish people as a result of transactions with the rest of the world
- Subsidies received by Ireland from the EU.

Imports of services (i.e. invisible imports)

- Irish people using the services of foreign carriers, e.g. British Airways, Lufthansa, etc.
- Spending by Irish holidaymakers on accommodation, meals and transport abroad
- Payment by Irish people or firms on services supplied by foreign companies, e.g. RTÉ and Irish cinemas paying foreign companies for the rights to show foreign films here
- Earnings of foreign artists, such as Travis, Oasis, Moby, etc. from Irish concerts
- All interest, dividends, profits and royalties paid by Irish people as a result of transactions with the rest of the world (including interest paid on the foreign part of national debt)
- Taxes paid by Ireland to the EU.

	1995 (€m)	1996 (€m)	1997 (€m)	1998 (€m)
Exports of services	10,487	11,875	14,069	17,568
Imports of services	18,599	21,387	26,498	35,732
Invisible balance	−8,112	−9,512	−12,429	−18,164
Source: CSO				

Table 29.2 Ireland's invisible balance, 1995–1998

Ireland's invisible balance for the years 1995–1998 is shown in *Table 29.2*. The invisible balance has been in deficit since 1985. There are two main reasons for this. First, many of the manufacturing companies operating in Ireland are subsidiaries of foreign companies, so the profits they make are 'repatriated' (i.e. sent abroad) to the parent company. This is included in imports of services. Second, the interest paid on the foreign part of national debt constitutes a large part of imports of services.

The balance of payments on current account is derived by adding the visible balance and the invisible balance together. When this is done, the answer is called the *net balance on current account*. This is shown in *Table 29.3*. In recent years the net balance on current account has been positive. In other words, the positive visible balance has been greater than the negative invisible balance.

	1995 (€m)	1996 (€m)	1997 (€m)	1998 (€m)
Balance of trade (visible balance)	+9,471	+11,118	+14,057	+18,880
Invisible balance	−8,112	−9,512	−12,429	−18,164
Net balance on current account	+1,359	+1,606	+1,628	+716
Source: CSO				

Table 29.3 Ireland's balance of payments on current account, 1995–1998

THE BALANCE OF PAYMENTS ON CAPITAL ACCOUNT

The capital account of the balance of payments records receipts and payments in respect of 'capital' items. It is divided into private capital transactions, official capital transactions and banking transactions. The balance of payments on capital account for the period 1995–1998 is shown in *Table 29.4*.

	1995 (€m)	1996 (€m)	1997 (€m)	1998 (€m)
Private capital transactions (including capital transfers)	−1,667	−58	−2,587	−3,406
Official capital transactions	30	48	−2,768	−1,594
Banking transactions	2,283	−1,561	−385	5,523
Change in external reserves	−1,832	70	957	−2,089
Capital account: net balance	−1,186	−1,501	−4,783	−1,566
Net residual	−173	−105	3,155	850
Source: CSO				

Table 29.4 Ireland's balance of payments on capital account, 1995–1998

Private capital transactions

Purchases of land, factory buildings, shares in companies, etc. are examples of private capital transactions. The purchase of shares in a foreign company by an Irish person is a capital outflow, while the purchase of shares in an Irish company by a foreigner is a capital inflow.

Official capital transactions

This category includes government borrowing, and the sale of government stock to foreigners by the Irish Government.

Banking transactions

This covers the change in the net external position of the banks. A plus sign here means an inflow of capital, and a minus sign means an outflow.

Change in external reserves

Change in external reserves is the increase or decrease in the country's holdings of foreign currencies.

A net inflow of capital will cause the external reserves to rise, while a net outflow of capital will cause the external reserves to fall.

Capital account: net balance

This is equal to the total of private, official and banking transactions plus or minus the change in external reserves.

Net residual

Net residual is the figure needed so that the balance of payments in its entirety can be balanced in the accounting sense.

It ensures an equivalence between all credit entries and all debit entries. It reflects errors which arise in recording various transactions in the balance of payments, as well as the omission of items for which no information is available.

Table 29.5 presents the current and capital accounts of the balance of payments for 1998. Notice that the balance of payments in its entirety must balance, that is, the total credits must equal the total debits.

Current account		(€m)	(€m)	(€m)
Visible trade	Exports of goods	57,852		
	Imports of goods	38,972		
	Balance of trade		18,880	
Invisible trade	Exports of services	17,568		
	Imports of services	35,732		
	Invisible balance		−18,164	
Net balance on current account				716
Capital account				
	Private capital transactions	−3,406		
	Official capital transactions	−1,594		
	Banking transactions	5,523		
	Change in external reserves	−2,089		
Capital account: net balance			−1,566	
Net residual			850	
				−716
Source: CSO				

Table 29.5 Ireland's balance of payments, 1998

Dealing with Balance of Payments Deficit

It should be obvious from these figures that the overall balance of payments must balance. When economists speak of a balance of payments deficit, they mean a deficit on the current account. Such a deficit would not be a source of concern to the government in the following circumstances.

- If the deficit followed a number of years of surpluses.

- If the deficit on the current account is covered by a surplus on capital transactions.

- If a large part of the deficit arises as a result of the importation of capital items (e.g. machinery) that will increase the future productive capacity of the country.

- If the deficit is as a result of exceptional items in this year's trading, which will not be repeated in future years, for example, the purchase of expensive machinery by the ESB or Bord na Móna, the purchase of new aeroplanes by Aer Lingus or Ryanair, etc.

- If a large part of the deficit arises as a result of the importation of raw materials for use in Irish factories. *Table 28.7* shows that over 60 per cent of Irish imports are classified as 'materials for further processing'.

However, if a deficit on the balance of payments on current account is a regular occurrence, then the government will regard it as cause for concern and will attempt to eliminate it. A persistent deficit means that the country is living beyond its means – it is purchasing more goods and services from other countries than they are buying from it. If such a situation were to persist indefinitely, there would be a continuous drain on the external reserves and international confidence in the country's currency would fall. For this reason the government will attempt to take corrective action. The following are some of the policies that a government may adopt to reduce a balance of payments deficit.

1. The government may try to reduce imports by using some of the methods of interference in international trade discussed in *Chapter 28* – tariffs, quotas, administrative barriers, exchange control or even embargoes. The powers of a government to use any of these measures will be limited if the country is a member of an international organisation such as the EU. Also, such action would most likely provoke retaliation from those countries most affected.

2. The government could pursue a policy of *import substitution*, that is, it could encourage home consumers to switch some of their spending from imported goods to similar home-produced goods.

3. A range of measures could be introduced to encourage exports – subsidies, tax relief, export credit insurance, organising trade fairs and exhibitions abroad, etc.

4. An incomes policy might be introduced, where only modest wage rises are allowed. Workers would buy fewer imports, while the competitiveness of exporters would be improved. Such a policy would not meet with the approval of trade unions.

5. The government could pursue a deflationary policy. By increasing taxation and reducing government spending, the government might succeed in reducing imports. However, such a policy would hit the demand for domestically produced goods as well, and could increase unemployment.

6. As a last resort, the government could devalue the currency.

DEVALUATION

Devaluation of a country's currency means reducing the value of the currency in terms of other currencies.

For example, suppose that initially €1 = $2. If the government now devalues the currency by 10 per cent, then €1 = $1.80. A government will devalue the currency only if there is a persistent deficit on the balance of payments, and if the other policies designed to correct this have failed. However, as we shall see later, devaluation of the currency is no guarantee that the balance of payments' position will improve.

THE EFFECTS OF DEVALUATION

1. Exports become cheaper

Devaluation makes exports cheaper. Suppose I am exporting hand-cut glass vases to the US at a price of €100 each. Before the devaluation, an American who wanted to buy one of these vases had to give $200 into his bank to get the €100 needed to buy one. However, after devaluation, an American must part with only $180 to get the €100 needed to pay me. Notice that the price of vases in euro has not changed, but to the American buyer they are cheaper as a result of the devaluation. Therefore, I would expect to sell more vases as a result of the devaluation.

2. Imports become more expensive

Devaluation makes imports more expensive. Suppose my neighbour imports jeans from the US to sell in her boutique. The American company which supplies the jeans charges $100 each for them. Before the devaluation, she had to give €50 to her bank to get the $100 needed for one pair of jeans. After the devaluation she must part with €55.55 (i.e. 100 / 1.80) to get the $100 she needs to buy one. Notice that the price of jeans in US dollars has not changed as a result of devaluation, but to the Irish buyer they are dearer. Therefore, she will probably import less of them.

3. Essential raw materials

Many of our imports are essential raw materials. Even though a devaluation means they now cost more, we must still buy them. The higher prices we must pay for imported raw materials will probably mean that the prices of the goods made from these raw materials will also increase.

4. Increase in cost of living

An increase in the cost of imports means an increase in the cost of living. Therefore a devaluation will cause inflation.

5. Boost to tourism

Devaluation will boost the tourist industry. If our currency is devalued, foreign tourists will find the cost of a holiday here (in their currency) has been reduced.

6. Higher repayments on foreign loans

The cost of repaying loans received from foreign banks will be higher as a result of devaluation. This is because such loans must be repaid in the currency of the lender. A large part of government borrowing is done with foreign banks so that a devaluation will increase the cost of servicing the government's debt.

REVALUATION

Revaluation of a country's currency means increasing the value of the currency in terms of other countries. For example, suppose that initially €1 = $2. If the government revalues the currency by 10 per cent, then the new rate of exchange is €1 = $2.20. A government will allow its currency to be revalued if it has a persistent surplus on the balance of payments. The economic effects of revaluation are the opposite of those listed above for devaluation.

EQUILIBRIUM RATE OF EXCHANGE

Consideration of devaluation and revaluation leads us to the concept of the equilibrium rate of exchange of a currency.

> The equilibrium rate of exchange is defined as the rate of exchange which ensures that exports are equal to imports.

This is the correct rate of exchange for that currency. If imports are continuously greater than exports, then exports may be too expensive. The currency is overvalued. In such a situation, devaluation is justified. If exports are continuously greater than imports, then exports may be too cheap. The currency is undervalued. In such a situation, revaluation is justified.

THE MARSHALL–LERNER CONDITION

We have seen above that devaluation makes exports cheaper and imports dearer. Will this always lead to an improvement in the balance of trade? The answer is no. The fact that exports become cheaper does not mean that more of them will be sold. This is particularly true of agricultural exports. Similarly, the fact that imports become more expensive does not mean that less of them will be bought. This is particularly true of essential imports, such as oil. Whether devaluation will improve the balance of trade depends on the elasticities of demand for exports and imports. This is expressed in the Marshall–Lerner condition as follows:

> A devaluation will improve a country's balance of trade if the sum of the elasticities of demand for exports and imports is greater than 1 (in absolute terms).

To understand this fully, we will now look at the effects of devaluation in two countries.

Example 1: Country A

Suppose Country A's international trade is as follows:
Exports: 1,000 items at €1.00 each.
Imports: 1,500 items at €1.00 each.
The balance of trade deficit €500.
The government decides to devalue the currency by 10 per cent. Suppose in Country A that the price elasticity of demand for exports is –1.5 and the price elasticity of demand for imports is –1.8.

BEFORE DEVALUATION

Exports = 1,000 items at €1.00 each = €1,000
Imports = 1,500 items at €1.00 each = €1,500
Balance of trade deficit (before devaluation) = €500

THE EFFECTS OF DEVALUATION

The price of exports falls by 10 per cent.
Since $PED_{(X)}$ = –1.5, the quantity of exports demanded rises by 15 per cent.
The price of imports rises by 10 per cent.
Since $PED_{(M)}$ = –1.8, the quantity of imports demanded falls by 18 per cent.

AFTER DEVALUATION

Exports = 1,150 items at €0.90 each = €1,035
Imports = 1,230 items at €1.10 each = €1,353
Balance of trade deficit (after devaluation) = €318

The overall result of the devaluation was an improvement in the balance of trade of €182. The deficit was reduced from €500 to €318. In Country A, the sum of the elasticity of demand for exports and the elasticity of demand for imports was 3.3. This is greater than 1, so devaluation will benefit the country. We can summarise by saying that the more elastic the demand for a country's exports and imports, the greater the improvement in its balance of trade as a result of a devaluation.

Example 2: Country B

Suppose Country B's international trade is as follows:
Exports: 1,000 items at €1.00 each.
Imports: 1,500 items at €1.00 each.
The balance of trade deficit is €500. The government decides to devalue the

currency by 10 per cent. Suppose in Country B that the price elasticity of demand for exports is –0.5 and the price elasticity of demand for imports is –0.4.

BEFORE DEVALUATION

Exports = 1,000 items at €1.00 each = €1,000
Imports = 1,500 items at €1.50 each = €1,500
Balance of trade deficit (before devaluation) = €500

THE EFFECTS OF DEVALUATION

The price of exports falls by 10 per cent.
Since $PED_{(X)}$ = –0.5, the quantity of exports demanded rises by 5 per cent.
The price of imports rises by 10 per cent.
Since $PED_{(M)}$ = –0.4, the quantity of imports demanded falls by 4 per cent.

AFTER DEVALUATION

Exports = 1,050 units at €0.90 each = €945
Imports = 1,440 units at €1.10 each = €1,584
Balance of trade deficit (after devaluation) = €639

The overall result of the devaluation was a disimprovement in the balance of trade deficit of €139. The deficit has increased from €500 to €639. In Country B, the sum of the elasticity of demand for exports and the elasticity of demand for imports is 0.9. This is less than 1, so devaluation will worsen the balance of trade.

EXCHANGE RATES

We have already defined the rate of exchange as the price of one currency in terms of other currencies. Like any price it depends on demand and supply. The greater the demand for a currency, the higher its price (i.e. its rate of exchange). The greater the supply of a currency, the lower its price. We will now consider the factors which affect the rate of exchange of a currency.

1. Volume of exports and imports

When exporters from the eurozone countries export goods, they expect payment in euro. Buyers of eurozone exports outside the eurozone will then have to exchange their own currencies for euro with which to pay the exporters. Therefore, the greater the demand outside the eurozone for eurozone exports, the greater the demand for euro, and consequently the higher the value of the euro.

When European importers buy foreign goods from outside the eurozone, they must pay for these goods in foreign currencies. The greater the volume of imports, the greater will be the supply of euro-seeking foreign currency, and consequently the lower the value of the euro. In general, countries which have a surplus on the balance of payments will have a strong currency, while those countries which experience balance of payments deficits will have weak currencies.

2. Speculation

Speculation is the buying and selling of currencies with a view to making profits. Speculators deal in currencies in exactly the same way as they deal in company shares. If speculators think the price of a currency will rise, they will purchase the currency now in the hope of making a profit. If speculators think that the price of a currency will fall, they will sell it now, and possibly buy it back again at the lower price. Factors causing speculation include political uncertainty, general elections, wars, recessions, poor trade figures, etc. If rates of exchange are not consistent internationally, then there is scope for *arbitrage operations*. This is defined as the purchase of an asset in one market and its sale in another in order to make profit.

A simple example will explain this. Suppose I have €10,000 and the following rates of exchange apply in Ireland:

> €1 = $2 (US dollars)
> €1 = £1.50 (sterling)

By exchanging my euro in an Irish bank, I can get $20,000 or £15,000. Suppose that at the same time in the UK the exchange rate between sterling and the US dollar is £1 = $1.50. By exchanging my €10,000 for sterling in Ireland, I get £15,000. If I switch this to the UK I can purchase $22,500. Now if I convert these dollars back to euro in Ireland, I will get €11,250.

3. Rate of interest

High interest rates in a country will result in a flow of money into that country, thereby strengthening the rate of exchange. Such funds which move from one country to another to take advantage of high interest rates are called *hot money*.

4. Actions of European Central Bank

The European Central Bank can affect the rate of exchange of a currency. We saw in *Chapter 22* that one of the primary tasks of the European Central Bank is to safeguard the integrity of the currency. The European Central Bank can intervene on foreign exchange markets in support of the euro. In other words, if demand for the currency is low, the European Central Bank can use some of its holdings of foreign currencies to purchase euro, thereby keeping its value (i.e. rate of exchange) high. Conversely, if the demand for euro is high, the European Central Bank can use euro to purchase foreign currencies, thereby preventing the value of the euro from rising too high.

PURCHASING POWER PARITY THEORY

Purchasing Power Parity was a theory put forward by the Swedish economist, Gustav Cassel (1866–1945). Cassel said that the exchange rate between one currency and another is in equilibrium when the domestic purchasing powers of the currencies are equal. In other words, if the rate of exchange between sterling and the American dollar is £1 = $2, then what costs £100 in Ireland should cost $200 in the US. Otherwise there would be scope for arbitrage operations, as explained above. The theory is not really valid. Many goods and services differ greatly in price from one country to the next, without any likelihood of prices converging. This is because trade is not completely free – there are trade barriers, transport costs, etc. Also, many goods and services cannot be traded internationally, e.g. houses, personal services, etc. For an interesting example of the purchasing power parity theory in operation, see the extract from *The Economist* at the end of this chapter.

TYPES OF EXCHANGE RATES

Fixed exchange rates

Under a system of fixed exchange rates, the value of a country's currency is fixed against all others. A value is chosen for the currency, and the government then undertakes to do whatever is necessary to keep the rate of exchange at that value. A system of fixed exchange rates has several advantages and disadvantages.

ADVANTAGES OF FIXED EXCHANGE RATES

1. The exchange risk in international trade is eliminated. In international trade, goods bought now are paid for in three months time. Without fixed exchange rates, importers face the risk of having to pay more than they expected. This would happen if the value of the currency fell between the date of purchase and the date of payment.
2. The exchange risk in international borrowing is eliminated. Those who have borrowed from foreign banks (including the government) know the full extent of their liabilities from the start.
3. There is no scope for currency speculation.

DISADVANTAGES OF FIXED EXCHANGE RATES

1. Large foreign reserves are required to cope with any crisis which may arise. For example, continuing balance of payments deficits will mean the supply of the currency on foreign exchange markets is greater than the demand. This will cause downward pressure on the rate of exchange. The government will have to intervene to maintain the value of the currency at the chosen rate.

2. To maintain the value of the currency, the government may be obliged to take measures to restrict imports. If a deflationary policy is pursued (i.e. reducing aggregate demand), then the demand for home-produced goods may also be hit.

Floating (or flexible) exchange rates

Under this system, the government does not choose a value for the currency, but allows the currency to move up or down according to demand and supply. A system of floating exchange rates also has several advantages and disadvantages.

ADVANTAGES OF FLOATING EXCHANGE RATES

1. The correct rate of exchange is automatically achieved. The rate of exchange at any time reflects the true strength of the currency at that time.

2. Governments do not need to hold large reserves of foreign currencies to intervene in support of the currency.

3. The balance of payments will be brought into equilibrium automatically. If exports are less than imports, the currency will fall in value. Therefore exports will be cheaper and imports dearer. Therefore, exports will rise and imports fall, until equilibrium is reached. Governments can pursue whatever economic policies they like, without having to worry about the balance of payments.

DISADVANTAGES OF FLOATING EXCHANGE RATES

1. They introduce an element of uncertainty into international trade. Suppose I buy goods from the US for $100,000 in January, when the rate of exchange is €1 = $2. I set aside €50,000 to pay the American company in three months time. If by that time, the rate of exchange has changed to €1 = $1.80, then I will have to pay €55,555 to get $100,000. Anything which increases uncertainty for importers and exporters is likely to reduce the volume of international trade.

2. Similarly, floating exchange rates may increase the cost of borrowing abroad.

3. Floating rates of exchange encourage currency speculation. If currencies are free to move up or down, then speculators will attempt to predict such movements in order to earn profits. The selling of large quantities of a currency by speculators in anticipation of a fall in its value may undermine confidence in that currency.

FIXED AND FLOATING EXCHANGE RATES – A BRIEF HISTORICAL SURVEY

1870–1914 The Gold Standard
We have already seen (in *Chapter 22*) that during the operation of the Gold Standard, a country's currency was fully convertible into gold. Since each currency's value was expressed in terms of gold, the Gold Standard represented a period of fixed exchange rates. All international debts were settled in gold. A country with a surplus on the balance of payments thus had an inflow of gold, which allowed the Central Bank to increase the money supply. This led to price increases, which in turn caused a drop in the demand for exports. This would continue until there was equilibrium on the balance of payments. The opposite would happen in the case of a country with a balance of payments deficit.

1914–1925 Floating Exchange Rates

1925–1931 The Gold Bullion Standard and the Gold Exchange Standard
In 1925, Britain adopted the Gold Bullion Standard, where the currency was only convertible into gold in large quantities. Other countries adopted a Gold Exchange Standard, where instead of holding gold (which earned no interest), they held sterling which was convertible into gold.

1931–1945 Floating Exchange Rates
Once the Gold Standard had finally broken down in 1931, there followed a period of uncertainty in international trade. The hardships caused by the Great Depression caused countries to engage in competitive devaluations to gain advantages on international markets. One country's devaluation was followed by another's so that no country gained as a result.

1945–1973 Fixed Exchange Rates Again
In 1944 a series of meetings of the major trading countries was held at Bretton Woods, USA. After the disruptions to world trade caused by the uncertainty of the 1930s and the Second World War from 1939 to 1945, it was felt that a system of fixed exchange rates was essential. The US dollar was fixed at $35 an ounce (in terms of gold), and it was agreed that all countries would express their currencies in terms of the US dollar. At the same meetings, the International Monetary Fund was set up. It provided loans to countries which were

experiencing balance of payments deficits to allow them intervene in support of the currency. Devaluation was allowed in extreme cases.

Fixed exchange rates worked well in the 1950s and 1960s. However, problems arose when the US itself experienced large deficits in the late 1960s and early 1970s and had to borrow from the IMF. These were largely caused by its involvement in the war in Vietnam. In 1971, the US terminated the convertibility of the dollar at $35 an ounce. By 1973, the system of fixed exchange rates had collapsed.

1973–1978 The Snake

In 1973 the EU countries attempted to fix member countries' rates of exchange against each other in a system known as The Snake. Because the countries were pursuing different economic policies over this period of time, the experiment failed. In 1979 the EU countries again attempted to introduce a system of fixed exchange rates with the creation of the European Monetary System.

1979–1999 The European Monetary System (EMS)

The EMS was established in 1979 with the aim of creating a stable monetary zone in the EU by limiting exchange rate movements. It was thus seen as a first step to a common currency for member countries. The ECU (European Currency Unit) was the currency unit of the EMS. The ECU was given a central rate against each member state's currency. The currency was then given a maximum divergence rate of + or –2.25 per cent from this rate, but these limits were widened on a number of occasions when the system came under pressure. Member states contributed to a fund which was used to support a currency if it appeared to be heading outside its permitted range. The burden of keeping currencies within the system was shared by the Central Banks of all member states.

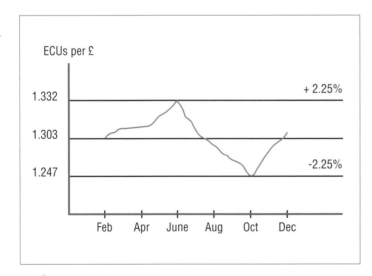

Fig. 29.2 The Exchange Rate Mechanism (ERM) of the European Monetary System

Figure 29.2 shows how the exchange rate mechanism of the EMS worked. The Irish pound's central rate was 1.303 ecus, so its value could move between 1.247 and 1.332. If the Irish pound approached either of these limits, the Central Banks would take action. For example, in June the Irish pound was approaching its upper limit. In this situation the Central Banks would sell Irish pounds and buy up other currencies, making the Irish currency more plentiful and thereby lowering its value. In October the pound is at the lower limit permitted, so the Central Banks buy up Irish pounds using their holdings of other currencies. They create a demand for the Irish pound and thus increase its value. Such an exchange rate system was called a *crawling peg system*. Despite its obvious advantages such a system had one major drawback – there was a possibility that the pegged rate might get out of line with underlying market conditions. Speculation against weak currencies would then occur.

The EMS was replaced in January 1999 by the exchange rate arrangements of the Economic and Monetary Union. These arrangements will be considered in the next chapter.

The following article, 'Big Mac Currencies' from *The Economist,* 19 April 2001, is an interesting example of the purchasing power parity theory in operation.

Fig 29.3 The Big Mac Index

Big Mac Currencies

It is time for our annual bite at burgernomics. *The Economist*'s Big Mac index was first launched in 1986 as a gastronome's guide to whether currencies were at their correct exchange rate. It is not intended to be a precise predictor of currency movements, but simply a way to make exchange-rate theory a bit more digestible.

Burgernomics is based upon one of the oldest concepts in international economics: the theory of purchasing-power parity (PPP). This argues that the exchange rate between two currencies should in the long run move towards the rate that equalises the prices of identical bundles of traded goods and services in each country. In other words, a dollar should buy the same amount everywhere.

Our 'bundle' is a McDonald's Big Mac, which is produced to more or less the same recipe in about 200 countries. The Big Mac PPP is the exchange rate that would leave hamburgers costing the same in each country. Comparing a currency's actual exchange rate with its PPP is one test of whether the currency is undervalued or overvalued.

The first column of the table shows local-currency prices of a Big Mac; the second converts them into dollars. The average price of a Big Mac in America is $2.54 (including sales tax). In Japan, Big Mac scoffers have to pay ¥294, or $2.38 at current exchange rates. The third column calculates PPPs. Dividing the yen price by the dollar price gives a Big Mac PPP of ¥116. Comparing that with this week's rate of ¥124 implies that the yen is 6% undervalued.

The cheapest Big Macs are found in China, Malaysia, the Philippines and South Africa, and all cost less than $1.20. In other words, these countries have the most undervalued currencies, by more than 50%. The most expensive Big Macs are found in Britain, Denmark and Switzerland, which by implication have the most overvalued currencies. Sterling, for example, is 12% overvalued against the dollar – less than two years ago, it was overvalued by 26%.

The greatest triumph of the Big Mac index has been in tracking the euro. When Europe's new currency was launched in January 1999, virtually everybody predicted that it would rise against the dollar. Everybody, that is, except the Big Mac index, which suggested that the euro started off significantly overvalued. One of the best-known hedge funds, Soros Fund Management, admitted that it chewed over the sell signal given by the Big Mac index when the euro was launched, but then decided to ignore it. The euro tumbled; Soros was cheesed off.

The average price today in the 12 euro countries is €2.57, or $2.27 at current exchange rates. The euro's Big Mac PPP against the dollar is €1 = $0.99, which shows that it has now undershot Mac parity by 11%. That, in turn, implies that sterling is 26% overvalued against the euro.

The hamburger standard

Country	Big Mac prices		Implied PPP* of the dollar 17/04/01	Actual $ exchange rate	Under(-) /over(+) valuation against the dollar (%)
	In local currency	In dollars			
United States†	$2.54	2.54	–	–	–
Argentina	Peso2.50	2.50	0.98	1.00	−2
Australia	A$3.00	1.52	1.18	1.98	−40
Brazil	Real3.60	1.64	1.42	2.19	−35
Britain	£1.99	2.85	1.28‡	1.43‡	12
Canada	C$3.33	2.14	1.31	1.56	−16
Chile	Peso1260	2.10	496	601	−17
China	Yuan9.90	1.20	3.90	8.28	−53
Czech Rep.	Koruna56.00	1.43	22.0	39.0	−44
Denmark	DKr24.75	2.93	9.74	8.46	15
Euro area	2.57	2.27	0.99§	0.88§	−11
France	FFr18.5	2.49	7.28	7.44	−2
Germany	DM5.10	2.30	2.01	2.22	−9
Italy	Lire4300	1.96	1693	2195	−23
Spain	Pta395	2.09	156	189	−18
Hong Kong	HK$10.70	1.37	4.21	7.80	−46
Hungary	Forint399	1.32	157	303	−48
Indonesia	Rupiah14700	1.35	5787	10,855	−47
Japan	¥294	2.38	116	124	−6
Malaysia	M$4.52	1.19	1.78	3.80	−53
Mexico	Peso21.9	2.36	8.62	9.29	−7
New Zealand	NZ$3.60	1.46	1.42	2.47	−43
Philippines	Peso59.00	1.17	23.2	50.3	−54
Poland	Zloty5.90	1.46	2.32	4.03	−42
Russia	Rouble35.00	1.21	13.8	28.9	−52
Singapore	S$3.30	1.82	1.30	1.81	−28
South Africa	Rand9.70	1.19	3.82	8.13	−53
South Korea	Won3000	2.27	1181	1325	−11
Sweden	SKr24.0	2.33	9.45	10.28	−8
Switzerland	SFr6.30	3.65	2.48	1.73	44
Taiwan	NT$70.0	2.13	27.6	32.9	−16
Thailand	Baht55.0	1.21	21.7	45.5	−52

* Purchasing-power parity: local prices divided by price in United States
† Average of New York, Chicago, San Francisco and Atlanta
‡ Dollars per pound
§ Dollars per euro
Source: McDonald's; *The Economist*

30

The International Economic System

In this chapter we shall examine the work of the major international economic institutions, especially as they relate to Ireland.

THE INTERNATIONAL MONETARY FUND

The IMF was set up by the Bretton Woods Agreement of 1944, and came into operation in March 1947. It now has 181 member countries. Its aims are:

1. To encourage co-operation between countries on monetary matters
2. To promote the expansion of world trade
3. To remove foreign exchange restrictions
4. To stabilise exchange rates
5. To facilitate a multilateral system of payments between member countries
6. To provide funds to those countries with temporary balance of payments difficulties, thereby eliminating the need for devaluation.

A member country had to declare the value of its currency against the American dollar, which was convertible to gold at $35 an ounce. In any one year a country was allowed to change its exchange rate parity unilaterally by up to 10 per cent. The country also had to contribute a quota based on its wealth, 25 per cent in gold and 75 per cent in its own currency. This fund was then used to help countries which had temporary balance of payments deficits. Such a country could obtain foreign currency from the fund. A country in debt to the IMF is obliged to seek its advice in relation to the measures needed to improve its balance of payments.

In 1969, the IMF created an international unit of account to distribute 'credits' to member countries. These credits are called *special drawing rights* (SDRs) or 'paper gold'.

Special drawing rights (SDRs) are credits issued by the IMF to member countries, which are a purely abstract form of reserve.

SDRs only exist as a book-keeping entry in a special IMF account. These sums are allocated to each member country in proportion to its IMF quota.

SDRs are used in the following way. Suppose a country has a deficit on its balance of payments. Since imports are bigger than exports, there will be downward pressure on the currency. This country will need to buy up its own currency in order to maintain its present value. It will need foreign currency for this purpose. This country can use its allocation of SDRs at the IMF to purchase foreign currency from another country with plentiful reserves. The IMF debits one country's SDR account and credits the other country's SDR account.

In 1976, major changes were made in the rules of the IMF. Members were no longer required to subscribe 25 per cent of their quota in gold. The IMF was authorised to sell its gold holding and use this revenue to give aid to the developing countries. Also, member countries are no longer required to adhere to fixed par values for their currencies.

Over the years, the IMF has introduced a number of 'special' funding arrangements to help countries suffering from acute foreign exchange difficulties. For example, a Systematic Transformation Facility was established in 1993 on a temporary basis to help member countries such as the former communist states of Eastern Europe out of severe payment problems caused by a shift away from trading at non-market prices to market-based trade prices.

Criticism of IMF

The IMF's increasing involvement in providing 'roll-over' credits to developing countries has led to criticisms that it has moved away from its core objective of dealing with short-term balance of payments problems to dealing with long-term aid issues. Many commentators argue that the IMF has extended its economic and political influence beyond its mandate by imposing increasingly restrictive conditions on loans to countries in crisis.

The IMF is based in Washington DC in the USA and is seen by many as promoting US interests and policies. Countries in crisis are very vulnerable to outside pressure.

IMF rescue packages usually involve some bitter medicine for countries in difficulties such as severe reductions in public expenditure. Because this may involve cutting back health or education spending such packages have been very unpopular in some countries. For example, in 1997–98 during the Asian crisis, Malaysia refused to accept any IMF assistance. In December 2001 the IMF told the Argentine government that it would not allow any further withdrawals from an agreed loan package as a result of failure to control spending. The IMF has proposed the idea of an international bankruptcy court to deal with similar cases in future as an alternative to bail-outs.

INTERNATIONAL BANK FOR RECONSTRUCTION AND DEVELOPMENT (IBRD) – THE WORLD BANK

The World Bank was also set up as a result of the Bretton Woods Conference in 1944 and has the same membership of 181 countries (*Figure 30.1*). Like the IMF it operates out of Washington DC in the USA.

The purpose of the World Bank is to facilitate capital investment for the development and reconstruction of member countries.

Each member country contributed to the Bank in proportion to its share of total world trade. The Bank raises additional finance by selling bonds on the world market.

Fig. 30.1 The World Bank headquarters in Washington DC

The bank makes loans either directly to governments or to projects which are guaranteed by the government. The most usual projects assisted are rural development and irrigation programmes, telecommunications, transport, water supply, etc. In the 1980s as a result of the growing debt crisis of the less developed countries, the bank made loans to poor countries to help them overcome balance of payments difficulties. There are two organisations affiliated to the World Bank:

1. The International Finance Corporation

The International Finance Corporation, created in 1956, can invest directly in private capital projects, as well as giving loans and guarantees. It can purchase shares in companies. It borrows from the World Bank and re-lends to private capital investors without government guarantee.

2. The International Development Association

The International Development Association was established in 1960. It gives long-term loans (up to 50 years) at very low rates of interest to the governments in the poorer developing countries, which have difficulty getting loans from other sources. These loans are mainly used for infrastructural development, e.g. roads, water supply, etc.

BANK FOR INTERNATIONAL SETTLEMENTS

The Bank for International Settlements was set up in 1930, and is often referred to as 'a Central Bank for Central Bankers' (*Figure 30.2*). Based in Basle, Switzerland, the bank is owned by 32 Central Banks, mostly from the main industrialised countries. It accepts deposits, makes short-term loans and carries out financial transactions for other international organisations. It acts as a clearing house for inter-bank transactions. The monthly meetings of directors have improved co-operation between Central Banks, especially in limiting currency speculation. It argues that the liberalisation in banking in recent years has created a need for international monitoring of money transfers across national borders. Also, it argues, that structures should be established to reduce the risks to depositors' funds and the danger of stock market crashes.

Fig. 30.2 The headquarters of the Bank for International Settlements in Basle (left of picture)

WORLD TRADE ORGANISATION (WTO)

The World Trade Organisation came into existence on 1 January 1995. One of the youngest of the international economic organisations, the WTO is the successor to the General Agreement on Tariffs and Trade (GATT) and is based in Geneva, Switzerland (*Figure 30.3*).

Fig. 30.3 WTO headquarters in Geneva

GATT was formed in 1947 at the end of the Second World War in an effort by the major trading nations to increase multilateral trade, reduce tariffs and quotas, and abolish preferential trade agreements. Negotiations between the members led to successive lowering of tariff barriers following eight 'rounds' of talks, commencing in 1947 and continuing up to the Uruguay round, which commenced in 1986 and did not conclude until 1994 with the setting up of the WTO.

Since 1947 substantial tariff reductions have taken place on manufactured goods. As a result merchandise exports grew on average by 6 per cent annually from 1950 to 2000. Total trade in 2000 was 22 times that of 1950. Economic growth in the major trading countries has been a direct result of the increase in world trade. An attempt to start a new trade round in Seattle in November 1999 ended in failure when up to 60,000 people took to the streets in anti-globalisation protests, claiming that WTO rules were biased in favour of wealthy countries (see *Figure 30.4*).

The earlier 'rounds' dealt mainly with tariffs but in later 'rounds' the scope of negotiations was widened to include progress on anti-dumping measures and non-tariff barriers. Liberalisation in telecommunications services, information technology products and financial services were the subject of talks between many member countries and these items have been put on the agenda for the latest round of talks which commenced in Doha, Qatar in November 2001. Agricultural products will also come under the spotlight at these talks, which will be a priority for developing countries. The draft text commits members to improve market access for farm products, reduce 'with a view to phasing out' agricultural export subsidies and cut trade-distorting domestic support.

It was agreed that WTO patent protection rules should not prevent countries

Fig. 30.4 Seattle – scene of anti-globalisation demonstrations in 1999

from taking measures to protect the health of their citizens. This will allow poor countries to produce cheap versions of drugs to fight AIDS, malaria and tuberculosis. On 11 December 2001, the WTO gained the membership of one fifth of the world's population when China became the 143rd member state.

Despite a commitment to developing trade worldwide, not everyone is in agreement with the policies of the WTO. Two conflicting views of the WTO are reproduced below.

A positive view

The World Trade Organisation is the only international organisation dealing with the global rules of trade between nations. Its main function is to ensure that trade flows as smoothly, predictably and freely as possible.

The result is assurance. Consumers and producers know that they can enjoy secure supplies and greater choice of finished products, components, raw materials and services that they use. Producers and exporters know that foreign markets will remain open to them.

The result is a more prosperous, peaceful and accountable world. Virtually all decisions in the WTO are taken by consensus among all member countries and they are ratified by members' parliaments. The risks of disputes spilling over into political or military conflict are reduced.

The WTO's agreements were negotiated and signed by governments. But their purpose is to help producers of goods and services, exporters and importers conduct their business. The goal is to improve the welfare of the peoples of the member countries.

From the WTO official website: www.wto.org

A negative view

Liberalizing your imports can be good if you have local firms that can make use of the cheaper imports to export to the world. But the firms must already exist and be able to take advantage of markets elsewhere. Markets elsewhere must be able to absorb the goods that you are able to produce. And the conditions in the country must already be good enough in terms of technology, infrastructure, education of the workforce, and so on. In countries where such conditions do not fully exist, then liberalizing imports would destroy local industry or farms. Nor would the country have the firms that would be able to export and counterbalance the cheaper imports...

We cannot press a country to liberalize before it is ready, because it will lead to a potential collapse of that economy. This is something that the WTO has to realise. The developed countries may want to export more to the developing countries, but if they don't have jobs and income and are not able to export, you are exporting to a country that is not able to import. In the end, you just end up with a world recession, which is what we are now seeing.

In the mind of the free-traders, the ideal situation would be zero industrial tariffs all over the world. But this would actually mean the death of local industry in many developing countries. The whole issue is whether we are going to have any domestic economy left in the developing world – either industry, services or agriculture. The situation is going to worsen in the next five to ten years. In the end, the WTO will have to come to its senses – not because of any ideology, but because of what is happening on the ground – that outright, all-out, big-bang liberalization is a disaster for the majority of countries in the world, and that this disaster will boomerang back on the developed countries in the form of lost markets, political instability around the world, and so on.

Excerpt from the article 'Why globalization is failing' by Martin Khor from Anita Roddick's book, Take it Personally.

Martin Khor is director of the Third World Network, an umbrella group of NGOs based in Penang, Malaysia.

International trading organisations

International trading organisations can be of three kinds:

A FREE TRADE AREA

This is a group of countries which agrees to remove all trade barriers (tariffs, quotas, export subsidies, etc.) between them. Each member can impose whatever measures it likes on trade with countries outside the free trade area.

A CUSTOMS UNION

This is a free trade area, where the member countries also agree to impose a common external tariff on trade with non-member countries.

A COMMON MARKET

This is a customs union where the free movement of labour and capital is also permitted between member countries.

THE EUROPEAN UNION (EU)

In 1957 six countries – Belgium, the Netherlands, Luxembourg, France, West Germany and Italy – signed the Treaty of Rome, which laid down the foundations of a common market between them. The primary objectives were to increase trade between member countries, so that wealth could be maximised and to initiate common policies in areas where it would be mutually beneficial to do so (transport, competition, working conditions, social affairs, agriculture, etc.).

Tariffs on goods moving between member states were gradually reduced so that within a 10-year period a common market in goods had been established. By July 1968 all internal tariffs were abolished and a common external tariff established. Steps were taken to facilitate the free movement of labour and capital across member states.

In 1973 Ireland, Britain and Denmark joined. Greece joined in 1981, and Spain and Portugal in 1986. Austria, Finland and Sweden joined in 1995, bringing the membership to 15 countries with a population of 380 million, accounting for almost 40 per cent of world trade. The EU is likely to enlarge further in the near future as another 12 countries have applied for full membership – Bulgaria, the Czech Republic, Cyprus, Estonia, Hungary, Latvia, Lithuania, Malta, Poland, Romania, Slovakia and Slovenia.

The Single European Act, which was adopted in 1987, provided the legal basis for the removal of the remaining barriers to the free movement of goods, services, labour and capital by the end of 1992. It contained almost 400 directives providing for common technical standards, product specification and labelling, transport regulations, telecommunications, etc. (see below). The EU also concluded a series of trade agreements with non-member countries, such as the preferential trading agreement of the Lomé Convention, giving 40 developing countries (some of the former colonies) access to European markets.

Another key element of the EU is its competition policy. Any arrangement which limits or distorts trade within the EU is discouraged – price fixing, market-sharing, abuse of dominant position, monopoly power, etc.

Institutions of the EU

THE EU COMMISSION

This is the cabinet (or executive) of the EU and is based in Brussels. It has 20 members, two each from Britain, France, Germany, Italy and Spain and one each from the other states. Each Commissioner is appointed for five years and is given one area of responsibility, e.g. agriculture, competition, regional policy, social affairs, etc. Each Commissioner proposes legislation in his/her area of responsibility. Although appointed by national governments, the Commissioners are obliged to act in the interests of the EU as a whole.

THE COUNCIL OF MINISTERS

The Council consists of representatives of the governments of the 15 member countries. Its membership changes, depending on which topics are being discussed. For example, if agricultural matters are being discussed, then the Council of Ministers consists of the Ministers for Agriculture of the 15 member states. It is in the Council of Ministers that the particular interests of the individual member states are put forward and discussed. Most decisions now require a qualified majority, although some require a unanimous agreement. The presidency of the Council of Ministers changes on a fixed rotational basis every six months.

THE EUROPEAN PARLIAMENT

This has 626 members, directly elected by the citizens of the EU every five years. It is intended to bring a measure of democratic control and accountability to the other institutions of the EU. It has steadily acquired greater influence and power through a series of treaties. These treaties, particularly the 1992 Maastricht Treaty and the 1997 Amsterdam Treaty, have transformed the European Parliament from a purely consultative assembly into a legislative parliament, exercising powers similar to those of national parliaments. The Parliament holds its sessions in Brussels and Strasbourg (see *Figures 30.5* and *30.6*). On 15 January 2002, the Irish MEP Pat Cox was elected President of the European Parliament (see *Figure 30.7*)

Fig. 30.5 The Leopold Building of the European Parliament in Brussels showing (a) the exterior and

(b) the inner chamber

Fig. **30.6** The Louise Weiss Building of the European Parliament in Strasbourg

Fig. **30.7** Mr Pat Cox, MEP, elected President of the European Parliament in 2002

THE COURT OF JUSTICE

The Court of Justice has 15 judges and nine advocates-general, based in Luxembourg. It ensures that laws are applied throughout the EU in accordance with the provisions of the Treaties.

THE COURT OF AUDITORS

The Court of Auditors monitors the sound management of the EU's finances. It has 15 members (one from each member state) and is also based in Luxembourg.

THE SINGLE EUROPEAN MARKET

In January 1993 the EU established the Single European Market. All remaining barriers to free trade, both tariff and non-tariff, were removed. The following are some of the measures agreed:

Removal of physical barriers

Immigration controls and customs checks have been completely removed (see *Figures 30.8* and *30.9*). There is no need for customs checks since customs duties have been abolished. Citizens will no longer have to queue up before police or immigration officials for passports and identity cards to be checked for immigration and security purposes.

Fig. 30.8 The barrier of customs checks has been removed by the Single European Market

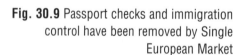

Fig. 30.9 Passport checks and immigration control have been removed by Single European Market

Goods transported from one member state to another were checked for statistical purposes, to control plant and animal diseases, to enforce quotas against external goods, to keep out banned goods (e.g. drugs). The mass of paperwork and the long delays at border crossings increased costs to the producer and ultimately increased prices for the consumer.

Removal of technical barriers

Different product regulations and standards – safety standards, health or environmental standards, standards for consumer protection – operate in each country. Such differences required expensive alterations to many goods, especially cars and electrical goods before they could move from one country to another. The EU has harmonised such standards so as to eliminate differences between countries which could hinder trade (see *Figure 30.10*).

Fig. 30.10 Technical barriers have been removed by the Single European Market

Free movement of people

From January 1992 all citizens of the EU, including students and pensioners, have been able to reside where they like in the EU, provided they register with the national health service in that country.

Recognition of professional and vocational qualifications

There is little point in extending a worker's right of residence if his/her qualifications are not recognised in all states. The absence of recognition was a major obstacle to labour mobility. Each country had its own requirements in training, qualifications and experience, which were very often not recognised in other countries. In 1989, a directive was issued establishing recognition of all professional qualifications of university level or equivalent. This came into force in 1991. This was followed by another directive on other qualifications. In addition, the EU has agreed the mutual acceptance of vocational training qualifications for apprentices. An EU vocational training card was introduced, providing proof that the holder had reached an accepted standard.

Free movement of capital

By the end of 1992 it was possible to open up a bank account anywhere in the EU, and to switch unlimited funds from one member state to another. A common market now applies in banking, insurance, information technology, etc. Common rules and regulations are applicable in all member states.

Transport

The EU has adopted common regulations in respect of transport within the EU, especially in the areas of air transport and road haulage. Deregulation has improved competition, thereby benefiting consumers who can avail of lower prices.

Energy and communications

Cross-frontier energy and communications networks have created closer links between countries.

Removal of fiscal barriers

For a single market to operate fully, all factors obstructing competition and creating price differences must be tackled. One such factor is the diversity in indirect taxes between different countries. As long as tax differences exist, there is an incentive for people living in border areas in high-tax countries to purchase goods in the low-tax country next door. In January 1993 the process of standardising VAT rates began. The policy of having similar tax rates and regimes across national frontiers is called tax harmonisation.

COMMON AGRICULTURAL POLICY (CAP) OF THE EU

The Common Agricultural Policy (CAP) has been the aspect of EU membership which has brought most benefits to Ireland. Up to 1991, three quarters of Ireland's gross income from the EU was received through the CAP. The aims of the CAP were as follows:

* To increase agricultural productivity
* To ensure a fair standard of living for those involved in agriculture
* To stabilise markets
* To guarantee regular supplies
* To ensure that supplies reach customers at reasonable prices.

How the CAP works

The CAP operates on three underlying principles:

* A single market for farm products applies throughout the EU. Free movement applies across national frontiers and a system of common prices is in operation
* There is a common tariff barrier on agricultural imports from outside the EU
* The costs of the system are paid from a fund to which all member countries contribute.

EU spending on agriculture is made through the European Agricultural Guidance and Guarantee Fund (EAGGF).

EUROPEAN AGRICULTURAL GUIDANCE AND GUARANTEE FUND (EAGGF)

The EAGGF has two sections, the guidance section and the guarantee section.

Guidance section
The guidance section (which accounts for only 5 per cent of EU farm spending) provides grants for the modernisation of farms in the EU's less developed

regions. It gives investment assistance, start-up assistance to young farmers and aid for improving the processing and marketing of agricultural products. The guidance section also finances the LEADER rural development initiative across the whole Union.

Guarantee section

The guarantee section pays for the guaranteed price system which is at the heart of the CAP. It also pays for buying-in by intervention agencies, direct income assistance, storage costs, marketing costs and export refunds.

The system of guaranteed prices was designed to provide a minimum income level for the EU's farmers. To achieve this the EU fixed the prices of many farm products at levels higher than the free market price. As has already been explained, the higher the price of a good, the higher the quantity supplied and the lower the quantity demanded. *Figure 30.11* shows the effect of a guaranteed price.

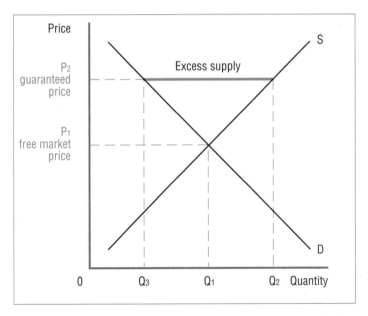

Fig. 30.11 Guaranteed prices can lead to excess supply

Suppose D and S represent the demand and supply curves, respectively, for beef. P_1 represents the price that would prevail if there were no intervention by the EU, and Q_1 is the equilibrium quantity. P_2 represents the minimum price guaranteed by the EU. At this price, the quantity supplied is Q_2 but only Q_3 is demanded. The quantity, $Q_2 - Q_3$ is the excess supply which the market does not want. This excess supply is bought up by the EU and disposed of at a later stage, mostly outside the EU. This stock includes the 'butter mountains' and 'wine lakes' to which reference is often made. Such intervention prices cover almost 90 per cent of products, including cereals, rice, sugar, dairy products, beef and lamb.

CAP success

Introduced in 1962, the CAP's first decade was a great success. Agricultural output grew steadily, leading to self-sufficiency for the original six member states, and low prices for consumers. However, in the early 1970s due partly to technological progress, substantial surpluses started to appear, causing the build-up of huge public stocks and a huge increase in agricultural spending. It was becoming clear that market management policies on their own could not solve the problems of European agriculture. Attention would have to be given to the social and economic environment in which farms operate. Accordingly, in the late 1970s and in the 1980s many changes were made to the CAP. Pricing policy for farm output was modified, market intervention was restricted, output was restricted (mainly by production quotas), and a system was put in place to control spending on agriculture. At the same time steps were taken to stimulate the development of rural areas – training for farmers, financial assistance for young farmers, a retirement scheme for older farmers, investment in modernising farm holdings, etc.

CAP problems

The CAP has been severely criticised over the years, both from within and outside the EU. It has been accused of penalising the consumer, who has to pay higher prices for food in the shops, and also must contribute more in taxes to pay for the costs involved in the CAP. Its critics also claim that it takes up too much of the EU budget. *Figure 30.12* shows that 47 per cent of total expenditure goes on agricultural policy.

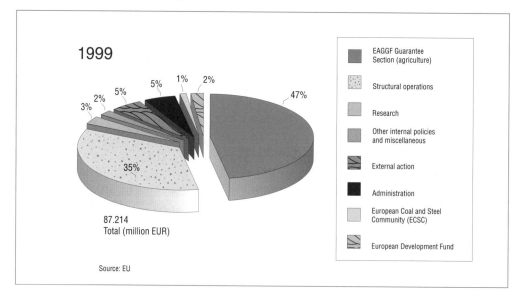

Fig. 30.12 The EU budget, 1999

Critics also point out that since those on low incomes spend a higher proportion of their income on food, the CAP imposes a greater burden on the poor. Also, the relative size of the farm sector varies in the member states. The more food a country produces, the more it gains from the CAP.

Britain and Germany pay most of the costs of the CAP, yet their farm sectors are the smallest in the EU. Also, pressure has been growing from outside the EU for changes in the CAP. The EU is self-sufficient in most food products, so imports from outside the EU are subject to major restrictions. This has led to US threats to impose additional tariffs on EU food products.

The US has seen its own position in world agriculture under threat as a result of EU export refunds. Between 1973 and 1988, the volume of agricultural production in the EU grew by 2 per cent per year, while internal demand increased by only 0.5 per cent per year. The EU is now an exporter of most foodstuffs. To get rid of surplus production, the EU refunds traders the difference between the world price and the EU price for any produce sold outside the EU. In the case of beef, export refunds make up almost 50 per cent of the total price received by the trader. Other food producing countries have been forced to give similar export refunds in order to hold onto markets.

CAP reform

The growing calls for CAP reform, particularly from Britain, led to the following decisions being taken in 1988.

- The introduction of guarantee thresholds for some products which would reduce open-ended production subsidies
- The application of milk quotas
- The introduction of a system of 'stabilisers' which would automatically cut price support when output exceeded a certain ceiling
- The restriction of the growth of annual spending on agriculture to 74 per cent of the growth of GNP in the EU.

In 1992, the EU undertook the most fundamental reform of the CAP in its 30-year history. The emphasis changed from price support to income support measures. The price support measures were seen as inefficient in that only a fraction of every pound spent actually goes to the producers. Also, large-scale producers derived most benefits from the CAP.

Agenda 2000

A further programme of CAP reform was put in place in 1999 (Agenda 2000). Market management instruments have been adjusted to restore greater balance to markets. A comprehensive rural development policy has been put in place with agriculture at its core, and the role of farmers in protecting the rural environment is recognised. A greater emphasis is placed on environmental awareness, animal welfare and quality products so as to consolidate the EU's agricultural status internally and on world markets. The new policy introduces a progressive reduction in support prices in several key sectors (cereals and beef from 2000, dairy products from 2005), with the intervention system downgraded to providing a safety net. As price support is scaled down, direct payments to farmers are being increased to guarantee them a stable income and a fair standard of living.

The reform also increases decentralisation. A portion of the direct payments in the beef and dairy sectors are now distributed in national budgets, with member states free to allocate them as they see fit, subject to EU competition rules.

Ireland and CAP

The importance of the EU's CAP to Ireland can be seen in *Table 30.1*. In 1999, Irish farmers received €1,723m in price supports and €106m in guidance payments. The CAP has been of immense benefit not just to agriculture but also to the economy in general. It has assisted the modernisation of farms and food processing firms, provided access for our food producers to a market of over 375 million people and increased farm incomes. In fact, Ireland has been a major beneficiary of the CAP, both as a result of direct transfers and also as a result of selling its goods on the higher priced European market.

Category	1996 (€m)	1997 (€m)	1998 (€m)	1999 (€m)
Guidance section of CAP	191	211	236	106
Guarantee section of CAP	1,733	1,930	1,619	1,723
EU Social Fund	321	344	398	266
EU Regional Development Fund	377	452	597	265
Cohesion Fund	174	207	143	290
Miscellaneous	22	37	24	29
Total	2,818	3,181	3,017	2,679
Source: Department of Agriculture				

Table 30.1 Irish receipts from the EU 1996–1999

EU STRUCTURAL POLICY

The Structural Policy objectives of the EU are classified as follows:

1. Promoting the development and structural adjustment of regions whose development is lagging behind.
2. Conversion of declining industrial regions.

3. Combating long-term unemployment.

4. Integration of young people into working life.

5. (a) Adjustment of production, processing and marketing structures in agriculture and forestry, and (b) development of rural areas.

The EU's Structural Funds are earmarked for the achievement of these objectives. The Structural Funds are:

*   The European Regional Development Fund (ERDF)
*   The European Social Fund (ESF)
*   The Guidance Section of the European Agricultural Guidance and Guarantee Fund (EAGGF)
*   The Financial Instrument for Fisheries Guidance (FIFG).

Ireland and Structural Funds

Ireland joined the European Union in 1973 as a peripheral and relatively poor state with average per capita income of only 62 per cent of the EU average. All of Ireland was designated as an 'Objective 1' region, which meant it was given priority status in the EU for the purposes of funding. In 1993 Ireland was one of four countries in the EU granted additional money for general infrastructural development from the Cohesion Fund set up under the Maastricht Treaty for this purpose.

*   The four priority areas for expenditure for Ireland were identified as:
*   Support for productive investment (industry, rural development, forestry, fishing, tourism)
*   Infrastructure (transport, Tallaght Hospital, power stations, computerisation of rural post offices)
*   Development of human resources (training, dealing with social exclusion, early school leavers programme, disability programmes)
*   Harnessing the potential of local initiatives (County Enterprise Boards, area partnerships, urban and village renewal).

Because of Ireland's very strong economic performance between 1994 and 1999, Ireland as a whole could not be classified as an 'Objective 1' region for the period 2000–2006. Accordingly, the government negotiated a reclassification of Ireland into two regions:

(a) The Border, Midland and Western (BMW) Region which has retained Objective 1 status for the full period 2000–2006.

(b) The Southern and Eastern (S&E) Region which will qualify for a six-year phasing out of Objective 1 Structural Funds up to the end of 2005.

> BMW Region – Border, Midland and Western Region
> S&E Region – Southern and Eastern Region

Figure 30.13 shows the regional classification of Ireland for Structural Funds.

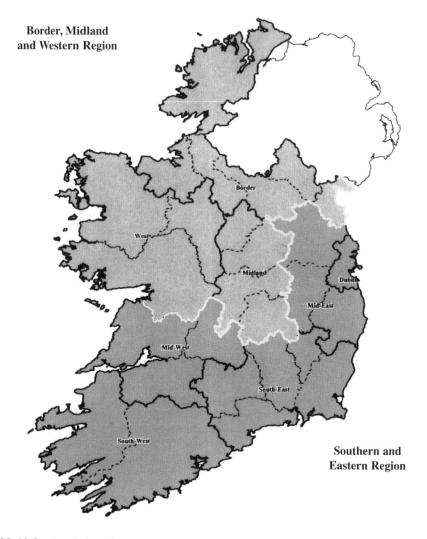

Fig. 30.13 Regional classification of Ireland for EU Structural Funds purposes (Source: NDP)

Ireland will obtain roughly €4.5 billion in Structural Funds for the period of the National Development Plan, 2000–2006. This is a reduction on our previous level of funding and reflects the fact that Irish per capita income has risen substantially in recent years. Funding levels for all 15 member states are likely to be lower in future with the likely expansion of the EU to include the less prosperous applicant countries of Central and Eastern Europe.

ECONOMIC AND MONETARY UNION (EMU): THE EURO ARRIVES

As early as 1970, the Werner Report put forward a plan for economic and monetary union in the EU. In February 1992 the Treaty on European Union was signed by the leaders of the 12 member states in the Dutch town of Maastricht. In a referendum held in June 1992, the Irish people approved of the Maastricht Treaty by a 2:1 majority, while in a similar referendum in Denmark, the Treaty was rejected by a small margin.

Economic and monetary union involves the unification of the economies of the member countries of the EU, through the introduction of a common currency – the euro – and the harmonisation of fiscal policies. Economic and monetary union was the final stage of a long process which started with the setting up of the EU in 1957. However, it received the necessary momentum with the setting up of the European Monetary System in 1979 that kept member states' national currencies fixed within certain bands.

The Maastricht Treaty set out a firm timetable for the achievement of complete economic and monetary union as shown in *Figure 30.14*. To achieve this, monetary and fiscal policies in all member states must be compatible.

Fig. 30.14 EMU – how it came about

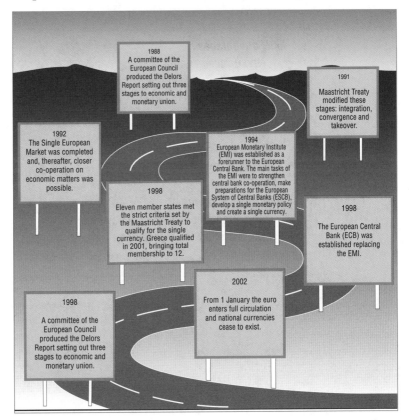

1988
A committee of the European Council produced the Delors Report setting out three stages to economic and monetary union.

1991
Maastricht Treaty modified these stages: integration, convergence and takeover.

1992
The Single European Market was completed and, thereafter, closer co-operation on economic matters was possible.

1994
European Monetary Institute (EMI) was established as a forerunner to the European Central Bank. The main tasks of the EMI were to strengthen central bank co-operation, make preparations for the European System of Central Banks (ESCB), develop a single monetary policy and create a single currency.

1998
Eleven member states met the strict criteria set by the Maastricht Treaty to qualify for the single currency. Greece qualified in 2001, bringing total membership to 12.

1998
The European Central Bank (ECB) was established replacing the EMI.

1998
A committee of the European Council produced the Delors Report setting out three stages to economic and monetary union.

2002
From 1 January the euro enters full circulation and national currencies cease to exist.

Advantages of EMU

EMU is seen as having a number of advantages. A single currency would remove all the risks and uncertainties associated with currency fluctuations. International trade between member states is free of transaction costs and speculation is discouraged. Inflation should fall, leading to cuts in interest rates. Employment in the poorer states should receive a boost as a result of the transfer of funds required to ensure economic cohesion. Finally, the euro will play a role comparable to the dollar or the yen on international financial markets. This would benefit companies and financial institutions in the EU.

Disadvantages of EMU

Economic and monetary union, however, would involve some reduction in national sovereignty, since a country's economic policy would have to be consistent with policies being pursued in the other member states. Member states would no longer be able to pursue independent national monetary policies, but would have an input into the drawing up of a unified monetary policy covering all eurozone countries.

Summary

EMU advantages
- No currency fluctuations
- Free trade between member states
- Speculation discouraged
- Fall in inflation
- Cuts in interest rates
- Increased employment
- Euro comparable to dollar or yen

EMU disadvantages
- Some reduction in national sovereignty
- No provision for independent national monetary policies

31

Economic Development and Growth

In the 80 years since independence, Ireland has made enormous progress in many different fields. Nowhere is this more apparent than in the area of economic development. Once almost exclusively dependent on agriculture, the country now has a wide range of manufacturing industries which employ 29 per cent of the labour force. GNP at constant prices increased by an average of 10 per cent per year from 1993 to 2000.

Because of the growth in output, the standard of living of Irish people has increased significantly over recent years. Increased incomes have enabled Irish consumers to choose from a wider range of goods and services than ever before. By 2000, 99 per cent of Irish households had a TV (49% had two or more) and 90 per cent a fixed line telephone, while 44 per cent had a mobile phone. Over 71 per cent had a microwave oven, 85 per cent a video recorder and 30 per cent a computer. Medical services and facilities have improved, and life expectancy has increased. Enrolment in second- and third-level education has increased dramatically, while a comprehensive social welfare system has been put in place. Our unemployment rate has fallen to less than 4 per cent.

The Irish economy of the period 1998–2002 has been called the Celtic Tiger – a phrase designed to show how closely our economic performance matches that of the so called Asian tiger economies.

There is no doubt that Ireland is ranked among the wealthy countries of the world. *Table 31.1* shows the world's richest and poorest countries, based on GDP per person in 1998. Ireland is ranked at 23rd in the list of wealthy countries. In fact, more than 88 per cent of the world's population has an average income per head which is lower than Ireland's.

If we look at the list of the world's 20 poorest countries, we note that 16 are in Africa, while the remaining four are in Asia. Even in the wealthiest of these, average income is less than 2 per cent of what an Irish person earns. In this chapter, we will identify the reasons for these huge income differences, and examine the long-term prospects for the millions of people who live in these less developed countries. We will see that economic growth involves costs as well as benefits. We will examine one theory which tries to explain the pattern of economic development, and we will study the different routes to economic progress chosen by a number of countries. At all times, we must be aware that increased wealth does not imply increased welfare. The inhabitants of a country at the top of the list in *Table 31.1* are not necessarily any happier as a result of their high incomes and the extra purchasing power that entails.

Highest GDP per capita, 1998					
Rank	Country	GDP ($)	Rank	Country	GDP ($)
1	Luxembourg	45,100	36	Netherlands Antilles	11,270
2	Switzerland	39,980	37	Portugal	10,670
3	Bermuda	39,060	38	Malta	10,100
4	Norway	34,310	39	Slovenia	9,780
5	Denmark	33,040	40	Réunion	9,680
6	Japan	32,350	41	Puerto Rico	9,110
7	Singapore	30,170	42	South Korea	8,600
8	United States	29,240	43	Barbados	8,580
9	Iceland	27,830	44	Guadeloupe	8,350
10	Austria	26,830	45	Argentina	8,030
11	Germany	26,570	46	Bahrain	7,640
12	Sweden	25,580	47	Liberia	7,390
13	Belgium	25,380	48	Libya	7,120
14	Netherlands	24,780	49	Saudi Arabia	6,910
15	Finland	24,280	50	Uruguay	6,070
16	France	24,210	51	Oman	5,960
17	Hong Kong	23,660	52	Czech Republic	5,150
18	United Kingdom	21,140	53	Chile	4,990
19	Australia	20,640	54	Brazil	4,630
20	Italy	20,090	55	Croatia	4,620
21	Qatar	19,520	56	Trinidad & Tobago	4,520
22	Canada	19,170	57	Hungary	4,510
23	**Ireland**	**18,710**	58	Gabon	4,170
24	United Arab Emirates	17,870	59	Poland	3,910
25	Brunei	17,530	60	Mexico	3,840
26	Bahamas	16,550	61	Mauritius	3,730
27	Israel	16,180	62	Slovakia	3,700
28	Macau	14,810	63	Malaysia	3,670
29	New Zealand	14,600	64	Lebanon	3,560
30	Spain	14,100	65	Venezuela	3,530
31	Kuwait	13,910	66	Estonia	3,360
32	Taiwan	12,040	67	South Africa	3,310
33	Cyprus	11,920	68	Turkey	3,160
34	Martinique	11,830	69	Botswana	3,070
35	Greece	11,740	70	Panama	2,990

Lowest GDP per capita, 1998					
Rank	Country	GDP ($)	Rank	Country	GDP ($)
1	Ethiopia	100		Nepal	210
	Myanmar	100	12	Tanzania	220
3	Congo	110	13	Chad	230
4	Burundi	140		Rwanda	230
	Sierra Leone	140	15	Burkino Faso	240
6	Guinea-Bissau	160	16	Mali	250
7	Eritrea	200	17	Cambodia	260
	Niger	200		Madagascar	260
9	Malawi	210	19	Yemen	280
	Mozambique	210	20	Sudan	290
Source: The Economist					

Table 31.1 World economies showing rich and poor in 1998

We will begin by making a distinction between 'economic development' and 'economic growth'.

Economic development is defined as an increase in output per person, which involves a fundamental change in the structure of society.

This is the task which faces the people of the underdeveloped countries. The fundamental change in the structure of society usually involves one or more of the following changes:

• Changes in the methods of farming

• Large-scale movements of people from rural to urban areas

• A change in the type of work done by the inhabitants of the country, e.g. a decline in the numbers involved in agriculture and a rise in the numbers in manufacturing and services.

Economic growth is defined as an increase in output per person which does not involve a change in the structure of society.

For example, if the output per person in Germany increased by 4 per cent this year, this would not involve large-scale movements of people or wholesale changes in work practices. It would occur as a result of an increase in investment by business people, and an increase in the efficiency of use of the factors of production. It should be clear, therefore, that development must take place before growth. Before a country embarks on the road to economic development, it usually has a high percentage (possibly 80%) of its workforce engaged in agriculture. Output per worker is low. An increase in the output per person engaged in agriculture is needed before any progress can be made. Less people will be needed in agriculture, and thus workers will be available for other jobs in manufacturing and services.

In many poor countries today, people are leaving rural areas and moving to large cities in search of jobs. As manufacturing increases in importance, some of the goods produced will be exported. With the money earned in this way, the country can buy basic machines and tools which will enable its workforce to be more productive. As output increases, the quality of services such as education, health, housing and transport improves and the process of development gathers momentum.

Rostow's Stages of Economic Growth

The American economist and historian, Walt Rostow, in his book, *The Stages of Economic Growth* (1960), put forward the view that all economies had to pass through five distinct stages on the road to economic development. In going from a poor agricultural society to a modern affluent high-consumption society, a country had to pass through the following five stages.

1. The traditional society

At this stage most people are engaged in subsistence farming. Output per worker is very low. The society is governed by a small wealthy ruling elite, while the majority of people have little or no prospect of improving their lot in life. Social customs and traditional values are very strong, and there is no framework within which new ideas can emerge.

2. The preconditions for take-off

At this stage of development, people become aware of the possibilities of improvements in production techniques. There is a growing awareness and acceptance of the benefits of new methods. Increases in output per worker occur in agriculture, and a manufacturing sector develops. Improvements take place in transport and communications, and a banking sector emerges. These changes may occur through the development of an export sector, where a natural resource is exploited by a foreign company, without any direct linkages to the remainder of the economy. Such a situation, where an advanced export-oriented sector exists alongside a traditional domestic sector, is called *dualism*.

3. The take-off

This is the really important stage. Obstacles to progress are removed, and economic growth becomes *self-sustaining*, that is, it does not require any external impetus. Agricultural output per worker increases further, so employment in manufacturing and services increases. More people move to the towns and cities, and the rate of investment increases.

4. The drive to maturity

The range of goods and services produced in the economy widens during this stage. Old industries decline in importance, and new ones emerge. More complex methods of production are used and the economy is engaged in import substitution. This means goods which previously were imported can now be made at home. Approximately 60 years after the start of the take-off stage, the economy reaches maturity.

5. The age of high mass consumption

Having reached maturity, the economy is characterised by high income per head. The basic needs of food, clothing and shelter have been met, and people turn their attention to the acquisition of consumer durable goods and the enjoyment of a wider range of services.

A sixth stage can be added where concern for the environment and the quality of life becomes more important than further increases in output. Technical progress allows a shortening of the working week and longer holidays, so that workers can enjoy greater leisure time. Additional resources are devoted to 'social' spending, i.e. health, education and social welfare. This stage is often referred to as the *post-industrial society*.

Evaluation of Rostow's theory

Rostow's theory has been criticised by economists on the following grounds:

- His analysis of the factors causing take-off and self-sustaining growth is very vague.
- The theory is based on the growth pattern of today's developed economies. As such, it may have no relevance to the challenges facing the underdeveloped countries. Conditions in all countries are different and what suited one will not necessarily work for another.
- The theory has also been criticised for not being 'people-centred'. Europe was seen as developed and thus offered a model towards which the underdeveloped countries should strive. The danger of repeating the mistakes of Europe was not pointed out.
- Increasing output does not necessarily narrow the gap between rich and poor. The notion that wealth would 'trickle down' to the poorest people has been shown to be false in many countries.

An analysis of the characteristics of the less developed countries will prove more useful in identifying what needs to be done than any effort to impose a pattern of development, as is implied in Rostow's theory.

CHARACTERISTICS OF LESS DEVELOPED COUNTRIES (LDCs)

1. Low income per person

LDCs have a low income per person. As can be seen from the figures in *Table 31.1*, less developed countries have a low income (GDP) per person. The value of total output is low, so output per person is low. Poverty is widespread, and all productive effort goes into supplying the basic needs of food, clothing and shelter. The scarcity of natural resources, and/or their incorrect use can contribute to the problem of low output. *Figure 31.1* shows some of the poorest countries of the world.

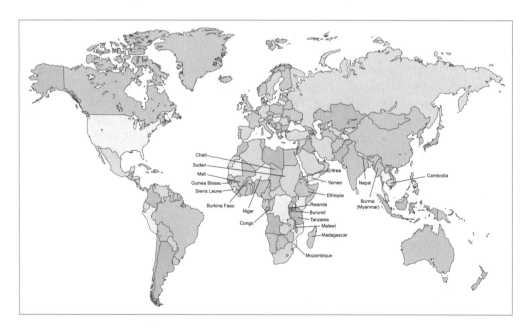

Fig. 31.1 The world's least developed countries as designated by the UN

2. Rapid population growth

Another contributory factor is rising population. LDCs have rapid population growth. The poorest countries in the world are the countries with the highest rates of growth of population. The very countries that have least resources to support increasing numbers of people are the countries which are experiencing the fastest population growth. *Table 31.2* shows the UN population growth projections for the period 2000–2015.

	Fastest growing populations, 2000–2015 (average annual growth %)				
1	West Bank & Gaza	3.82	11	Burkina Faso	2.78
2	Yemen	3.27	12	Saudi Arabia	2.75
3	Liberia	3.25	13	Congo – Brazzaville	2.70
4	Afghanistan	3.21	14	Jordan	2.64
	Somalia	3.21	15	Mali	2.63
6	Oman	3.19	16	Ghana	2.59
7	Uganda	3.06		Iraq	2.59
8	Congo	2.94	18	Benin	2.55
9	Niger	2.94		Bhutan	2.55
10	Angola	2.83		Madagascar	2.55
Source: The Economist					

Table 31.2 Fastest growing populations

Of the 20 countries which are expected to have the fastest growth in population, 13 are in Africa and seven in Asia. An annual growth rate of 3 per cent is sufficient for the population to double in 23 years. The reasons for rapid population growth in these countries are examined in more detail in *Chapter 32*. The implications of this population growth are obvious. Any modest increase in output which these countries have achieved has, in many cases, been more than outweighed by an increase in population. The share of output available to each individual will fall in such circumstances.

3. High proportion engaged in agriculture

LDCs have a high proportion of the labour force engaged in agriculture. *Table 31.3* shows the 20 countries which are most economically dependent on agriculture. Some 13 of these 20 countries have already appeared as the poorest countries in the world in *Table 31.1*. In many cases, they cannot supply their own needs and depend on outside aid. Agriculture in these countries is characterised by:

- Very low output per worker, i.e. rural underemployment
- Very little use of machinery (see *Figure 31.2*)
- Shifting cultivation
- Irregular rainfall, i.e. periodic droughts which seriously affect cereal crops
- Absence of the 'green revolution'. The green revolution was the increase in agricultural output achieved in some countries (e.g. China and India) by

the use of new high-yielding varieties of crops such as wheat and rice (see news article below from *The Economist*, 8 November 2001)

- Bad farming practices which cause long-term damage to the soil. Land overuse and misuse has occurred. Deforestation is taking place at an annual rate of 4 per cent in many West African countries. Creeping desert (or desertification) is another major problem affecting agriculture. The Sahara is estimated to be expanding southwards by 6 km per year (see *Figure 31.3*).

Countries most economically dependent on agriculture (% of GDP from agriculture)					
1	Guinea-Bissau	62		Rwanda	47
2	Congo	58		Kyrgyzstan	47
3	Albania	54		Tanzania	47
	Burundi	54	14	Uganda	45
5	Central African Rep.	53	15	Sierra Leone	44
	Laos	53	16	Cameroon	42
	Myanmar	53		Togo	42
8	Cambodia	51	18	Niger	41
9	Ethiopia	50	19	Chad	40
10	Mali	47		Nepal	40
Source: The Economist					

Table 31.3 The 20 countries most economically dependent on agriculture – percentage of GDP from agriculture in 1998

Fig. 31.2 Agriculture in less developed countries makes little use of modern machinery, relying instead on traditional methods

The following article from *The Economist*, 10 November 2001, shows the challenges facing agriculture worldwide in feeding an ever-increasing population.

Feeding the five billion

Predictions that people would multiply beyond their capacity to feed themselves ...have repeatedly been proven wrong. In 1798 Thomas Malthus foretold famine just as farm yields were taking off. To his credit, he later admitted that he was wrong. Not so Paul Ehrlich, an American biologist who wrote in 1969: "The battle to feed humanity is over. In the 1970s hundreds of millions of people will starve to death." They didn't.

The world's population grew much as expected, but food output more than kept pace. During the 1960s and 70s, a 'green revolution' swept the developing world. Millions of farmers started using higher-yielding hybrid seeds, chemical fertilisers, pesticides and weed-killers.

The results were remarkable. For example, Mr Ehrlich had predicted that by the mid-1970s, India would be so obviously beyond hope that America would stop sending food aid. Yet by 1990, India was exporting surplus grain. Chinese rice farmers, using similar techniques, raised production by two-thirds between 1970 and 1995. By one estimate, the green revolution saved a billion people from starvation.

There were some side-effects. Governments subsidised the new chemicals, which encouraged their over-use. This damaged the environment in many parts of the developing world. But the main worry about the green revolution is that it has run out of steam. There are still areas – mainly in Africa – where its techniques have yet to be tried. But in most of the developing world, the gains in productivity from it are tailing off.

Globally, 800 million people are still mal-nourished. Heavily sub-sidised farmers in rich countries produce enough surplus food to feed the hungry, but not at a price the hungry can afford. Even if the rich world's surplus were simply given to the poor, this would not solve the problem. Most poor people earn their living from agriculture, so a deluge of free food would destroy their livelihoods. The only answer to world hunger is to improve the productivity of farmers in poor countries.

This will be difficult. The developing world's population is growing fast, but the amount of land available for cultivation is not. To feed the 2 billion new mouths expected by 2025, new ways must be found to squeeze more calories out of each hectare....

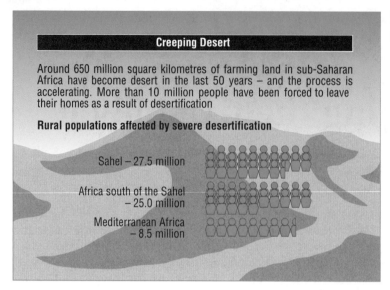

Fig. 31.3 Creeping desert

4. Dependence on one crop

LDCs are often heavily dependent on one crop. The less developed countries are very dependent on primary products such as tea, coffee, cocoa, rubber, tropical fruits, etc. Most of these products are perishable, and they are usually exported in their raw state. Consequently, the greater share of the profits from these products accrues to large multinational companies in the USA and Europe. These companies pay low rates of pay to the workers in the less developed countries and repatriate the bulk of their profits. Many poor countries are heavily dependent on one or two products, the prices of which can fluctuate widely on international markets. The World Bank's Development Report (2000/2001) shows that three quarters of LDC exports were primary products or raw materials. There is oversupply of many of these products. Industrial plastics have reduced the demand for copper, tin and rubber. The production of artificial sweeteners (in the USA) has led to a fall in the demand for sugar. *Table 31.4* shows the problem of overdependence facing some countries.

5. Uneven distribution of wealth

LDCs have an uneven distribution of wealth. Any wealth which exists in the poorest countries is concentrated in the hands of a small ruling elite. The affluence of such people is in stark contrast to the poverty in which most people are forced to live. In Africa, very few of these countries are democracies. Most are military dictatorships or 'one-party states', where the ruling elite has a vested interest in maintaining the status quo. Because of this, political instability is a major problem and revolutions and attempted coups are

Country	Leading export	Percentage (%) of total exports
Nigeria	Crude oil	91.3
Botswana	Diamonds	79.4
Burundi	Coffee	73.4
Angola	Petroleum	70.9
Zambia	Copper	70.6
Liberia	Iron ore and concentrates	55.1
Uganda	Coffee	53.7
Bangladesh	Clothing	52.3
Guinea	Bauxite and alumina	51.6
Afghanistan	Dried fruit and nuts	51.3
Chad	Cotton	48.9
Mali	Cotton	48.4
Somalia	Live animals	44.3
Rwanda	Coffee	43.2
Central African Rep.	Diamonds	42.2
Niger	Uranium	39.4
Ethiopia	Coffee	36.1
Source: UN, 2000		

Table 31.4 The problem of overdependence – leading exports as a percentage of total exports for selected countries

common. In fact, many African governments spend more on arms and military equipment than they do on health, education or agriculture.

6. Lack of resources for investment

In LDCs there is a lack of resources for investment. A country generates the money it needs for investment by saving – in other words, by producing more than it consumes. Two problems face LDCs here.

* Because they are so poor, it is very hard for them to save anything. Incomes are at (or below) subsistence levels
* Most capital goods needed will have to be imported, so foreign exchange is required.

7. Poor terms of trade

LDCs have poor terms of trade. In *Chapter 28* we saw that LDCs had experienced many unfavourable movements in their terms of trade. This means that for a given amount of exports, they can buy less imports. During the 1980s and 1990s, the prices of goods they imported (oil, machinery, vehicles, etc.) increased considerably, while the prices of goods they exported (mostly primary food products, hardwoods and ores) fell. *Figure 31.4* shows Zambia's terms of trade from 1990 to 1999. We can deduce from this that the prices it got for its exports fell steadily over the decade, while the price it had to pay for its imports continued to rise. Apart from the oil producing countries, worsening terms of trade was a feature of practically all LDCs during the last decade.

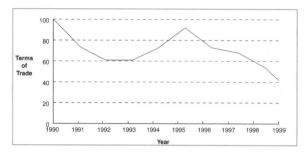

Fig. 31.4 Zambia's terms of trade, 1990–1999 (*Source:* UNCTAD)

8. Poor living conditions

Living conditions are poor in many cities in the LDCs. Because of rural poverty and underemployment in agriculture, many people have left the land and moved to the cities in search of jobs (see *Figure 31.5*). Unemployment has increased and those that do find work must accept very low pay and very bad working conditions. There is much disease, an absence of clean water and proper sewage facilities, and a serious shortage of housing. Millions of people live in slums and shanty towns on the outskirts of the big cities (see *Figure 31.6*). In 1990, 98 million people lived in eight cities of more than 10 million people. The UN estimates that by 2015 this will have risen to 378 million people in 23 such cities. Nearly all the increase will take place in developing countries. By 2025 four out of five urban dwellers will live in the developing countries and some of these will be among the poorest people in the world. The rise in urban population will continue because cities are perceived as having an advantage in the area of education and healthcare as is shown in *Figure 31.7*.

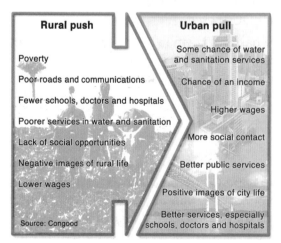

Fig. 31.5 Reasons for movement from rural to urban areas in LDCs

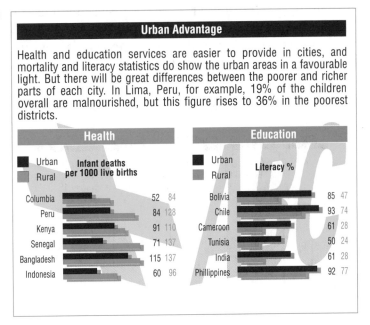

Urban Underclass

The faster cities grow, the bigger the proportion of their population which lives in slum or squatter settlements.

Estimated minimum living in unauthorised or slum conditions for selected Third World cities.

Nouakchott Mauritania	64%
San Salvador, El Salvador	63%
Guayaquil, Ecuador	60%
Delhi, India	56%
Mexico City, Mexico	44%
Lima, Peru	40%
Manilla, Phillipines	40%
Nairobi, Kenya	40%
Bangkok, Thailand	25%

Fig. 31.6 Urban underclass (*Source:* Congood)

Fig. 31.7 Urban advantage
(*Source:* UN)

Urban Advantage

Health and education services are easier to provide in cities, and mortality and literacy statistics do show the urban areas in a favourable light. But there will be great differences between the poorer and richer parts of each city. In Lima, Peru, for example, 19% of the children overall are malnourished, but this figure rises to 36% in the poorest districts.

Health

Urban / Rural — Infant deaths per 1000 live births

	Urban	Rural
Columbia	52	84
Peru	84	128
Kenya	91	110
Senegal	71	137
Bangladesh	115	137
Indonesia	60	96

Education

Urban / Rural — Literacy %

	Urban	Rural
Bolivia	85	47
Chile	93	74
Cameroon	61	28
Tunisia	50	24
India	61	28
Phillipines	92	77

9. Low levels of adult literacy

LDCs have low levels of adult literacy. *Table 31.5* shows the countries with the lowest adult literacy rates. A low rate of adult literacy is a major obstacle to growth. Illiterate people are unable to take advantage of new technology or learn new skills.

Rank	Country	Percentage (%) adult literacy	Rank	Country	Percentage (%) adult literacy
1	Niger	14.3	11	Guinea	37.9
2	Burkina Faso	20.7	12	Nepal	38.1
3	Gambia	33.1	13	Mauritania	38.4
4	Afghanistan	33.4	14	Bangladesh	38.9
5	Guinea-Bissau	33.6	15	Mozambique	40.5
6	Benin	33.9	16	Pakistan	40.9
7	Sierra Leone	34.3	17	Central African Rep.	42.4
8	Senegal	34.6	18	Yemen	42.5
9	Ethiopia	35.4	19	Côte d'Ivoire	42.6
10	Mali	35.5	20	Bhutan	44.2

Source: The Economist

Table 31.5 The least literate countries – adult literacy rates, 1997

10. Huge foreign debts

LDCs have a huge foreign debt problem. By 1999, the combined total of foreign debt in the less developed countries was estimated at over $2,900 billion. Most of us think that huge transfers of funds are made every year from the rich countries to the LDCs. In fact, the opposite is now true. Since 1983, there has been a net flow of funds in the opposite direction (i.e. from the LDCs to the wealthy countries), as is shown in *Figure 31.8.*

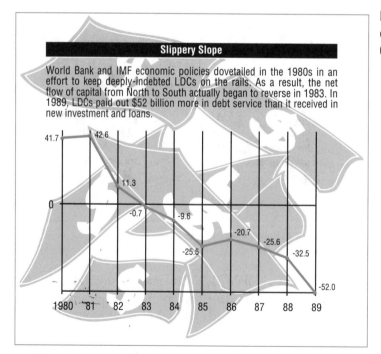

Slippery Slope

World Bank and IMF economic policies dovetailed in the 1980s in an effort to keep deeply-indebted LDCs on the rails. As a result, the net flow of capital from North to South actually began to reverse in 1983. In 1989, LDCs paid out $52 billion more in debt service than it received in new investment and loans.

Fig. 31.8 The debt crisis of the LDCs (Source: Congood)

The origins of the debt crisis are to be found in the oil crisis of 1973, when the price of oil quadrupled. The oil producing countries (Kuwait, Saudi Arabia, etc.) had more money than they could consume or invest, so they deposited huge amounts with banks in the wealthy countries (USA, Japan and Western Europe). These banks then recycled this money to governments in the poor countries, who were trying to pay for the rising cost of their imports, especially oil. Interest rates were low, and the banks felt safe giving loans to governments. Very little of this money was used to improve the lot of the people. Much of it was transferred by those in power to other foreign bank accounts (*capital flight*), some was used to build up foreign reserves (and so have a higher future credit rating) and some was used to service previous loans. Matters became serious in the 1980s because of the following situations that developed:

- The price of LDC exports fell on world markets, while the price of their imports continued to grow

- Interest rates rose because some wealthy countries (especially the USA) borrowed heavily at this stage. Between 1978 and 1984, the total interest payments of Latin American countries more than trebled

- In 1982, Mexico announced that it could not repay its debts. Argentina and Brazil later made similar statements.

The IMF became involved in *'debt rescheduling'*, i.e. changing the terms of the debt to make it easier to pay. This involved cancelling some debts, extending the period of repayment of others and lowering interest rates. However, such rescheduling ('Structural Adjustment') carried with it a price. Countries had to have balance of payments equilibrium within a few years and were obliged to cut back on public spending. There had to be strict control of the money supply.

Such adjustment programmes are deeply resented in many poor countries, because of the assumption that the poor nations were solely to blame for the debt crisis. The poor countries were not responsible for increasing interest rates or for the decisions to grant the loans in the first place. Furthermore, the burden of adjustment has fallen most heavily on the poorest people in these countries, since reduced public spending means less money for health, education and housing.

Table 31.6 shows debt service paid and aid received in 1999 for selected countries. As can be seen from this table, in all cases but one the cost of servicing the debt exceeded the amount of foreign aid received. Concern about the huge burden of debt falling on the poorest countries of the world led to the formation of Jubilee 2000, an organisation dedicated to the cancellation of debt for the poorest countries of the world as they faced into the new millennium (see *Figures 31.9* and *31.10*). Although the aim of total debt cancellation was not achieved, some progress was made in this regard and substantial debts were written off by certain creditors. Many high-profile individuals and celebrities from the world of showbiz and pop music lent their support to the campaign.

Country	Debt service paid	Aid received	Debt service as a percentage of Aid received
Angola	1144	261	438
Bolivia	494	206	240
Cameroon	549	190	289
Côte d'Ivoire	1449	366	396
Gambia, The	21	14	156
Ghana	524	255	205
Guyana	105	29	362
Honduras	366	298	123
Kenya	716	195	367
Myanmar	97	29	330
Vietnam	1410	257	548
Yemen, Rep.	157	157	100
Zambia	439	347	126

Source: Global Development Finance 2001, World Bank

Table 31.6 Debt service versus aid figures for 1999 for selected countries

Rich World, Poor World

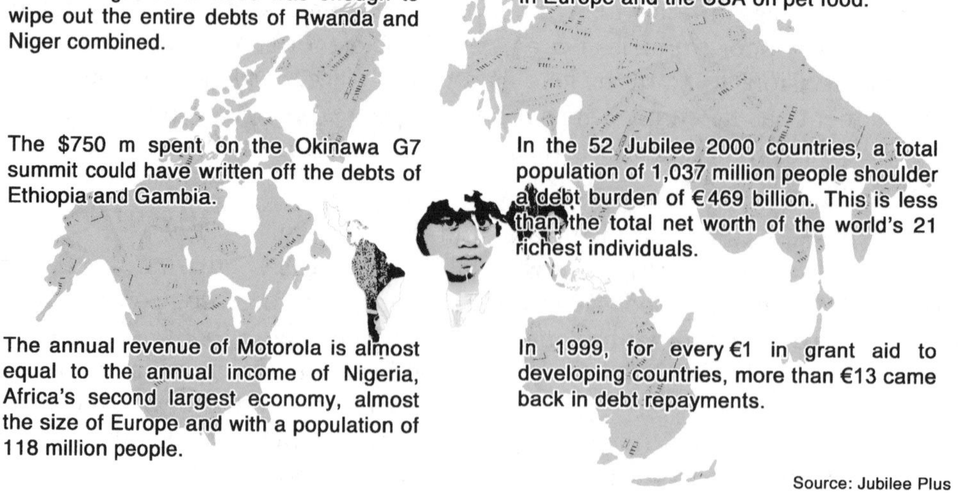

The income the Japanese firm Nintendo expected to earn on US sales of its Pokemon games in 2000 was enough to wipe out the entire debts of Rwanda and Niger combined.

The cost of providing basic healthcare and nutrition for all would be less than is spent in Europe and the USA on pet food.

The $750 m spent on the Okinawa G7 summit could have written off the debts of Ethiopia and Gambia.

In the 52 Jubilee 2000 countries, a total population of 1,037 million people shoulder a debt burden of €469 billion. This is less than the total net worth of the world's 21 richest individuals.

The annual revenue of Motorola is almost equal to the annual income of Nigeria, Africa's second largest economy, almost the size of Europe and with a population of 118 million people.

In 1999, for every €1 in grant aid to developing countries, more than €13 came back in debt repayments.

Source: Jubilee Plus

Fig. 31.9 Rich World, Poor World

Fig 31.10 Bono and Bob Geldof meet with Pope John Paul II as part of the Jubilee 2000 campaign

Summary of economic characteristics of LDCs

1. Low income (output) per person.
2. Rapid population growth.
3. A high proportion of the population are involved in farming but output is low.
4. Overdependence on one product.
5. Unequal distribution of wealth.
6. Shortage of savings and investment).
7. Unfavourable terms of trade.
8. Slums and shanty towns in the cities.
9. A low rate of adult literacy.
10. A huge 'debt crisis'.

STRATEGIES FOR DEVELOPMENT

Countries have tried a range of strategies to achieve economic development, with varying degrees of success.

1. *Self-sufficiency.* This is where the country attempts to produce as much of its own needs as possible. Exports are encouraged while imports are curtailed. **Example**: India.
2. *'Trickle down' policy.* This is where the country imposes little or no restrictions on industry in the hope that rapid growth will bring benefits

that eventually will trickle down to the poorest sections of society. **Example**: Brazil.

3. *Export-led growth.* This is where a country concentrates on the mass production of cheap, reliable consumer goods, taking advantage of its low-wage rates to undercut established suppliers. **Example**: Taiwan, South Korea.

4. *Central planning.* State planning and public ownership of the means of production. A state agency plans production on the basis of the existing resources. Any profits made are used to improve healthcare, education, etc. **Example**: Cuba.

WHAT IS REQUIRED FOR DEVELOPMENT TO TAKE PLACE?

For development to take place, the following are required:

1. Foreign aid

In 1970, the UN set a target of 0.7 per cent of GNP as the amount of aid which the wealthy countries should set aside for Official Development Assistance (ODA). This target has only been achieved by five countries. Much aid is 'tied aid', that is, it is based on political and trade factors rather than economic necessity. Ireland spent €464 on ODA in 2002, or 0.45 per cent of GNP, with a commitment to achieve the 0.7 per cent target by 2007.

2. Improvements to the infrastructure

An inadequate infrastructure will deter much needed investment. Consequently, governments and international aid agencies should give a high priority to improving the infrastructure. Land drainage and irrigation schemes, roads, housing, factories, etc. are all required if the economy is to prosper.

3. Increased output from the agricultural sector

This would increase the number of workers available for the other sectors of the economy, and reduce dependency on outside food aid.

4. Increased trading opportunities

This is extremely important. The slogan 'Give us trade, not aid' has become popular in many LDCs. While wealthy countries have given aid, many of their trade policies have closed the door to the exports of the LDCs. The classic example of this is the Multi-Fibre Arrangement (MFA), whereby LDC exports of textiles are strictly limited by quota. The World Bank estimates that the share of LDC exports that face non-tariff barriers is 20 per cent, or about twice the share of wealthy countries' exports facing such barriers. If the poor countries are to develop, they must have unrestricted access to all markets. Also, there is scope for increased trade between the LDCs themselves.

5. Education is a priority

No significant improvement in living standards is possible when a majority of the inhabitants of a country cannot read or write. Most education spending should go initially to establishing primary schools. As the country develops, additional resources need to be channelled into secondary education and job training schemes.

6. A change in attitudes is required

Upward and downward mobility must be possible to reflect the competence of the individual. Greater tangible reward must be given to workers, many of whom at the moment see the fruits of their labour going to foreign multinational companies or as tax to the government to pay debt charges.

7. Capital is required

The capital–output ratio is the number of extra units of capital required to produce one extra unit of output per year. If €5 extra capital is needed to produce €1 extra income (output) per year, then the capital output ratio is 5. If output in an economy is to grow by a modest 2 per cent per year, then investment (capital formation) of 10 per cent is required, plus an additional amount to cover depreciation.

8. Peace and political stability

Peace and political stability are required before economic development can proceed. Most of the military conflicts in the world today occur in the poorest countries (e.g. Ethiopia and Mozambique). Too many of the poorest countries in the world spend more on military equipment than on necessary social spending.

BENEFITS OF ECONOMIC GROWTH

1. Economic growth increases the standard of living of a country's inhabitants. Consumers have a wider choice of goods and services, increased spending power, more leisure time, etc.

2. Increased output should lead to a greater demand for workers (and other factors of production) to produce that output. When growth involves the use of previously unemployed resources, it is termed costless growth.

3. Economic growth provides the resources (i.e. tax revenue) with which the government can undertake a range of spending on projects considered worthwhile, e.g. improved infrastructure, better education and health services, etc.

4. Economic growth alleviates poverty in two ways. First, higher social welfare payments are possible because of increased government revenue. Second, increased demand in the economy should lower the numbers unemployed as explained above.

COSTS OF ECONOMIC GROWTH

1. The benefits of growth are unlikely to be distributed evenly. Some will gain rapidly, while others may be left behind. Workers whose skills are no longer needed because of new technology may find themselves unemployed if they are unwilling or unable to undergo retraining. This is especially true of older workers. Firms may be unwilling to make expensive training schemes available to older workers with a short remaining working life.

2. Damage to the environment has been an unfortunate consequence of economic growth. The developed countries of the North have grown accustomed to lifestyles which are consuming most of the earth's resources and causing the bulk of pollution. The USA has 4.5 per cent of the world's population, uses 24 per cent of the world's energy, and emits 22 per cent of all carbon dioxide. India has 17 per cent of the world's population, uses 3 per cent of the world's energy and emits 3 per cent of all carbon dioxide. The world must abandon self-destructive practices in favour of 'sustainable development'. A sustainable society is one that manages its economic growth without causing irreparable damage to the environment. By balancing economic and environmental concerns, it can meet the needs of its citizens without damaging the prospects of future generations.

3. Economic development in the past involved large-scale migration. Those in search of jobs had to move from rural to urban areas. There are a number of costs here. There is the cost to the workers in terms of the upheaval in their lifestyles – the loss of the traditional way of life with which they were familiar, the disruption to family life, the increased cost of accommodation and travel in large cities, etc. Also there are the additional costs associated with the growth of cities – pollution, traffic congestion, noise, crime, vandalism, stress, etc.

4. We have already seen that economic development and growth require the sacrifice of current consumption. People must be prepared to save part of their income. The money saved can be used for investment, that is, the creation of capital goods. Thus, the country will have a higher standard of

living in future. This aspect of growth is called the opportunity cost of growth.

5. We have already stated that an increase in wealth does not mean an increase in welfare. Increased wealth does not always bring happiness. Many of the major social problems of the 20th century – drug addiction, suicide, divorce and stress-related illness are features of the wealthiest countries.

An increase in wealth does not mean an increase in welfare.

The following article outlines the arguments of the organisation Jubilee Plus for the cancellation of debt of the world's poorest countries.

Campaign Statement from Jubilee Plus, 2001

In Africa, the UN estimates that the payment of foreign debts costs the lives of seven million children each year. That's one every five seconds.

A problem we can solve. Third World countries owe the world's richest nations over £1,000m. This is a practical proposal. If the rich nations cancelled enough debt to half poverty in the world's 50 poorest countries by 2015, Britain's share of the debt would be less than 4 pence per person per week!

If you borrow money surely you should pay it back? No. Debt relief is nothing new. In 1953, Germany was granted massive debt relief after its wartime defeat. With 50% of its debts cancelled it could rebuild its shattered economy and create today's prosperity. Shouldn't other countries struggling to recover from war, like Mozambique, be given the same fresh start?

If you borrow more than you can repay you are not forced to starve. Instead you are declared bankrupt and you start afresh with a clean slate. But there is no international bankruptcy law. So people in the Third World are forced to pay back money borrowed decades ago, often by unelected dictators. If your parents ran up huge debts would it be fair if you were made to pay?

If a Third World country simply stopped paying its foreign debts then the US, Britain and other rich countries would turn very nasty very quickly and force them to pay. The foreign assets of a country would be seized: its sources of desperately needed capital goods and spare parts virtually eliminated. In many countries even food imports would be curtailed.

Who owes whom? 300 years ago, European countries had already plundered over 185 tonnes of gold and 16,000 tonnes of silver from the Americas. For Europe to pay it back – with interest – would now weigh more than the earth. And this is just a fraction of the spoils of colonialism! So who really owes whom? The Jubilee 2000 campaign was one of the biggest international non-governmental movements in recent years. The year 2000 is over, but the campaign continues now as Jubilee Plus.

Globalisation refers to the tendency for markets to become global, rather than national, as barriers to international trade are removed, and the tendency for large multinational companies to supply these global markets.

The following article argues that globalisation will not solve the problems of food supply for the poor countries of the world.

Myth: Globalization will end world hunger

Reality: The globalization of agriculture fails to address the world's hunger crisis. In fact it makes it worse. During the past two decades, the total amount of food in the world has increased, but so has hunger.

The main problem is that globalisation of food production pushes small, self-reliant farmers off their lands and replaces them with large chemical and machine-intensive corporate farms. It does not emphasize food for hungry local communities. Instead, it encourages exports resulting in mono-cultures – a single crop grown over thousands of acres. These crops are usually luxury items cultivated for export and are notoriously vulnerable to insect blights and bad weather, and cause soil infertility.

Global biotechnology companies claim they have the answer to world hunger. But biotech production does nothing to solve local hunger problems. Does anyone believe that the invention of biotech plants whose seeds are sterile – forcing farmers to buy new seeds every year – has anything to do with stopping hunger? The biotech industry's goal is not to feed the hungry, only to feed itself.

A recent United Nations study confirms that the world already has enough food. The problem is one of distribution. Global trade rules put food production and distribution in the hands of agribusiness giants, supplanting the traditional system of local production for local consumption.

The world is producing the wrong kind of food, by a process that leaves millions of people, landless, homeless, cashless and unable to feed themselves.

From **Take it Personally** *by Anita Roddick (Thorsons, 2001).*

32

The Economics of Population

This chapter examines the economic aspects of population. The relationship between population and living standards will be discussed. We will examine world population trends and the problems caused in less developed countries by rapid population growth. Finally, we will examine the most recent data on Irish population, as revealed in the Census of Population of Ireland, 1996, and *Population and Labour Force Projections 2001–2031* (published in July 1999).

INTRODUCTION

The statistical study of population characteristics is called demography. Demographic information for most countries is derived principally from two sources:

* Registration of births and deaths
* A count of the inhabitants of the country taken every few years (i.e. a census of population).

While information gathered in this way is very reliable for the developed countries, the figures for less developed countries cannot be considered as 100 per cent accurate.

TERMS USED IN STUDY OF POPULATION

The birth rate

The birth rate is the average number of live births in a year per 1,000 population.

This varies widely from country to country, as is shown in *Table 32.1*. It depends, among other things, on the age structure of a country's population. It will tend to be higher if there is a large proportion of women of childbearing age in the population. Ireland's birth rate in 2001 was 15.3.

Highest birth rates		
1.	Somalia	52.3
2.	Afghanistan	51.3
3.	Uganda	51.1
4.	Niger	48.7
5.	Angola	48.4
Lowest birth rates		
1.	Bulgaria	8.8
	Latvia	8.8
3.	Czech Republic	8.9
	Estonia	8.9
5.	Italy	9.0
Source: The Economist		

Table 32.1 Birth rates – number of live births per 1,000 population per year (annual average for period 1995–2000)

The fertility rate

The fertility rate is the average number of children born to a woman who has completed her childbearing years.

It varies widely from country to country, as can be seen in *Table 32.2*. In poor countries, children are regarded as essential to supplement household income and support the old. In wealthy countries, children are seen as expensive to rear and educate. Ireland's fertility rate in 1998 was 1.93 (which is below the replacement rate of 2.1).

Highest fertility rates		
1.	Yemen	7.60
2.	West Bank and Gaza	7.30
3.	Somalia	7.25
4.	Uganda	7.10
5.	Afghanistan	6.94
Lowest fertility rates		
1.	Spain	1.15
2.	Romania	1.17
3.	Czech Republic	1.19
4.	Italy	1.20
5	Bulgaria	1.23
Source: The Economist		

Table 32.2 Fertility rates – average number of children per woman (annual average for period 1995–2000)

The death rate

The death rate is the average number of deaths in a year per 1,000 population.

High death rates can be due to:

- An inability of countries to produce enough food to supply their needs, e.g. Ethiopia

- A shortage of medical facilities and clean water, which leads to the spread of disease and a low-life expectancy, e.g. Sierra Leone and Afghanistan

- Long-running internal conflicts, wars, etc., e.g. Sierra Leone, Afghanistan, Angola

- A high proportion of the population in the older age groups, e.g. Hungary, Russia.

Table 32.3 shows death rates for selected countries. Ireland has a low death rate at 7.9 per 1,000 population.

High death rates	
Sierra Leone	25
Malawi	23
Afghanistan	21
Hungary	14
Russia	14
Low death rates	
Saudi Arabia	4
Turkey	6
Canada	7
France	9
Spain	9
Source: The Economist	

Table 32.3 Death rates in selected countries (annual average for period 1995–2000)

The density of population

The density of population is the average number of people per square kilometre.

It is derived as follows:

$$\frac{\text{Total population of a country}}{\text{Total land area of a country}}$$

Table 32.4 shows population density for a number of selected countries. Ireland's density of population in 2000 was 53.

Country	Population/km^2
High density	
Hong Kong	6,628
Singapore	5,771
Bangladesh	897
Netherlands	386
United Kingdom	241
Low density	
Australia	2
Canada	3
Argentina	13
Norway	14
Finland	15
Source: The Economist	

Table 32.4 Density of population in selected countries, 2000

The infant mortality rate

The infant mortality rate is the average number of deaths a year per 1,000 live births.

Table 32.5 shows the huge differences in infant mortality rates between the developed and underdeveloped countries. Ireland has one of the lowest infant mortality rates in the world with a rate in 2001 of 6.

Highest infant mortality rates	
1. Sierra Leone	182
2. Angola	170
3. Niger	166
4. Afghanistan	165
5. Liberia	157
Lowest infant mortality rates	
1. Finland	4
Japan	4
Norway	4
Singapore	4
Sweden	4
Source: The Economist	

Table 32.5 Infant mortality rates, 2001

Life expectancy

Life expectancy is a statistical projection of the length of an individual's life based on probabilities and assumptions of living conditions, medical care, natural disasters and other factors.

Table 32.6 shows significant differences between developed and underdeveloped countries in this regard, with inhabitants of poorer countries having much lower life expectancy.

Country	Life expectancy (years)
Japan	80
Canada	79
Australia	78
UK	77
Ireland	**76**
South Africa	54
Nigeria	50
Afghanistan	46
Zambia	40
Sierra Leone	38
Source: *The Economist*	

Table 32.6 Life expectancy for selected countries, 2000

The natural increase

The natural increase is the extent to which total births exceed total deaths during a period of time.

For example, in 2000 there were 54,239 registered births in Ireland, and 31,115 registered deaths. Therefore, the natural increase in that year was 23,124.

Net migration

Net migration is defined as the difference between outward migration (emigration) and inward migration (immigration) during a period of time. It is calculated as follows:
Net migration = increase in population – natural increase

For example, in the five-year period 1991–1996, the population of Ireland rose by approximately 100,000. Since the natural increase was about 90,000, net migration was therefore 10,000. The number of people entering the country was 10,000 bigger than the number going out.

WORLD POPULATION – A GROWING PROBLEM

In 2001 the United Nations Population Fund released new forecasts for population growth. Total world population reached 6.1 billion in mid-2000 and is currently growing at an annual rate of 1.2 per cent, or 77 million people a year. Six countries account for half of this population growth – India, China, Pakistan, Nigeria, Bangladesh and Indonesia. By 2050, world population is expected to be between 7.9 billion (low variant or estimate) and 10.9 billion (high variant) with a medium variant of 9.3 billion. (See *Figure 32.1*).

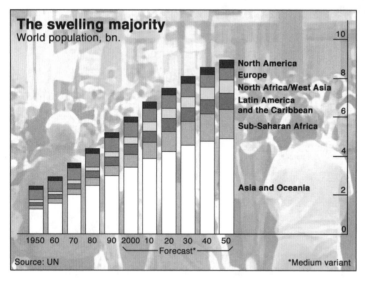

Fig. 32.1 World population in billions with future projections (Source: UN)

The population of the most developed countries presently at 1.2 billion will change little over the next 50 years because fertility levels are expected to remain close to or slightly less than the replacement level. The population of the less developed countries is projected to rise steadily from 4.9 billion in 2000 to 8.2 billion in 2050 (medium estimate), even allowing for declining fertility rates and the impact of the AIDS epidemic in some African countries. Also some improvement has occurred in life expectancy for these countries which will also lead to increasing population. Over 85 per cent of the world's population in 2050 will live in the developing countries, which are experiencing great difficulty coping with their current populations. At present, three out of four people live in developing countries. It is not surprising that

Fig. 32.2 China has one of the fastest growing populations

many people are as pessimistic about the situation as the economist Malthus was in the late 18th century (see *Chapter 33*).

Today, 80 per cent of deforestation results from population growth. If the numbers grow as predicted, the UN estimates an extra 5.9 million square km of land will have to be turned over to farming, roads and urban development. This is almost equal to the total size of protected natural areas on Earth today. Most good agricultural land is already being cultivated, and each year spreading deserts, inadequate irrigation and overuse take millions of acres out of production. Between 1980 and 1990 an estimated 8 per cent of the world's tropical forest was cut, burned or otherwise destroyed (*Figure 32.3*). Farms may

Fig. 32.3 Forests as a renewable resource are threatened by deforestation and pollution

Fig. 32.4 The world's fish stocks are in danger from overfishing and pollution

become more productive but they will hardly match the increases in productivity of the past. Whether agricultural output can keep pace with population growth is an open question. The output of the seas is coming under threat as a result of pollution and overfishing (see *Figure 32.4*). Also, the ability of the world to process many wastes is now being called into question.

Pessimists point to water scarcity and stagnating levels of cereal output arising from diminishing returns from the use of fertilisers. Optimists point to the development of new fertilisers and irrigation systems, and hybrid high-yielding strains of crops. They argue world hunger has more to do with war, poverty and poor food distribution than with the failure of farming to produce enough food.

Demographic pattern in less developed countries

We have seen in the last chapter that less developed countries have a very low GNP per capita. GNP per capita can only be increased if total output rises faster than population. Unfortunately, population growth in many of the poorest countries of the world far exceeds the increase in output, so that income per person is falling.

In the past, less developed countries had high birth rates and high death rates. High birth rates were common because children were seen as necessary for supplementing family incomes and as providing support for their parents in old age. High death rates were the result of disease, malnutrition, lack of hygiene, inadequate medical facilities, lack of a clean water supply, etc.

In recent times, the death rate in many less developed countries has fallen. This is due to a number of factors – better medical facilities, vaccinations against

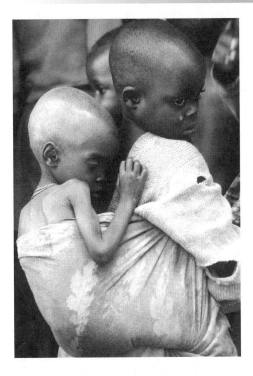

Fig. 32.5 The people of many African states suffer from regular food shortages and rely heavily on foreign aid

diseases, overseas aid programmes, the development of crops which are more resistant to disease, etc. (*Figure 32.5*). However, no reduction has occurred in birth rates. The result is the population explosion which is now taking place in many of these countries. For example, Angola experienced an average annual rate of growth in population of 3.3 per cent between 1990 and 2000. If this rate of growth continues, its population will double in about 20 years.

There are many reasons why the population continues to rise in these poorer countries.

1. EARLY MARRIAGE

In many less developed countries, early marriage is the norm, and in some it is rigidly enforced.

2. HIGHER PERCENTAGE OF POPULATION UNDER 15

Even though infant mortality is very high by European standards, some reduction has taken place. As a result, a very high proportion of the population of many African, Asian and South American countries is under 15. Therefore, many girls are now moving into the childbearing age group. In Nigeria, 43 per cent the population is under 15 years of age and one third of all births are to teenagers. *Table 32.7* shows the percentage of the population aged under 15 in selected countries.

High percentage of population under 15	
Uganda	50.1
Congo	48.3
Niger	48.2
Somalia	48.1
Angola	47.5
Low percentage of population under 15	
Italy	14.3
Spain	14.5
Japan	14.8
Greece	14.9
Germany	15.5
Source: The Economist	

Table 32.7 Percentage of population under 15 years in selected countries, 2000

3. UNSUCCESSFUL GOVERNMENT MEASURES TO CURB POPULATION

Government efforts to curb the growth in population have failed in many countries. Contraception programmes have been opposed on religious grounds. China with a population of 1,256 million in 2000 has a one child per family policy. Sterilisation programmes have been attempted in India, without much success. The population there grew at an average annual rate of 1.75 per cent from 1990 to 2000 and is now also over one billion. Other countries have reduced children's allowances in an attempt to curb the growth of population.

Summary of demographic characteristics of less developed countries

* High birth rates
* High fertility rates
* High death rates
* High infant mortality rates
* High percentage of the population aged under 15.

RECENT IRISH POPULATION TRENDS AND CHARACTERISTICS

The Census of Population 2002 is a detailed stocktake of everybody who was in the country on 28 April 2002. Apart from being a headcount of the population, the Census provides us with a breakdown of the population by age, sex, marital status, occupation, travel to work, educational qualifications, etc.

Each household is given a Census form which must be filled in carefully and is later collected by Census enumerators. Preliminary results were published within three months and full results will be published within two years.

The 2002 population is likely to be the highest since 1871. The Central Statistics Office estimated the population to be 3.84 million in April 2001. With births exceeding deaths by about 20,000 each year, and with net inward migration over the past number of years, the population for April 2002 could be as high as 3.9 million.

A census of population is usually taken every five years, and provides the government with vital data to assist in effective policy-making, planning and decision-taking, e.g. school building needs, hospitals, roads, infrastructural requirements, etc.

The most recent Irish census of population for which full data is available was taken on 28 April 1996. A number of interesting features have emerged from this census.

- *Total Population.* The population of Ireland on 28 April 1996 was 3,621,035 persons compared with 3,525,719 in April 1991. This represents an increase of 95,316 persons or 2.6 per cent. *Table 32.8* gives the population of each province, county and county borough, and the changes since 1991.

- *Regional distribution.* The rise in population is not evenly distributed across the country. Some rural counties have experienced a very small drop in population – Leitrim (–1.1%), Longford (–0.5%) and Monaghan (–0.1%), but this is much smaller than the fall in the previous five years. It suggests that the slide in rural population has been halted. Some 29 per cent of the population live in Dublin city and county, exactly the same as five years earlier.

- *Gender.* The number of females (1,823,439) exceeded the number of males (1,797,596) by 25,843, reinforcing the pattern set in 1991.

- *Age.* Compared to our European neighbours our population is relatively young, with 23.9 per cent of it less than 15 years old. Only 11.5 per cent of our population was more than 65 years old. The population aged over 65 is projected to double by 2031.

- *Dependency ratio.* Ireland has a high dependency ratio. This is defined as:

$$\text{Dependency ratio} = \frac{\text{Number of people aged under 15 and over 65}}{\text{Number of people aged between 15 and 65}}$$

Province, county or county borough	Population		Change in population 1991–1996	
	1991	1996	Actual	Percentage
LEINSTER	**1,860,949**	**1,921,835**	**60,886**	**3.3**
Carlow	40,942	41,616	674	1.6
Dublin	1,025,304	1,056,666	31,362	3.1
of which				
Dublin Co. Borough	478,389	480,996	2,607	0.5
Dun Laoghaire-Rathdown	185,410	189,836	4,426	2.4
Fingal	152,766	167,433	14,667	9.6
South Dublin	208,739	218,401	9,662	4.6
Kildare	122,656	134,881	12,225	10.0
Kilkenny	73,635	75,155	1,520	2.1
Laois	52,314	52,798	484	0.9
Longford	30,296	30,138	−158	−0.5
Louth	90,724	92,163	1,439	1.6
Meath	105,370	109,371	4,001	3.8
Offaly	58,494	59,080	586	1.0
Westmeath	61,880	63,236	1,356	2.2
Wexford	102,069	104,314	2,245	2.2
Wicklow	97,265	102,417	5,152	5.3
MUNSTER	**1,009,533**	**1,033,045**	**23,512**	**2.3**
Clare	90,918	93,914	2,996	3.3
Cork	410,369	420,346	9,977	2.4
of which				
Cork Co. Borough	127,253	127,092	−161	−0.1
Cork County	283,116	293,254	10,138	3.6
Kerry	121,894	125,863	3,969	3.3
Limerick	161,956	165,017	3,061	1.9
of which				
Limerick Co. Borough	52,083	52,042	−41	−0.1
Limerick County	109,873	112,975	3,102	2.8
Tipperary North Riding	57,854	57,944	90	0.2
Tipperary South Riding	74,918	75,364	446	0.6
Waterford	91,624	94,597	2,973	3.2
of which				
Waterford Co. Borough	40,328	42,516	2,188	5.4
Waterford County	51,296	52,081	785	1.5
CONNACHT	**423,031**	**432,551**	**9,520**	**2.3**
Galway	180,364	188,598	8,234	4.6
of which				
Galway Co. Borough	50,853	57,095	6,242	12.3
Galway County	129,511	131,503	1,992	1.5
Leitrim	25,301	25,032	−269	−1.1
Mayo	110,713	111,395	682	0.6
Roscommon	51,897	51,881	−16	0.0
Sligo	54,756	55,645	889	1.6
ULSTER (PART OF)	**232,206**	**233,604**	**1,398**	**0.6**
Cavan	52,796	52,903	107	0.2
Donegal	128,117	129,435	1,318	1.0
Monaghan	51,293	51,266	−27	−0.1
STATE	**3,525,719**	**3,621,035**	**95,316**	**2.7**
Source: CSO				

Table 32.8 Population of each province, county and county borough, and actual and percentage change, 1991–1996

- *Density of population.* This was low in Ireland at 51 persons per square km, compared to an EU average of 142.

- *Migration.* This has been the most important and the most changeable factor affecting Ireland's population in recent years. During the period 1986–1991, the estimated net migration level was –134,000. During the following period 1991–1996, estimated net migration was +5,700, reflecting increased economic activity and more employment opportunities. The available evidence since then shows upward movements in both the natural increase and in net inward migration resulting in an annual average increase in population of around 1 per cent. *Table 32.9* shows estimated migration in the years 1992–1998. Over the past three to four years there has been a steady decline in the number of emigrants coupled with a corresponding rise in the number of immigrants, reflecting the exceptionally strong performance of the Irish economy and labour market over this period.

Year ending April	Out-migration	In-migration	Net migration
1992	33.4	40.7	7.4
1993	35.1	34.7	–0.4
1994	34.8	30.1	–4.7
1995	33.1	31.2	–1.9
1996	31.2	39.2	8.0
1997	29.0	44.0	15.0
1998	21.2	44.0	22.8

Figures in thousands

Source: Population and Labour Force Projections 2001–2031, CSO

Table 32.9 Estimated migration 1992–1998

- *Life expectancy.* The 1996 census showed male life expectancy to be 73 years and female life expectancy to be 78.7 years, slightly less than most EU countries in both cases.

EMIGRATION

Emigration has been a feature of Irish history since the Great Famine of the 1840s. Very high levels of emigration persisted in the second half of the 19th century. The population remained almost stationary between 1921 and 1951. This was because the natural increase was offset by emigration. Emigration was particularly heavy during the depressed years of the 1950s. The factors contributing to emigration are usually classified as 'push' and 'pull' factors.

Push factors are those factors prevailing within their own country which cause people to leave, for example, lack of jobs, lack of promotional opportunities for those with jobs, low pay, political or religious factors, etc.

Pull factors are those conditions in other countries which make working and living there seem attractive. Such factors include more opportunities of employment, higher rates of pay, better social life, opportunities for more training and career development, a desire to travel and to experience life in other countries. etc.

Economic effects of emigration

The economic effects of emigration are the same as the economic effects of a declining population and are considered below.

1. REDUCTION IN DEMAND FOR GOODS AND SERVICES

A declining population will lead to a reduction in the demand for goods and services. Many firms in Ireland cater exclusively for the home market. A reduction in population reduces their potential market and may thus lead to closure and the loss of jobs. It will also discourage investment.

2. INCREASED DEPENDENCY RATIO

There is an increase in the dependency ratio. This is the number of people who are economically inactive relative to those who are economically active (see above). Emigrants are mostly people aged between 15 and 65. Emigration reduces the number of people in the economically active age groups. Consequently, the 'tax base' (i.e. the pool of people who can be taxed) is reduced. Rates of tax will, therefore, be higher if public services are to be maintained at existing levels.

3. RETURN ON EDUCATIONAL INVESTMENT

Many of those who leave are third-level graduates or those who have received state-funded training. There is therefore no direct financial return to the state for the money spent on such education and training. However, if some of these emigrants return and use the skills acquired abroad in the provision of goods and services here, then there is a return to the state.

4. BRAIN DRAIN

Strict immigration requirements are now laid down in many countries. Potential emigrants must have the skills or qualifications required abroad. Many of the brightest and best of our workers have been enticed abroad by the prospects of higher salaries, better conditions, etc. Such emigration by highly skilled people is called the 'brain drain'. Additional state funding may be required for the training of those without the necessary skills, so as to increase their employment prospects either at home or abroad.

5. Higher Wage Rates

Because of the increased international mobility of highly skilled workers, there is pressure on Irish employers to pay wage rates comparable to those available abroad.

6. Level of Unemployment

Emigration has in the past kept the level of unemployment below what it otherwise would have been. This has been a very important consideration for Irish governments in the years before the Celtic Tiger brought labour shortages.

7. Curtailment of Services

Certain services require a minimum population before they can be profitable, for example, newspapers, local radio, etc. In the case of transport, a declining population may lead to the curtailment of certain services, e.g. buses or trains operating less frequently.

8. Low Morale

High emigration can have a depressing effect on national morale.

The economic effects of a rising population are the opposite of those listed above.

IMMIGRATION

As we have seen above a major feature of our population in recent years has been the level of immigration into the country. In 2000, Ireland had an inward migration rate of 5.3 per 1,000 population, the second highest in the EU (after Luxembourg) and more than twice the EU average (see news article at end of chapter). Because of the unprecedented levels of growth in the economy in the late 1990s, young skilled Irish workers no longer felt compelled to seek employment overseas. Also the record level of jobs created attracted significant numbers of former emigrants back to the country, most of whom had acquired additional skills, qualifications and experience while abroad. Also there has been a huge increase in the number of work permits granted to non-nationals in recent years as the economy struggled to fill the available vacancies.

OVERPOPULATION, UNDERPOPULATION AND OPTIMUM POPULATION

> A country is said to be overpopulated if a rise in population would cause a fall in average income.

In other words, there are not enough resources in the country to support more people, without a fall in the standard of living. In this case, there are decreasing returns to labour.

> A country is said to be underpopulated if a rise in population would cause a rise in average income.

In this case, there are under-utilised resources which could be brought into production if there were more people in the country. There are increasing returns to labour. Such countries (e.g. Canada and Australia) may encourage immigration to overcome their labour shortages.

> A country is said to have an optimum population when it has the best number of people, given its economic resources.

In recent years Ireland has witnessed an influx of immigrants, both non-Irish and returning emigrants.

Ireland having the second-highest immigration in the EU is noted by the *Sunday Business Post*, 30 December 2001, while the return of Irish skilled workers is outlined in the *Irish Independent* on 11 January 2002.

Ireland has second-highest immigration in EU

By Niamh Connolly

The highest migration flows ever into the Republic were recorded in the 12 months up to April 2001, according to new figures obtained by this newspaper.

Figures to be released in a labour report by the employment agency FÁS this week reveal the highest level of migration into this country since the Central Statistics first recorded data in the 1950s.

In 2000 the Republic had an inward migration rate of 5.3 per 1,000 population – the second highest of all EU members states after Luxembourg, and more than twice the rate for the EU as a whole.

The number of people entering this country to work in the year up to April 2001 rose by over 9 per cent on the previous year to 46,200. At the same time, emigration dropped to its lowest level since 1987, at just 19,900.

The two events contributed to the highest net inward migration rate in the 12 months to April 2001 ever recorded – at 23,300 – representing a jump of 31.5 per cent on the previous 12 months.

"Both a decline in the number of people emigrating and an increase in the number immigrating were responsible for the turnaround in net migration flows experienced in Ireland," said the FÁS report.

Separate figures show that more work permits were issued in the first nine months of 2001 than at any other time. From January to September 2001, more than 26,000 permits were issued – a 46 per cent increase on 2000.

The figure is "even more impressive when it is considered that the number of permits issued in 2000 was nearly three times that of 1999," said the report.

Eight nationalities, mostly Eastern European, accounted for half of all the work permits issued in 2001: Latvian, Lithuanian, Polish, Romanian, Czech, Ukrainian, Philippine and South African.

Three quarters of work permits were issued to immigrants taking up work in the services sector, and within the services industry two subsectors – catering, at 26 per cent, and medical and nursing at 6 per cent – accounted for nearly a third of all permits issued. One in 13 work permits went to those entering industry, and three in 20 to immigrants gaining employment in agriculture, forestry and fisheries.

The figures show that the proportions of permits issued to Europeans expanded from 9 per cent in 1993 to 56 per cent in 2001. The proportion issued to Asians declined over the same period from 51 per cent to 22 per cent.

Ireland experienced an inflow of 18,400 per year in each year since 1996, while about 110,600 more people entered the country than left over this six-year period.

Immigration patterns have changed in recent years. The relative size of inflow from Britain and the US declined, while immigrants from the 'rest of the world' increased, particularly since 1999.

There were 17,000 immigrants from the 'rest of the world' category in 2001 – 72 per cent more than in 1999. In contrast, the number of immigrants from Britain, the rest of the EU and the US was 28 per cent lower in 2001 than in 1999.

The Tánaiste, Mary Harney, this month announced a tightening of the work permit scheme from January 2, to ensure employers offer first choice of available jobs to Irish or other EU nationals.

From this date applications for new work permits will not be accepted unless they are accompanied by a letter from FÁS confirming that all efforts have been made by the employer to find an Irish or EU national to fill the vacancy.

Over 123,600 Irish people returned to Ireland from 1996 to 2001, accounting for nearly half of the 255,000 immigrants. British nationals were the second largest group, accounting for 17 per cent of inflows.

The figures show that the share of immigrants accounted for by returning Irish emigrants has decreased from 54.5 per cent in 1999, to 39.5 per cent in 2001, while the share of the 'rest of the world' nationals increased from 9.3 per cent in 1999 to 26.7 per cent in 2001.

The report notes that the migration data relates to the 12 months to April of each year, and so does not capture the implications of the economic slowdown experienced in Ireland during the second half of 2001, nor the ramifications of terrorist attacks on the US on September 11.

Ireland gains as skilled workers return

By Brendan Keenan

Ireland is one of several countries which has benefited from returning emigrants who acquired high-tech skills abroad, the Paris-based OECD says in a new report.

More and more highly skilled workers are moving abroad for jobs, encouraging innovation to circulate and helping to boost economic growth around the globe, according to the study, *International Mobility of the Highly Skilled*.

It identified over 500 Irish citizens with science or engineering degrees working in the USA in 1999.

Proportionate to population, this was more than the 7,000 British citizens, which was the biggest single number, and three times South Korea's total of 2,000.

Research on the Irish experience by Alan Barrett of the Economic and Social Research Institute (ESRI) suggests that the flow of immigrants from 1994–97 added 1.5pc to Irish economic growth, kept wages of skilled workers almost 5pc lower than they would have been but, as result, knocked 0.7pc off unemployment.

Returning emigrants had higher qualifications than average, and there is evidence that they increased their skills while abroad.

During the emigration peak in 1988, 26pc of those with third level education left, as did 15pc of those with second level qualifications.

Non-Irish immigrants also had higher than average qualifications.

"These findings suggest that Ireland in the 1990s was particularly attractive to high-earning people," Dr Barrett says.

The report concludes that greater co-operation between sending and receiving countries is needed to ensure a fair distribution of the benefits of labour flows.

The main increase in flows has been from Asia and Central and Eastern Europe into North America, Australia, Germany and Britain.

CHAPTER 33

History of Economic Thought

This chapter provides the student with an introduction to the development of economic ideas, so that he/she can see how the content or subject matter of economics evolved through the years. In this regard it is important to note that no theory or set of ideas is instantly accepted but must serve the test of time, and must be judged according to the standards (social, political and economic) prevailing at the time. Progress in any field of study involves the rejection of previously held theories, the refining or modification of others and the development of new ones, in the light of changing circumstances and the ever-increasing store of knowledge at our disposal. *Table 33.1* lists the various schools of economic thought, the period in which their ideas were promoted and the associated economists. *Table 33.2* gives a brief outline of ideas developed by the respective schools.

School of economic thought	Period promoted	Associated economists
Mercantilism	16th-17th century	Sir Thomas Mun; Jean Baptiste Colbert
Physiocrats	18th century	François Quesnay
Classical economists	18th-19th century	Adam Smith; Thomas Robert Malthus; Jean Baptiste Say; David Ricardo; John Stuart Mill
Socialism	19th-20th century	Karl Marx
Neo-classical economics	Late 19th century	Alfred Marshall; William Jevons; Carl Menger; Leon Walras
Keynesian economics	20th century	John Maynard Keynes
Monetarism	20th century	Milton Friedman

Table 33.1 Development of economic thought

School of economic thought	Some economic ideas promoted
Mercantilism	State intervention; balance of foreign trade; economic self-sufficiency; tariffs on imports; exploitation of colonies
Physiocrats	No state intervention; rule of nature; preserving private property; importance of agriculture; laissez-faire policies
Classical economists	Freedom of individual; minimum state intervention; manufacturing equal status as agriculture; labour theory of value; division of labour; subsistence theory of wages (Iron Law of Wages); law of markets (Say's Law); theory of rent; distribution laws changeable; large-scale production leading to growth; benefit of trade unions
Socialism	Inequality in distribution of weath; class division based on private property and wealth; labour exploited by capitalists; replacement of capitalism by socialism; social welfare system; labour theory of value based on labour needed to produce item
Neo-classical economics	Theory of value based on concept of utility; marginal utility of a good; price and output determined by 'elasticity'; demand and supply interacting; concept of short run and long run
Keynesian economics	Problem of recessions; disequilibrium; governments to regulate economy; fiscal policy; role of aggregate demand in determining output; reducing unemployment
Monetarism	Controlling inflation; control of money supply; high interest rates; laissez-faire principles; privatisation; market de-regulation; supply-side economics

Table 33.2 Overview of economic ideas

MERCANTILISM

This is the name given to the set of ideas put forward by several European writers in the 16th and 17th centuries, who were called 'Mercantilists'. The word 'mercantilist' means 'pertaining to trade'. These writers were living at a time when the nation states were developing and merchants were increasing in importance because of the huge growth in the volume of international trade. The following is a summary of the main economic arguments advanced by the Mercantilist writers.

1. State intervention might be necessary in economic matters to ensure that conflicts between competing groups could be resolved. Thus there was a need for a strong political authority in a country. This need took precedence over the rights of the individual.

2. The state should at all times seek to advance or improve its position, even if this is at the cost of neighbouring states. Greater wealth required increased political power.

3. There was a direct and fundamental link between the wealth of a country and the balance of its foreign trade. The greater the excess of exports over imports, the greater the build up of gold and silver in the country. The accumulation of large reserves of gold and silver was seen as the ultimate objective of the state, and the yardstick by which its prosperity could be judged.

4. Economic self-sufficiency was advocated. The state should at all times seek to encourage the consumption of domestically produced goods. Consumption of foreign goods was seen as a vice. Manufacturing was the method by which value could be added to the natural resources or raw materials of a country.

5. To make the balance of trade as favourable as possible, governments should impose tariffs on imports, give subsidies to exporters, and create licensed trading companies with exclusive rights to trade in particular areas.

6. The exploitation of colonies was seen as having two advantages. First, colonies provided a source of raw materials which could be shipped to the 'mother country' and processed so that extra revenue could be gained. Second, colonies provided a market for manufactured goods or surplus produce from the 'mother country', so that extra revenue might also be gained in this way.

Evaluation of Mercantilism

1. Mercantilists have been criticised for equating the wealth of a country with its stock of gold and silver. They did not understand the link between an increase in the money supply and inflation. Unless accompanied by an increase in the production of goods and services, the accumulation of gold and silver resulted only in increased prices for goods and services.

2. Mercantilists argued strongly in favour of self-sufficiency and national advantage. This led to distrust and rivalry between nations which fuelled later conflicts.

3. Mercantilists did not see that international trade could be beneficial to all countries, that is, they were ignorant of the operation of the principle of comparative advantage.

Among the best-known Mercantilists were Sir Thomas Mun (1571–1641) and Jean Baptiste Colbert (1619–1683).

THE PHYSIOCRATS

This is the name given to a group of 18th-century French philosophers and economists, led by François Quesnay (1694–1774) (*Figure 33.1*), who disagreed with the Mercantilists about the origin of wealth.

Fig. 33.1 François Quesnay

The following is a brief summary of their main beliefs.

1. Unlike the Mercantilists, they did not believe in state intervention in economic affairs. 'Physiocracy' means 'rule of nature', and the Physiocrats believed that there existed a natural order or set of rules. Human laws were at best imperfect, and should be kept to a minimum. These laws should reflect, as far as possible, natural laws or the laws of the Universe. The role of the state should, therefore, be limited to upholding the laws of nature and preserving private property.

2. Unlike the Mercantilists, who stressed the importance of manufacturing, Physiocrats argued that agriculture was the main source of wealth. In fact, they argued, all wealth ultimately derives from the soil. Agriculture creates wealth, whereas manufacturing merely changes the nature of wealth and/or its ownership. Those who were not involved in agriculture were considered to be members of a 'sterile' or non-productive class.

3. Again in marked contrast to the views of the Mercantilists, they argued against protectionism and in support of free and unrestricted trade. They were among the first to advocate 'laissez-faire' in economic matters. They believed that society in general would be served if individuals were left to pursue their own interests, without any restrictions imposed by the state.

4. François Quesnay in his famous work, *Tableau Economique* (Economic Table), published in 1758, made the first attempt to analyse the interdependence of various sectors of the economy. This was a chart or diagram that traced the flow of money from one sector of society to another. Quesnay, who was a surgeon by profession, compared the movement of resources from one sector of the economy to another to the flow of blood through the human body.

Evaluation of Physiocrats

1. The Physiocrats provided a firm foundation for later writers who wished to analyse the workings of an economy in greater detail.

2. Most writers on economic matters since the Physiocrats have accepted the notion of a set of natural laws on which all human actions should be based, and have stressed that the aim of government should be to make the laws of the state reflect as closely as possible these natural laws.

THE CLASSICAL ECONOMISTS

The 'Classical School' of economics is the name given to those writers of the 18th and 19th centuries who argued in favour of the maximum freedom for the individual and the minimum state intervention in economic affairs. They wanted business to be able to grow unhampered by the restrictions of government, and thus they opposed protectionist policies in international trade. Their writings coincided with the Industrial Revolution in Britain and the development of capitalism, and provided the framework within which economic issues were perceived throughout the 19th century and into the early part of the 20th century. We will now consider the contributions of the five main classical writers – Smith, Malthus, Say, Ricardo and Mill – to the development of economic thought.

Adam Smith (1723–1790)

Adam Smith was born in Kirkcaldy, Scotland in 1723 and entered Glasgow University at the age of 14 (*Figure 33.2*). He won a scholarship to Oxford where he spent six years. He later returned to Scotland where he lectured, first at Edinburgh University and subsequently at Glasgow University, following his appointment there as Professor of Moral Philosophy.

From 1764 to 1766 he toured France where he came into contact with the writings of the Physiocrats. His major work, *The Wealth of Nations*, was first published in 1776 and laid the foundations for the future development of the subject. The following is a summary of the main points of *The Wealth of Nations*:

Fig. 33.2
An engraving from 1790 by Kay showing 'The Author of the Wealth of Nations' – Adam Smith

1. Smith rejected the Physiocratic view that all wealth had its origin in agriculture, and gave equal importance to manufacturing.

2. Smith adopted a labour theory of value. He said that the value of an item was determined by the amount of labour necessary to produce it.

3. Smith believed that individuals pursuing their own selfish interests actually worked for the benefit of society as a whole. He argued that if free to pursue his own self-interest, each individual was 'led by an invisible hand to promote an end that was no part of his intention'. To earn profits, businessmen must produce what customers want, and price was the signal to businessmen to produce the goods which the public most wanted. Products in great demand commanded high prices and thus yielded the most profits. Smith was a powerful advocate of completely free markets as the means of achieving economic harmony. If a good was in short supply its price would rise, and other producers would be attracted into the industry. Conversely, if a surplus existed, prices fell and some firms left the industry. Therefore, competition ensured the efficiency of markets. Smith had outlined the essential features of perfect competition (see *Chapter 12*).

4. He believed strongly in the division of labour as a means by which total production (and therefore wealth) could be increased. By the division of labour he meant the allocation of the labour force in such a way that each worker concentrated on only one task in the production process.

5. He was an advocate of free international trade. He believed that countries, like individuals, should specialise. International trade meant countries could not only consume items that they were unable to produce, but also find an outlet for excess or surplus produce.

6. While he was opposed to government intervention in economic affairs, Smith did see a limited role for a government in providing the framework within which private enterprise could flourish. The state was responsible for national defence, the legal system and the provision of public works (i.e. building up the infrastructure). These essential services should be funded by taxation. Taxation should be based on the following rules or canons:

   (a)   Ability to pay
   (b)   Certainty with regard to the amount to be collected
   (c)   Convenience of payment
   (d)   Low cost of collection.

7. While in favour of businessmen being allowed to pursue their own interests without restriction, Smith was aware of the dangers of unlimited competition, as is shown by his statement that: 'People of the same trade seldom meet together even for merriment and diversion, but the conversation ends in a conspiracy against the public, or on some contrivance to raise prices'.

Evaluation of Smith's contribution to economics

1. There were many shortcomings in Smith's analysis of an economic system. He argued that the price of an item depended on its cost of production, and neglected the effects of supply and demand.

2. Like earlier writers, he made the unnecessary distinction between 'productive' labour (manufacturing goods) and 'non-productive' labour (supplying services).

3. Smith was writing before the worst effects of the Industrial Revolution became apparent. He did not concern himself with the social issues arising from laissez-faire – poverty, low wages, long working hours, bad working conditions in factories, exploitation of women and children, etc.

4. Also it is naive to assume that individuals pursuing their own advantage will always benefit society as a whole.

5. Despite these faults, Smith's contribution to the development of the subject cannot be overestimated. He produced the first complete assessment of the workings of an economy, and provided the framework in which subsequent contributions to the subject were made.

Thomas Robert Malthus (1766–1834)

Malthus was educated at St John's College, Cambridge, where he studied mathematics and philosophy. He then entered the Church of England and became a country parson. He was subsequently made Professor of History and Political Economy at the East India Company's College at Haileybury, and is considered to be the first professional economist.

Malthus is mostly remembered for his entirely pessimistic work, *Essay on the Principle of Population*, which was first published in 1798. In this essay, he argued that while population grew in a geometric progression (2,4,8,16,32...), food production could only increase in an arithmetic progression (1,2,3,4,5...). Therefore, as time passed, the gap between population and food production would grow wider, and this ensured that mankind could never rise above a subsistence standard of living.

The only checks on the growth of population were 'moral restraint' (limits on the size of families), 'vice' (birth control) and 'misery' (famine, war and disease). He had no faith in the ability of the English working classes to exercise moral restraint, he opposed birth control, so he saw no other outcome from rising population than widespread 'war, pestilence and famine'. Thus, he was pessimistic about the future of mankind, saw no prospect for economic progress and earned for economics a reputation as a dismal science. This view of society was very controversial and Malthus's writings attracted much criticism.

Malthus accepted the subsistence theory of wages (or Iron Law of Wages as it was also called).

> The Law of Wages asserts that if wages rise above the subsistence level (i.e. the minimum level required for survival), an increase in population results, which again forces wages down to the subsistence level.

This was a very popular idea at the time with employers since it allowed them to justify the payment of low wages to their workers.

A less well-known part of Malthus's work was his attempt to explain the over-production of some goods. Unemployment resulted when more was produced than consumed. Malthus argued that the reason for this was excessive saving which reduced the demand for goods. A century was to elapse before Keynes addressed this problem when writing during the Great Depression of the 1930s.

Evaluation of Malthus's contribution to economics

1. Malthus's gloomy forecast concerning population growth and widespread starvation did not prove correct for a number of reasons.

   (a) The vast continent of America was developed as a major food producer and exporter.

   (b) Improvements in transport and storage meant food items became more widely available and were less subject to perishability.

   (c) Improvements in food production techniques, e.g. mechanisation of farming, higher yielding crops, etc. meant that output of food could be increased without increasing the land area devoted to agriculture.

   (d) As people's incomes increased, the birth rate dropped, proving that the subsistence theory of wages is not correct. As standards of living increase, there is a tendency for average family size to fall rather than rise.

2. Nevertheless, Malthus is to be credited with focusing attention on the issue of overpopulation which is still very much a problem in many underdeveloped countries today. Malthus's theories are still relevant in those parts of the world where famine is an ever-present threat.

Jean Baptiste Say (1767–1832)

A French economist, Jean Baptiste Say began lecturing in economics in 1816, and in 1831 was appointed Professor of Political Economy at the College de France. He is chiefly remembered for his *Treatise on Political Economy*, published in 1803, which contained what later became known as the Law of Markets (or Say's Law).

> Say's Law is usually summarised as 'supply creates its own demand'.

Say explained this as follows: people work, not for its own sake (indeed work is unpleasant), but only to obtain goods and services which they desire. In an economy that practises division of labour and exchange, each person does not attempt to supply all his needs directly. Rather, he produces those goods at which he is best, and exchanges his surplus goods for the surplus goods of others. The very act of production, therefore, constitutes the demand for other goods. Thus, there can never be overproduction of goods. Each man's production (supply) constitutes his demand for other goods, and so, the aggregate demand must equal the aggregate supply.

If at times some income was saved and not spent on the goods of others, the end result would still be the same. The accumulation of savings would lead to a drop in interest rates. This would lead to a rise in demand for capital goods, while it discouraged savings. Therefore, the system was self-adjusting and full employment would be maintained. Say's analysis obviously failed to explain how a deficiency in aggregate demand could cause unemployment. The role of savings in regulating demand was not satisfactorily explained until Keynes's writings in the 1930s.

David Ricardo (1772–1823)

Born in London, the son of Jewish parents, Ricardo had little formal education, but set himself up as a dealer on the Stock Exchange, where he made a fortune while still a young man. He retired from business aged 42 and devoted the remainder of his life to studying and writing about economics. He became a Member of Parliament (MP) for an Irish constituency in 1820 but died suddenly in 1823. His major work was *Principles of Political Economy and Taxation*, published in 1817, which dominated Classical economics for the next 50 years.

Ricardo is chiefly remembered for his theory of rent, which like Malthus's population theory had pessimistic conclusions. By rent, Ricardo meant the difference between the value of output produced by the best land and that produced by the worst land in use.

Ricardo's theory can be summarised in the following way. If the population of a country is fairly small, its food requirements can be supplied from the use of only the best (i.e. most fertile) land. Rents would be low, but the fertile land would yield high output and high profits. Landowners would then want to increase output to gain even more profits. This caused an increase in the demand for labour, which resulted in wages rising above the subsistence level.

Like Malthus, Ricardo accepted the subsistence theory of wages. He therefore argued that the rise in wages above the subsistence level would cause population to increase. This would lead to a greater demand for food, which would necessitate the cultivation of less fertile land. The price of food would rise to cover the extra cost of production involved in using less fertile land. This would lead to extra-high profits (i.e. rent) accruing to the owners of the most fertile land. This extra profit to the wealthy landowners was seen by Ricardo as being a burden on the productive (i.e. industrial) sector. This was because the landowners were assumed to spend these profits in a wasteful manner, thereby reducing the amount of capital available for industry.

Evaluation of Ricardo's contribution to economics

Ricardo, like all the main economists of his time, believed that there should be no intervention by the state to restrict free international trade. He opposed tariffs and developed the theory of comparative advantage to show that the benefits of free trade could be spread among all the countries engaged in trade.

Like Adam Smith, he used the labour theory of value, even though he accepted that this was, at best, only a partial explanation of value. However, his main legacy to economics is the law of comparative advantage, which is still used to show the advantages of free trade between nations. Ricardo also developed the theoretical side of the subject, which had a profound influence on the methods adopted by later writers.

John Stuart Mill (1806–1873)

John Stuart Mill was subjected to severe educational pressure by his father, who believed strongly in the benefits of a formal education (*Figure 33.3*). By the age of 13, he had learned Latin, Greek, mathematics, algebra and philosophy and had read all the major works on economics.

Fig. 33.3
John Stuart Mill

Not surprisingly, he had a nervous breakdown in his mid-twenties. In 1823 he joined the East India Company and worked there for 35 years. Like Ricardo, he also became an MP. His main work, *Principles of Political Economy*, published in 1848, was a review of the main economic theories of his day. This book was a huge success and remained the main textbook for students of economics until the beginning of the 20th century. The main points of Mill's work are summarised below.

> 1. He argued that while the laws of production are fixed, the laws governing distribution are open to change. Wealth can be distributed more fairly by taxation on the excess earnings of one sector (most likely, wealthy landowners). Therefore, he saw a more active role for government than earlier writers. Government intervention was not to be condemned if it improved the lot of the majority of citizens.

2. Mill accepted Say's Law and regarded overpopulation as impossible.

3. He discussed 'increasing returns to scale' and saw that the advantages of large-scale production led to the growth of very large firms in some industries.

4. Mill accepted that trade unions might be necessary to counterbalance the increasing power of employers.

5. He accepted the subsistence theory of wages.

6. He analysed the role of supply and demand in the determination of price.

THE RISE OF SOCIALISM

The 19th century saw many social and political changes, which were linked to the changing economic order. The development of capitalism and the excesses of the Industrial Revolution had led to huge inequality in the distribution of wealth. Poverty flourished in the midst of abundance. Appalling working conditions, bad housing and inadequate wages were the order of the day for many families. There was no social welfare system, such as we have today, to protect the old, the sick and the unemployed. All Classical writings on economics, even those of JS Mill, accepted the existence of rigid class divisions based on the ownership of private property and wealth.

It was inevitable, therefore, that there would be a strong reaction to the worst features of capitalism, as it developed in the 19th century. The strongest condemnation of the system is to be found in the writings of Karl Marx.

Karl Marx (1818–1883)

Karl Marx was born in Trier, Germany in 1818, the son of a Jewish lawyer (*Figure 33.4*). He attended university at Bonn and Berlin where he studied philosophy. Marx received his doctorate from Jena University in 1841 but his well-known political beliefs ensured that he did not get the university lectureship he wanted. He became editor of a German newspaper which the government later suppressed because of its political editorials. Marx was forced to flee to Paris in 1843. There he married Jenny Von Westphalen, the daughter of a German baron, and began his lifelong friendship with Friedrich Engels, a wealthy businessman who supported the Marx family financially and encouraged his interest in economics.

Fig. 33.4
Karl Marx

Marx and Engels jointly wrote *The Communist Manifesto* which was published in 1848. This was a very short book which was intended to outline the nature of the communist system, to reveal the historical process of change and to provide a strategic policy for the working class.

Marx returned briefly to Germany in 1848, where labour unrest was growing, but he was again forced into exile. In 1849 he settled in London, where he remained until his death in 1883. Most of his 34 years in London were spent on his great work, *Das Kapital.* This work of over 2,500 pages was published in separate stages. Volume 1 appeared in 1867. The remaining volumes, edited by Engels, were published posthumously in 1885 and 1894. Marx's basic economic ideas were similar to the Classical writers in that he accepted a labour theory of value, but his approach was completely different. For Marx, there was no 'invisible hand' producing harmony throughout society. He was interested in the process of change and evolution, while the Classical writers dealt with a stationary state. His economics were only a part of his overall social and political theory.

His fundamental belief was that capitalism contained within it the seeds of its own destruction. Just as capitalism replaced feudalism, communism would replace capitalism. Capitalism was to be seen as a necessary stage along the road which would eventually lead workers to the socialist state, where they would have full control over all means of production and where wealth would be distributed fairly.

How Socialism would Replace Capitalism

Marx argued that workers were paid subsistence wages by the employers. He said that the value of a good was the value of the amount of 'necessary labour' required to produce it. The value of goods produced by a worker was more than the wages paid to the worker, the difference being a surplus (or profit) to the employer. Capitalists, therefore, exploit labour which is the only factor capable of producing wealth. Unlike labour, capital creates no surplus, since the price paid for it by the employer represents its addition to the income of the employer.

The capitalists want to make as much profit as possible and so they demand more labour. However, the increased demand for labour will cause wages to rise (above subsistence level). Capitalists' profits are then squeezed, so they seek out ways of lowering their wage costs. New machines which do away with the need for many workers will be installed. If some firms introduce new labour-saving machines, others will be forced to do likewise, so unemployment rises dramatically. This adversely affects capitalists in two ways:

1. Because machines are replacing labour, profits will be reduced, since only labour can generate profits.

2. Because there is more unemployment, there will be a reduced demand for the goods produced by the capitalists.

The process continues as capitalists try to gain advantages by the introduction of new machinery. However, the result is smaller profits and more unemployment. Sooner or later, many firms get into trouble, either going out of business altogether or being taken over by large firms. As recession hits harder, businessmen buy up machines cheaply and workers are forced to accept low wages (since unemployment is so high). Workers become 'de-skilled' – skilled craftsmen become simply 'machine minders'. Workers are alienated and working conditions worsen. This process repeats itself again and again.

Production is concentrated in the hands of fewer and fewer capitalists, while more workers end up in the 'industrial reserve army' of the unemployed. Eventually, the workers organise themselves, a revolution occurs and the capitalist system is overthrown. It is replaced by a socialist state where workers control the means of production, and unlimited progress is possible.

Evaluation of Marx's contribution to economics

1. Marx's writings cannot be defended on purely economic grounds. His labour theory of value, which states that the value of an item is determined by the labour needed to produce it, was borrowed from Smith and Ricardo, and is a gross simplification of reality.

2. Marx also argued that capitalists accumulate more capital and get richer, while workers cannot share in the increased wealth because wages remain at subsistence levels. In *The Communist Manifesto* Marx argues that as capitalism progresses, there is 'a corresponding increase in the mass of poverty, oppression, enslavement, degeneration and exploitation'. The 20th century provides overwhelming evidence that, in fact, the opposite is true. As profits increase, so do wages. Wages have improved dramatically and so have working conditions. Legislation to protect workers' rights has been a feature of most 'capitalist' countries, while trade unions have ensured that steady improvements have taken place without the need for violent revolution. Marx assumed that workers would only organise when unemployed, but again the opposite is true.

3. His view of technical improvements contradicted his own labour theory of value. If labour were the only source of surplus value, why would capitalists choose to replace labour with machines?

4. His view of history has also proved to be inaccurate. The divisions between the social classes have become blurred in most countries, as workers share in the increased prosperity brought about by capitalism. Profits in capitalist countries have not declined, as Marx predicted. Nor does socialism appear inevitable now. Capitalism is flourishing in more

countries than ever before, including those previously under communist rule, such as the countries of Eastern Europe and the former Soviet Union. Moreover, according to Marx, the advanced capitalist countries would be the first to embrace communism; instead, it is in these countries that communist ideas have had least impact.

5. While Marx wrote a great deal about the overthrow of capitalism, he did not explain what type of society would emerge to replace it. Nor did he explain why the process of historical change would suddenly stop, once a communist state had been established. His methods of analysis have also been criticised. He highlighted cases of exploitation but ignored the improvements that were occurring in many areas. The historian, Paul Johnson, goes further. In his book *Intellectuals* he concludes that 'so far as we know, Marx never set foot in a mill, factory, mine or other industrial workplace in the whole of his life'.

6. In defence of Marx, it must be said that he focused attention on the plight of the working class at a time when other writers ignored the issue. His doctrines on alienation, exploitation, the weaknesses of capitalism and class warfare have, according to his followers, been at least partially responsible for governments taking action to improve working conditions and create a more caring society. Also, he was the first economist to analyse the forces of change in an economy, even if his approach was faulty. Marxists today argue that despite the improvements that have taken place, exploitation of workers still occurs, most notably in the less developed countries, and the distribution of wealth is as unequal as ever.

NEO-CLASSICAL ECONOMISTS

It should be obvious that all the economists discussed above had failed to answer the most fundamental economic question – what determines the value of a good? Many writers in the latter part of the 19th century turned their attention to the so-called 'paradox of value'. Why is it that water which is essential to life has little value, while diamonds which are of little use have great value? Karl Marx, like Smith and Ricardo before him, found the answer in the labour theory of value. The high value of diamonds was explained by the great amount of labour involved in their discovery, extraction, cutting, polishing, etc., while water was easily acquired. Even these writers knew that the labour theory of value was unsatisfactory. If A takes twice as long to make a unit of output as B, does this mean that A's output is twice as valuable as B's?

The solution to the problem of value was based on the concept of utility. This idea was arrived at separately by three economists at roughly the same time – an Englishman, William Jevons (1835–1882), an Austrian, Carl Menger

(1840–1921) and a Frenchman, Leon Walras (1834–1910). These and other economists of the late 19th century, who accepted the main framework of Classical laissez-faire economics, while adopting a theory of value based on utility, are sometimes known as Neo-classical economists.

The utility of a good was defined as the use or satisfaction a person gets from consuming that good. Therefore, it is entirely subjective, that is, it varies from one person to another.

The marginal utility of a good was defined as the extra utility derived from consuming one more unit of the good. Total utility increases as consumption increases, while marginal utility declines as consumption increases.

The paradox of value can be resolved by using these concepts. Water is consumed in vast quantities and its total utility is immense. However, it is cheap because its marginal utility is low. Diamonds are in short supply, with a low total utility, but a high marginal utility, and therefore, a high price.

Alfred Marshall (1842–1924)

The English economist, Alfred Marshall, who became Professor of Political Economy at Cambridge in 1855, published *Principles of Economics* in 1890. In this work, he refined the ideas of the earlier Classical writers and used mathematical methods to explain how price and output were determined. He adopted the marginal utility theory of value, and invented the term 'elasticity' to describe the response of demand to small changes in price.

Marshall put forward the famous 'scissors' analogy to explain how demand and supply interact to achieve market equilibrium. One blade of the scissors is demand, the other supply. It was neither possible nor necessary to see which blade does the cutting since they are both interdependent. Marshall also introduced to economics the concepts of the short run and the long run. *Principles of Economics* remained the main textbook for students of economics up to the Great Depression of the 1930s.

KEYNESIAN ECONOMICS

John Maynard Keynes (1883–1946)

In the early 20th century, economists chiefly concerned themselves with further refinements to the main economic ideas of the Classical writers. They overlooked one very serious shortcoming of the earlier theories – they ignored the problem of recessions. Some economists accepted, without question, Say's Law – that supply creates its own demand – and therefore claimed that recessions were impossible. Most of them took the less extreme view that if recessions occurred, they would last only a short period of time. If unemployment existed, they argued, competition among the unemployed for scarce jobs would force wages down until firms found it attractive to take on extra workers again.

Similarly, if investment were too low, rates of interest would fall until savings and investment were made equal once more. In this way, throughout the economy, any disequilibrium would be temporary, because markets were flexible and prices would adjust to reach a new equilibrium. So any recession could only be temporary, while markets were adjusting, and a new equilibrium was being reached. However, these economists were to be proved wrong by the Great Depression, which started in the United States in 1929, and then spread to Europe where it lasted well into the 1930s. It became clear that an alternative economic theory was required to explain the problem of recessions. Such an explanation was provided by John Maynard Keynes.

Keynes was born at Cambridge in 1883 (*Figure 33.5*). He was educated at Cambridge University, where he studied economics under Alfred Marshall. After a period in the civil service, he became a lecturer at Cambridge, and in 1911, became editor of the *Economic Journal*. During the First World War (1914–1918), Keynes held a post at the Treasury [the British Department of Finance], and represented Britain at the Peace Conference in Versailles in 1919.

Fig. 33.5
John Maynard Keynes

He argued strongly against the imposition of huge reparation payments on Germany, on the grounds that such payments would disrupt world trade and cause a depression. His advice was ignored, so he resigned, and in his book, *The Economic Consequences of the Peace*, he forecast with great accuracy the economic chaos that followed in the 1930s. He also severely criticised the decision of the government to return to the Gold Standard in 1925, at the rate of exchange that prevailed before the War. He returned to the Treasury during the Second World War (1939–1945), where he acted as an economic advisor to the government. He was one of Britain's leading figures at the Bretton Woods Conference in 1944, which led to the setting up of the International Monetary Fund. He died in 1946.

Keynes's major work, *The General Theory of Employment, Interest and Money*, was published in 1936 and marked a completely new departure in economics. In this book, he explained how recessions happen, and how governments can act to avoid them. We have already looked in detail at Keynes's theory on interest rates (*Chapter 20*) and his theory on how national income is determined (*Chapter 24*), so what follows here is only a brief summary of his position.

If there is unemployment, he argued, this is the result of an insufficient demand for goods and services in the economy. Wages are not always flexible downwards, and even if they were, a general cut in wages would lower consumption, income and aggregate demand. Keynes argued that if the level of investment by businessmen was insufficient to generate a level of income which would achieve full employment of resources in the economy, then the government was justified in increasing its own spending. This would have the same effect as increased investment.

The widely held economic view of the time was that increased government spending, by means of a current budget deficit, would cause more problems than it would solve. A balanced budget was regarded as equally important for a government as for a household. Many economists felt that a budget deficit would divert funds from the private sector, which was more productive, to the state sector, which would use them less efficiently. It was not until Keynes had explained his theory clearly in *The General Theory of Employment, Interest and Money* that his views became more widely accepted. According to Keynes, the job of the government is to regulate the economy. If no regulation is undertaken, booms and recessions will occur. If there is a shortage of aggregate demand, the government should step in, and, by increasing its own expenditure, ensure that the economy achieved its full potential. Thus the use of fiscal policy as an instrument of macroeconomics was the greatest legacy of Keynes.

Keynesians and neo-Keynesians

Those economists who are in broad agreement with the general economic arguments put forward by Keynes are called 'Keynesians' or 'neo-Keynesians'. While it must be stressed that these writers do not constitute a single united group in agreement on all economic issues, they generally tend to support the following propositions.

PROPOSITIONS SUPPORTED BY NEO-KEYNESIANS

1. Aggregate demand plays a very important role in determining the level of output.

2. Economies can settle at positions with high unemployment, where unemployment shows no tendency to fall.

3. Governments, mainly by the use of fiscal policy, can increase aggregate demand to reduce unemployment.

These ideas were largely unchallenged until the 1970s, when the new economic doctrine of 'monetarism' began to attract attention. At the same time, a more extreme Keynesian group of writers emerged, arguing that disequilibrium could persist indefinitely, because of interactions between the various sectors of the economy. Once an economy left equilibrium, no amount of price flexibility could guarantee its return to full employment. Therefore, there was even more justification for the use of fiscal policy to regulate the economy.

MONETARISM

Fig. 33.6
Milton Friedman

This is the name given to the theory of macro-economics which suggests that monetary policy should be the main instrument used by the government to manage the economy. This view contrasts sharply with Keynesian theory, which stressed fiscal policy.

Monetarism first emerged in the 1960s when it seemed that Keynesian theories were unable to come up with solutions to the economic problems of that time, particularly inflation. Monetarist ideas became more prominent during the 1970s, first in the United States, where they found their clearest expression in the writings of Milton Friedman (born 1912) (*Figure 33.6*), and then in Britain, where the Conservative governments of Margaret Thatcher were influenced strongly by the desire to control inflation.

The following is a summary of the main arguments advanced by monetarist economists.

1. An increase in the money supply will lead to a rise in inflation. Any increase in the amount of money in circulation will cause prices to rise. Therefore, a policy of increasing government expenditure to reduce unemployment, as advocated by Keynesians, would not result in higher output, but only in higher prices. The use of budget deficits to increase aggregate demand and reduce unemployment was seen as inappropriate and futile.

2. By keeping strict control of the money supply, it is possible to control the rate of inflation. By limiting the availability of loans, and by keeping interest rates at a relatively high level, consumer borrowing could be controlled. Also, wage rises would be moderate, since companies would not be able to afford to pay high wages.

3. The reduction in inflation achieved in this way would increase international competitiveness. Exports would be relatively cheaper abroad and so the volume of exports would rise. Therefore investment would rise and unemployment would be reduced.

4. Monetarists advocate a return to the principles of laissez-faire, with a minimum of state intervention. A healthy private sector is the means of achieving economic growth, and therefore the selling off of state companies to the private sector ('privatisation') is regarded as desirable.

5. Another aim should be the 'deregulation' of markets, that is less supervision and control of private companies by the government.

6. Supply-side economics is the name given to the economic doctrine which emerged in the 1980s which advocated control of the economy by the use of supply-side policies. Such policies were advocated by monetarists in preference to the demand management policies of the Keynesians. Anything that attempts to influence the supply of labour or the supply of goods can be called a supply-side measure. Examples of such policies are:

(a) Cutting income tax to increase the difference between the take-home pay of a worker and what an unemployed person gets on social welfare.

(b) Introducing laws against monopoly in order to encourage more competition.

(c) Diminishing the ability of trade unions to interfere with the free working of the labour market.

(d) Introducing measures to improve the mobility of labour.

(e) Reducing the benefits available to the unemployed so as to increase their incentive to find work.

(f) Restricting the growth of the money supply in order to control inflation, and so increase investment.

These policies have in turn been criticised by many writers. The following strong attack by Susan George (from *Take it Personally,* Thorsons 2001) argues that 'neo-liberalism' (a name for the underlying philosophy of the above policies) has been cleverly promoted as the normal and correct state of affairs.

Neo-liberalism and the decline of 'the public good'

By Susan George

Some 50 years ago if you had seriously proposed any of the ideas and policies in today's standard neo-liberal toolkit, you would have been laughed off the stage or sent off to the insane asylum. At least in the Western countries at that time, everyone was a Keynesian, a social democrat or a social-Christian democrat, or some shade of Marxist. The idea that the market should be allowed to make major social and political decisions; the idea that the state should voluntarily reduce its role in the economy, or that corporations should be given total freedom, that trade unions should be curbed and citizens given less, rather than more, social protection – such ideas were utterly foreign to the spirit of the time.

However incredible it may sound today, the IMF and the World Bank were seen as progressive institutions. When they were created at Bretton Woods in 1944, their mandate was to help prevent future conflicts by lending for reconstruction and development and by smoothing out temporary balance of payments problems. They had no control over individual government's economic decisions nor did their mandate include a license to intervene in national policy.

In the Western nations, the Welfare State and New Deal had got under way in the 1930s but their spread had been interrupted by World War II. The first order of business in the post-war world was to put them back in place. The other major item on the agenda was to get world trade moving and this was accomplished through the Marshall Plan, which established Europe once again as the major trading partner for the USA.

On the whole, the world has signed on for an extremely progressive agenda. The great scholar Karl Polanyi published his masterwork, *The Great Transformation* in 1944, a fierce critique of 19th century industrial, market-based society. Over 50 years ago, Polanyi made this amazingly prophetic and modern statement: "To allow the market mechanism to be the sole director of the fate of human beings and their natural environment... would result in the demolition of society." But Polanyi was convinced that such a demolition could no longer happen in the post-war world. Alas, his optimism was misplaced: the whole point of neo-liberalism is that the market mechanism should be allowed to direct the fate of human beings. The economy should dictate its rules to society, not the other way around.

So what happened? How did neo-liberalism ever emerge from its ghetto to become the dominant doctrine in the world today?

- Why can the IMF and the World Bank intervene at will and force countries to participate in the world economy on unfavorable terms?

- Why is the Welfare State under threat in all the countries where it was established?
- Why is the environment on the edge of collapse?
- Why are there so many poor people in both the rich and the poor countries at a time when there has never existed such great wealth?

One explanation for this triumph of neo-liberalism – and the economic, political, social, and ecological disasters that go with it – is that neo-liberals have bought and paid for their own vicious and regressive "Great Transformation." They have understood, as progressives have not, that ideas have consequences. Starting from a tiny embryo at the University of Chicago with the philosopher-economist Friedrich von Hayek and his students like Milton Friedman, the neo-liberals and their funders have created a huge international network of foundations, institutes, research centres, publications, scholars, writers, and public relations hacks to develop, package, and push their ideas and doctrine relentlessly.

They have built this highly efficient ideological cadre because they understand that if you can occupy peoples' heads, their hearts and their hands will follow. The ideological and promotional work of the Right has been absolutely brilliant. They have spent hundreds of millions of dollars, but the result has been worth every penny to them because they have made neo-liberalism seem as if it were the natural and normal condition of humankind.

What is neo-liberalism?

"Neo-liberalism" is a set of economic policies. You can see its effects as the rich grow richer and the poor grow poorer. Neo-liberalism in a nutshell:

THE RULE OF THE MARKET
Liberating "free" enterprise from any bonds imposed by the government no matter how much social damage this causes.

CUTTING PUBLIC EXPENDITURE FOR SOCIAL SERVICES
like education and health care and water supply, all in the name of reducing government's role.

DEREGULATION
of laws that could reduce profits, including measures to protect workers and the environment.

PRIVATISATION
Selling state-owned enterprises, goods, and services to private investors. Although done in the name of greater efficiency, which is often needed, privatisation concentrates wealth into fewer hands and makes the public pay more.

ELIMINATIING THE CONCEPT OF "THE PUBLIC GOOD"
and replacing it with "individual responsibility." Pressurising the poorest people to find solutions to their lack of health care, education, and social security and branding them, if they fail, as "lazy."

Appendix

SOURCES OF INFORMATION

This textbook provides students with a basic understanding of the economic issues which confront all of us in the everyday business of living. Every effort has been made to include the most up-to-date economic information available. However, a textbook used in isolation will not really enable the student to fully appreciate the workings of an economic system. It is necessary to supplement the textbook with selective use of other sources of information. The following lists should point students in the direction of those sources. Nowadays, there is a wealth of information provided on the internet and web addresses are supplied where available.

Newspapers

DAILY

- *The Irish Times* – Friday business supplement   *www.ireland.com*
- *The Irish Independent* – Thursday business supplement   *www.independent.ie*
- *The Irish Examiner* – Friday business supplement   *www.examiner.ie*
- *The Financial Times* – leading British finance newspaper   *www.ft.com*

WEEKLY

- *The Sunday Business Post*   *www.sbpost.ie*
- *The Sunday Independent*   *www.independent.ie*
- *The Sunday Tribune*   *www.tribune.ie*
- *The Sunday Times*   *www.sunday-times.co.uk*

Magazines

- *Business & Finance* – weekly   *www.businessandfinance.com*
- *The Economist* – leading British weekly publication   *www.economist.com*
- *Business Plus* – monthly   *www.bizplus.ie*

Additional sources

1. BANKING AND FINANCE

- *Central Bank Quarterly Report*   *www.centralbank.ie*
  The Central Bank's overview of the national economy's recent performance and examines outlook for future in light of international developments, etc.
- *Bank Brief*   *www.ibis.ie*

The Irish Banks' Information Service (IBIS) publishes three issues yearly containing articles on banking and related matters for second-level business students. Contact IBIS at Nassau House, Nassau Street, Dublin 2. Tel: (01) 6715299.

2. THE EUROPEAN UNION

www.europarl.ie
www.europa.eu.int

- A wide range of booklets and videos are available from European Union House, 43 Molesworth Street, Dublin 2. Tel: (01) 605 7900. Excellent examples include:
  - *The Common Agricultural Policy*
  - *How Does the European Union Work?*
  - *A Community of Fifteen: Key Figures.*

3. ECONOMIC DEVELOPMENT

www.irlgov.ie

- Country profiles relating to Ireland's foreign aid are produced by the Department of Foreign Affairs.

4. LABOUR AND EMPLOYMENT

www ictu.ie

- Videos and various material on workers' rights and the problem of unemployment are available from the Irish Congress of Trade Unions (ICTU), 31-32 Parnell Square, Dublin 1. Tel: (01) 889 7777.

Government publications

THE CENTRAL STATISTICS OFFICE (CSO)

www.cso.ie

The CSO publishes information on the following topics:
- Census of Population of Ireland – every five years
- Quarterly National Household Survey – quarterly
- The Live Register – monthly
- Economic Series – monthly
- Trade Statistics – monthly
- Statistical Bulletin – quarterly
- The Statistical Yearbook – annually
- Census of Industrial Production – annually.

School resources

BUSINESS 2000

www.business2000.ie

Woodgrange Technologies in association with *The Irish Times* and the Business Studies Teachers Association of Ireland produce an excellent set of laminated case studies for use in the classroom with an accompanying CD-ROM. Topics covered include the Central Bank, the Department of Finance and the National Treasury Management Agency. The resource is updated annually. Contact Business 2000 Teachers Support Desk, Woodgrange Technologies Ltd, 25 Merrion Square, Dublin 2. Tel: (01) 435 2500.

Index